AF476964

FUTURBALLA

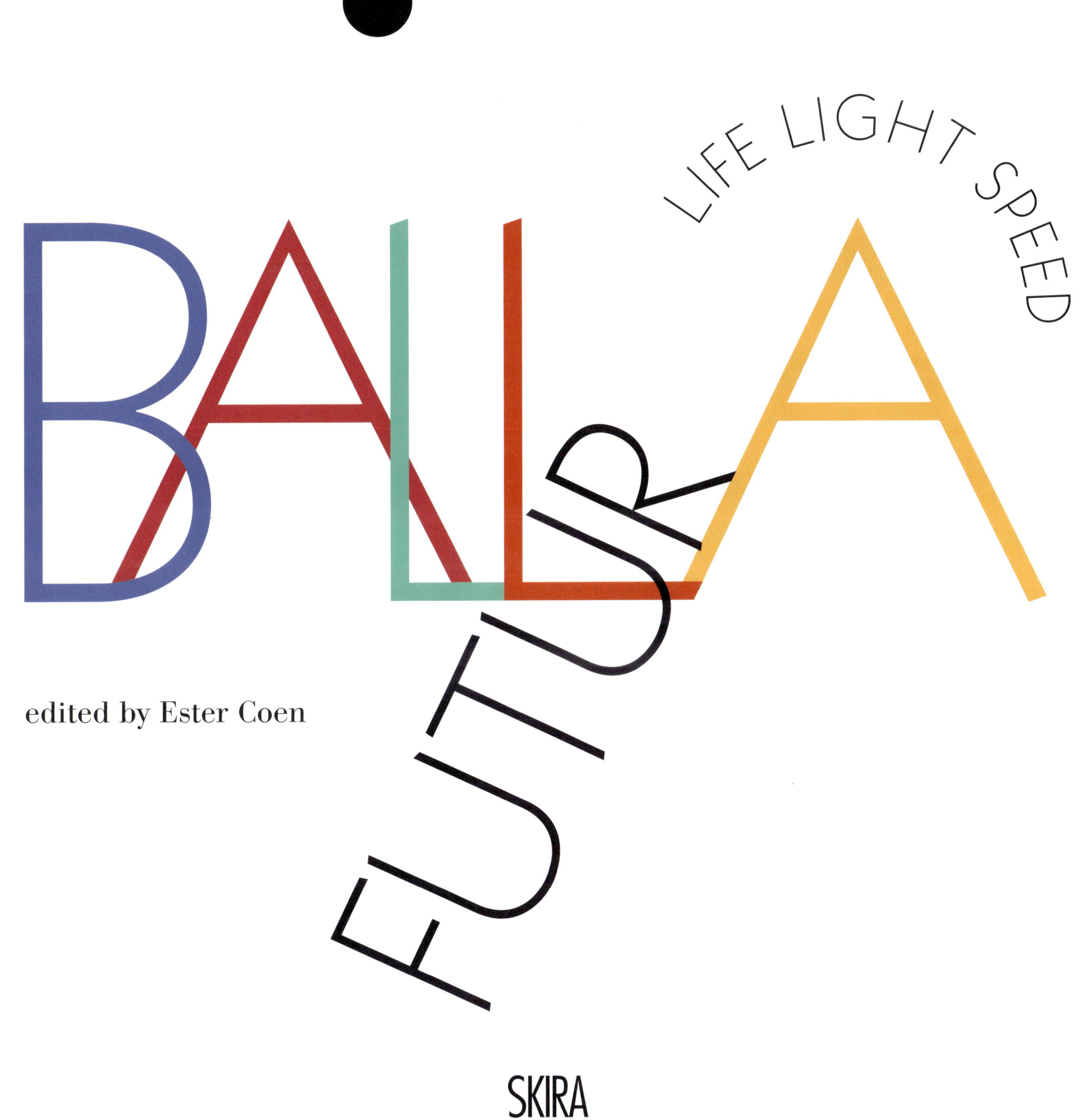

edited by Ester Coen

SKIRA

Design
Marcello Francone

Editorial Coordination
Vincenza Russo

Editing
Marco Abate

Layout
Serena Parini

Iconographical Research
Paola Lamanna

Translations
Paul Metcalfe for *Scriptum*, Rome

First published in Italy in 2016 by
Skira Editore S.p.A.
Palazzo Casati Stampa
via Torino 61
20123 Milano
Italy
www.skira.net

Printed and bound in Italy. First edition

ISBN: 978-88-572-3386-4

Distributed in USA, Canada, Central & South America by Rizzoli International Publications, Inc., 300 Park Avenue South, New York, NY 10010, USA.
Distributed elsewhere in the world by Thames and Hudson Ltd., 181A High Holborn, London WC1V 7QX, United Kingdom.

Photo Credits
© 2016. BI, ADAGP, Paris/Scala, Firenze: p. 40 right
© 2016. DeAgostini Picture Library/Scala, Firenze: p. 147 right
© 2016 Digital Image The Museum of Modern Art, New York/Scala, Firenze: pp. 80 top, 104, 149; cat. 84
© 2016. Foto Scala, Firenze/bpk, Bildagentur für Kunst, Kultur und Geschichte, Berlin: p. 174
© 2016. Foto The Philadelphia Museum of Art/ Art Resource/Scala, Firenze: pp. 148, 161 top left
© 2016. White Images/Scala, Firenze: p. 163 right
© Accademia Nazionale di San Luca, Roma: cat. 7
© La Biennale di Venezia, ASAC, Fototeca: p. 29 top
© Collection Stedelijk Museum Amsterdam: cat. 59
© Collezione Peggy Guggenheim, Venezia (Solomon R. Guggenheim Foundation, New York): cat. 67
© Dorotheum, Wien: cat. 12
© Estorick Collection, London/ Foto Ezio Buzzegoli, Progetto Futurahma: cat. 52
© Farsettiarte, Prato/ Foto Industrialfoto, Firenze: cat. 19, 20, 21, 74
© Fondazione Federico Cerruti per l'arte/ Foto Ernani Orcorte, Torino: cat. 4, 63, 76
Foto Luca Carrà, Milano: cat. 28a-b, 29a-b, 53, 62, 69, 77, 88, 90a-b, 92a-b, 95a-b, 96a-b, 97, 98, 99, 101, 102, 104a-b, 107, 108, 110a-b, 111, 112
Foto Giuseppe Schiavinotto, Roma: cat. 1, 58
© Galleria Russo, Roma – Istanbul: cat. 13, 55, 56
© Galleria d'Arte Moderna, Milano / Foto Luca Carrà, Milano: cat. 3, 23, 66
© Galleria d'Arte Moderna, Roma / Foto Giuseppe Schiavinotto, Roma cat. 5
© Galleria Nazionale d'Arte Moderna e Contemporanea di Roma. "Su gentile concessione del Ministero dei Beni e delle Attività Culturali e del Turismo" / Foto Giuseppe Schiavinotto, Roma: cat. 8, 9, 10, 61, 78, 79, 80, 81, 82, 83
© GAM - Galleria Civica d'Arte Moderna e Contemporanea, Torino/ Archivio Fotografico "Su concessione della Fondazione Torino Musei": cat. 25-26 (Studio Gonella 1986), 27 (Studio Gonella 1985), 30 (Studio Gonella 2014), 31 (Studio Gonella 2007), 32 (Studio Gonella 2014), 33 (Paolo Robino 2016), 34 (Studio Gonella 1986), 35 (Studio Gonella 2014), 36 (Paolo Robino 2015), 37 (Studio Gonella 2014), 38 (Foto Padovan 2007), 39 (Studio Gonella 2014), 40-41 (Studio Gonella 1986), 42 (Studio Gonella 2006), 43 (Studio Gonella 1986), 47 (Studio Gonella 2012), 48 (Studio Gonella 1985), 51, 94, 108 bottom (Studio Gonella 1985)
© MART - Museo di Arte Moderna e Contemporanea di Trento e Rovereto/Archivio Fotografico e Mediateca: cat. 49, 65, 72, 86
© Museo del Novecento, Milano/ Foto Luca Carrà, Milano: cat. 2, 60, 85
© RMN-Réunion des Musées Nationaux / distr. Alinari: p. 161 top, centre
© Segretariato Generale della Presidenza della Repubblica, Roma / Foto Giuseppe Schiavinotto, Roma: cat. 6
© Sotheby's, Milano: cat. 18
© Gian Enzo Sperone, New York: cat. 44, 45, 46, 70, 71, 73, 75, 89a-b, 91a-b, 94a-b, 100a-b, 103, 105a-b, 106a-b
© Tate, London 2016: cat. 68
Agence Bulloz / RMN-Réunion des Musées Nationaux / distr. Alinari: p. 78 bottom
Archivi Alinari, Firenze: pp. 26 top, 79, 132
ARCHIVIO GBB / Contrasto: p. 40 left
Bridgeman Images / Archivi Alinari: pp. 69, 78 top, 118, 139 top left
Cambridge University Library: p. 108 top
Courtesy of The Lewis Walpole Library, Yale University: p. 163 left
Encyclopaedia Britannica / Getty Images: p. 115
Foto Marc Gouby: cat. 22
Foto Cesare Pagliero, Savigliano: cat. 11
Hulton Archive/Getty Images: p. 139 bottom
MONDADORI PORTFOLIO / Electa / Sergio Anelli: p. 70
Omikron / Getty Images: p. 109 bottom
Photo © The Israel Museum, Jerusalem by Elie Posner: cat. 64
Photo Bruno Bani, Milano: cat. 109
Photograph by Tom Loonan: cat. 54
Photograph Courtesy of Sotheby's, Inc. © 2016 : cat. 93, 113
Raccolte Museali Fratelli Alinari (RMFA) - donazione Morpurgo, Firenze © Alinari: p. 37 top
P. Schälchli, Zurich: cat. 57, p. 129
Science & Society Picture Library / Getty Images: p. 139 top right
SCIENCE SOURCE/Getty Images: pp. 109 top, 161 left
George Silk/Getty Images: p. 85 bottom
"Su concessione del Ministero dei Beni e delle Attività Culturali e del Turismo – Galleria Nazionale di Parma" / Foto Annarita Ziveri, Archivio Fotografico Soprintendenza SBEAP di Parma e Piacenza: cat. 24
Paolo Vandrasch fotografo, Milano: cat. 50
Wolfsoniana - Palazzo Ducale Fondazione per la Cultura, Genova: p. 157
www.atlanteditorino.it: p. 25

Under the August Auspices
of the President
of the Italian Republic

FUTURBALLA
Life Light Speed

Alba, Fondazione Ferrero
29 October 2016 – 27 February 2017

The exhibition is a project of
Fondazione Piera, Pietro e Giovanni Ferrero
Maria Franca Ferrero, *President*
Edo Milanesio, *Secretary General*

Superintendency for the Archaeological, Artistic and Environmental Heritage of the Metropolitan City of Turin
Luisa Papotti, *Superintendent*

Superintendency for the Archaeological, Artistic and Environmental Heritage of the Provinces of Alessandria, Asti and Cuneo
Egle Micheletto, *Superintendent*

GAM – Galleria Civica d'Arte Moderna e Contemporanea, Turin
Carolyn Christov-Bakargiev, *Director*

With support from
The Piedmont Region
Sergio Chiamparino, *President*
Antonella Parigi, *Head of the Culture and Tourism Department*

Compagnia di San Paolo
Francesco Profumo, *President*
Piero Gastaldo, *Segretary General*

Fondazione Cassa di Risparmio di Cuneo
Giandomenico Genta, *President*
Andrea Silvestri, *Chief Executive*

Under the auspices of
The Piedmont Region

The City of Turin
Chiara Appendino, *Mayor*
Francesca Paola Leon, *Head of the Culture Department*

The Municipality of Alba
Maurizio Marello, *Mayor*
Fabio Tripaldi, *Head of the Culture and Tourism Department*

Exhibition
Ester Coen, *Curator*

Committee of Honour
Carolyn Christov-Bakargiev
Cristiana Collu
Rudi Fuchs
Luisa Papotti
Philip Rylands
Claudio Salsi
Janne Sirén

Board of Consultants
Danilo Eccher
Eva Menzio

Organization
Fondazione Ferrero
Mario Strola, Elena Torchio, *general management*
Flavio Bonifacio, *graphic design and installation management*
Gabriele Bottero, Giuliana Sarotto, *administration*
Edoardo Borra, *publishing supervision*
Margherita Campanello, *press office*
Emanuela Delpiano, *educational activities*
Cristina Manzone, *secretarial services*
Giuseppe Pansi, Giuseppe Songia, *technical supervision*
Laura Rolfo, Monica Torrero, *supervision of exhibition assistance services*
Renata Vandenbemden, *Web communications*

Sincere thanks to Piero Bianucci for advice and cooperation

Press Office
Studio Esseci di Sergio Campagnolo

Installation design
Danilo Manassero
with Eva Menzio

Implementation and installations
Alpiq Intec Italia
Audiosystem
C.S.A.
CUBAR
EK
Espert
Eurofiere
Martinetti F.lli Decorazioni
OR. VE. CA.
Studio Forte
Studio Saracco e Lanzetti

Publialba
IGP Decaux
L'Artigiana
L'Artistica
Publiproget

Restoration
Doneux & Soci
Barbara Ferriani
Luigi Parma
Cornici Villa
Soseishi

Assistance with handling
Cesare Pagliero

Insurance
Aon S.p.A. Insurance & Reinsurance Brokers
AXA Art, primary company

Transport
Arteria

Guided visits
Itinera Servizi Turistici

Visitor assistance
Senior Ferrero personnel
Staff Ferrero S.p.A.
Pupils of the P. Gallizio, G. Govone and L. Cocito high schools in Alba

Surveillance
Ferrero Management Services - Sicurezza industriale
Telecontrol

Catalogue
Ester Coen, *Editor*

Texts
Vincenzo Barone
Ester Coen
Giorgio Muratore
Luca Francesco Ticini

Assistance with editing and critical apparatus
Zelda De Lillo

Documentary
FuTurBalla (Italy, 2016)
Directed by Priscilla Benedetti

Expert advice and texts
Ester Coen and Maria Baiocchi

Iconographic research
Graziella Gnozzi

Narrator
Remo Girone

Editing
Studio Cliché, Rome

We thank Nicoletta Pallini Clemente for her kind permission to show the film *Balla et le Futurisme* (France, 1972), directed by Jack Clemente, awarded the Silver Lion for best documentary at the Venice Film Festival.

List of Lenders
Accademia Nazionale di San Luca, Rome, Carlo Lorenzetti, Francesco Moschini
Albright-Knox Art Gallery, Buffalo, Janne Sirén
Archivio dell'Opera di Duilio Cambellotti, Rome, Marco and Alessandro Cambellotti, Fabrizio Russo
Estorick Collection of Modern Italian Art, London, Roberta Cremoncini
Fondazione F.C. per l'ARTE, Rivoli
Galleria d'Arte Moderna, Milan, Marina Lampugnani, Paola Zatti
Galleria d'Arte Moderna, Rome, Claudio Parisi Presicce, Maria Catalano
GAM – Galleria Civica d'Arte Moderna e Contemporanea, Turin, Carolyn Christov-Bakargiev, Virginia Bertone
La Galleria Nazionale, Rome, Cristiana Collu
MART, Museo di arte moderna e contemporanea di Trento e Rovereto, Gianfranco Maraniello
Museo del Novecento, Milan, Marina Lampugnani, Claudio Salsi
Palazzo del Quirinale, General Secretariat of the Presidency of the Italian Republic, Ugo Zampetti, Louis Godart
Peggy Guggenheim Collection, Venice – Solomon R. Guggenheim Foundation, New York, Philip Rylands
Stedelijk Museum, Amsterdam, Beatrix Ruf, Bart Rutten
Tate, London, Sir Nicholas Serota, Frances Morris
The Israel Museum, Jerusalem, James S. Snyder, Tanya Sirakovich
The Museum of Modern Art, New York, Glenn D. Lowry, Ann Temkin

We thank the private collectors who preferred to remain anonymous for their kindness and cooperation in lending works

Particular thanks to
Alessandro, Patrizia and Vittorio Balla, Guido Donati and Elena Gigli for their helpful and cooperative response to the exhibition project.

Thanks for their cooperation
Ministry of Cultural Heritage and Tourism
General Directorate for Museums
Ugo Soragni, Director General
Antonio Tarasco, Director of Service I – Museum Collections
Giuliano Romalli, Certification of Cultural Interest

Daniela Porro, Director of the Regional Secretariat of the Ministry of Cultural Heritage and Tourism for the Lazio region

Mario Francesco Lamparelli, Exhibitions Department of the Superintendency for the Archaeological, Artistic and Environmental Heritage of the Metropolitan City of Turin
Virginia Bertone, Chief Curator of the GAM Collections, Turin
Flavia Barbaro, Head of the GAM Department of Education, Turin constant points of reference for the exhibition project

Mario Chiriotti, Piedmont Region, Directorate for the Promotion of Culture, Tourism and Sport

Rosaria Cigliano, Compagnia di San Paolo, Head of Art and Cultural Heritage Section

Andrea Silvestri, Francesco Bertello and Valentina Dania, Fondazione Cassa di Risparmio di Cuneo

Ferrero Group
H.E. the Ambassador Francesco Paolo Fulci, President of Ferrero S.p.A.
Giuseppe Addezio, Laura Airaghi, Carlo Bonino, Giovanni Barile, Chiara Berzanti, Ettore Bologna, Davide Bracco, Martino Caretto, Franco Carrer, Paul Chibe, Gianluca Colombo, Giuseppe D'Angelo, Alessandro D'Este, Diego Daniele, Domenico Dogliani, Lucia Farruggio, Filippo Ferrua, Mario Garetto, Nicola Gaverina, Franco Genovese, Diego Giordano, Davide Messa, Roberto Mollo, Jeanne Murphy, Andrea Nappo, Valter Nicoletti, Nemio Passalacqua, Nunzio Pulvirenti, Costanza Quaglia, Alessandro Ronco, Cristiano Santarelli, Vladimiro Sinatti, Fabio Timelli, Alberto Tinivella, Massimo Tonello, Aldo Uva

Senior Ferrero personnel, retired and working

AON S.p.A. Insurance & Reinsurance Brokers for expert advice on insurance matters

Thomas Amman Fine Art, Zürich
Dorotheum, Vienna
Farsettiarte, Prato
Galleria dello Scudo Arte Moderna e Contemporanea, Verona
Galleria Russo, Rome
Sotheby's, New York - Milan
Sperone Westwater, New York

Acknowledgements

The organizers and curator wish to express their warmest gratitude to all those involved in various ways in the production of the exhibition and apologize for any involuntary omissions

Christopher Adams, Rosamaria Agostoni, Luisa Albanese, Serena Aldi, Ezio Amuro, Arianna Angelelli, Maria Baiocchi, Roberta Barbaro, Attilio Begher, Stefania Bertelli, Roberto Binello, Enrico Boglione, Caterina Bon di Valsassina, Arianna Bona, Debora Bonandrini, Filippo Bosco, Laura Bosso, Ombretta Bracci, Roberto Brunelli, Massimiliano Caldera, Alice Calloway, Angelo and Silvia Calmarini, Carla Caputo, Kelly Carpenter, Marella Caracciolo Chia, Mauro Carbone, Luigi Carlon, Luca Carrà, Assunta Caruso, Edoardo Casolari, Maria Grazia Conti, Maria Cristina Corsini, Paolo Curti, Clarenza Catullo, Clara Colnaghi, Francesco D'Agostino, Anna Maria De Gregorio, Laura Ada De Luca, Nicola Del Roscio, Mario De Simoni, Bettina Della Casa, Pier Ugo Demarziani, Massimo Di Carlo, Lino Di Gioia, Elena Dolino, Claudia Dwek, Ursula Esposito, Alexander Estorick, Michael Estorick, Loredana Faletti, Franco Faranda, Frediano Farsetti, Daniela Ferrari, Gianluca Ferrero, Monica Ferri, Ileana Florescu Franchetti, Giancarlo Fontana, Laura Fornara, Federico Forquet, Giuseppe Forte, Gaia Franchetti, Pietrarco Franchetti, Caitlyn P. Frank, Simonetta Fraquelli, Bruno Gabetti, Matthew Gale, Silvia Gallarato, Marco Gallo, Luisa Gallucci, Anna Maria Gambuzzi, Claudio Gandino, Federica Garoglio, Marina Gerra, Danka Giacon, Haim Gitler, Giorgia Giuffrida, Davide Gribaudo, Holly Hughes, Noemi Icardi, Jillian Jones, Adina Kamien-Kazhdan, Sanne Klinge, Daniel Kobrinski, Verena Koja-Perlhefter, Matteo Lafranconi, Paolo Lamberti, Rachel Laufer, Cristina Lavagna, Luciano Marengo, Alessia Margiotta Broglio, Maria Stella Margozzi, Stefano Marson, Martina Marucco, Daniela Matteu, Deborah McCauley, Carmine Miccolis, Massimo Mininni, Valeria Moratti, Luisa Morozzi, Marco Mozzone, Anna Odenato, Fabio Olivieri, Giuseppina Ornaghi, Marina Paglieri, Alfredo Pallesi, Christian Palmers, Riccardo Passoni, Valentina Pastorelli, Massimo Pellisseri, Cristina Pereno, Marco Perrone, Federica Pirani, Tania Pistone, Nicola Poeta, Giovanna Prini Sette, Annalisa Ricciardi, Enzo Riggio, Bianca Roagna, Famiglia Roger, Ettore Rosboch, Fabrizio Russo, Livio Sacco, Grazia Salviati, Michelle Samson, Daniele Sansanese, Ernesto Saracco, Silvio Scafoletti, Catherine Scrivo Baker, Agnese Sferrazza, Rina Sghedoni, Alberto Spallanzani, Catherine Spurrell, Andrea Staub, Chiara Stefani, Simone Strummiello, William Swainger, Samantha Sweeney, Laura Testa, Barbara Tomassi, Alessandro and Simonetta Tosti, Soledad Twombly, Marco Vallora, Henk van Doornik, Hadewych van Heugten, Hetty Wessels, Annarita Ziveri.

Wunderkammer

The exhibition *ProToBalla. The Turin of Balla's Youth*, curated by Virginia Bertone and Filippo Bosco, will be held at the GAM – Galleria Civica d'Arte Moderna e Contemporanea in Turin from 5 November 2016 to 27 February 2017

Ferrero celebrates the firm's 70 anniversary with great pride and gratification in 2016. Among all the initiatives undertaken to mark this major milestone, it is a great pleasure to include *FuTurBalla*, an exhibition of international importance curated by Ester Coen for Fondazione Ferrero. Running from October 2016 to February 2017, it features the extraordinary painter Giacomo Balla, a crucial link between Italian art and international avant-garde.

Life, *Light* and *Speed* are the keywords that will guide and accompany visitors through the rooms and the show as the essential themes of Balla's art: from the social realism of moving works on the outcast and oppressed to Divisionism; from the *Iridescent Interpenetrations* and studies on the perception of light through the analysis of movement all the way to Futurism.

The first work on show is dated 1894 and the last are from the 1920s, thus presenting an overview of a history unique in the world of art, the history of a drive that involved the whole of society and characterized the taste and lifestyle of an entire age.

The long and rigorous research carried out by the curator has made it possible to gather together in Alba works of inestimable value on loan from illustrious public and private collections at the national and international levels, offering the opportunity to gaze upon extraordinary masterpieces seldom lent for exhibitions.

I am indebted to Ester Coen, whose critical expertise has made it possible to construct a complete exhibition that paints a precious and definitive portrait of Giacomo Balla.

I am most grateful to Carolyn Christov-Bakargiev, director of the GAM - Galleria Civica d'Arte Moderna e Contemporanea in Turin, for her unfailing support and her decision to stage *ProToBalla. The Turin of Balla's Youth* in the museum's Wunderkammer, thus strengthening the bonds of synergy between our institutions and offering the visitor a broad and varied range of cultural opportunities.

Sincere thanks are also due to the superintendencies for archaeology, fine arts and the environment of the metropolitan city of Turin and the province of Alessandria, Asti and Cuneo for their constant collaboration and to the Piedmont Region, the Compagnia di San Paolo and the Fondazione Cassa di Risparmio di Cuneo for their support that enhances the value of our initiatives.

I also thank the city of Alba and all the local institutions that have contributed with their proposals to create an interesting and fruitful relationship of cooperation for the benefit of visitors and students.

Maria Franca Ferrero
President of the Fondazione Piera, Pietro and Giovanni Ferrero

The successful collaboration between the Ferrero Foundation and Turin's Galleria Civica d'Arte Moderna e Contemporanea (GAM) now continues with the *FuTurBalla* exhibition in Alba. This rigorous, scholarly project, developed by Ester Coen, offers an important opportunity to examine key moments in the career of Giacomo Balla, who left Turin, the city of his birth, for Rome in 1895. The rich harvest of studies produced in recent years have recognized Balla's major role on the art scene of the 20 century, above all for his ability to combine Italian art with the early international avant-garde through Futurist modernity.

This realization is the result of a slow discovery that began with the crucial exhibition held in 1963 at the Galleria d'Arte Moderna in Turin, fully renovated and reopened to the public just four years earlier. Curated by Enrico Crispolti, the event was strongly supported by Vittorio Viale, then director of Turin's municipal museums, who described it in his introduction to the catalogue as "the first complete retrospective" of Balla's work. As he wrote, "Turin thus brings one of its great sons home again and finally presents a broad and genuine examination of his painting. The Galleria Civica is proud to have undertaken and performed this task and duty in the hope that significant works of the artist's heroic period will soon enter these new premises to fill the inexcusable gap."

This hope was to be fulfilled and now the museum can boast a precious Balla collection, a large slice of which is on show in Alba. We refer to the studies known as *Iridescent Interpenetrations*, key evidence of an exploration of colour, vibration and decoration that was to lead around 1912 to work of an abstract character based on the dynamic optical decomposition of light.

As in the earlier case of the exhibition of works by Felice Casorati, the generous support of the Ferrero Foundation has made it possible for the Wunderkammer of the GAM to host an exhibition, curated by Virginia Bertone and Filippo Bosco, in conjunction with the one in Alba.

Entitled *ProToBalla. The Turin of Balla's Youth*, it examines the painter's links with the city, from documentation of the poverty-stricken Borgo del Rubatto district, where Balla was born in 1871, to his friendships and complex artistic development. This dialogue with Piedmontese painting continued until 1907, the year when Balla produced his extraordinary *Portrait of Clelia Ghedini Marani*, now in the GAM, and Giuseppe Pellizza da Volpedo – whose explorations of Divisionism and Symbolism were a crucial point of reference for the young Balla – died by his own hand.

Carolyn Christov-Bakargiev
Director of the GAM - Galleria Civica d'Arte Moderna e Contemporanea, Turin

Our best wishes to the Fondazione Piera, Pietro e Giovanni Ferrero, the curator Prof. Ester Coen and all the organizers of the *FuTurBalla* exhibition for the success of an event that we have gladly allowed to take place under the aegis of the Piedmont Region and that adds cultural lustre to the province of Alba, the region and the country as a whole.

Initiatives like this must in fact constitute an opportunity not only to promote the territory, its traditions and its strengths, thus further enriching the range of cultural and tourist attractions that draw national and international visitors to Piedmont in ever greater numbers, but also for residents and "next-door neighbours" to broaden their knowledge of the area.

I have always been struck by Giacomo Balla's continual experimentation and international horizons, present both in his personal development and in his artistic trajectory, constantly in search of new stimuli, path-breaking approaches and revolutionary fusions of ideas and techniques.

Balla's work as a whole, from his early social realism to the definitive spheres of Futurism, illustrates his ability to link Italian art with the international avant-garde and combine intellectual contributions and concrete action at the highest level in accordance with a particularly Piedmontese way of thinking and doing.

In paying tribute to this great artist, the Ferrero Foundation once again displays its ability to act as a cultural multiplier and a cornerstone of regional development.

I am sure that the illustrious masterpieces from public and private collections on show will offer not only art lovers but also and above all families and young people an opportunity for insight into a slice of Italian history that is important in both artistic and social terms, a period in which progress was inspired and propelled by change and a drive for modernity.

Sergio Chiamparino
President of the Piedmont Region

The Compagnia di San Paolo believes very strongly in supporting the knowledge, preservation and appreciation of our cultural heritage as a tool to create development for the community. Through the adoption of different but complementary methods, it acts accordingly to support cultural institutions of the highest rank on initiatives capable of contributing to the common good.

These convictions underpin the decision to support museum projects for exhibitions capable both of furthering studies in the art-historical sphere and of prompting reflections to foster the growth of the general public.

FuTurBalla is in fact particularly significant by virtue of a curatorial approach of unquestionably great interest and scholarly value that will shed new light on Giacomo Balla's work and life. The prestige and expertise of the Ferrero Foundation also guarantee that the event will meet the highest standards of quality, efficiency and economic sustainability and play its part as one of the major attractions drawing flows of visitors into the territory.

Finally, not least through its rich educational programme, the initiative will help to foster an interest in art and its most meaningful expressions among ever-larger sections of the public.

We therefore wish to thank all those who have worked on the exhibition, which will hopefully help to establish the image of Piedmont as a key point of cultural production and reflection in the international panorama.

Compagnia di San Paolo

Support for top-level artistic events capable of enhancing the cultural attractions of our province, fostering social cohesion and generating major returns in terms of income and tourism for the local territory is one of the goals pursued by Fondazione Cassa di Risparmio di Cuneo (CRC) through its activities. Such efforts are essential above all at the present time, when the availability of resources in the cultural sphere is subject to constant and general reduction at all levels.

The exhibition of works by the Turinese artist Giacomo Balla offers a precious opportunity made possible by the collaboration between Fondazione Ferrero, committed to making modern Italian artists more widely known through major events, Galleria d'Arte Moderna in Turin, the Superintendency for Fine Arts of Piedmont and Fondazione CRC. Visitors will be able to enjoy a unique and original experience developed on the basis of a rigorous and painstaking research, feasting their eyes on masterpieces from museums and collections inside and outside Italy that could otherwise be hard to see. This synergy between public and private bodies in our region offers deep insight into the life and work of the Piedmontese painter, a penetrating observer of early 20th-century society and extraordinary model for the artistic and cultural movements of subsequent decades.

It is with great pleasure that Fondazione CRC lends its support to this event, which will offer visitors a unique and enriching experience and the province an important opportunity to enhance its lustre in Italy and all over the world.

Giandomenico Genta
President of the Fondazione CRC - Cassa di Risparmio di Cuneo

The exhibition offered to us by the Ferrero Foundation every two years has by now become an appointment that the city of Alba could hardly do without, not only for the tens of thousands of visitors it attracts every time but also for the cultural enrichment it provides.

The artist featured on each occasion is one of Piedmontese roots, able to make a new and unique contribution to art, thus winning renown far beyond the regional borders. Needless to say, this description is also largely applicable to the Ferrero company itself.

On the basis of solid academic training, Giacomo Balla succeeded in giving new expression to a reality in the throes of change. He experimented with the representation of movement, almost as though seeking to reproduce on canvas the miracle revealed by the new technique of cinematography. Beneath his unquestionable and disconcerting technical ability lay a vision of the world that endeavoured to give an intellectually adequate response to a reality undergoing radical transformation. While the movement of which Balla is one of the most famous members may well inspire misgivings today, given the aspects that made Futurism a champion of anti-democratic views and a forerunner of Fascism in certain respects, this cannot blind us to the fascination of many of its artistic results.

Much of Balla's best can be seen in this exhibition, which features works from the most renowned museums and the most illustrious private collections. The fact that they have been made available on loan so generously speaks volumes about the reputation enjoyed by the initiatives of the Ferrero Foundation.

Like the others before it, this event has the further unquestionable merit of not only offering visitors the opportunity for passive contemplation of what is on show but also endeavouring with different tools to foster a deeper understanding among the young, at whom an extensive array of educational activities is aimed. In conclusion, let it be repeated that what is offered here is an opportunity for cultural growth that should not be missed. For this I thank the Ferrero Foundation in the name of the city as a whole.

Maurizio Marello
Mayor of Alba

CONTENTS

LIFE

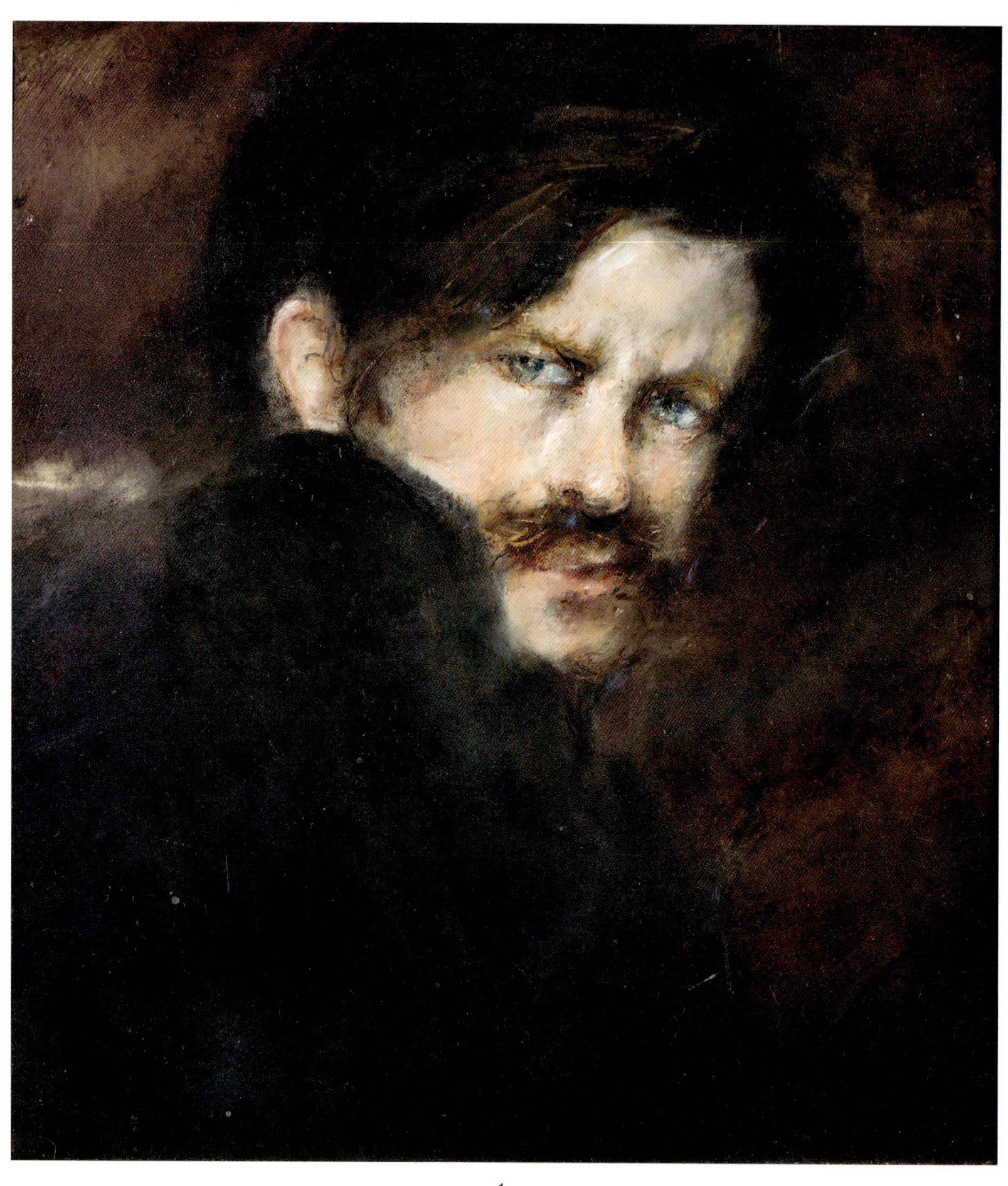

1

Autoritratto (Self-Portrait), c. 1894
oil on photographic paper, 33.9 x 29.8 cm

Life

Ester Coen

It was just a few months after the birth of Giacomo Balla in Turin on 18 July 1871 that Rome became the new capital of Italy.[1] Turin, the political focal point of the Risorgimento and capital up to the early years after national unification, was impoverished in its role by the departure of the court and all the administrative apparatus and plunged into a phase of severe economic depression, only to recover through transformation into an industrial centre of extraordinary importance in the space of a few years (fig. 1).

Balla's mother decision to move to Rome in 1895, during a still uncertain period in the recently unified country's history, bound up above all with the fear of not being able to offer her only child any prospects in a city where career possibilities were hard to glimpse.[2] A life devoted to art was still a distant dream and Rome appeared from afar to be a place of great dynamism, with countless activities under way to set a city of just 200,000 inhabitants on an equal footing with the modern metropolises north of the Alps (fig. 2). Vast sums and supporting means were deployed in a colossal undertaking to redraw the map of the city in relation to the demands of its new and important role. The urban planning scheme of 1883 envisioned the development of the railway system and the construction of entire districts to house the new entrepreneurial class and a cosmopolitan bourgeoisie attracted by the beauties of Rome, but above all by the potential for major investment, the prospects of immediate economic and speculative developments or the possibility of a safe haven from turbulent political situations. In this short period Rome experienced the inebriation of sudden and unexpected rebirth. Dialects mixed with accents of various origins, words from distant countries, sharply distinguished intonations, tastes and styles of rare eclecticism and original extravagance in a singular *lingua franca*. The simple words of the young Balla, his quick impressions of the newly explored city, capture the things seen in the beauty of bright and varied colours: "I visited St Peter's. Fine piece of landscape behind with the church of San Giovanni. I was really impressed by the Colosseum, especially in its overall effect of grandeur. The countryside around it is nice even in the rain. I must re-

1. Map of Turin in 1880. Via Moncalieri is on the other side of the river from Piazza Vittorio where was born Balla

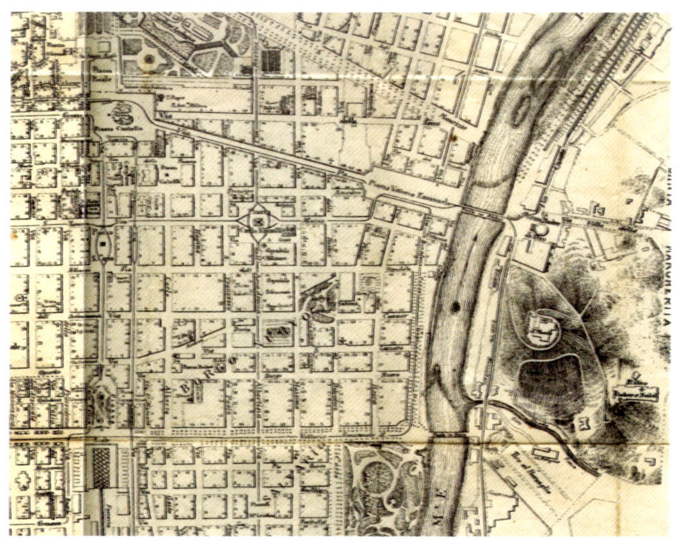

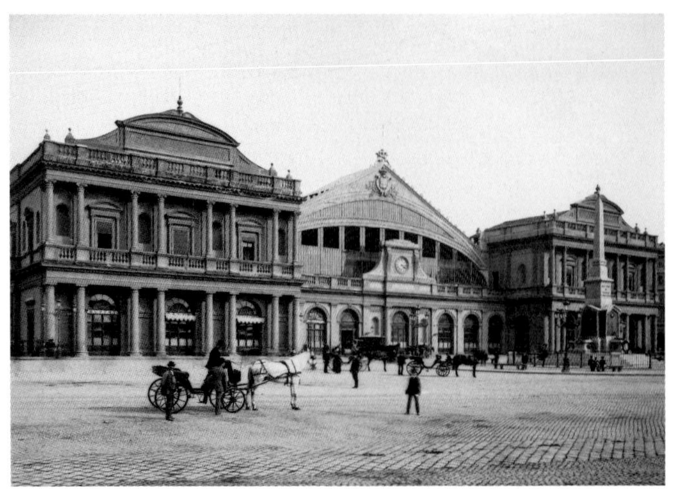

2. Termini railway station in Rome at the end of the 19th century

3. Giacomo Balla in the Roman countryside near Sacrofano, c. 1896

member the countryside by St Peter's. The countryside is very clean, which is why I like it. Found a nice piece of stone in the area near the Capitol. Painting by Guercino with great chiaroscuro. I don't like the filthy streets: be careful not to get used to them. You meet a lot of eccentrics. You see foreigners throwing money around and living it up. I should do caricatures of them."[3] Concise strokes of a pen ready to capture the two aspects on which the artist was to construct his simple and great work in the course of an entire lifetime. In a contemplative relationship with nature in its quintessential forms, in the feeling of absolute oneness with every element of the universe, in an emotive palpitation of the senses arising at the same time out of passionate participation in the loftiest expressions of the human intellect (fig. 3). The beauty and charm of the landscape and a careful reading of the great masters of the past, his first spiritual guides. In the walks through the streets of a Rome with plebeian characteristics, surrounded by countryside stretching in towards the centre, the stops in museums constituted moments of high culture and training. It was Guercino, rather than Caravaggio, that caught an eye resolutely alert to accentuated perspective and shafts of light enhancing colour but not form. A precise choice that eludes any dramatic sense of representation. It is the combination of objective material and awareness that reveals the deep, analytical truth of reality, a reflection of the mystery of creation. It was the years in Turin with the lithographer Pietro Cassina and then the photographers of the Bertieri family[4] that trained the eye of the young Balla in the twofold singularity of the precise, rigorous study of detail on the one hand and precise visual trajectories based on unusual and personal angles on the other. It is as though the care and precision of the technique of engraving and the transversal direction of the mechanical

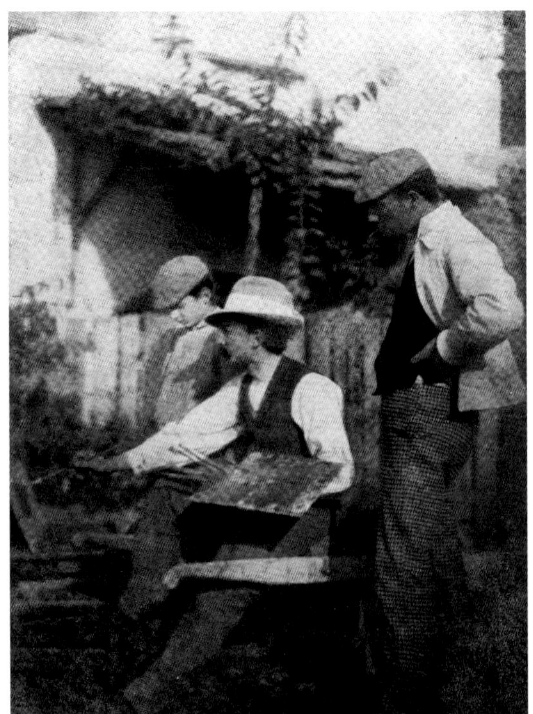

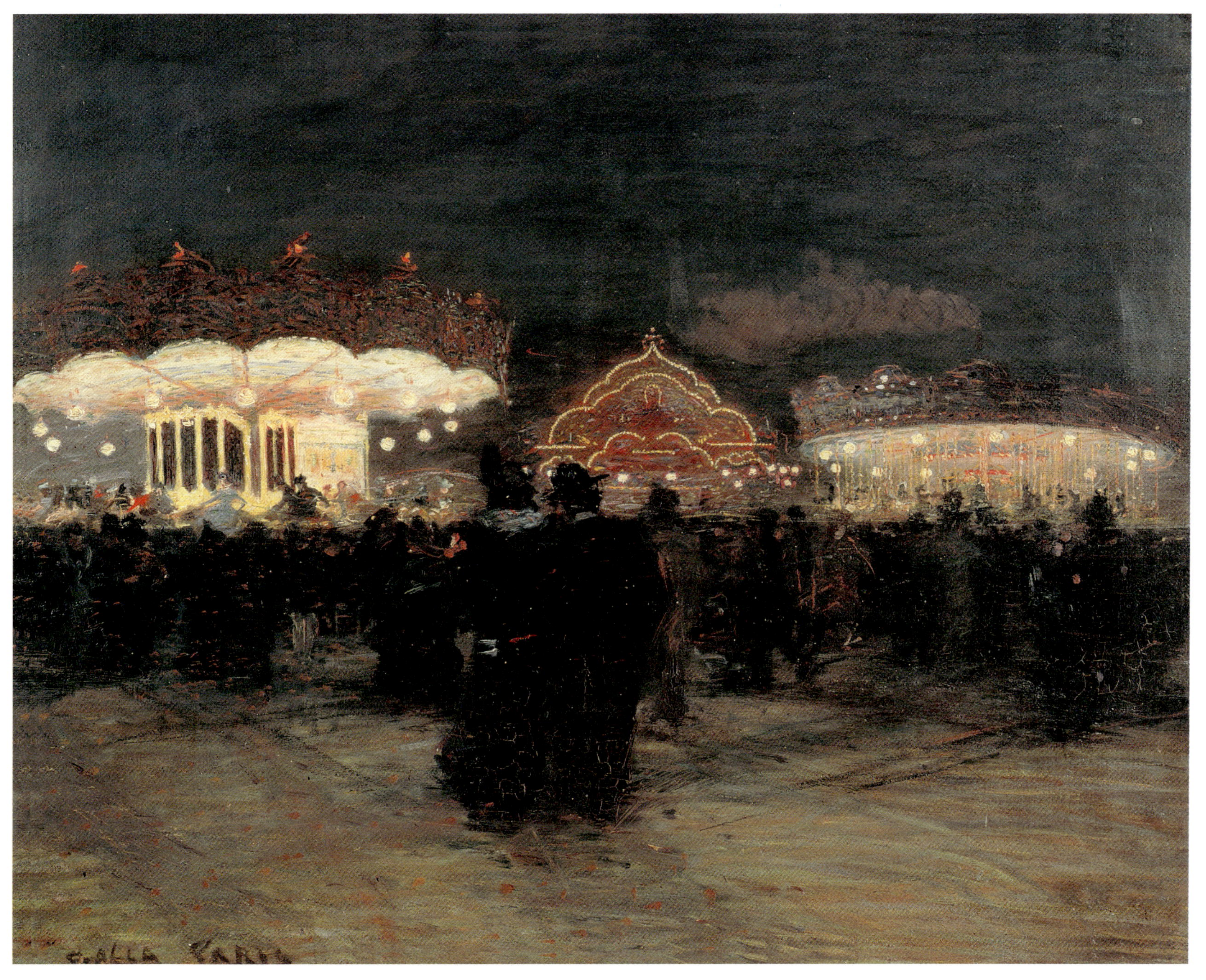

2

Fiera parigina (Parisian Fair), 1900
oil on canvas, 65 x 81 cm

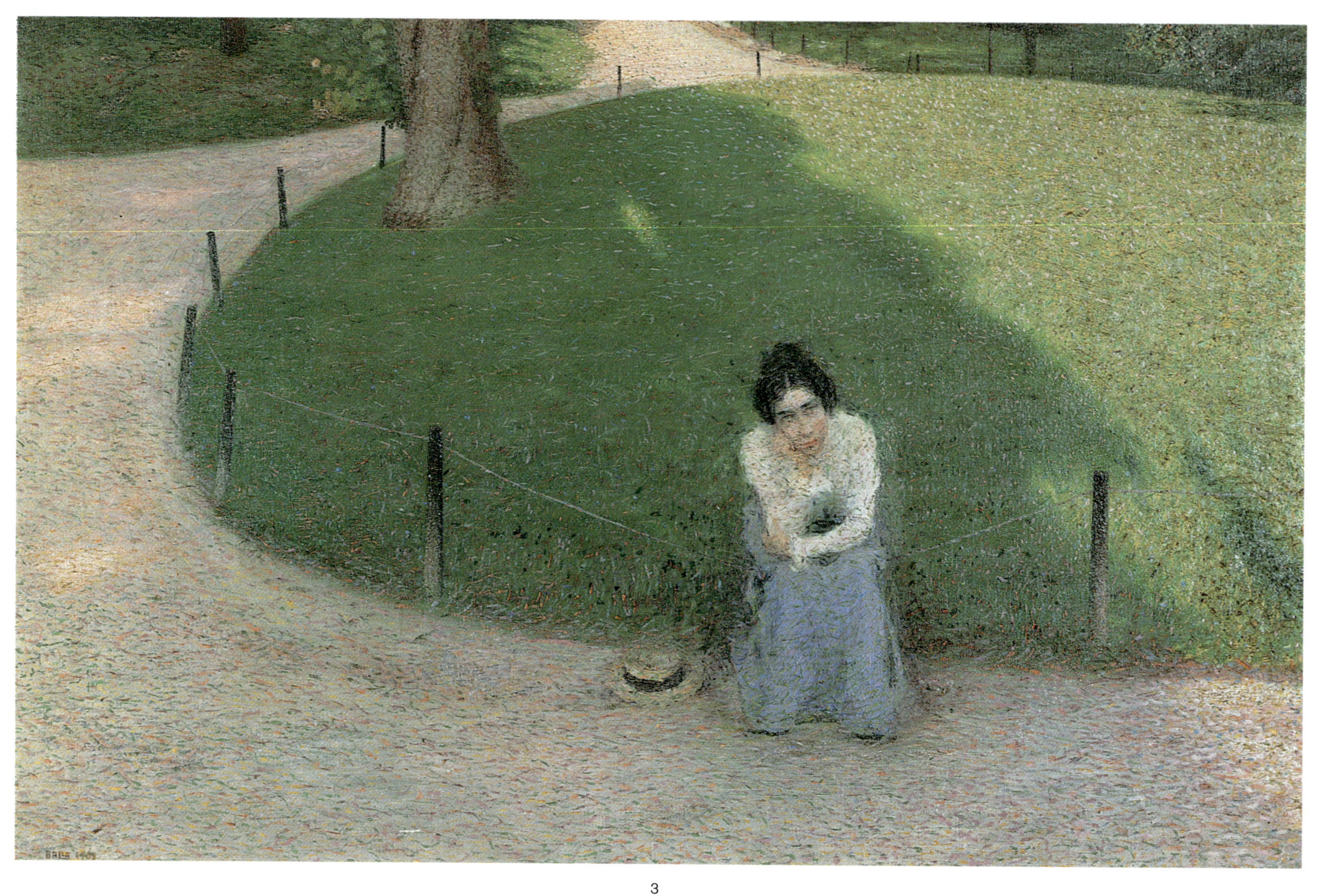

3

La fidanzata al Pincio (The Girlfriend at the Pincio), 1902
oil on canvas, 60.5 x 90 cm

4. Giacomo Grosso
Supremo convegno (*Supreme Meeting*), 1895
Lost work

4a. Giacomo Grosso's painting, *Supremo convegno* (*Supreme Meeting*), shown at the first Venice Biennial in 1895

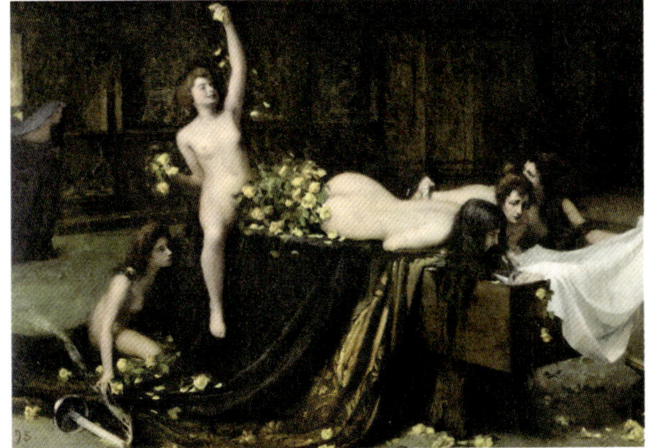

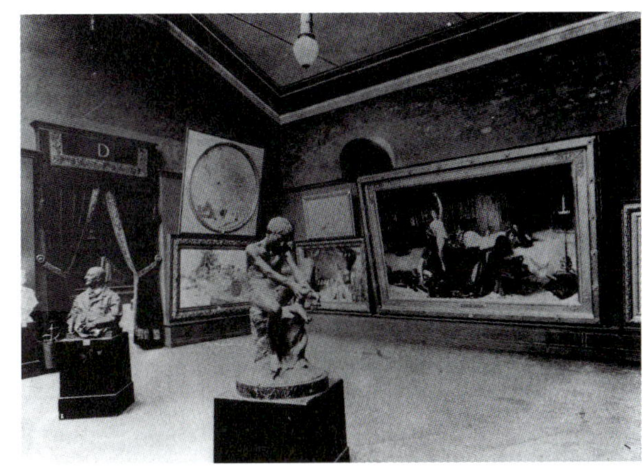

lens (fig. 5) together had left the indelible imprint of a whole way of looking at things. Still strongly inspired by French positivism and the application of new scientific methods to the spheres of knowledge, this period also bore witness to major technological innovations, systematic doctrines and extraordinary discoveries. It was not therefore by chance, in this cultural climate, that Balla not only attended Giacomo Grosso's (figs. 4-4a) lectures and courses of painting but was also so struck by the theories of Cesare Lombroso as to follow his investigations into criminal anthropology and Darwinian determinism. He may have been fascinated by medical research into deviant behaviour and figures marked by a pitiless society with the brand of exclusion or infamy. He could also have been attracted by the studies of physiognomy launched with a view to taxonomic definition of types such as the criminal, the politician, the revolutionary, the lunatic (figs. 6a-f). Some sign of the persistence of these interests can perhaps be seen in the fact that the first graphic and pictorial impressions of the early years in Rome,[5] traces of which have survived, were caricatures – "autosmorfie" or "macchiette" – of a world of craftsmen and street hawkers (fig. 7). The snapshot-like capturing of an expression, the mirror of a secret, inner psyche, became an essential tool to address a genre in which Balla was to be a very great master, namely the portrait (fig. 8). It was, however, above all with the world of outcasts that he had strong feelings of empathy,[6] the guiding thread of a personal exploration, of his truest vision. It is this vision and his extraordinary ability to penetrate the simplest aspects of life that gave birth in 1902 to one of the most innovative and intriguing canvases of the century, namely *Fallimento* (*Bankruptcy*). It presents the door of a shop closed for the reason indicated in the title[7], with a degree of realism visible in the penetrating details of the bluntest representation.

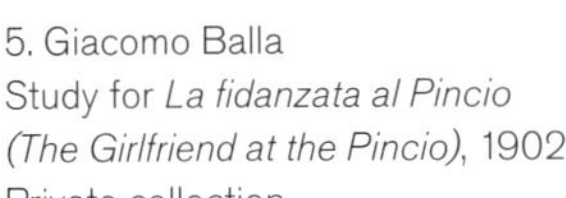

5. Giacomo Balla
Study for *La fidanzata al Pincio* *(The Girlfriend at the Pincio)*, 1902
Private collection

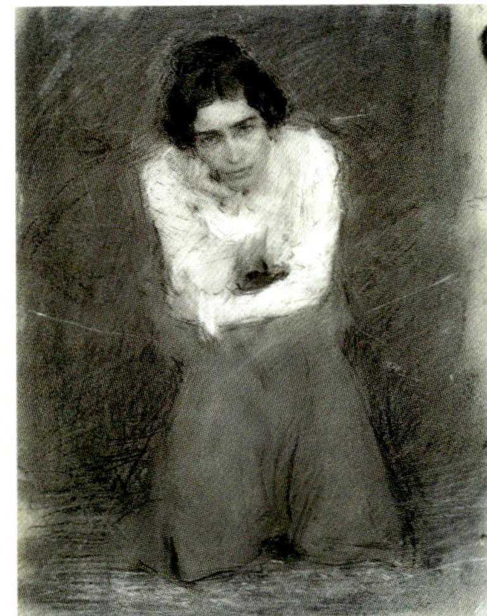

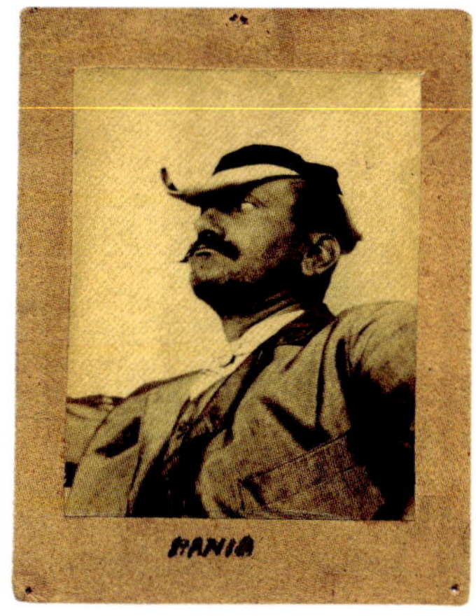

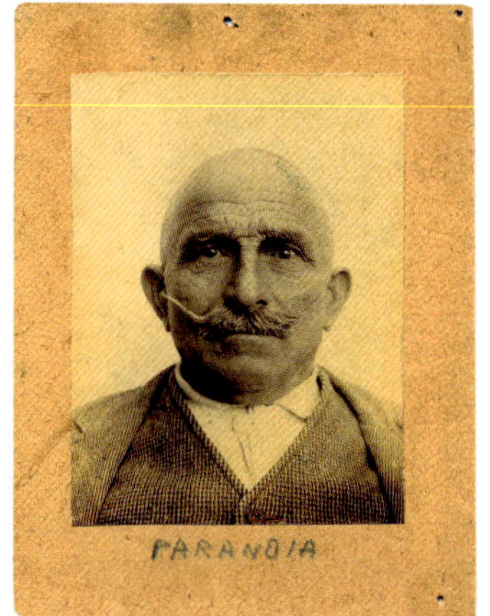

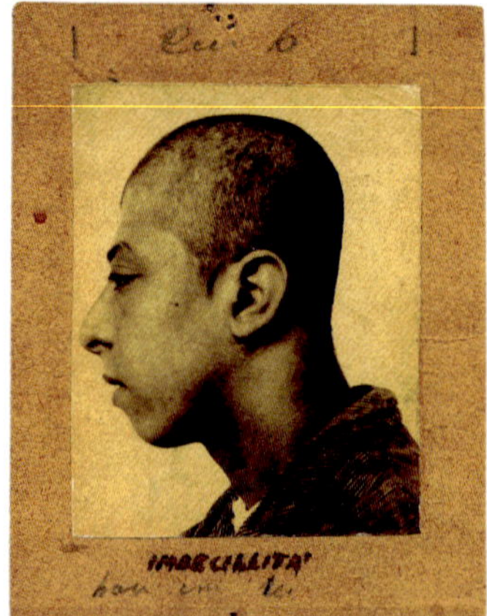

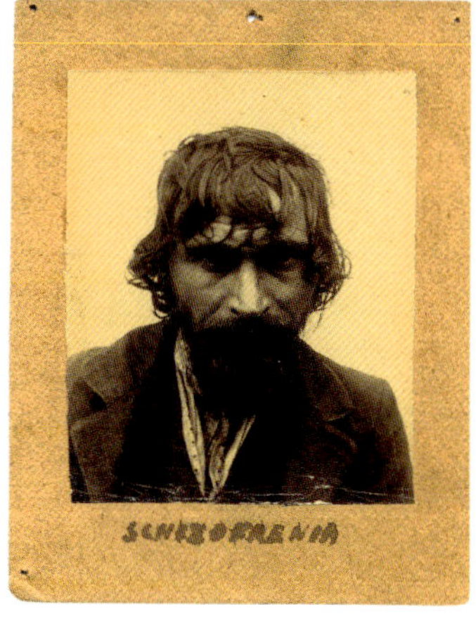

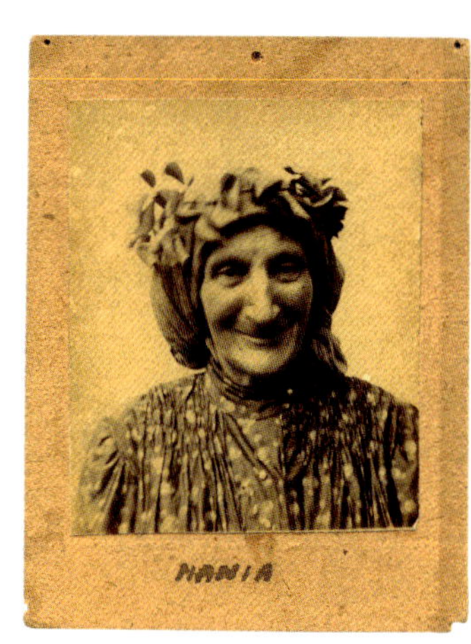

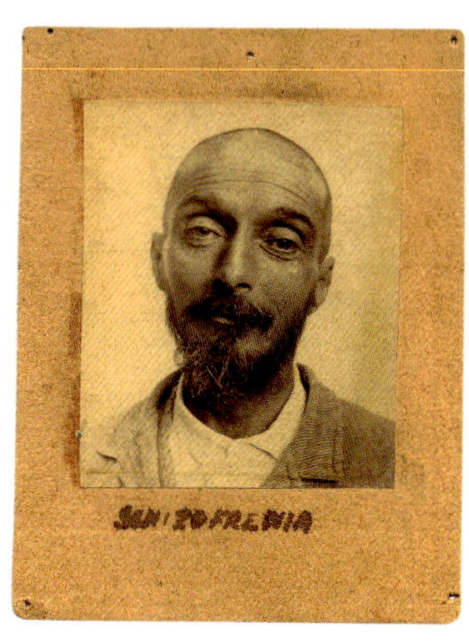

6a-f. Mental hospital in Reggio Emilia: series of photographs showing patients with different illnesses, c. 1900
Turin, Museo di Antropologia Criminale Cesare Lombroso

7. Giacomo Balla
Macchietta romana (*Roman Caricature*), 1898
Private collection

At the same time, however, Balla inverts the realism and transforms it into something very modern indeed, with his sharp definition and the oblique perspective that truncates part of the façade to deviate the frontality into a strongly tilted fragment. It is the extraordinary ability of a skilled hand that turns reality upside-down, starting from the objective element and creating a different vision that sublimates it in an unconventional dimension. "Gripping objective matter with all my strength gives birth to the reaction of the subjective abstract my painting *Fallimento* objective matter not on a par."[8] Thus he wrote years later to his pupil and friend Umberto Boccioni, perhaps recalling criticisms of undue attachment to reality (fig. 9). A few lines of absolute concision, fully aware of the force of impact of the simple translation of phenomena by attuning the objective to the subjective to the point of transfiguration of their physical essence. From Turin to Rome, emotive identification with the fringes of society excluded from every activity

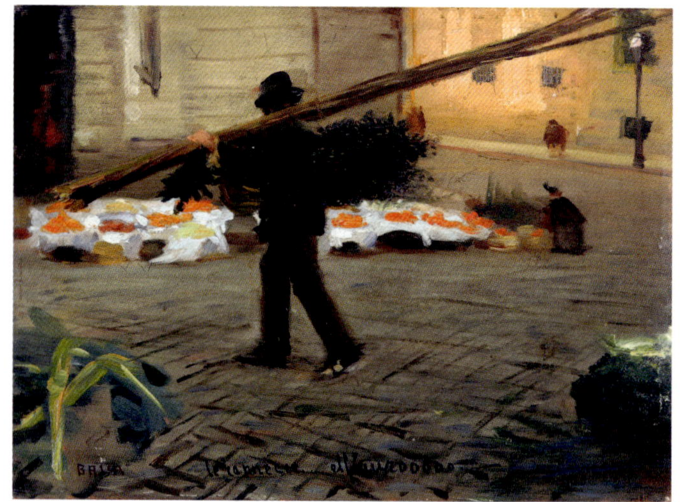

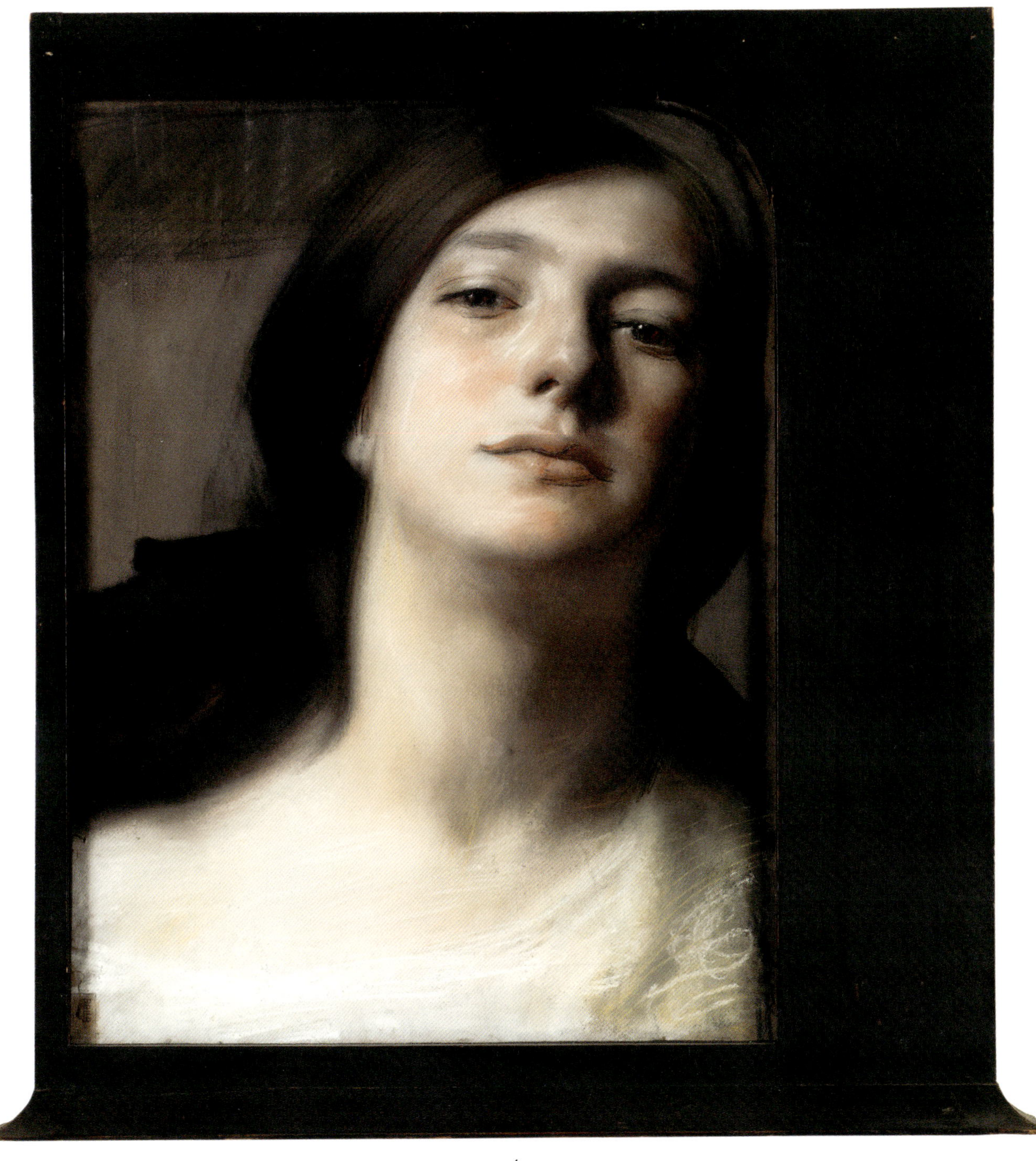

4

La seducente – Enrichetta (The Charmer – Enrichetta), c. 1902
crayon on paper, 45 x 36 cm

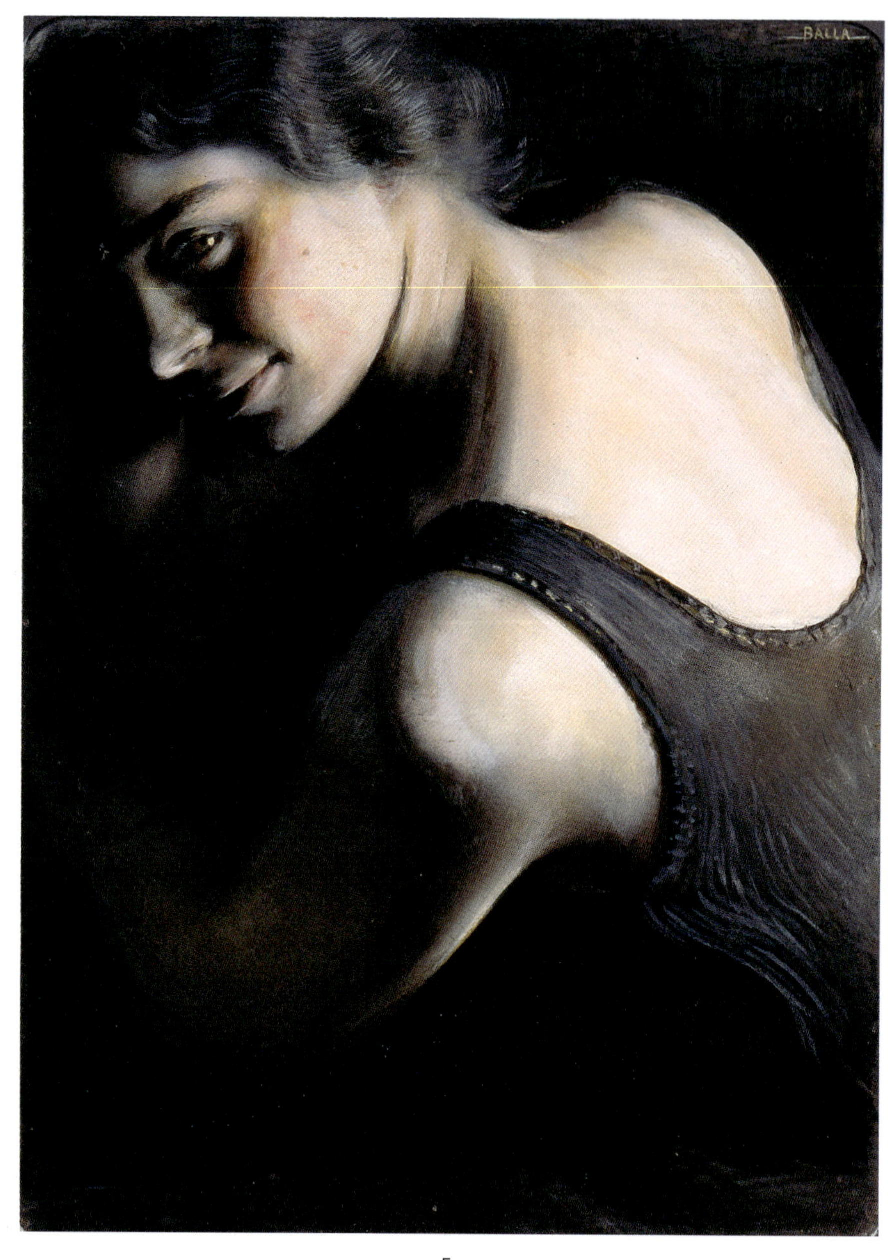

5

Il dubbio (Doubt), 1907–08
oil on paper, 67 x 50 cm

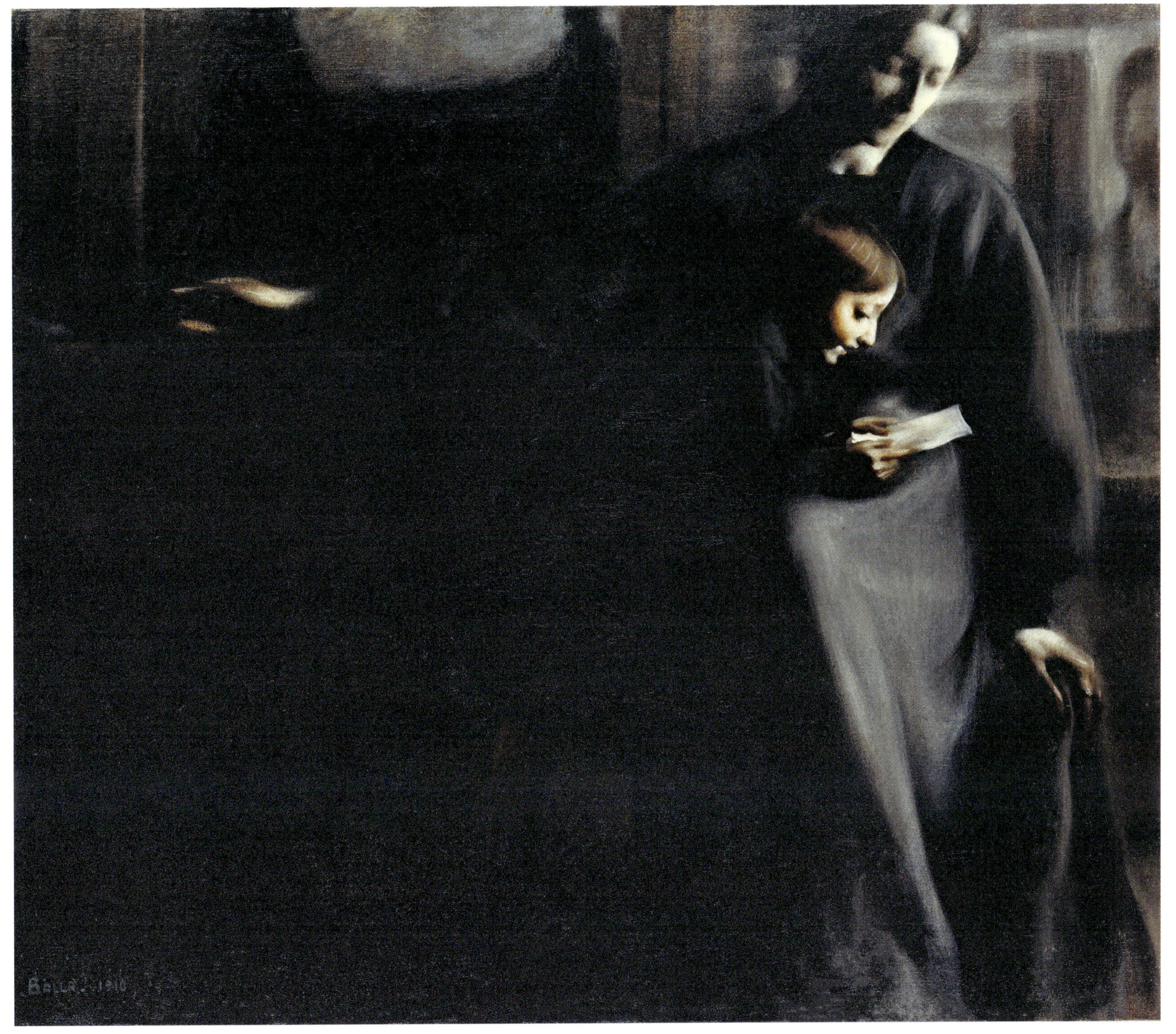

6

Affetti (Attachment), 1910
oil on canvas, 115.5 x 130 cm

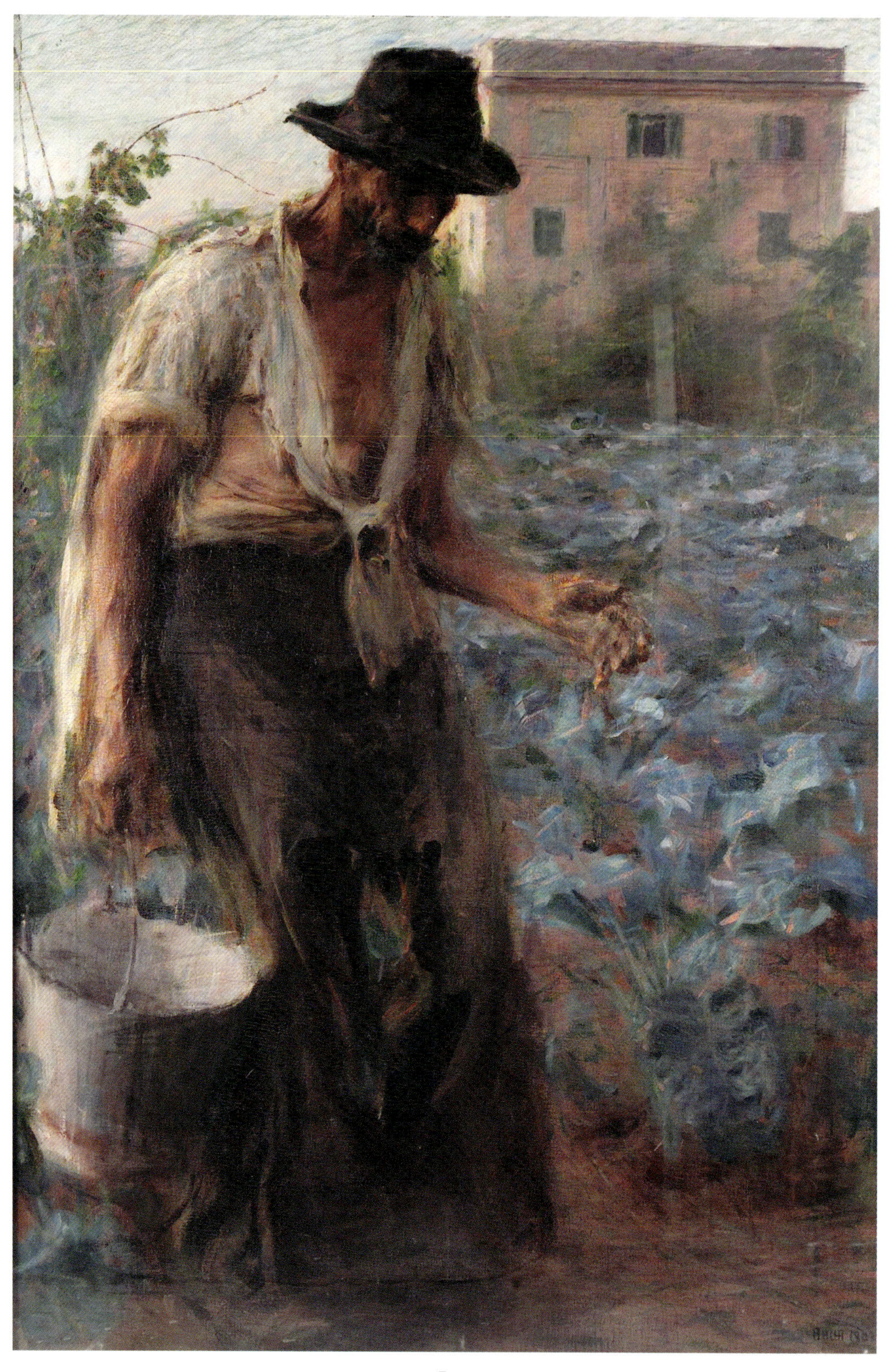

7

Il contadino (The Peasant), 1902
oil and tempera on canvas, 175 x 115 cm

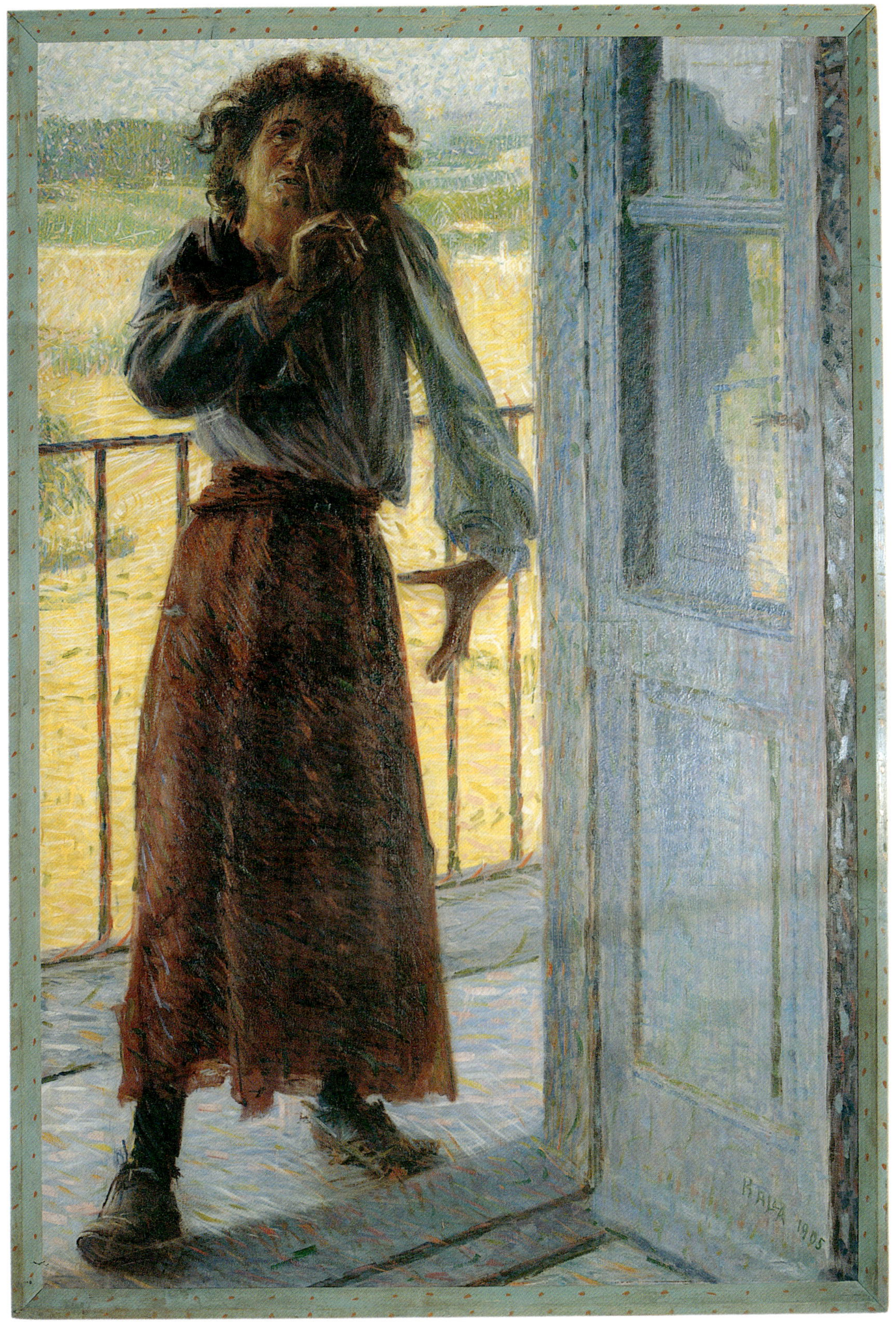

8

La pazza (The Madwoman), 1905
oil on canvas, 175 x 115 cm

and every feeling of compassion grew parallel to the contradictions of a city unable for decades to elevate itself to the rank of a capital city. "Much greatness but all scattered and sad. The nauseating horror of the old districts. Linen hanging from windows on a rope held away from the wall with a stick. Entire loads of washing, long drapes dangling, shirts, white linen and then a jumble of coloured linen. The mixed odour of rancid oil and poverty."[9] This was the pitiless comment of Émile Zola on his arrival in Rome at the end of 1894, an image of the city to which he added further touches of colour in the days that followed: "What a strange thing the natural history of Rome is in this modern revival! The old trunk still attempting to blossom. The dream of Rome as capital dates from 1860 and everything has been sacrificed to this necessary, inevitable, patriotic idea. A fight against the very nature of the city they are intent on resuscitating at all costs in spite of the physical obstacles. The leaden weight of antiquity. Ancient Rome forced to become a modern Rome. The *Urbs* of the ancient and future eras. And the enthusiasm in the pride of this conception. The inebriation and the inevitable defeat on the emergence of the reality: an enormous city built for a population that does not exist, the modern capital run aground on the real city with its lack of communications, mortal outer ring of sterile land and dead river. Pride has dreamt of what reality cannot deliver. What an astounding and interesting case, what a page in the natural history of a city."[10] A great polemicist and keen observer of political events, the French writer reveals all the drama of the wave of speculation in that historical period and the doom of the aristocrats and entrepreneurs who wanted to build "the third Rome",[11] the Umbertine Rome that Balla now observed through eyes sharpened by the study of anatomy and composition. A Rome torn between reconstruction and disintegration (fig. 10) that Robert Musil could still describe in 1913 as simultaneously repellent and mysterious: "Piazza Montecito-

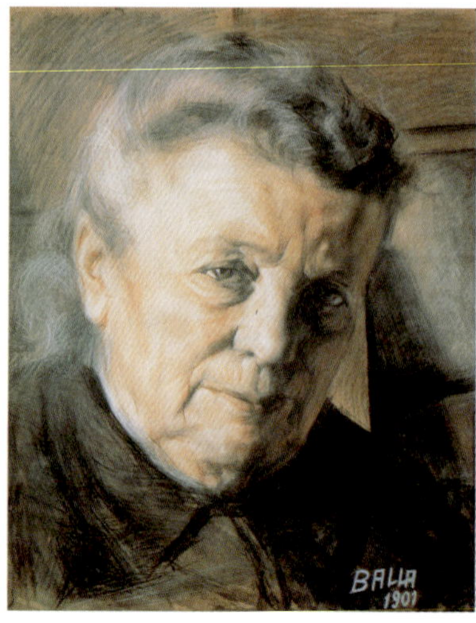

8. Giacomo Balla
Ritratto della madre
(*Portrait of the Artist's Mother*), 1901
Rome, Galleria Nazionale

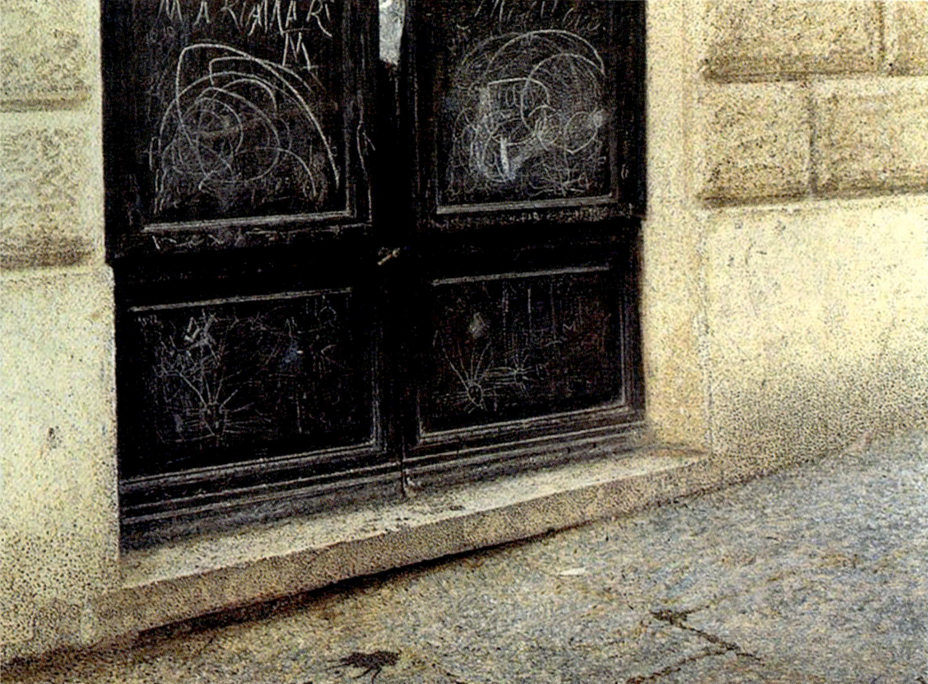

9. Giacomo Balla
Fallimento (*Bankruptcy*), 1902
Private collection

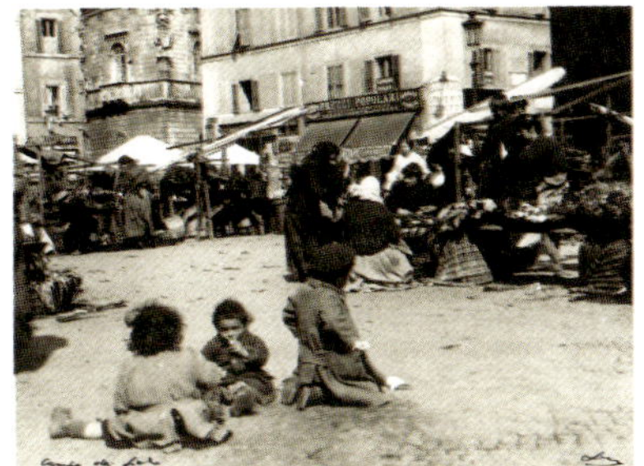

10. Campo de' Fiori in Rome in the late 19th century

rio, in front of the parliament building, in the middle of dense traffic, I saw a baker run bare-chested across the street, towards the urinal or driven by some other need. Here in Rome I saw a horse laugh. It was on Viale della Regina. An elegant, small, young carriage horse. It was hitched to a wall (there was a tavern or a carter's yard, something with a courtyard, foliage and cane fencing set back from the row of houses on the unpaved roadside to the left) and being currycombed by a groom."[12]

Slightly farther along, however, it looked wild and barbaric: "Big palms with trunks like gigantic pineapples. The leaves as though coloured with an emulsion of dust. Their shape is Cubist, futuristic, ugly but eternal: the same feeling as you get from elephants. A cactus in the upper part of the climb to the Pincio, completely suffocated by stones, with holes at the base of the leaves like the holes in Palaeolithic stone axes. But its life has gone on around those parts. The life here is as tough as this cactus."[13]

After first staying with an uncle, a royal huntsman at Palazzo Quirinale, and then in humble lodgings in the vicinity of the railway station and Piazza delle Terme, Balla and his mother moved in 1896 into a small shop on the street in Via Piemonte (figs. 11-11a) in the new Ludovisi district, filled with the homes of rich middle-class families, mostly arrived from the north. Elegant private houses in various styles sprang up in the space of a few years in the area between Porta Pia and Via Veneto, where the first big hotels were built, bounded to the south, towards the Termini station, by the Palazzo delle Finanze, inaugurated in 1876. These homes, small architectural gems of a whole range of types – many of which designed and built by Carlo Pincherle, the father of Alberto Moravia, Giulio Podesti and the better-known Ernesto Basile – were also to be the stage of unbridled eccentricity, albeit for only a few decades. The district of rich industrialists, businessmen and important political

11. A view of Via Piemonte, where Giacomo Balla had a combined home and studio as from 1896

11a. Giacomo Balla and his mother in the home and studio on Via Piemonte

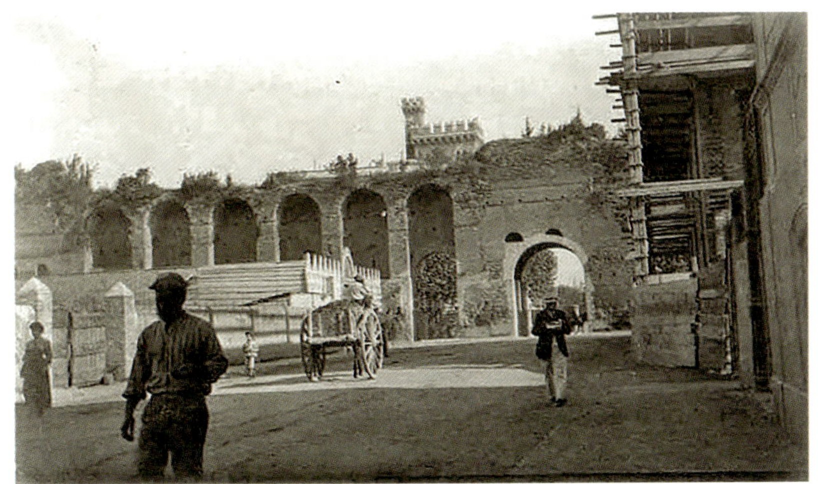

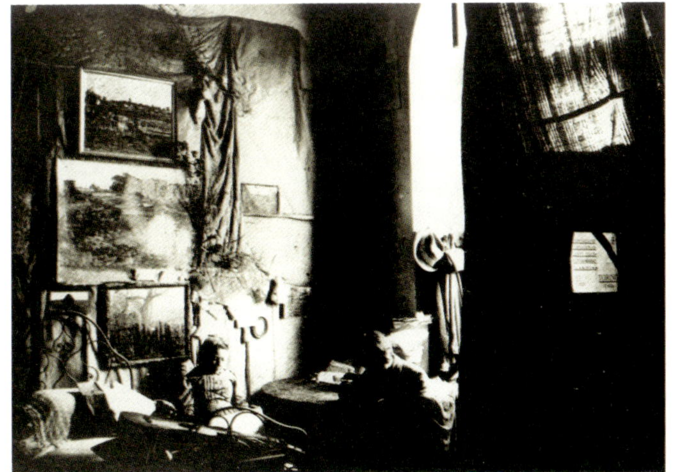

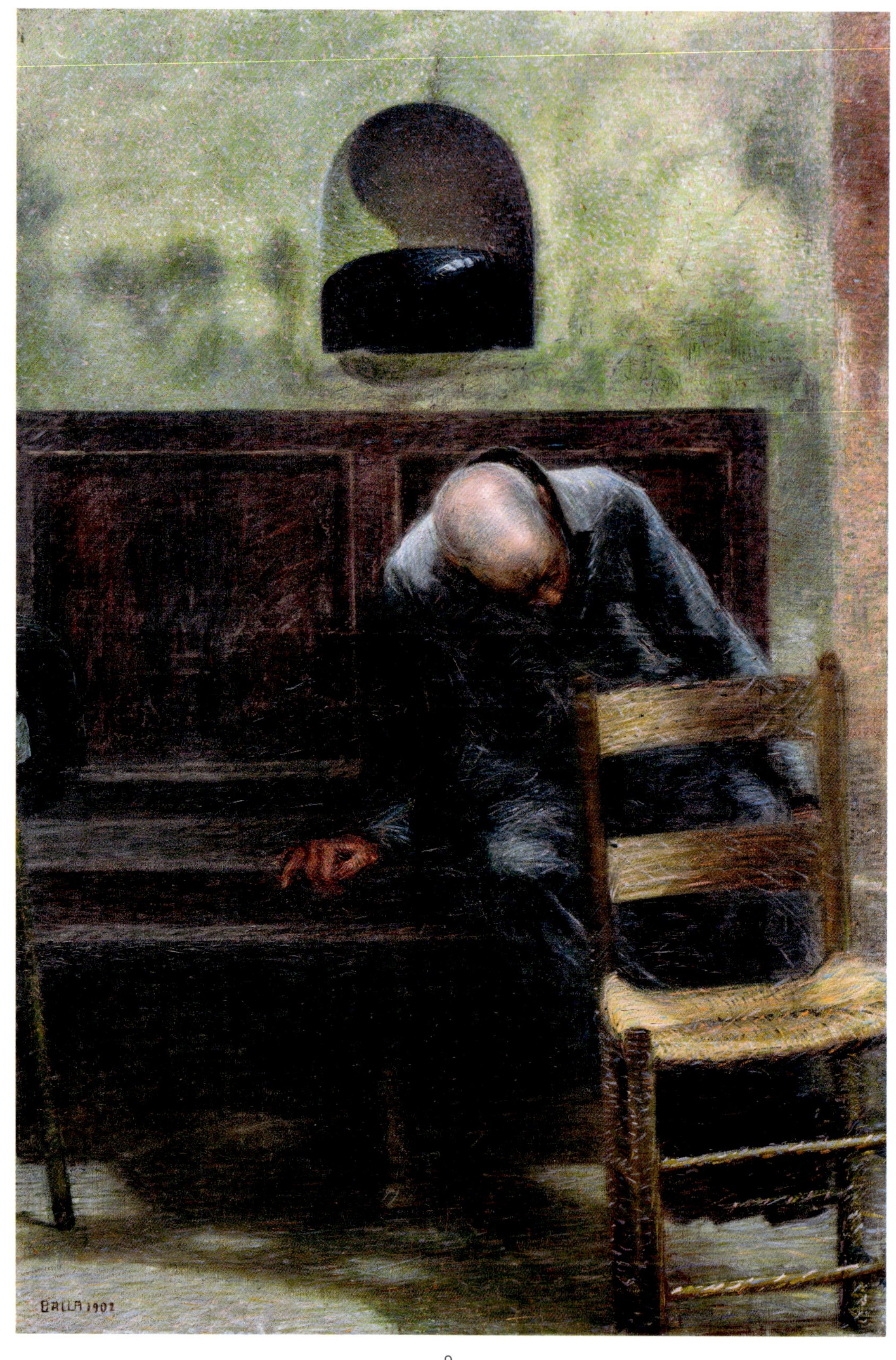

9

Il mendicante (The Beggar), 1902
oil on canvas, 175.5 x 115 cm

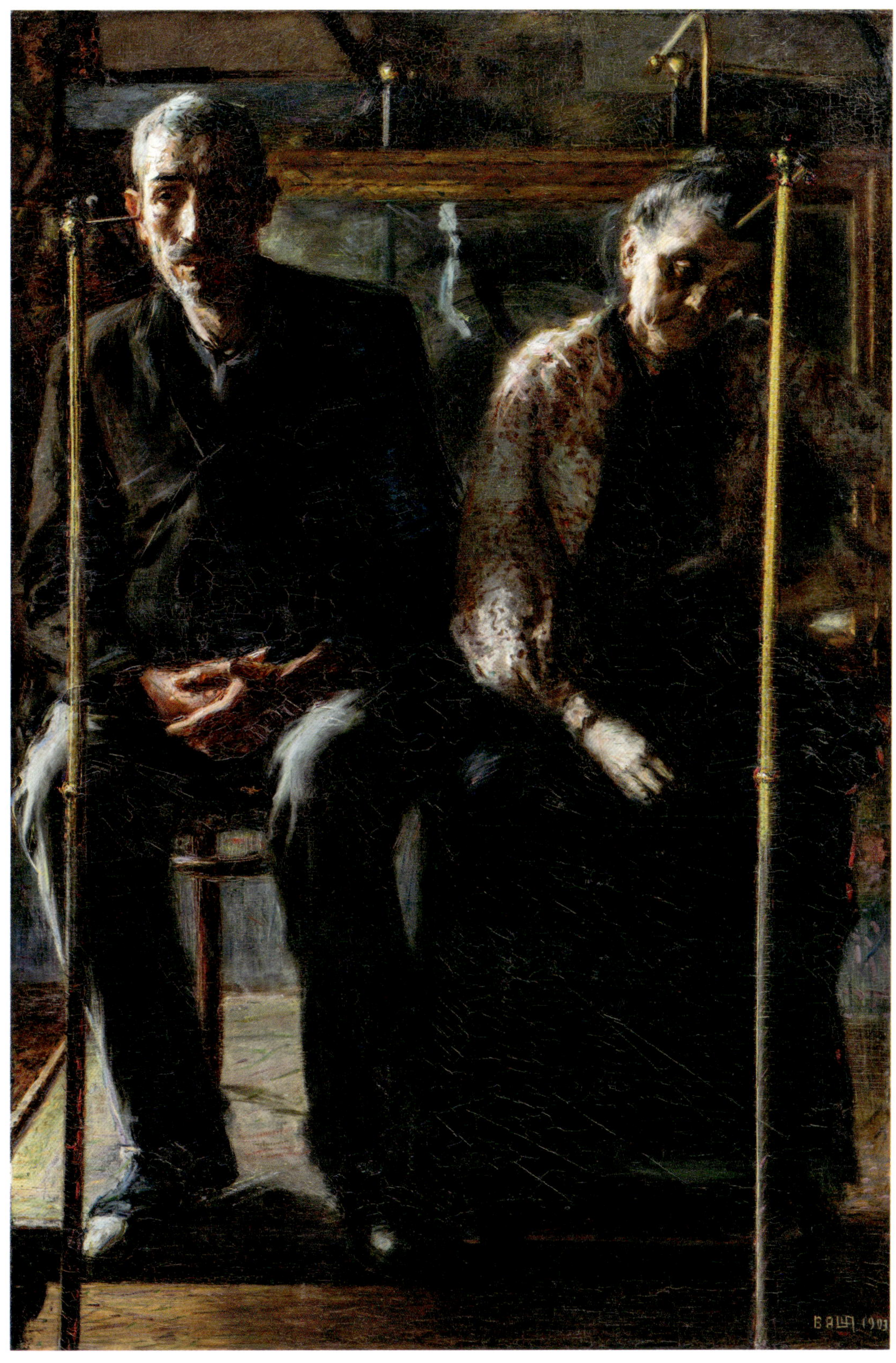

10

I malati (The Sick), 1903
oil on canvas, 175 x 115 cm

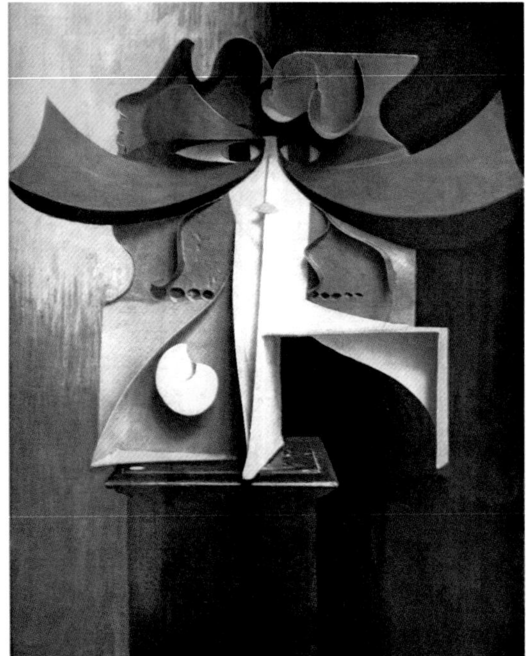

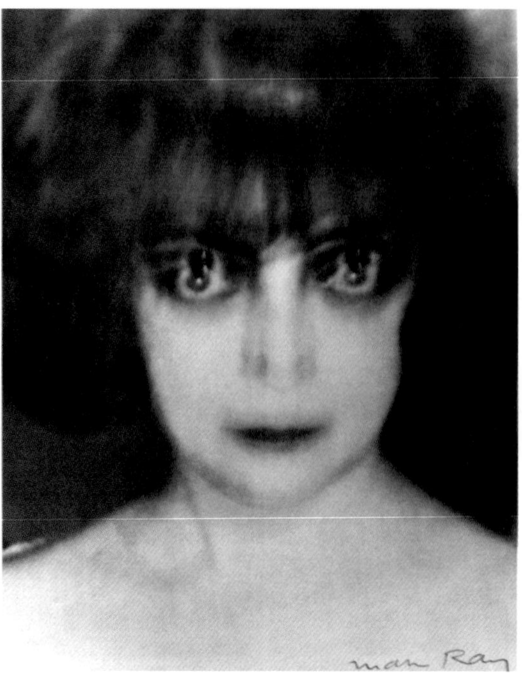

12. Giacomo Balla
Ritratto della marchesa Casati
(*Portrait of the Marchesa Casati*), c. 1916
Lost work

12a. Man Ray
Marquise Casati, Le portrait de mon âme,
1922

figures like Rudinì and Rattazzi was also inhabited as from the beginning of the new century by very odd and off-beat figures floating between sophisticated crepuscular poetry, dark mystery cults and esoteric rituals of initiation on the one hand and the impetus of aesthetic explorations running parallel to the progressive thrust of contemporary life on the other. The period saw Queen Elena and the Queen Mother visit the Argentinian sculptress Lola Mora in the studio beside her beautiful house with a tower with a conical roof in Via Dogali,[14] and Count Lulù[15] Primoli, "last of the Napoleonids" and brother of the better-known Giuseppe or Gegé, set up a studio in a building on Via Sallustiana.[16] A photographer known for his work, he was described as the "highly refined, cultured and intelligent but tragically pastist son of a Bonaparte, master of all courtesy and all erotic-sentimental oddity" by Filippo Tommaso Marinetti[17] after a party "in honour of the maimed" spent in the company of his "Futurist friend" the Marchesa Luisa Casati di Soncino, an extremely singular and unconventional figure,[18] ethereal and evanescent but with very marked features. The Princess Mananà Pignatelli d'Aragona Cortés, another resident of Via Piemonte living just a few steps away from what had been Balla's simple combined room and studio, was instead mysteriously nocturnal and shrouded in darkness. A sculptress, she is known from a portrait with a haunted gaze against a background of the deepest blue by Adriana Bisi Fabbri, an artist close to Boccioni. The muse of Boldini and then Man Ray, the Marchesa was immortalized with eyes of mica and a wooden heart[19] (figs. 12-12a) by Balla in the second half of the 1910s

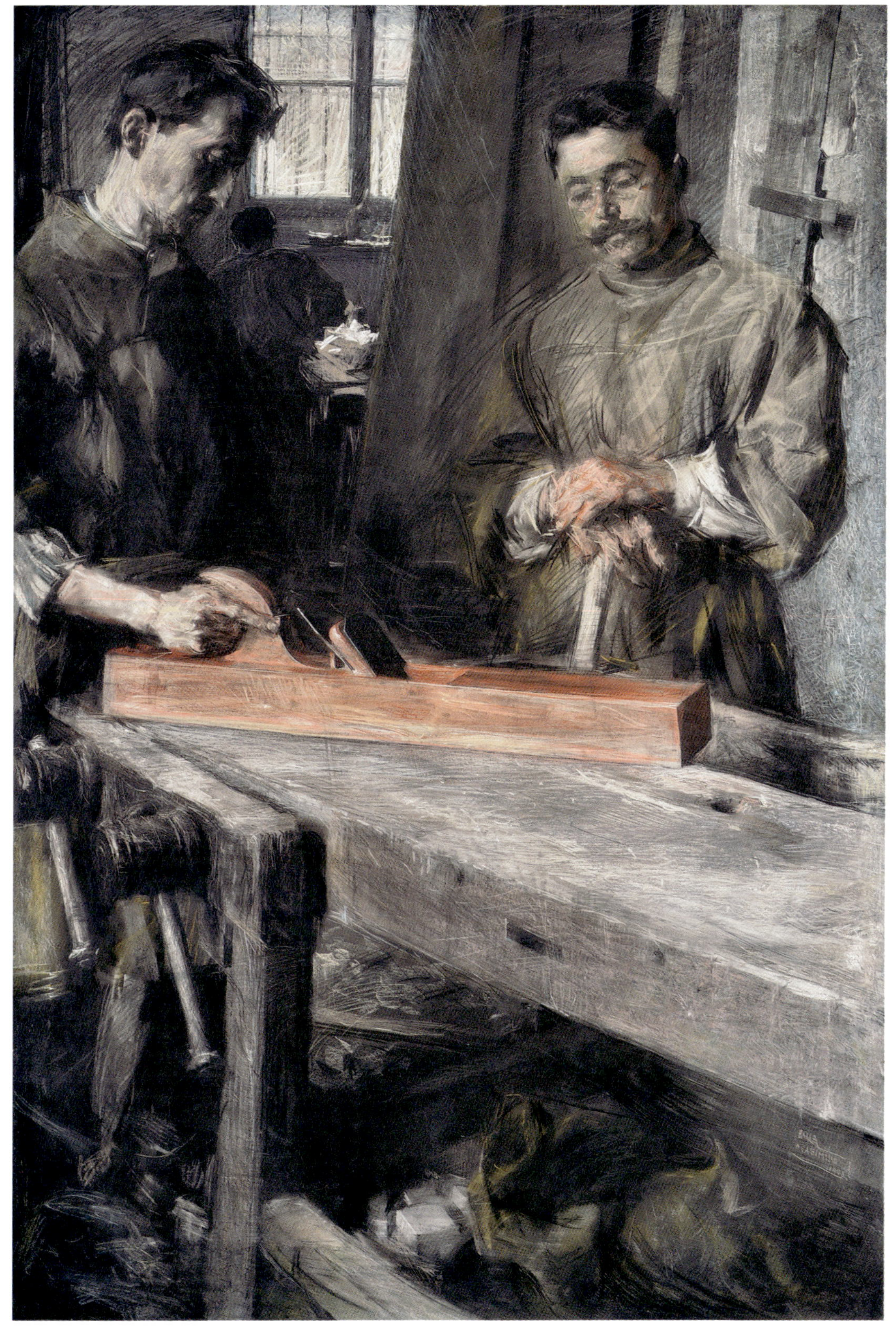

11

La pialla nuova (The New Plane), 1903
crayon and charcoal on paper, 172 x 112 cm

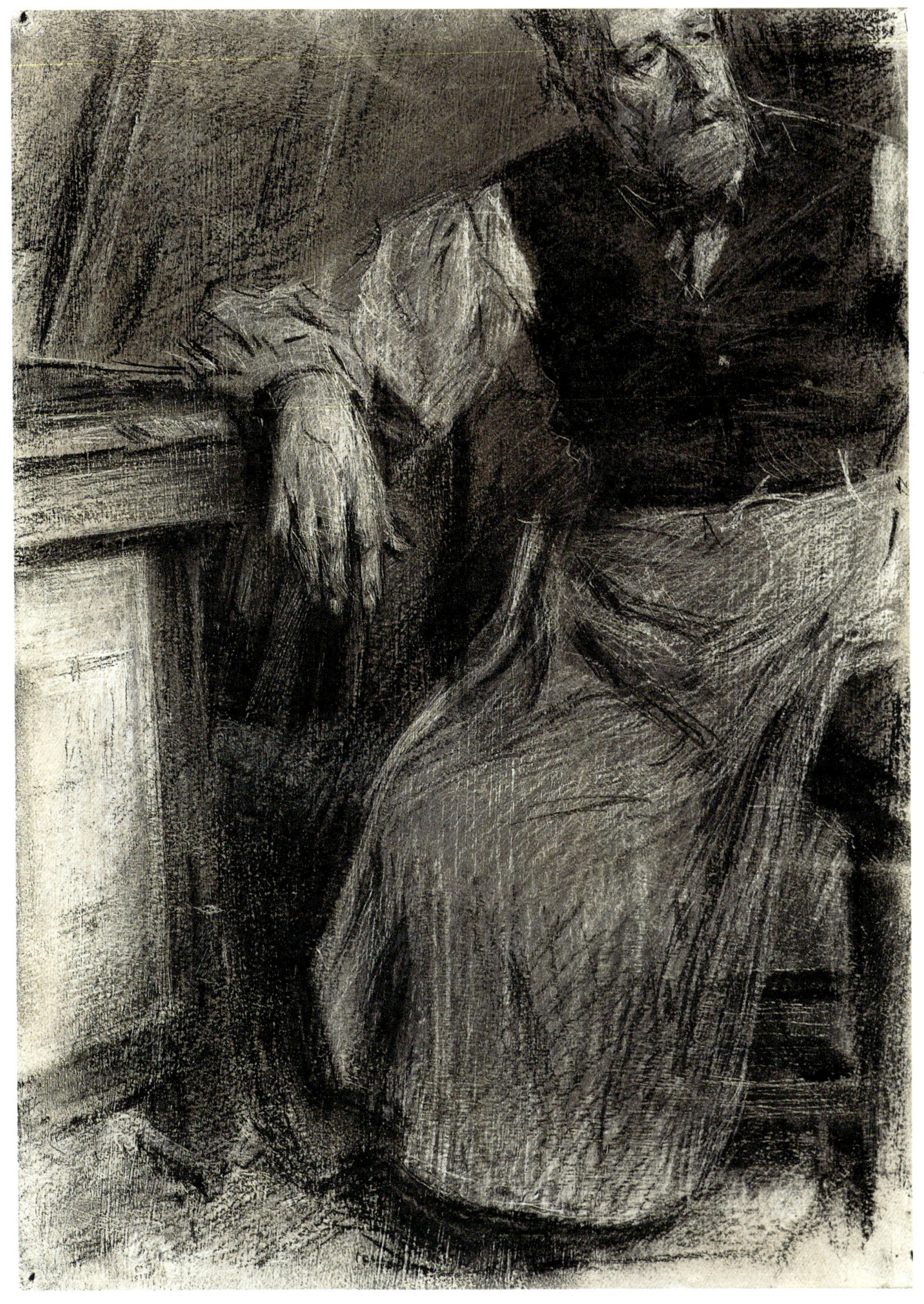

12

Il falegname Mariano (Mariano the Carpenter), 1903
graphite, charcoal and white lead on paper, 32.5 x 23 cm

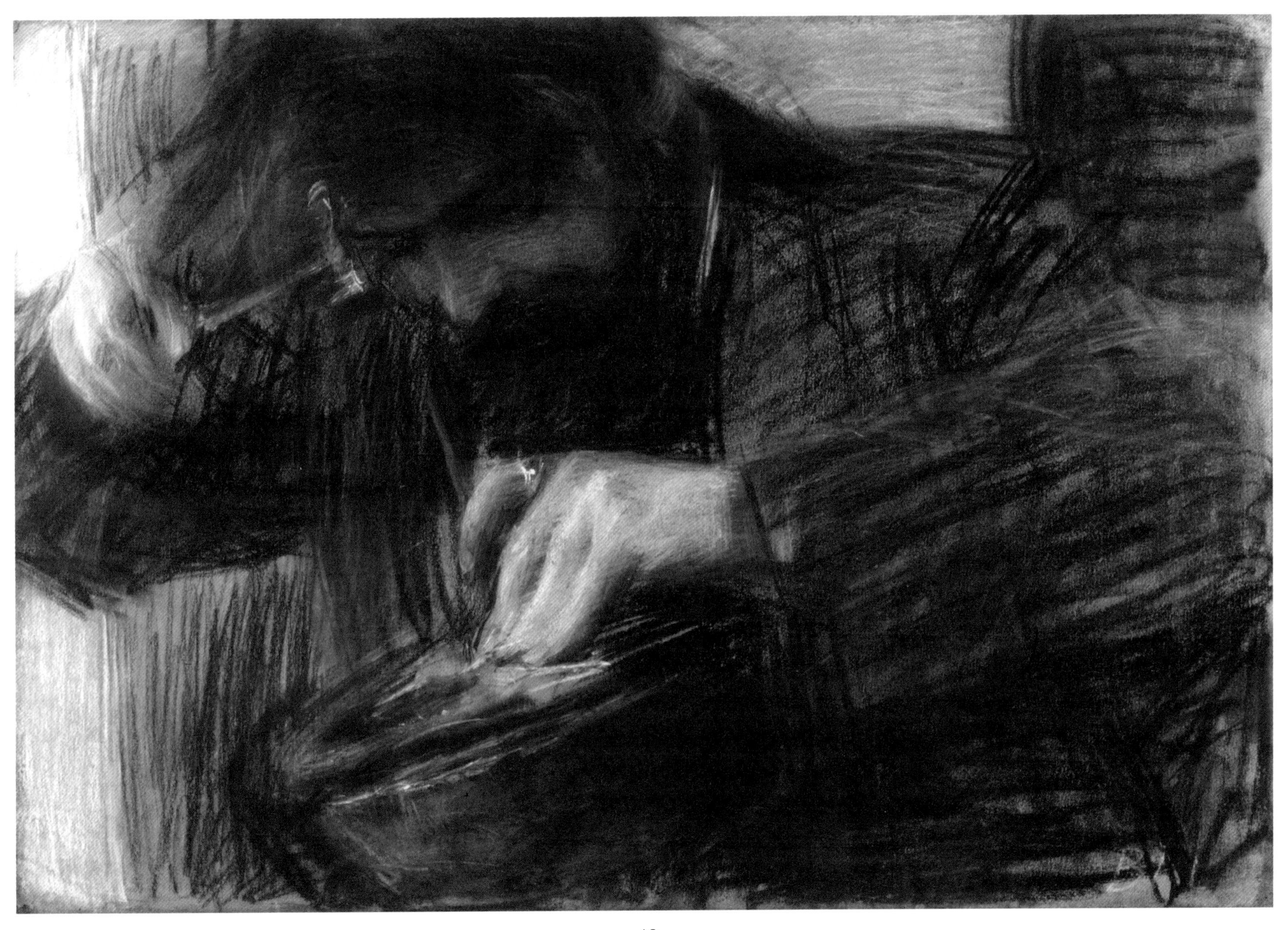

13

Il cesellatore – Ritratto di Duilio Cambellotti
(The Painstaking Artist – Portrait of Duilio Cambellotti), 1906
charcoal and white lead on paper, 44.5 x 63 cm

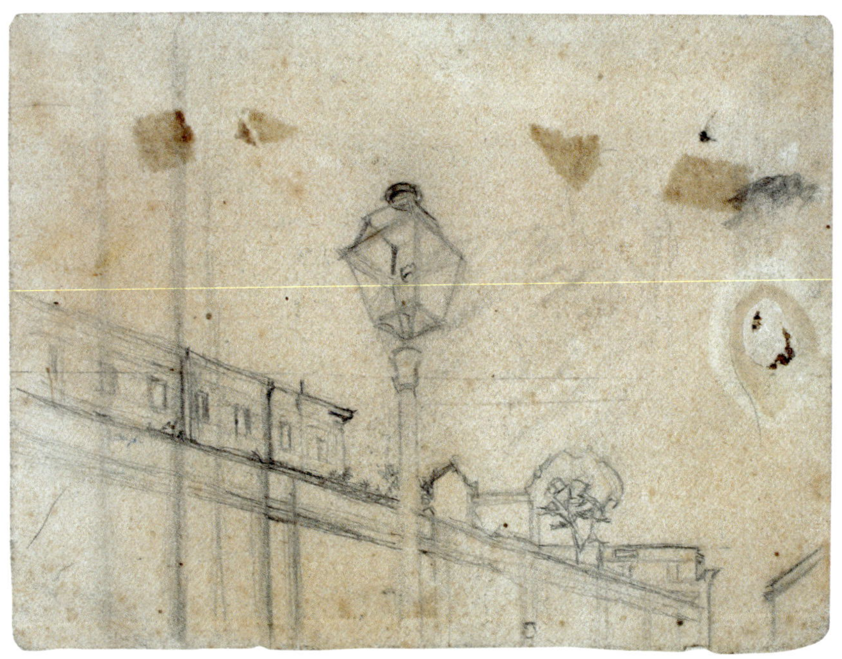

14

La giornata dell'operaio (The Worker's Day), 1904
pencil on paper, 8.8 x 10.8 cm

15

La giornata dell'operaio (The Worker's Day), 1904
pencil on paper, 9 x 10.8 cm

16

La giornata dell'operaio (The Worker's Day), 1904
pencils on paper, 12.6 x 10.3 cm

17

La giornata dell'operaio (The Worker's Day), 1904
pencil on paper, 11.2 x 12.7 cm

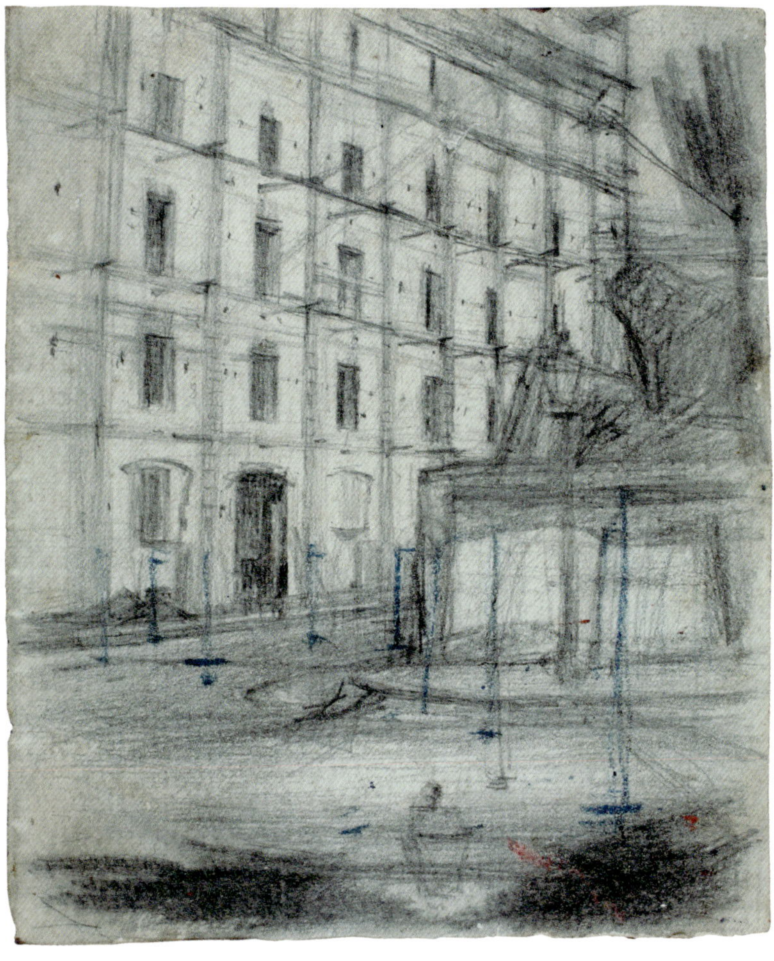

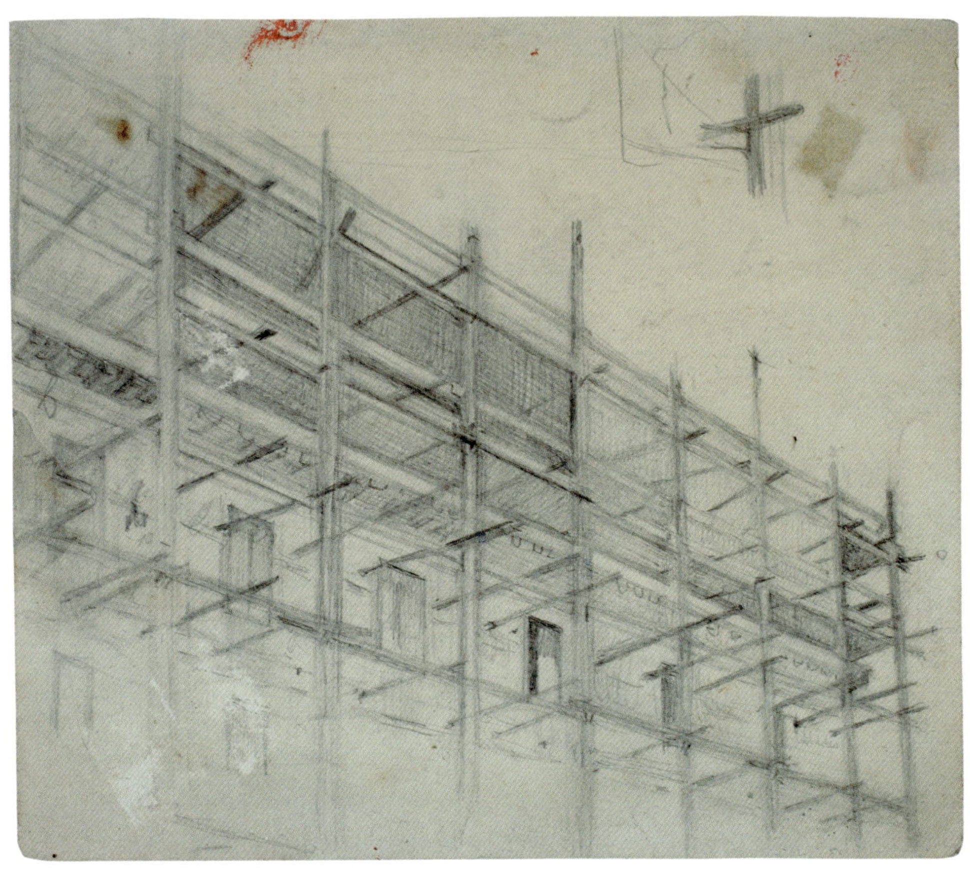

in a Futurist sculpture that captures her likeness despite the abstraction of its soaring lines.

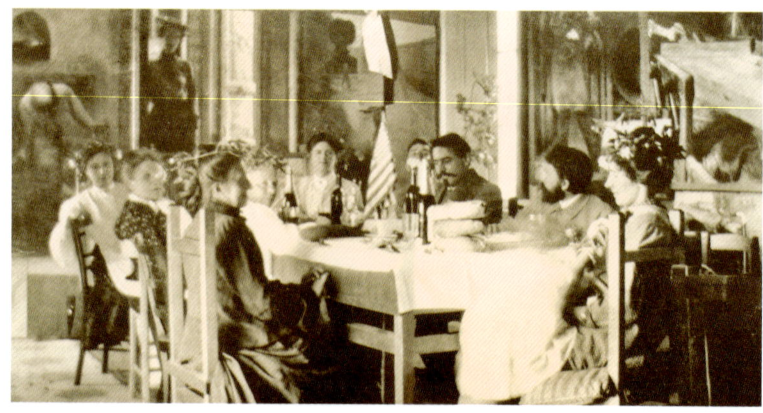

13. Giacomo Balla with family and friends in the studio on Via Parioli, c. 1906. *Il mendicante* (*The Beggar*) can be seen in the back on the left

As from his first Roman period, Balla was a magnet, the centre of attraction for a group of female pupils, intellectual, highly cultured and above all from a sophisticated, elegant world far removed from his artistic and family background. One singular personality that stands out amongst them is Martha Heimann, the future wife of Robert Musil, who described her master as follows: "When I lived in Rome – starting in 1897 –, he was a perfectly normal painter, of importance for his extraordinary technique. He had a weakness for socialist ideas.[20] He believed that art should be exclusively at the service of the people and all that counted was its good and so on ... a bit like it is for the Soviets. He was an Italian from the north, small, with very regular features, blond hair and beard, like some images of Christ. He was extraordinarily uneducated. He thought, for example, that you had to cross the sea to get from Rome to Berlin. He may have become more cultured under the guidance of Marinetti, and was in fact to convert to Futurism later on."[21]

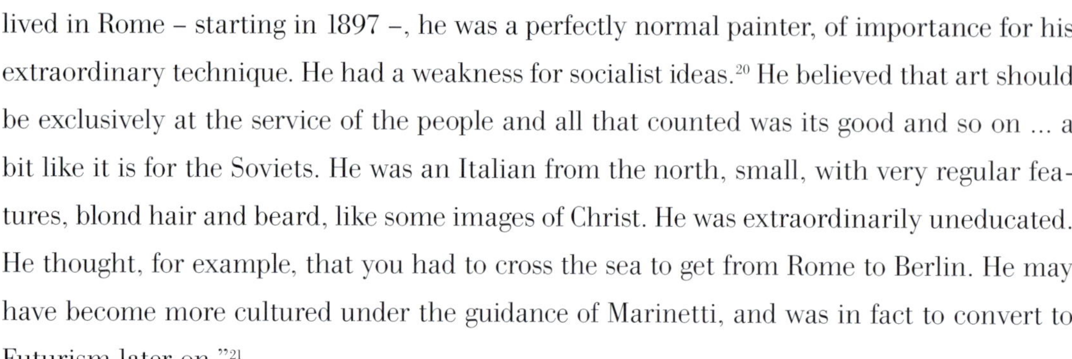

In this highly varied context, veering between Verismo, Dannunzianism[22] and Mitteleuropa, Balla appears to have accentuated the emotional impulse that led him ever closer to the world of the poverty-stricken and suffering in an impetus of fraternal charity and certainly not of external aesthetic sensibility. Following the example of the painting and subject matter of Angelo Morbelli, the strong, silent scenes of desperate solitude at the Pio Albergo Trivulzio in Milan, and of the struggles of workers and socialists by Pellizza da Volpedo,[23] a friend known and frequented in Turin and Rome, Balla chose to represent the abandonment and misery of the poor and outcast in a series of paintings. Another model was the incredibly acute eye of Gustave Caillebotte, with Degas the master of a new definition of perspective through the accentuated tension of compositional line, who in 1875, before the Italian artists, had opened up and dilated the pictorial distance in his depiction of men scraping a parquet floor in a downward-looking perspective. Balla was to describe that moment in a series of autobiographical notes written in the third person: "Surrounded by beggars, lunatics, hooligans, consumptives and paralytics, with these wretched beings, rejects of civilization, outcast by all, Balla studies, lives, suffers and is himself cast out by the ignorant and derided for his excessive pity" and "after more struggles and obstacles, he explodes with the polyptych ironically entitled *I viventi* [*The Living*], a work of new truth and tragically human feeling that made a deep impression on the public together with another entitled *Fallimento*."[24]

The polyptych, comprising four works of equal size, was actually envisaged as consisting of about fifteen more scenes in addition to those he worked on between 1902 and 1905. *Il mendicante* (*The Beggar*) and *I malati* (*The Sick*), works more strongly inspired by this climate of feeling, provide important evidence of the spatial presence of these huddled, crouching figures, crippled by a life of hardship (fig. 13). They also bear lucid witness to a new visual construction, highlighted – as in the case of the elderly couple – by the interplay of black and white, which accentuates details of deep despair. Or, in the case of the old man asleep, the diagonal of the chair and the white-haired head, giving the impression of the dynamic and dramatic presentation of a painful situation. Balla embeds the marks of suffering in accentuated verticality, highlighting the essential characteristics of the person but above all defining a new visual perspective through a strongly linear approach. His was a silent revolution, a radical departure from the art of the period in Rome,[25] a modern way of penetrating the subject's soul and developing the internal trajectories of the figuration, of penetrating the primal spirit of the very idea of representation with the gaze of a living lens, a vibrant mind and magnificent pictorial technique. Balla started from the traditional forms peculiar to painting, from the boundaries of the image, isolating every single detail from its outline of reality. While the polyptych had been structurally divided in ancient times into a number of elements joined by hinges or other devices serving to open out and fold back the panels, he maintained this system but separated the parts so as to transform each one into the defined principle of a system, each the icon of its own truth. Thus it was for the triptych, based in ancient times and especially during the Middle Ages on a comple-

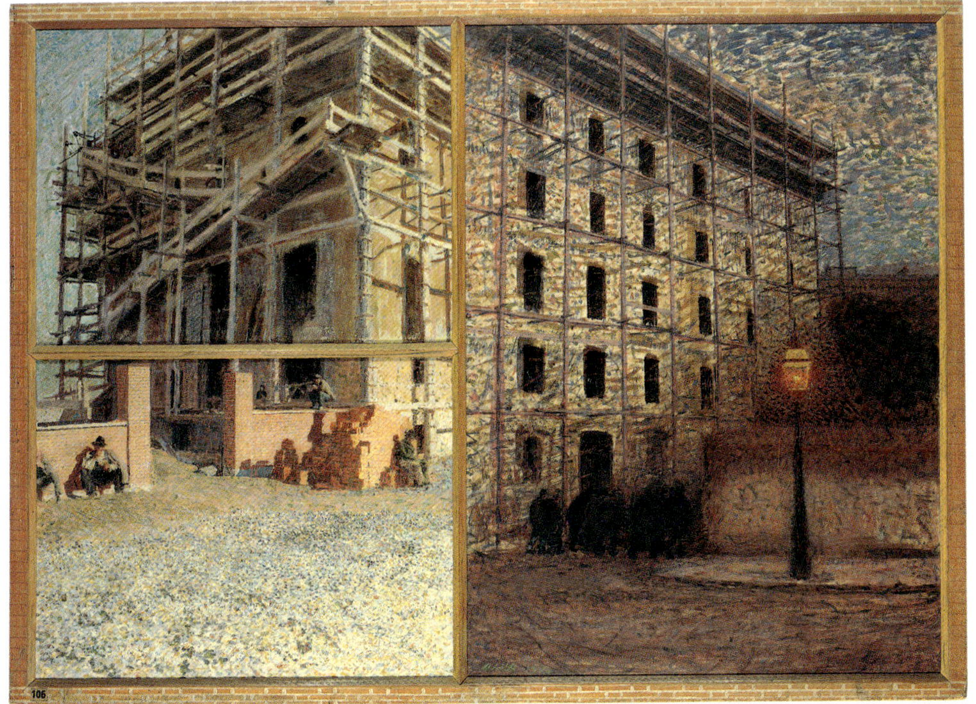

14. Giacomo Balla
La giornata dell'operaio (*The Worker's Day*), 1904
Private collection

18

Ritratto di donna e due paesaggi
(Portrait of a Woman and Two Landscapes),
c. 1905
oil on panel, 40 x 97 cm

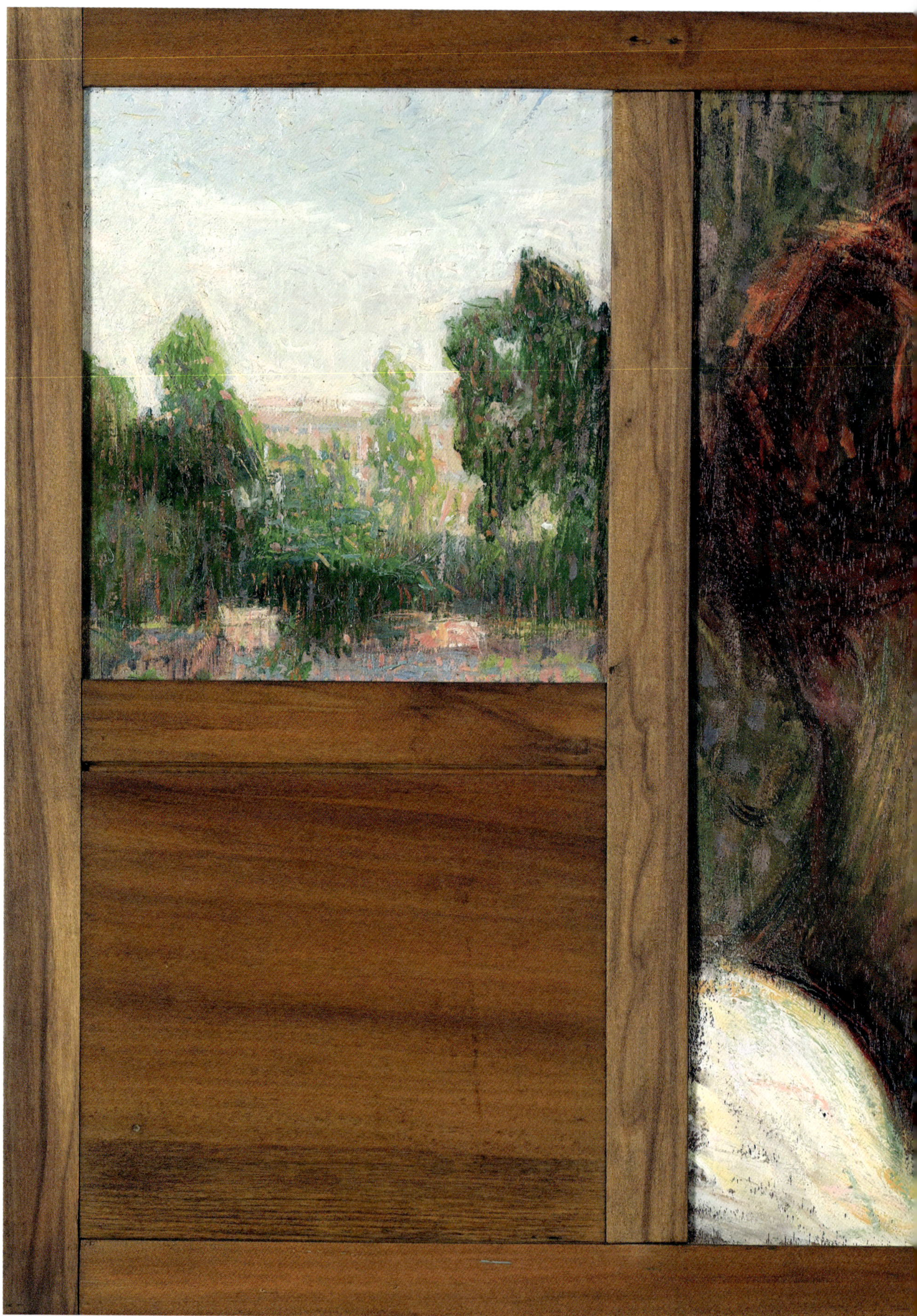

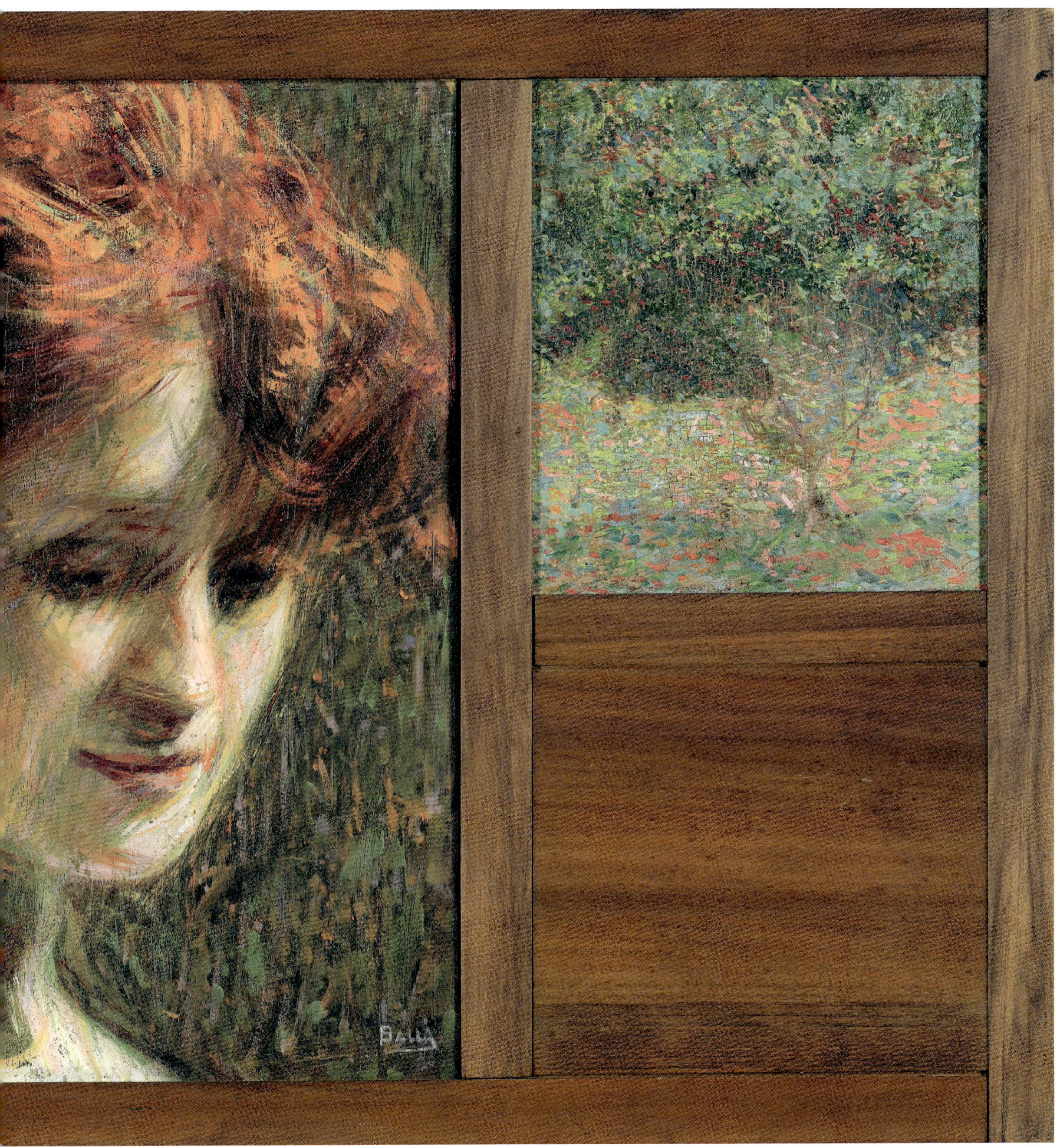
BALLA

mentary concept of hierophanies and then revived in the 19th century as a decorative set or romantic narrative in three acts. Balla took up the idea, as in *La giornata dell'operaio* (*The Worker's Day*) of 1904 (fig. 14), and intensified the three-part structure in the title but radically altered its nature. There are in fact only two views of buildings[26] separated on the same edge by a strip of wood, the part on the left being then divided into two equal parts by another element. The structure and title both maintain the fiction. A multistorey building on the right appears to correspond in type and size to the one in which Balla lived at Via Piemonte 119, the address on the visiting card that he designed and painted in watercolour, where he described himself in 1898 as "Architetto Pittore", architect and painter. The one on the left could instead be a building on the other side of the road on the corner with Via Sardegna, still under construction in 1903. A view of places distinguished in the simply juxtaposed visions, in daylight and at dusk, the worker's day. The artist observes the residential buildings from two angles, constructs opposing views, combines the styles of different edifices and eliminates the street separating them. He unites two perspectives in a single space. In the half illuminated by the midday sun, with the workers stopping for lunch, Balla overlaps the parts slightly so as to permit a synchronous rotation of the gaze that is imperceptible at first. In the other section, the light of a lamppost shows the dark mass of workers moving away against the façade of heterogeneous colours, hurried, lively, vital and vibrant. The three-part structure makes it possible to create a scene where the images are formed in accordance with a different logic, with limited depth and a visual field of limited radius. The details presented with the utmost precision belong to his practice of exploring and penetrating the objective world, which led him to pick up the most detailed aspects of phenomena. As his friend Guido Chialvo observed, "Every day without fail, in the vicinity of Via Piemonte, you find *Giacomo Balla, Ballin* to his friends, eminent caricaturist and intelligent painter. He is always exploring the environment. For me, he says, form does not exist. It is colour that must give everything, absolutely everything. And in fact our friend pays little or no attention to form and achieves amazing effects with colour alone, which does not alter the fact that *Ballin* is a perfect draughtsman, capable of building wonderful planes out of form when he wants."[27] As we can see in the studio-apartments where Balla worked, also from the spatial arrangement of the sketches, arrayed together with the paintings to form a single reality of "wonderful planes", his is a microcosm within a macrocosm, an atom in the boundless universe, examined with a sort of binocular perception in perfect harmony with the close-up view of life in a district and a street from which he seldom strays. Time and space are locked in the rhythm of a new modality, simply sensed but deeply modern and in line with the advances made by physics in those years. In the two other great paintings of the polyptych *I viventi*, produced in the new accommodation of a former monastery on Via Parioli,[28] the figures of the mad woman and the farmer[29] open up to colour, eliminating the strong contrast of black and white. The palette glows with countless shades, the mark of an increasing interest in the decomposition of light and its primary elements. The subjects are the same but the painting is more vigorous and dynamic now and the silhouettes eschew chiaroscuro. In the background we see the new landscape of Villa Borghese in the distance, the dome of St Peter's far away and the fields of the Sebastiani vineyard[30] just past his balcony. In the countryside on the outskirts of Rome, bordering a few hundred yards away with the park recently purchased by the City Council, where Balla was to find subjects for numerous drawings and paintings. His sense of solidarity with the oppressed, gradually tempered by a great empathy with nature, is expressed in a dialectical confrontation of all the principles previously experimented with. The artist's eye was, however, always to show particular regard, almost love, for the world of craftsmen, workers and other artists close to him in the attempt to reinvent a history. The greatest intensity is found in the pastels, with long streaks of variegated and ever-changing material, in which Balla portrayed his friends Giovanni Prini and Duilio Cambellotti in the very act of creation, like the carpenters

15. Giacomo Balla
Salutando (*Waving Goodbye*), 1908
Private collection

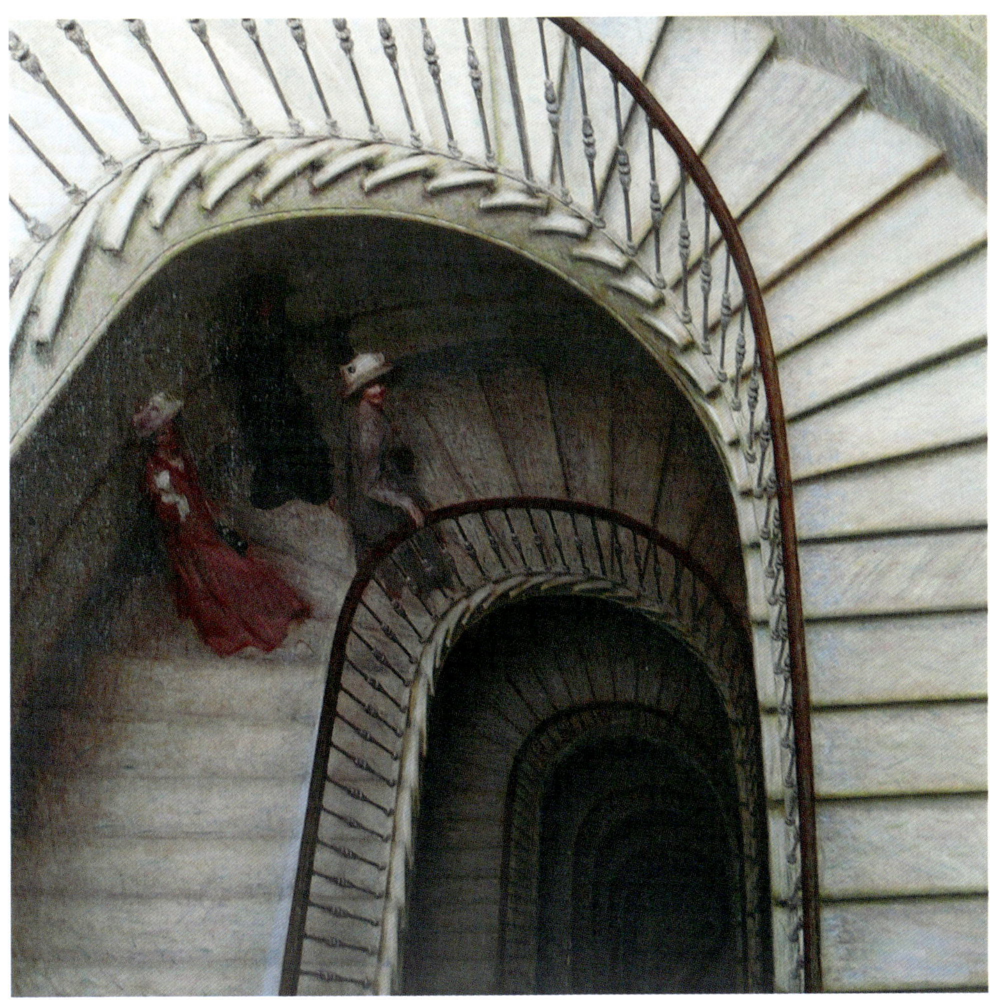

16. Giacomo Balla
Parco dei Daini (*The Deer Park at Villa Borghese*), 1910
Rome, La Galleria Nazionale

at work in their busy shop. The most intimate aspects of the personality of each one are captured with speed and precision in a detailed study of viewpoints, where colour is not immediately the protagonist, even though the body and soul of a dynamic and luminous dimension are moulded in that extraordinarily masterly glow of chromatic combinations.

The countryside also inspired other accents, however, as the expanses of grain and yellow springtime flowers seen from the window of the new studio make the paintings glow with new reverberations. At the same time, the lines of the future development of his work are defined with ever-greater clarity. As in *Salutando* (*Waving Goodbye*) (1908) (fig. 15), where the process of continual action is indicated by the gerund of the title, developed in the view of three women descending a spiral staircase as seen from above. Or in the large polyptych of the *Parco dei Daini* (*The Deer Park at Villa Borghese*) (1910) (fig. 16), where the slight stagger of the left-hand part of *La giornata dell'operaio* reappears between the panels. The overall effect of spatial elongation and breadth is unique. Seen in close-up, the effect disintegrates in harmony with the very structure of the painting in a lens-like analysis of detail studied in connection with the time of the artist's vision. As Balla was to state, "Landscape and nature were my source of inspiration as from the Villa Borghese triptych. I analyzed nature scientifically in all its elements to observe the metamorphoses it undergoes in time and space. Individual photograms impinge on the retina and constitute snapshots and segments of a constant process of becoming. Painting and photography achieve an exceptional feat: photographing the invisible."[31]

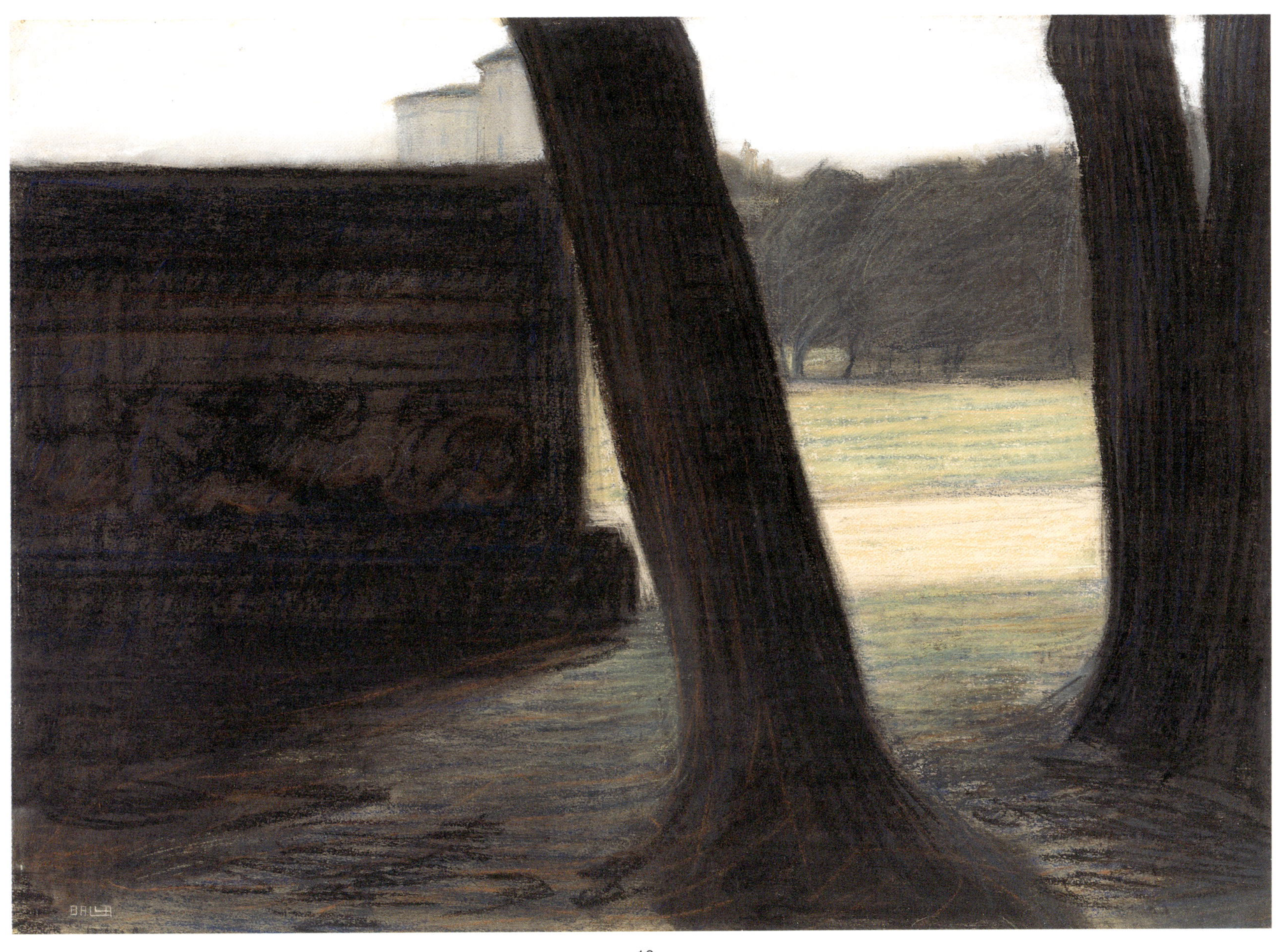

19

Villa Borghese – Le torri del museo
(Villa Borghese – The Towers of the Museum), c. 1905
crayon on paper, 38 x 52 cm

[1] Rome was proclaimed capital on 3 February 1871.
[2] Not least because he had already been forced to find occasional jobs in order to go on studying.
[3] This brief note, attributed to the year of Balla's arrival in the new capital, is found in the important three-volume biography by his daughter Elica Balla, *Con Balla*, Multhipla Edizioni, Milan, 1984, vol. I, p. 36.
[4] See Giovanni Lista, "Divisionismo e visione fotografica", in *Balla La modernità futurista*, exh. cat. (Milan, Palazzo Reale, 15 February – 2 June 2008, curated by Lista, Paolo Baldacci and Livia Velani), Skira, Milan, 2008, pp. 1–13, for a detailed study of Balla's formative years in Turin including his study of music, attendance at the Accademia Albertina and apprenticeship to the lithographer Cassina and then the photographer Bertieri, whose son Pilade, a painter, was to remain in contact with the artist until the last years of his life, as attested by Elica Balla.
[5] As appears evident also from last part of the phrase quoted, for which see note 1.
[6] In addition to any personal predisposition, one of the primary reasons for the artist's compassion and sensitivity to certain subjects may have been the fact that he was born on Via Moncalieri in Borgo Rubatto by the Gran Madre, "one of the residences of Turin's laundry workers", and spent the early years of his life before moving to Corso San Maurizio 19 on the other side of the river (see *Divisionismo e visione fotografica*, op. cit., p. 2).
[7] As Gino Severini, his pupil together with Umberto Boccioni in that period, recalled years later, "If there had been an old shoe in a landscape, he would have painted it too. He once painted a picture entitled *Fallimento* showing the bottom part of the door of a shop closed for bankruptcy. The shutters no longer opened, abandoned, dirty, covered in figures and hieroglyphics in chalk by children, certainly suggested abandonment and sadness. There was a magnificently depicted ball of spit in a corner of the stone step. It was a fine and personal painting regardless of its subject and the spirit of realism (or *verismo*, as it was then called) in which it was executed." *La vita di un pittore*, Edizioni di Comunità, Milan, p. 24 (first published by Garzanti, Milan, in 1946).
[8] Letter to Boccioni (Milan, private collection) written in 1914 after receiving a copy of Boccioni's *Pittura Scultura Futuriste* and subsequent to his pupil's response to the criticism of Futurism for its overly material use of objects, expressed by Giovanni Papini in "Il cerchio non si chiude!", *Lacerba*, II, 5, 1 March 1914.
[9] Entry dated Wednesday, 31 October 1894 in the diary kept by Zola (*Journal de Voyage à Rome*, in *Oeuvres complètes*, ed. H. Mitterrand) to make notes for the setting of his novel *Rome*, part of the trilogy *Les Trois Villes* (1893–98), featuring the Abbé Pierre Froment and including *Lourdes* and *Paris*. The pages of *Rome* appeared simultaneously in *Le Journal* in Paris and *La Tribuna* in Rome from December 1895 to May 1896, the year of its publication in Paris by G. Charpentier et E. Fasquelle.
[10] Ibid., entry for Thursday, 8 November 1894.
[11] Ibid., Thursday, 1 November 1894: "Masters of Rome, the Italians decided to build the third Rome, the great modern capital of Italy. They announced this, declaring their pride and the blood of Augustus. The idea was to show the pope what a unified Italy could make of the capital. It was all supposed to be done in a score of years after 1875.
"What drove everything was, however, the idea of lucrative speculation on the sale of land. What was bought for a hundred sous a metre was sold for a hundred francs. A site was like stock passed from hand to hand, all of this inflamed by national pride and profit. There's the story of Prince Ludovisi, who was offered six million for his villa and took it. On seeing the value rise and hoping that it would go on rising, he then bought back his lands at fifty francs to sell them again for a hundred. This game cost him the six million of the sale and another twelve out of his own pocket. Similar things happened everywhere. Great prelates engaged in speculation. The pope himself is said to have lost 23 million, most of the treasure left by Pius IX. The collapse happened because they built with no restraint and without wondering about who was going to live in the new houses. On the one hand, the local population has only doubled and the masses expected have never arrived. On the other, they have made the mistake of building quality houses that the lower classes could not afford to rent.
"And so no rent is coming in and the houses are left empty to deteriorate. Tenants are needed to save the situation, to get things back on an even keel, but tenants wealthy enough to make the houses profitable to their owners. Everything suggests, however, that no such event will take place any time soon. The sums gambled so far and swallowed up by the building in Rome are estimated at a billion. It was all done too well and in too much of a hurry.
"The huge ministry of finance on Via XX Settembre is empty. The Bank of Italy on Via Nazionale is a grim joke. I'll have to go into all this financial side. But how deeply ironic it is with this national pride leading to ruin and the pope losing millions on a capital city he loathes."
[12] Robert Musil, *Tagebücher, Aphorismen Essays und Reden*, ed. Adolf Frisé, Rowohlt Verlag, Hamburg, 1955. I am grateful to Giovanna Bonasegale for bringing these diaries to my attention.
[13] Ibid.
[14] The building at Via Romagna 17 now houses the Banca Marche. Though altered over the years, it still retains its original structure.
[15] Louis or Luigi.
[16] At number 43.
[17] F.T. Marinetti, *L'alcova d'acciaio: romanzo vissuto*, chapter 12, *Una festa napoleonica*, Vitagliano, Milan, 1921, pp. 139 and 141.
[18] For extensive photographic documentation of this legendary figure, renowned also for the scarcely imaginable excesses and eccentricity of the festivities held in her Venetian palace, the Ca' Venier dei Leoni, see Scot D. Ryersson and Michael Orlando Yaccarino, *The Marchesa Casati*, Abrams, New York, 2009. See also Dario Cecchi, *Coré: vita e dannazione della marchesa Casati*, L'inchiostroblu, Bologna, 1986.
[19] The sculpture, entitled *La marchesa Casati con il cuore di mica e gli occhi di legno* and known from the photograph featured on the cover of the weekly magazine *Il Mondo*, Sunday, 30 March 1919, V, 13, Sonzogno, Milan, has been lost for decades.
[20] In Rome Balla was part of a group of artists and intellectuals including Giovanni Cena, Sibilla Aleramo, his future brother-in-law Alessandro Marcucci, Giovanni Prini and Duilio Cambellotti. As Gino Severini also recounts in his memoirs,

socialist ideas informed their lives and constant efforts on behalf of the disinherited and the new paupers created by the situation in Italy. The group focused its ethical and educational efforts in particular on Rome rural area, with its pockets of ignorance, as attested by the presentation of a hut from there with paintings by Balla inside Rome Expo of 1911. The hut was set up at the crossing with Via Flaminia on the way to the city's new Galleria d'Arte Moderna designed by Cesar Bazzani.

[21] See the interesting biography by Marie-Louise Roth and Annette Daigger, *Un destin de femme: Martha Musil: l'amante, l'épouse, la soeur*, P. Lang, Bern, 2006, p. 46.

[22] An assiduous habitué of high society during his years in Rome, Gabriele D'Annunzio described the capital as a pit of the worst corruption in his novel *Le vergini delle rocce* (Fratelli Treves, Milan, 1896, pp. 43–44): "It was the time when the efforts of Rome's destroyers and constructors reached the murkiest depths of industriousness. Clouds of dust spread together with a kind of craze for lucre like an evil whirlwind, seizing not only the servile, kith and kin of brick and mortar, but also the aloof heirs of papal entailments, who had previously looked down disdainfully on the intruders from the windows of mansions built of travertine and unshakeable beneath the crust of centuries. The magnificent houses – founded, renewed and strengthened through nepotism and partisan war – stooped one by one, slithered in the new mire, sank and disappeared. The illustrious wealth built up in centuries of joyful plunder and splendid patronage were exposed to the risks of the stock exchange."

[23] Balla saw the painting at the first Turin Quadrennial in 1902, where he also took part, as noted by Efisio Aitelli ("Esposizione Quadriennale di Belle Arti in Torino", *Emporium*, XVI, 94, October 1902, p. 268): "By Balla, so celebrated in Rome, there is *Sentiero* [*Path*], a work full of sweet poetry." The artist had spent long time working on this during a seven-month stay in Paris in 1900 and 1901. As he wrote to his future wife: "If it doesn't get too wintry and cold I'll be able to finish the painting I'm working on in the country (in which I'll try to explain what love is). My nerves are so taut that it feels like being made of steel. If the picture comes out as I feel it, we'll see how far suggestion can take you." *Con Balla*, op. cit., p. 85. Aitelli was referring to the enthusiastic response to the thirteen works, including numerous portraits, shown by Balla a few months earlier in Rome (LXXII Esposizione della Società degli Amatori e Cultori di Roma, February–June 1902).

[24] *Con Balla*, op cit., pp. 131–32.

[25] For a major survey of the Roman art scene in those years, see *Aspetti dell'arte a Roma dal 1870 al 1914*, exh. cat. (Rome, Palazzo Barberini), ed. Anna Maria Damigella, Paola Frandini, Dario Durbé and Gianna Piantoni, De Luca, Rome, 1972. See also Giovanna Bonasegale, 'L'Ottocento nelle collezioni della Galleria Comunale d'arte moderna e contemporanea di Roma: identità di una raccolta', in *GCAMC. Catalogo Generale delle Collezioni. Autori dell'Ottocento*, ed. Cinzia Virno, Rome, 2004, 2 vols.; Giovanna Bonasegale, 'Immagini riflesse tra pittura e fotografia', in *La poesia del vero. Pittura di paesaggio a Roma tra Ottocento e Novecento da Costa a Parisani*, exh. cat. (Macerata, Palazzo Ricci and Camerino, Complesso Museale di San Domenico), De Luca, Rome, 2001, pp. 20–28.

[26] And not of the same building, as claimed in most of the literature.

[27] *Le serate italiane*, 15–31 August 1896, III, XV–XVI; in *Con Balla*, op. cit., p. 50. Guido Chialvo, a lecturer on law, was secretary of Istituto di belle arti in 1906 and, together with its director Ettore Ferrari, a leading figure in the Masonic lodge of Palazzo Giustiniani.

[28] Obtained with the help of Ernesto Nathan, whose daughters were pupils of Balla. Nathan was also Grand Master of the Grande Oriente d'Italia Masonic lodge (1896–1903 and 1917–19), where his place was taken by Ettore Ferrari in 1904 when he was elected mayor of Rome. Giorgio Amendola, who lived in the same street with the family (his Lithuanian mother Eva Kühn, fascinated by Marinetti's vitalism, adopted the literary name of Magamal for her writing) and was a neighbour of Balla's, recalls those places in *Una scelta di vita* (Rizzoli, Milan, 1978, p. 7): "The best years of my childhood were spent in the house on Via Paisiello. At the end of 1912 the road ran through the old Sebastiani vineyard, which was being turned into the district named after the owner, who had begun the construction work. The road started from Villa Borghese, on the side with the museum and the Parco dei Daini, and went straight through the fields as far as Viale Parioli. The buildings completed and inhabited were few, there were large stony areas separating them from the huge tenements built for office workers alongside the Via Salaria. Our home, number 15, was the most modest of the villas and houses already seeking to impart pretentious tone to what was to become a smart residential district."

[29] The façade of the building in the background corresponds to that of the one at Via Parioli 8, built at the end of the 19th century. The drawings made for its "reconstruction and partial elevation" are still in Rome's municipal archives (Archivio Capitolino, no. 1291, 31 March 1896).

[30] After the approval of the Sanjust urban planning scheme of 1909, the entrepreneur and engineer Adolfo Sebastiani – whose father was portrayed by Balla in the lost work *Proprietario* (*Owner*) (see Giovanni Lista, *Balla*, Edizione Galleria Fonte d'Abisso, Modena, 1982, n. 98, p. 131) – obtained permits as from 1911 to divide his land facing Villa Borghese into building lots. After the demolition of the former monastery, Balla and his family stayed from 1926 to 1929 with his friends and collectors the Ambrons (Amelia Almagià Ambron had been one of his pupils at the beginning of the century). The Ambrons also owned the now demolished Villa Villegas-Tavazzi, designed in the Moorish style by Ernesto Basile and built in 1887 on the corner of Viale Parioli and Via Stoppani. A painting of 1926 shows his daughter Luce in the tiled patio in an Arab-like pose with transparent veils shimmering between pink and purple.

[31] Roberto Quarta, *Roma segreta: i luoghi dell'esoterismo nella città eterna*, Mediterranee, Rome, 2014.

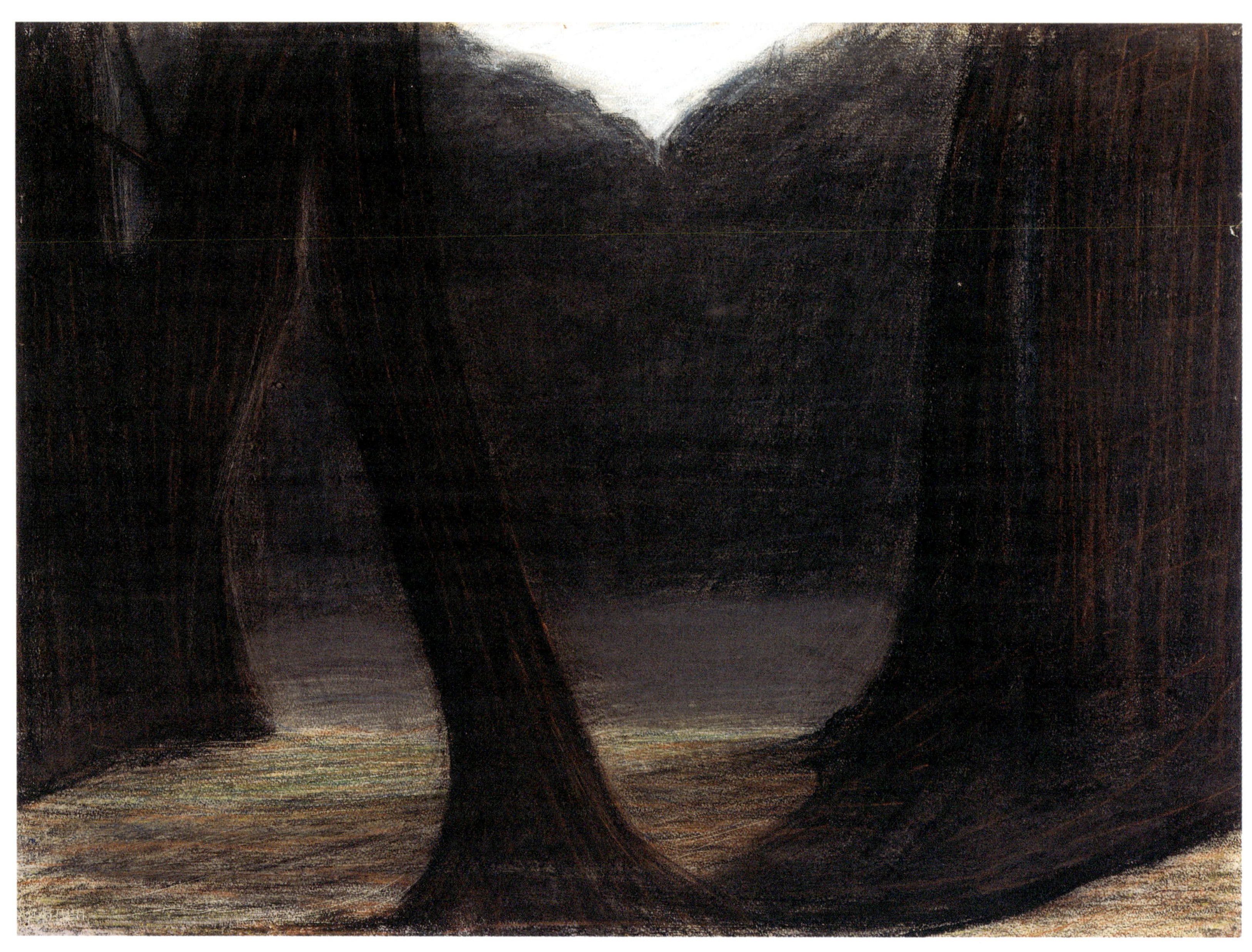

20

Villa Borghese – Tronchi
(Villa Borghese – Tree Trunks), c. 1905
crayon on paper, 38.5 x 52 cm

Balla's Rome: Vineyards, "campagna", villas and "villini"

Giorgio Muratore

Balla moved to Rome as a young man in the mid-1890s, just after the Banca Romana scandal, and was swept up in a city undergoing complete dynamic and dramatic transformation, a vast and endless building site.
Having arrived at the Termini railway station at the end of January 1895, he saw the city with the eyes of Segantini, Pellizza, Previati and Morbelli, and the spirit of Tolstoy.

Only recently proclaimed the capital, Rome was subjected over the short space of about a decade to accelerated change in both concrete and symbolic terms that radically altered its physical structure, image and even memory.

Those were the years of major public works like the Vittoriano, the parliament building and the Palazzo di Giustizia, of major urban-planning projects in the Esquilino, Castro Pretorio and Prati districts, and the construction of the massive Tiber embankment as well as waves of building speculation like the one that saw the destruction of numerous historical edifices, above all the splendid Villa Ludovisi.

The young artist from Turin arrived in the city and walked out of the station, leaving the recently erected Dogali obelisk behind him and proceeded towards the Baths of Diocletian and the Piazza Esedra with the fountain in the middle, yet to be embellished by Rutelli, and the buildings around still under construction. He discovered a world of building sites, new edifices and ancient monuments overwhelmed by a would-be European modernity that was still struggling to attain the metropolitan status of a great capital city through callow use of a new eclectic vocabulary. Market gardens, vineyards, nymphaeums, ruins, fountains, ravines, city walls, shrines, ancient roads, entire villas, water and age-old pines were swallowed up in those last years of the 19th century by the new urban layout, the building frenzy, the somewhat sketchy plan of streets and squares, the slightly gloomy idea of a city unquestionably born out of the hurried reflections developed by a handful of Piedmontese planners – midway between military and civil engineering, often also with the psychological characteristics of the pen-pusher and the yokel – on the simplified model of experiences similar in some respects to others in Europe at the turn of the century but more often of very different breadth and substance.

Paris, Berlin, Vienna and Barcelona but also Naples and above all Turin were the prototypes to which methodological, formal, typological and linguistic reference was widely made for the work on Rome. The urban models of the new districts, the huge squares, the great arteries, the arcades and the compact blocks all attempted – albeit not always successfully – to create the image of modernity and efficiency that the culture of the new dominant class strove to project in support of its political ideals, economic ambitions, symbolic expectations and above all material interests. Following the Haussmann model, De Merode had already embarked between the Esquilino, the Baths of Diocletian and Palazzo del Quirinale on a radical process of urban reorganization with the new Termini railway station as its barycentre. The same obsession with renewal is still attested by the choices of vocabulary made by architects in the period between national unification and the end of the century to endow the figurative aspects of those imposing transformations with form and meaning.

A lively debate on the "national style" saw the participation of the finest minds, who flocked to Rome en masse from all over the country. The often conflicting suggestions and interpretations of the various creators of the new Italian architecture thus found the ideal place for verification and possible confirmation of their ideas in the crucible of this great opportunity and its differentiated structure, organized above all on the basis of major competitions and professional openings. Names and figures like Promis, Selvatico, Boito, Poggi, Alvino, Cipolla, Basile, Sacconi and Calderini – corresponding substantially to the various regional developments that had for years, from Turin to Milan, Venice to Florence, Naples to Palermo, been doggedly in search of a path to modernity expressed through the various languages of architecture – were evoked by students and imitators as indispensable points of cultural and disciplinary reference to endow the various choices of "style" and "vocabulary" with strength and substance.

The architects and above all the civil engineers active in those years – including Canevari, Koch, Piacentini, Sacconi, Manfredi, Tatti, Cipolla, Pistrucci, Azzurri, Leonori, Busiri Vici, Passarelli, Calderini, Barucci, Janz and Street, to name just a few – endeavoured with professional expertise and civil commitment to combine international and national experience, to infuse the dialectal accent of the Roman academic province with the experimental dimension of new materials and technologies, pursuing forms and languages capable of imparting meaning and congruity to the image of the new architecture of the capital and the country as a whole. Historical styles were revived, reworked and interwoven repeatedly in an attempt to distil from the various forms of contemporary eclecticism at the national and international level a new common vocabulary capable of imparting universal

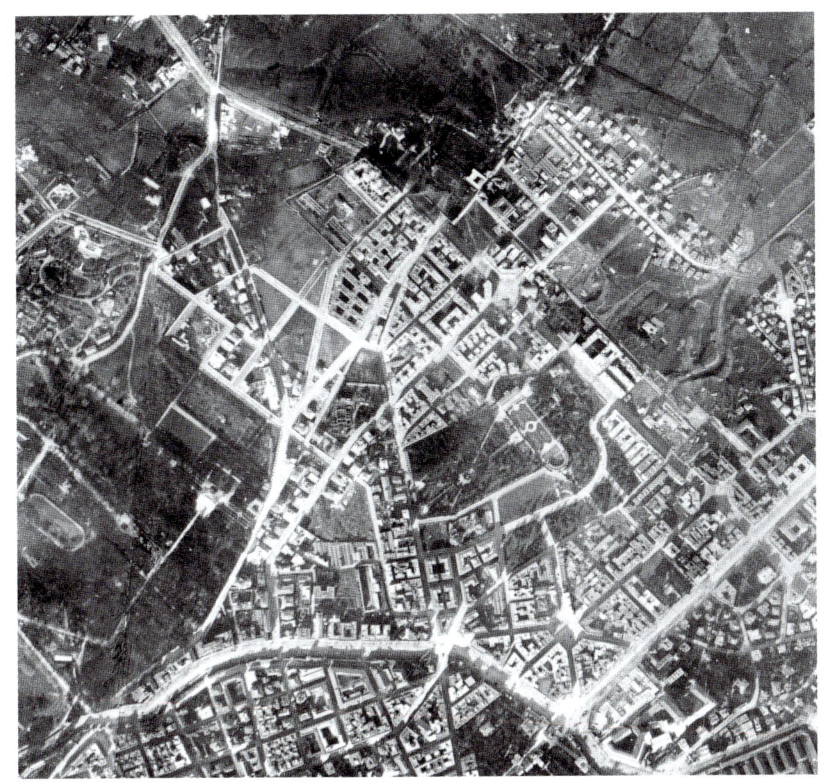

1. Rome from an aeroplane, scale 1:10,000, photomosaic by Umberto Nistri, February 1919

meaning to the new architecture so as to embrace also the work of great international masters like Viollet-le-Duc, Semper, Schinkel, Garnier, Haussmann and Sitte.

The result of this uninterrupted series of attempts and experiments was what we all know and what still survives to a great extent before our eyes today: a city that radically transformed its traditional cultural references and customary rhythms of life as well as the very scale of its spaces, streets and squares (fig. 1).

As F. Marion Crawford wrote in *Don Orsino* (1892), one of his well-known novels set in Rome: "He who was born and bred in the Rome of twenty years ago comes back after a long absence to wander as a stranger in streets he never knew, among houses unfamiliar to him, amidst a population whose speech sounds strange in his ears. He roams the city from the Lateran to the Tiber, from the Tiber to the Vatican, finding himself now and then before some building once familiar in another aspect, losing himself perpetually in unprofitable wastes made more monotonous than the sandy desert by the modern builder's art. ... Old Rome is gone. The narrow streets are broad thoroughfares, the Jews' quarter is a flat and dusty building lot, the fountain of Ponte Sisto is swept away, one by one the mighty pines of Villa Ludovisi have fallen under axe and saw, and a cheap, thinly inhabited quarter is built upon the site of the enchanted garden. The network of by-ways from the Jesuits' church to the Sant'Angelo bridge is ploughed up and opened by the huge Corso Vittorio Emanuele. Buildings which strangers used to search for in the shade, guide-book and map in hand, are suddenly brought into the blaze of light that fills broad streets and sweeps across great squares. The vast Cancelleria stands out nobly to the sun, the curved front of the Massimo palace exposes its black colonnade to sight upon the greatest thoroughfare of the new city, the ancient Arco de' Cenci exhibits its squalor in unshadowed sunshine, the Portico of Octavia once more looks upon the river."

Too much has certainly been said and written about the umpteenth "sack" of Rome then perpetrated and about the often excessive tendency towards simplification and schematicism of the planning proposals adopted and connected in an overly elementary way with the inexorable mechanisms of profit and speculation on areas suddenly and mysteriously transformed into building land. The history of cities is made up also and sometimes above all of this, however, and the events of Rome as the new capital could obviously not remain immune. The famous building crisis of the 1880s with its terrible wave of bankruptcies, failed banks, halted construction sites, strikes and the illicit occupation of suddenly abandoned buildings bears witness to a complex reality where the Roman market found itself caught up in a far broader financial crisis on the European scale and, for this reason too, ended up the victim of a situation originating elsewhere and of its own failure to detect the symptoms of collapse in time.

All this is captured once again in the prose of F. Marion Crawford: "Rome was very gay that year [1888], to compensate for the shortness of its playtime. Everything was successful, and every one was rich. People talked of millions less soberly than they had talked of thousands a few years earlier, and with less respect than they mentioned hundreds twelve months later. Like the vanity-struck frog, the franc blew itself up to the bursting point, in the hope of being taken for the louis, and momentarily succeeded, even beyond its own expectations. No one walked, though horse-flesh was enormously dear and a good coachman's wages amounted to just twice the salary of a government clerk. Men who, six months earlier, had climbed ladders with loads of brick or mortar, were now transformed into flourishing sub-contractors, and drove about in smart pony-carts, looking the picture of Italian prosperity, rejoicing in the most flashy of ties and smoking the blackest and longest of long black cigars. During twenty hours out of the twenty-four the gates of the city roared with traffic. From all parts of the country labourers poured in, bundle in hand and tools on shoulder to join in the enormous work and earn their share of the pay that was distributed so liberally. […] Thousands upon thousands of workmen who had come from great distances during the past two or three years were suddenly thrown out of work, penniless in the streets and many of them burdened with wives and children. There were one or two small riots and there was much demonstration, but, on the whole, the poor masons behaved very well. The government and the municipality did what they could, what governments and municipalities can do when hampered at every turn by the most complicated and ill-considered machinery of administration ever invented in any country. The starving workmen were by slow degrees got out of the city and sent back to starve out of sight in their native places. The emigration was enormous in all directions. […] The French banks had decided that it was no longer profitable to finance the Italian, which in turn stopped lending to the construction companies. The buildings left unfinished for lack of funds and abandoned for an in-

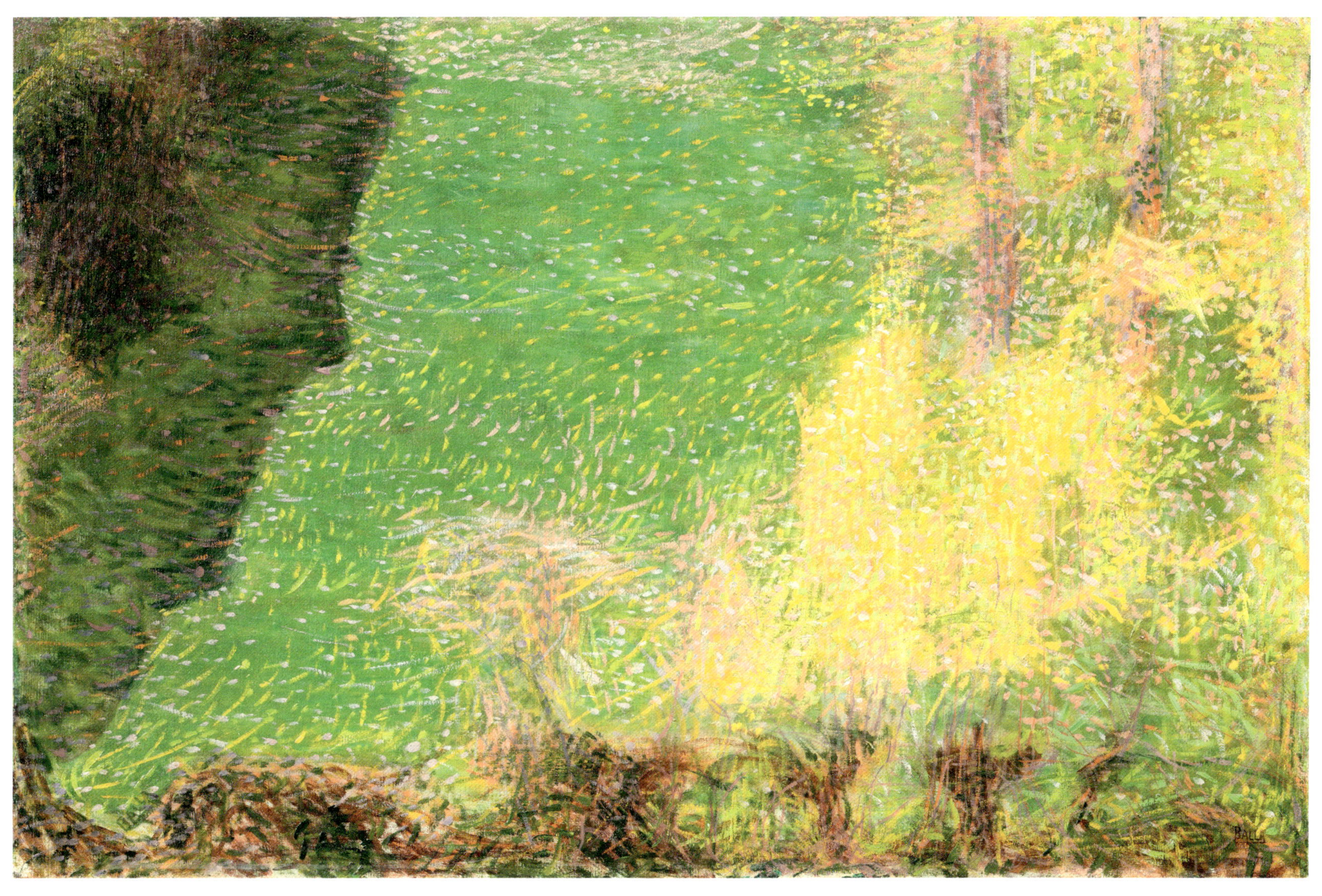

21

Germogli primaverili – Paesaggio di Villa Borghese
(Springtime Buds – Landscape of Villa Borghese), 1906
oil on canvas mounted on panel, 51 x 76.3 cm

definite length of time gave the new Rome a ghostly, unsightly appearance that saddened the eyes and hearts of so many of its old admirers, aghast at the havoc wrought, all the more ruinous for having been perpetrated in the name of civilisation […] The dismal ruins of that new city which was to have been built and which never reached completion are visible everywhere. Houses seven stories high, abandoned within a month of completion rise uninhabited and uninhabitable out of a rank growth of weeds, amidst heaps of rubbish, staring down at the broad, desolate streets where the vigorous grass pushes its way up through the loose stones of the unrolled metalling. Amidst heavy low walls which were to have been the ground stories of palaces, a few ragged children play in the sun, a lean donkey crops the thistles, or if near to a few occupied dwellings, a wine seller makes a booth of straw and chestnut boughs and dispenses a poisonous, sour drink to those who will buy. But that is only in the warm months. The winter winds blow the wretched booth to pieces and increase the desolation. Further on, tall façades rise suddenly up, the blue sky gleaming through their windows, the green moss already growing upon their naked stones and bricks."

We are reminded of the journal in which Zola captured all the drama of the Roman situation in equally vivid terms as the basis for *Rome*, the second novel in his trilogy *Les Villes*.

Meanwhile, the great public construction projects went on growing in this bleak panorama: the Vittoriano, towering with its massive bulk over the Capitol in symbolic opposition to the dome of St Peter's, and the gigantic Palazzo di Giustizia near Castel Sant'Angelo, an assertion of the finally regained secular nature of the newly unified country and its capital city. It was in fact precisely the crisis in the building sector of the late 1880s that served, paradoxically enough, to speed up the work on the colossal palace of justice: "The edifice under construction, an immense skeleton with an external framework of timber, soared to what appeared a disproportionate height. The moon of the last autumnal nights bathed it in an icy, silvery glow, giving the whitish scaffolding and above all the black holes of the unframed windows a eerie, sinister appearance. There was silence all around. Thus immersed in stillness, the enormous skeleton appeared to be sleeping too […] But no sooner had dawn broken, delineating the outline of Castel Sant'Angelo down there on the left at first vaguely and then with growing clarity, than groups of labourers appeared with a gradually increasing hubbub of voices […] the banging of hammers, screeching of saws and scraping of trowels spreading mortar, all the noisy construction work got underway in an ever greater wave of sound […] First it was wasteland with hardly enough grass to graze livestock, then the digging started and the foundations were laid for one building, then two, three, twenty, a hundred, sprouting like mushrooms. And so another big city rose beside the old one."

The purple prose of Evelina Cattermole, better known as Contessa Lara, thus clearly delineates the confused but vital concrete dimension of the new city designed to overshadow St Peter's and hide it from the eyes of the new Italians. The foundations were thus laid of a new modern and cosmopolitan city designed to supplant the decay, the real and metaphorical rot of the old regime, with its functional structures.

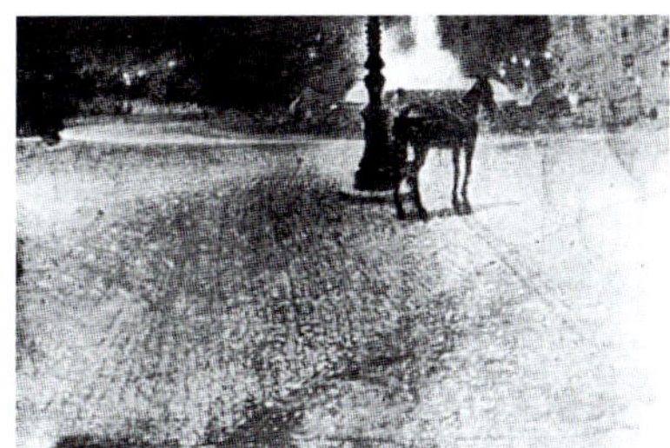

2. Giacomo Balla
Il pertichino, 1898
Lost work

A new city that was supposed to house a new mankind and was to inspire at least two of the great interpreters of that cultural climate, namely D'Annunzio and Pirandello. It is certainly no coincidence that the latter took precisely this context as the setting for the life of his Serafino Gubbio, symbol and metaphor of the new professions, cinematography in this case, that were coming to replace the old, traditional trades.

We thus imagine Balla's first steps in Rome as taking him from Termini to the Palazzo del Quirinale, where his uncle was lodged as royal huntsman, passing through the interminable construction site of an administrative and residential city where the huge ministries of finance, agriculture, commerce, industry and war as well as the Bank of Italy were still rising together with housing made to measure for the lower middle-class office workers required to man the bureaucratic machinery of a state still under construction, not far away from the great villas and eclectic houses of aristocrats, bankers, industrialists and entrepreneurs of all kinds crowded into the new capital.

Lack of steady work and a situation of authentic poverty forced the young Balla into makeshift arrangements in the Termini area around the corner from the station, between Piazza delle Terme and Via Montebello, in a context of old and new buildings often designed to house recent immigrants in search of fortune in cheap accommodation, cramped spaces and furnished rooms on an often precarious basis. Even his later and more stable lodging on Via Piemonte is still indicative of a situation of evident hardship, where the small place on the street offered barely enough space for the everyday activities of the small family, reunited once again after the mother's arrival in the capital.

These years also saw the ripening and confirmation of some social elements in the painting of Balla, who was evidently overwhelmed by experiences "on the street" that were necessarily everyday occurrences in areas like the ones where he usually lived. The spirit of his sketches with street scenes and the hallucinatory, distressing and dramatic atmosphere still to be found in *Il pertichino* (fig. 2) provide confirmation of this.

The Rome the painter knew in those early years was therefore not really very Roman, consisting mostly of marginal, peripheral situations, areas of recent immigration and construction sites, the new districts making up what has been known for a long time as "Piedmontese" Rome.

In later years, the "studio" at Via Piemonte 119 (fig. 3)– a room on the street on the ground floor of an anonymous building of the Umbertine period, where Balla plied his trade as "architect and painter" (according to his business card) as from the closing years of the century – was then to prove a useful vantage point, albeit precarious, to observe the city at a significant location near the Aurelian Walls. It was indeed located in the middle of a district that was to accommodate the new homes of the wealthier middle classes, often newly arrived in the capital from the provinces, as well as the studios of numerous artists in search of fortune, like him, practically looking onto the countryside near what was to become one of his favourite places and subjects, namely Villa Borghese, still highly suburban or indeed rustic and immersed in its original aura (fig. 5).

Space was found in this setting for the sumptuous studio of the Sienese painter Cesare Maccari, author of the large-scale frescoes in the Senate and the Palazzo di Giustizia, situated a few yards away from Balla's in a neo-Gothic edifice recently built near the ancient nymphaeum of the Horti Sallustiani. There was also the "mystical workshop" of Francesco Randone, Balla's great friend and fellow Turinese, housed in two towers of the ancient Aurelian Walls opposite the studio on Via Piemonte together with his art school (the Scuola di Arte Educatrice) and kiln. The esoteric "Master of the Walls" was often assisted there by a group of artist friends including Giovanni Prini, Ettore Ximenes and Balla as well as Ferruccio Ferrazzi, Lorenzo Cozza and Raffaele De Vico later on.

The district brutally erected on the site of Villa Ludovisi, one of the city's most renowned parks, offered an inexhaustible range of types, models and styles of construction to which the leading engineers and architects of the day contributed to lend form and substance to the aspirations of a social class that held the political, economic, entrepreneurial and cultural reins of the entire country (fig. 1). The most active in this context include Ernesto Basile, Garibaldi Burba, Carlo and Andrea Busiri Vici, Filippo Galassi, Giovan Battista

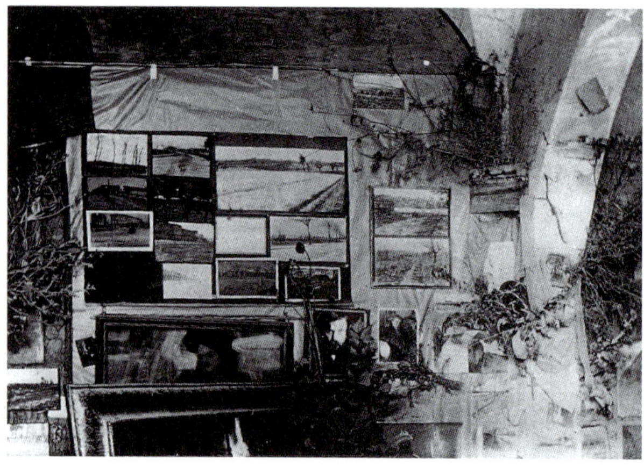

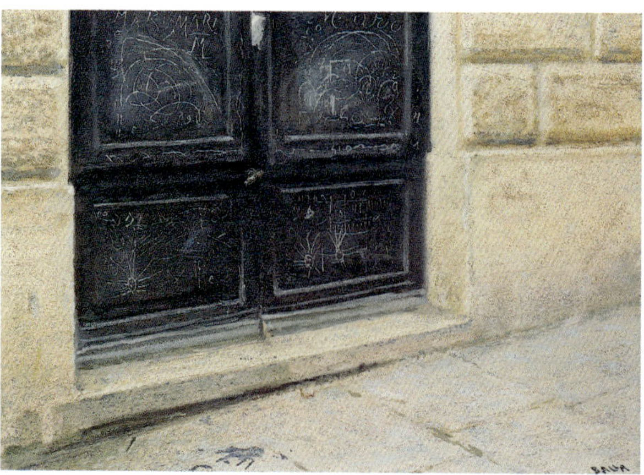

3. Giacomo Balla's studio on Via Piemonte with the upper part of the painting *Il pertichino* visible in the bottom left corner

4. Giacomo Balla
Study for *Fallimento* (*Bankruptcy*), 1902
Private collection

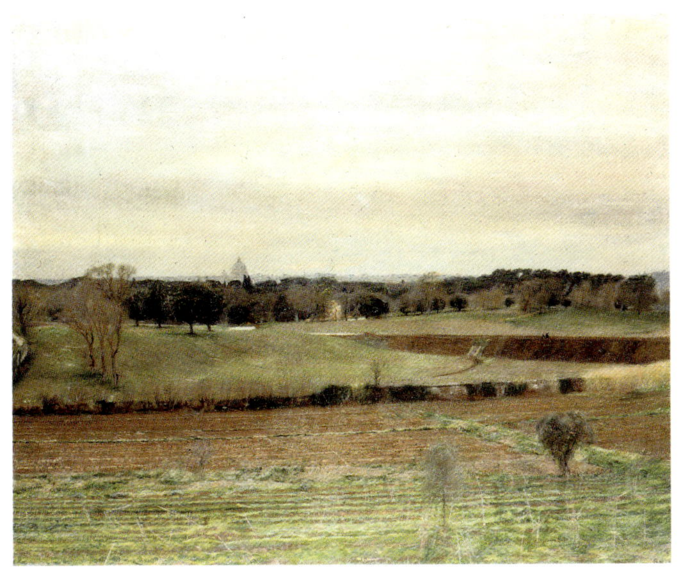

5. Giacomo Balla
Villa Borghese dal balcone
(*Villa Borghese from the Balcony*), c. 1907
Private collection

Giovenale, Gaetano Koch, Aristide Leonori, Giulio Magni, Giovanni Mascanzoni, Giovan Battista Milani, Tullio Passarelli, Pio Piacentini, Carlo Pincherle, Quadrio Pirani, Giulio Podesti, Luigi Rolland and Giovanni Sleiter, to mention just a few, sufficing in any case to give an idea of the high quality of this professional class.

This period also saw Balla's stay in Paris and his search for new spaces of investigation and experimentation. While the former in particular appears to have been a frustrating existential experience, confronting the young Turinese artist, now Roman by adoption, with a metropolitan reality that he found daunting, the influence on his artistic sensibility of the Paris Expo then under way should not be forgotten. Focused entirely on electricity and therefore light, the event can hardly not lie at the origin of the fundamental investigations and prototypal dynamic-visual reflections on the same theme that Balla was to develop – and with what results – in the years to come.

Much the same could be said of the experience in Turin two years later.

The International Exhibition of Decorative Art held in Turin in 1902 was in fact a crucial turning point. An authentic watershed between the 19th-century academic tradition and the latest ground-breaking developments in various parts of Europe ushering in the new century, the event perfectly encapsulated the complexity of the multiple explorations under way, whose legacy was largely to be reinterpreted and reworked in its various formulas by Italian Futurism just a few years later.

We shall therefore take advantage of this circumstance to open up the discourse on Futurist innovation to a broader area of European culture and encompass the subject of a more global modernization of creative thought and aesthetic inquiry rooted in the vast area affected by the technological progress of the two previous centuries, starting from the new dimensions of the contemporary city as from at least halfway through the 19th century. In this sense, the phenomenon of Futurism, in both the narrow and the broad sense, impacted the vital nerve centres of contemporary international culture, hooking up with Walter Benjamin's reflections on the metropolis, mass consumption and society, industrialization, scientific and technological discoveries and communication, and finally coming at the end of the century to meld with the most relevant issues of the debate on the city and aesthetics still alive and kicking in Balla's day. As from at least the mid-19th century, an attitude of attraction and repulsion had in fact developed towards machinery, technology and their derivatives with a radical impact on the aesthetic of the late 19th and early 20th centuries. The names of Jules Verne, Zola, Poe and Tolstoy already suffice to give an idea of the scenario onto which the collective consciousness at the turn of the century projected its hopes and fears, its technological nightmares and metropolitan angst. Suffice it to recall the extraordinary reflections of Tony Garnier and Auguste Perret on the theme of the industrial city, the "American" contamination of Loosian architecture, the metropolitan dimension of many Viennese buildings by Otto Wagner, the proto-expressionistic fantasies of Scheerbart, Bruno Taut, the Luckardt brothers and Mendelsohn, and the key episode of the German Werkbund from Muthesius to Behrens all the way to the early Gropius and the young Le Corbusier, in order to realize the extent of the cultural ferment of the time and its evolution as derived to a large extent also and above all from the specific work of the Italian Futurists. The urban scenario thus acted as a background for the most significant figurative contributions of artists like Balla, Boccioni, Depero, Marchi, Pannaggi, Paladini, Sironi and Prampolini while architects and scenographers lent physical substance to the dreams of painters, poets, writers and artists. The city with its growth, development, opportunities and new creative, aesthetic, architectural and technological dimensions became the subject, setting and protagonist of a dialectical understanding of the needs of contemporary mankind with all its contradictions and complexity of values, symbols and meanings, also and above all ideological.

All of this took shape in Turin in the ephemeral form of an epoch-making exhibition, a point of intersection between Viennese and Parisian developments, where Italian culture also managed to hold its own, above all in the pavilions featuring automobiles, photography and cinema.

The young Balla was necessarily aware of all this in addressing the themes of social life, machinery, time, speed and above all light in terms of his artistic sensibility on his return to Rome.

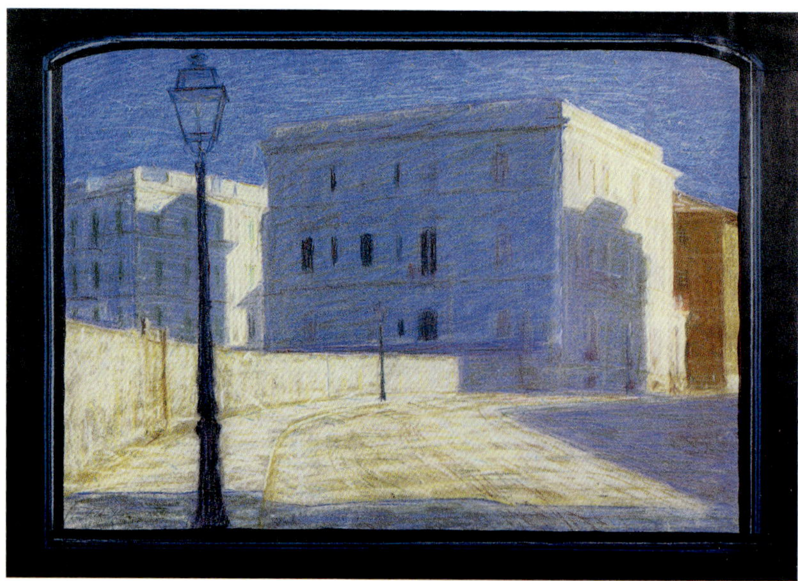

6. Giacomo Balla
Via Po, c. 1904
Private collection

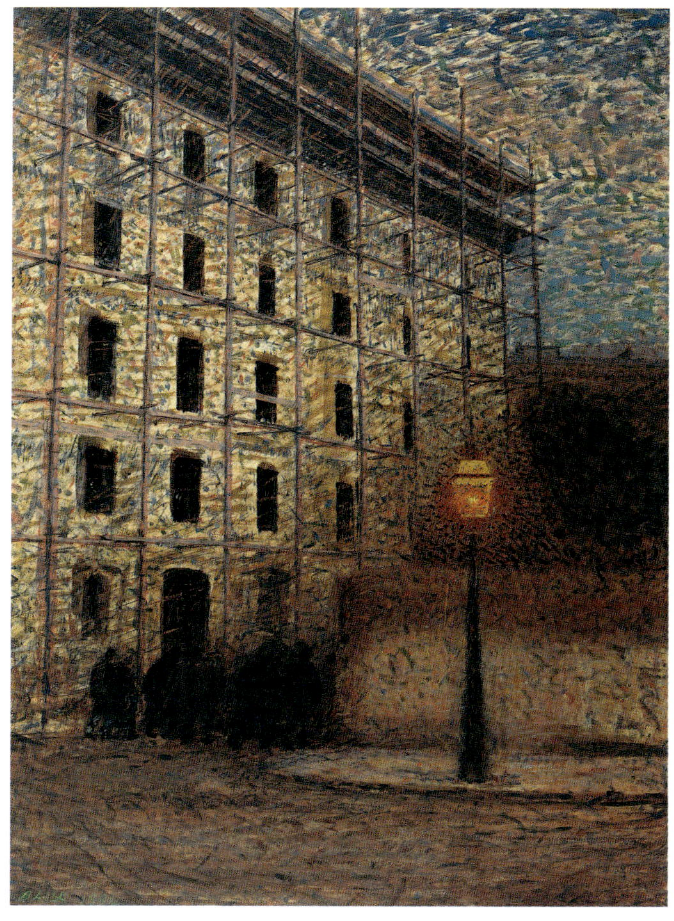

7. Giacomo Balla
La giornata dell'operaio (*The Worker's Day*), detail, 1904
Private collection

Wandering through his neighbourhood in the vicinity of the new Via Veneto, Balla faithfully recorded the reality and contradictions of a city in a simultaneous state of expansion and crisis. The dramatic nature of this awareness is fully represented by *Fallimento* (*Bankruptcy*) (fig. 4).

These were also the years of key works like *La giornata dell'operaio* (*The Worker's Day*) (fig. 7), which encapsulates a numerous series of reflections on the theme of the growing city in the symbolic image of a construction site with a building under erection and scaffolding, all fragments of a more complex vision of the city seen in its development through the dynamics of successive phases of the day cadenced by light and its "movement". The buildings that sprang up around the artist's studio on Via Piemonte, above all in the area of Via Po (fig. 6), attracted his attention and were subjected to painstaking analysis in depth, focusing above all on the more characteristic elements of the building site, like rough masonry and scaffolding. The houses and buildings under construction thus came to play a leading part in a contemporary urban story where time, light and space cadence the worker's daily toil. Balla's life was lived in this period predominantly in the new districts outside Porta Salaria. The streets leading off the Via Salaria by Villa Albani were home to his dearest friends as well as the artisans who supplied his needs, and he painted numerous works in that area, where rusticity still survived alongside an urban dimension ever more firmly established every day.

Particularly marked by the work of Carlo Busiri Vici, Giulio Magni, Giovan Battista Milani, Tullio Passarelli and Gino Coppedè, the area was the point where the working-class tenement blocks of the initial urban growth outside the city gates and outside the urban planning framework came into contact with the middle-class urban development of the Pinciano, Salario and Parioli districts, characterized by the smaller residential buildings known as the *villino* and the *palazzina*. The former gave rise above all to exercises in style, the endless hybridization of historical models with vocabularies ranging from the Romanesque to the Gothic, the Renaissance to the Baroque, the Moorish to the Mediterranean, the Turkish to the Indian, the Rococo to the Flemish, in an inexhaustible drive for self-representation of an upper middle class particularly prey to the need for status symbols, often verging on the kitsch.

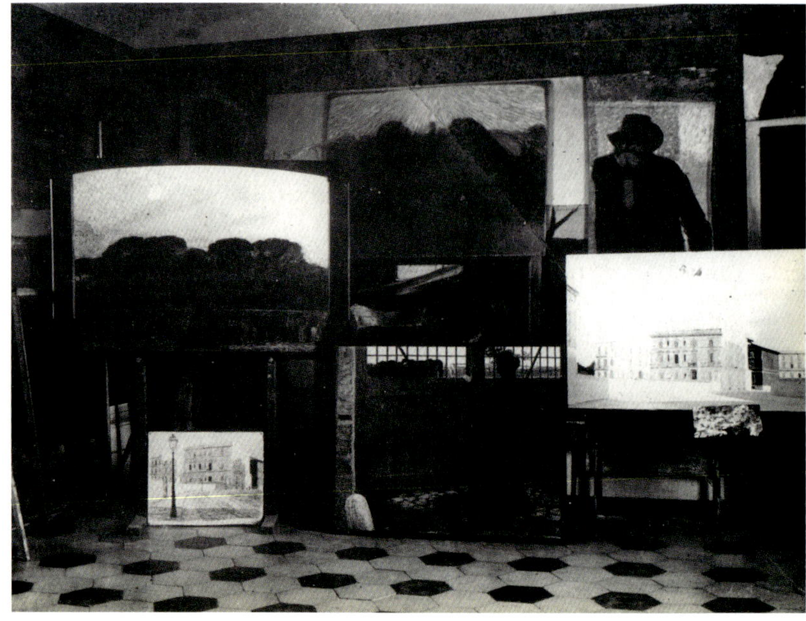

8. Giacomo Balla's studio on Via Parioli around 1908

This was to be the "high" area of Rome, developed outside the Aurelian Walls in substantial continuity with the Ludovisi district, the scene of the major speculation launched by the Società Generale Immobiliare shortly after the unification of Italy to meet the large-scale demand for quality real estate expressed by a new affluent society representing the expectations of the early decades of the new century, as described in the novels of Alberto Moravia and Ercole Patti. These were the places of Balla's day-to-day life in the early years of the 20th century, the scene of his most frequent contacts, the metamorphic setting that was to enfold him for over twenty years. The place, scene and subject of his most cherished reflections, which found their moments of greatest enchantment and contemplation in the as yet unspoilt spaces around the Galleria Borghese and its tree-shaded, secret gardens. Balla moved in these places, never too far from home and the homes of those closest to him, and obtained stimuli to reflect on nature, the evolving city, the transformation of light, time and space. What attracted him was always the omnipresent construction site of a city growing and developing in the background, the irresistible dynamics of a shapeless urban organism that swallowed up places and their history in the relentless metropolitan dynamics of modernity. Balla interpreted and bore witness to all this first-hand and left us an exemplary record of the daily succession of events. It is above all the attention with which he observed the dynamics of the building sites that attests to his precise desire to go beyond any initial impressionistic reading of things and events, and investigate in depth a metamorphic process that made construction one of the most specific and characteristic factors of contemporary society.

La giornata dell'operaio (fig. 7) attests authoritatively to this in its metamorphic, dynamic and realistic description of a building site, a three-part assemblage showing two different buildings, one presumably at the crossroads of Via Po with Via Salaria, not far from the home of the Marcucci family and therefore the carpenter's shop on Via Basento, the other probably close to the studio in Via Piemonte.

The move to the new accommodation in the long wing of an old monastery on Via Parioli (later renamed Via Paisiello) – obtained through the good offices of the mayor to be Nathan from the Sebastiani family, owners of the surrounding land – was an event with a deep and lasting impact on the entire evolution of Balla's work.

A place to live and work, a domestic and existential scenario, the new home (fig. 8) also became a vantage point to observe the city from a very special angle and later the meeting place of the Roman avant-garde. By virtue of its position on a key axis of development for the evolution of modern Rome, in the vicinity of one of the capital's finest historical villas with views extending past Villa Balestra to the slopes of Monte Mario and the dome of St Peter's, it offered crucial insight into the dynamics of development that turned a peripheral and still agricultural area characterized by vineyards, fields, market gardens, haystacks and rustic taverns into one of the capital's most upmarket and sought-after residential districts in the short space of twenty years. Balla experienced, enjoyed and suffered all of this, recording the great and small transformations and leaving in his boundless work of those crucial years a sort of diary in images bearing persuasive and fascinating witness to the definitive loss and disappearance of a world, a history and a memory to make way for the new reality of the short 20th century. In the space of a few years, Balla's rustic "red house" was surrounded, besieged and then finally destroyed by fashionable, eclectic and often vulgar buildings, in a relentless wave of speculative expansion. A leading part in this exemplary chapter in the history of Roman urban planning was played precisely by Sebastiani, the subject of the famous portrait *Il proprietario* (*The Owner*), who divided the entire area between Viale Rossini, Via Mercadante and Viale Parioli up into building lots with the aid of his son, an engineer, and initiated one of the most successful real estate operations of the early 20th century. In an area already marked by the presence of renowned architects like Koch, Pistrucci, Sleiter, Piacentini, Pincherle, Busiri Vici and Galassi, Sebastiani employed trusty associates like Frezzotti and then

9. Giacomo Balla
La fila per l'agnello (*Queuing for Lamb*), 1942
Private collection

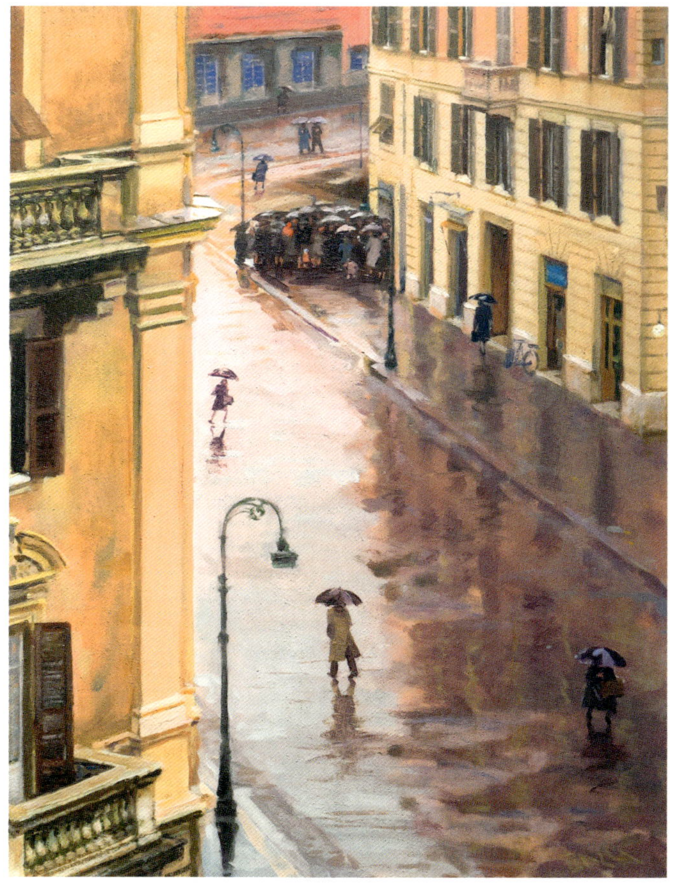

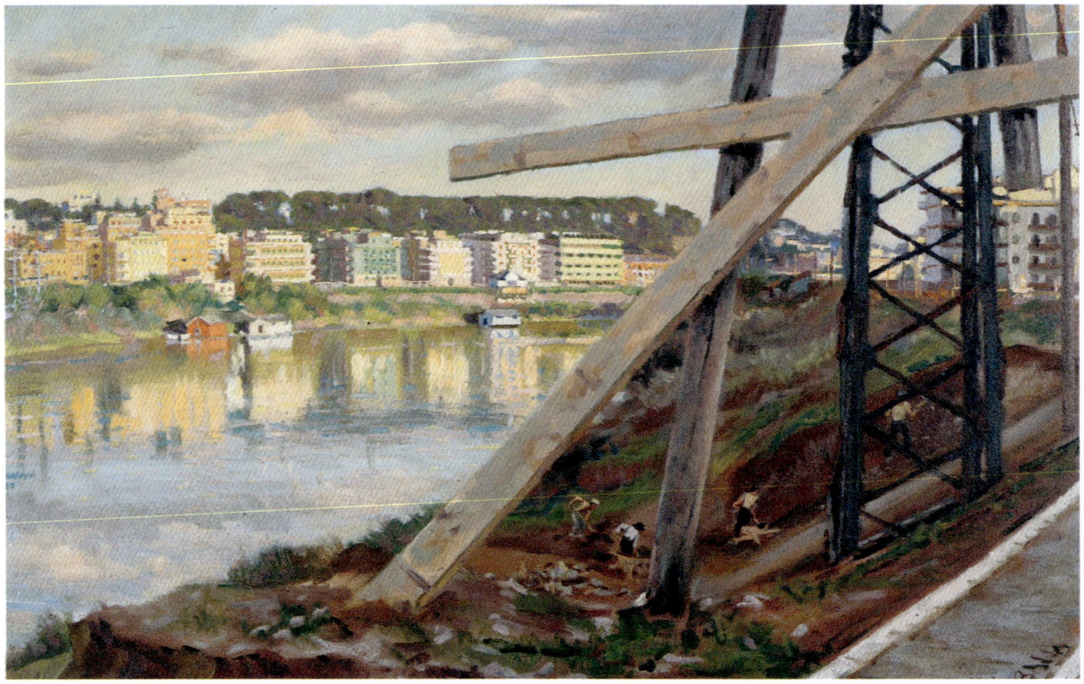

10. Giacomo Balla
La città che avanza (*The City Advancing*), 1942
Private collection

Foschini to erect a series of quality buildings, partly for the family's own use. In the short space of a few years, the landscape lost its panoramic, rural and agricultural characteristics definitively to become the location of a pretentious but anonymous middle-class district, as clearly attested also by some views of Balla's home produced around 1920 by his neighbour Armando Spadini, who lived opposite on Via Paisiello at the intersection with Via Porpora.

Balla evidently suffered from this violent and inevitable environmental metamorphosis and promptly recorded the changes. An episode recalled in by his daughter Elica in her memoirs is exemplary in this sense: "Not far away … stood a magnificent pine, right where they planned to build a square. By agreement with the men working in the streets, the painter had a fence put up around it and was thus able to save the magnificent pine in what is now Piazza Pitagora."

The national Expo held in 1911 to celebrate the fiftieth anniversary of Italy's unification also left major imprints in Balla's work, as he depicted, years later, the construction of the external staircase in front of the monumental Galleria d'Arte Moderna built for the occasion by Cesare Bazzani.

While the dramatic departure from his home in Via Paisiello left Balla still obsessed with the city's growth, he continued to gravitate around the symbolic focal point of Villa Borghese and its surroundings. Having found temporary accommodation for some time after the eviction and demolition in nearby parts of the Parioli district like Villa Ambron, he finally moved through the good offices of his friend Biancale into the block on Via Oslavia recently built in the early 1920s, not far from Piazza Mazzini, by the Istituto romano per le Case Popolari, then ably directed by Alberto Calza-Bini, which reserved a small proportion of its public housing for the city's artists. His friend Cambellotti had also taken advantage of this opportunity and moved his home and studio some time earlier into a block on the Lungotevere Flaminio near Piazza Perin del Vaga.

The view from that position in the middle of the Vittorie district was now very different from the rustic panorama of Via Paisiello. Balla was now in the heart of the compact city, as attested by the disconcerting stretch of Via Montello immortalized in his famous *In fila per l'agnello* (*Queuing for Lamb*) (fig. 9).

In his most recent works, however, Balla still pursued with realistic determination the urban ideal that had fascinated him since the dawn of the century. His extraordinary view of the road alongside the Tiber, seen through a dramatic interweaving of metal in the foreground with the pines of Villa Balestra in the background, offers us once again that idea of a city rising (figs. 10-11) that had already played such a part in defining the poetic, linguistic and theoretical horizons of early Futurism.

Bequeathing us the most vivid and authentic record of the new Rome of the 1930s and 40s, where we find the signs of new architecture once again, embedded in a long stretch of the new Tiber waterfront, with the buildings erected by Rossi, Di Castro, Gra and De Renzi, Balla returned to the origin of his visions, where the pines of Rome still provide scenery but this time for the now consolidated, constructed, compact city. Now old, Balla went back to the places of his first Roman attachments, the very spot where thirty years earlier, in 1911, he and his friends Marcucci, Cambellotti, Cena, Celli and Aleramo built the famous hut that housed, among the materials of the newly founded schools for the rustic population of the Roman countryside, one of his most dramatic and disquieting works: the monochrome portrait of Tolstoy.

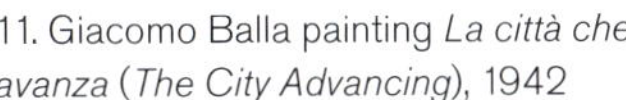

11. Giacomo Balla painting *La città che avanza* (*The City Advancing*), 1942

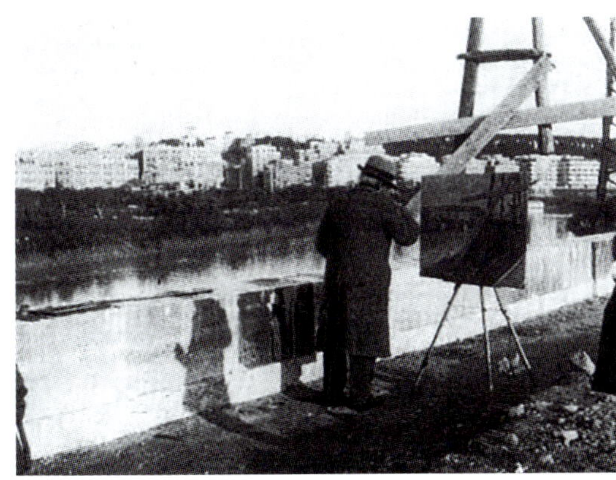

LIGHT

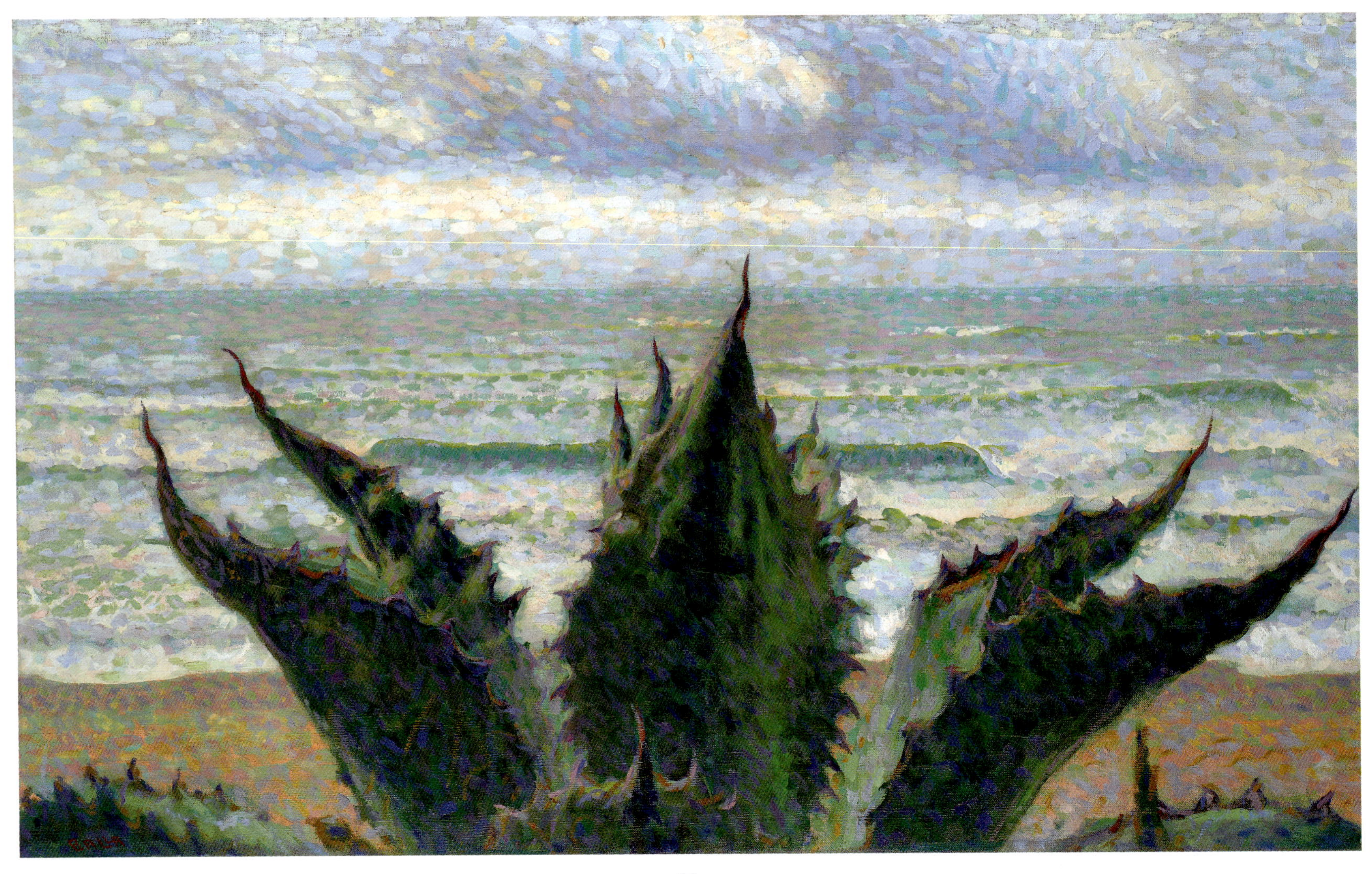

22

Agave sul mare – Il mare di Anzio
(Agave by the Sea – The Sea at Anzio), 1908
oil on canvas, 90 x 143 cm

Light

Ester Coen

"Now that the sky is no longer the vague blue background of the pictures invented by pastists, it is a vault that captures and envelops us. And then, it is all over with objective painting. What we pursue is the representation, the projection of a thought on canvas, coloured algebra and geometry ..."[1] Giacomo Balla was nearly fifty in 1919, just under ten years after signing the manifesto of Futurist painting and about seven after his studies on the interpenetration of colour,[2] better known as *Compenetrazioni iridescenti* (*Iridescent Interpenetrations*), an original attempt to explore the elementary structures of vision and painting with renewed sensibility and an experimental, analytical vocabulary.

Reckless, fearless and daring, Balla accepted the invitation of Filippo Tommaso Marinetti and Umberto Boccioni to join the ranks of the new warriors for art with great enthusiasm in 1910. This awakened a hidden side of his apparently calm, Olympian character. The spontaneous, impulsive energy of a previously curbed revolutionary spirit suddenly broke free. With unbridled impetus, he took up the new challenge with ardour and vitality to the point of putting all the works of his early period on sale in 1913. On the threshold of fame, Balla repudiated the past with uncommon determination. His was a genuine rejection and at the same time – and perhaps above all – a symbolic gesture. One chapter ended and another began (fig. 1).

1. "Fu Balla" ("The Late Balla"), sale of works from the artist's pre-Futurist period at the Galleria Giosi, April 1913

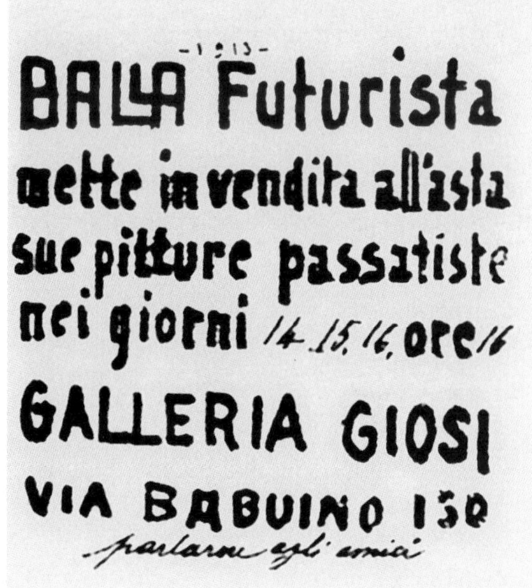

Impenetrable mystery shrouds Balla and his work between 1910, when he signed the general and technical Futurist manifestos on painting, and 1912, the date of his first stay in Germany (fig. 2); a mystery that prepared the group for the real battle, one to be fought on foreign soil. An aura of secrecy surrounds the images and themes of pictorial representation, noisily covered by the shouting, din, racket, riot and confusion of the Futurist soirées, as all the signatories waited to find the right key to strike up a choral battle hymn together and light the fuse of the explosive mixture that was to blow up in the great capital cities of Europe. All this was not to happen, however, until February 1912 in Paris at the Galerie Bernheim-Jeune[3] (fig. 3). Balla's *Lampada ad arco* (*Street Light*) is listed in the catalogue of that exhibition as *Lumière électrique*, no. 27, but the evidence available and the lack of any mention in the press suggest that it was not shown. Because it was not sufficiently in line with the work of the Milanese Futurists? Because it would have been too expensive to transport a single painting from Rome?[4]

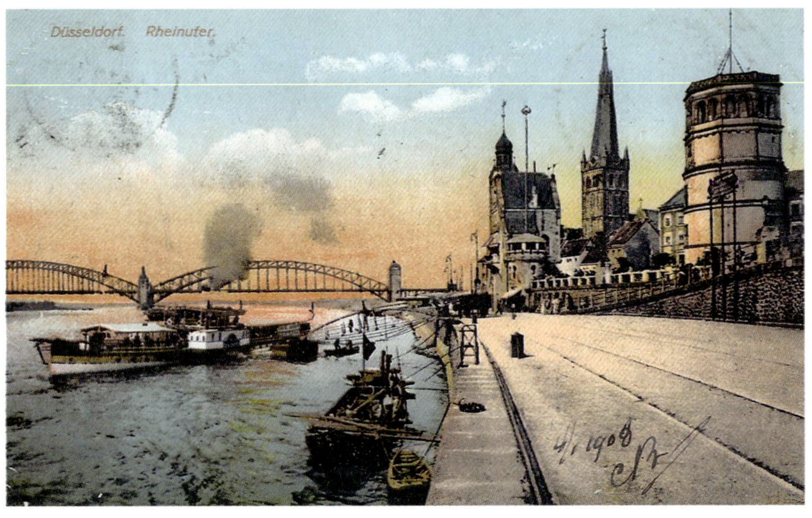

2. View of Düsseldorf from the Rhine on a postcard of 1908

Even though *Lampada ad arco* was not shown in the group's first public show, perhaps because of its overly Divisionist character or the persistence of naturalistic overtones, Balla's adherence to Futurist theory and practice was already under way. In 1912, in the wake of the chronophotographic experiments, he commenced his analysis of the progress of a temporal dimension in successive stages of development with *Dinamismo di un cane al guinzaglio* (*Dynamism of a Dog on a Leash*) in paratactic sequence with the *Bambina che corre sul balcone* (*Girl Running on a Balcony*), both presumably painted between the summer and the end of the year on his return from Germany. In the latter work the accent falls in particular with greater insistence on the reduction of colour to broad strokes in order to emphasize the articulation of movement in space. It was in those few months of frenzied activity and enthusiasm that he tackled the subject matter of modernity to transform the earlier compositional principles into a more dynamic and vibrant surface.

For Balla, Divisionism was not the pure application of scientific theories of chromatic decomposition, as it was for the painting of French Neo-Impressionists Georges Seurat and Paul Signac, but rather the result of the slow evolution of a personal technique grounded on the study of nature rather than the synthesis or abstraction of cold, rigorous principles. It was a development based also on continuity with the history of Italian painting and the greatness of artists chosen as spiritual guides for a constructive trajectory, such as Giovanni Segantini, Giacomo Grosso, Angelo Morbelli and Giuseppe Pellizza da Volpedo, to mention just some of the most significant names for his technical, intellectual and moral formation. This path led Balla to analyze luminous phenomena not in the French way, through the contrasting or complementary juxtaposition of basic colours, but through the reverberation of primaries, perfectly calibrated in quantity by brushwork capable of rendering the vibrations of light. Short dabs of paint and long, narrow streaks of greater or lesser thickness reflect at the same time full awareness of the most recent scientific investigations, regarded as openings for an interpretation of reality, not only pure empirical verification[5] or simple tools for objective correspondence or symmetry with physical phenomena.

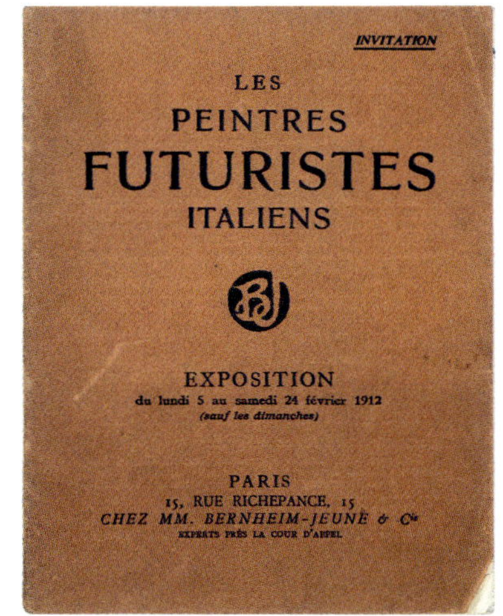

3. Cover of the catalogue of the Futurists' exhibition at the Galerie Bernheim-Jeune, Paris, February 1912

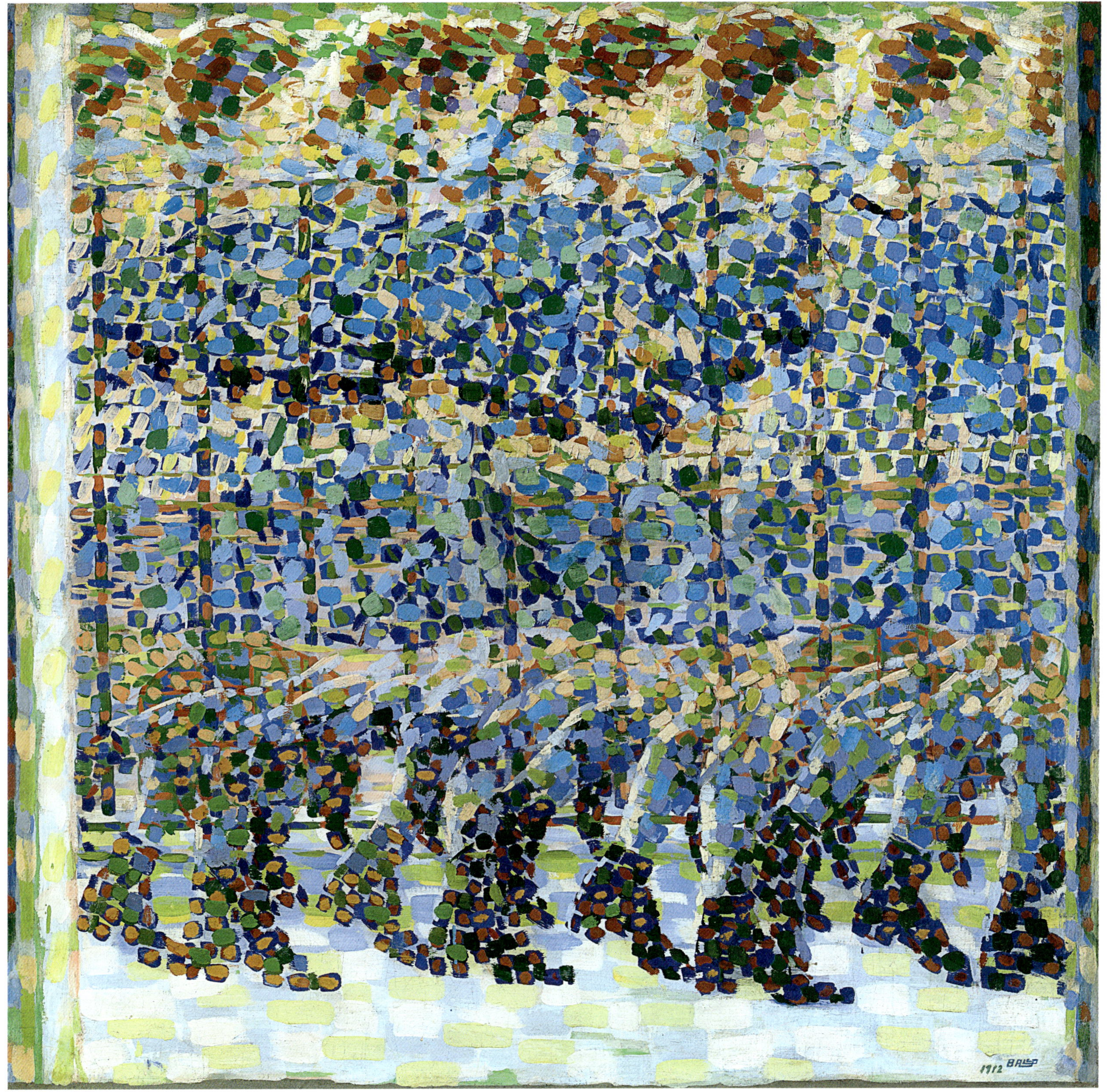

23

Bambina che corre sul balcone
(*Girl Running on a Balcony*), 1912
oil on canvas, 130 x 130 cm

Balla had spent seven long months in Paris from the autumn of 1900 to the spring of 1901 (fig. 4) as assistant to Serafino Macchiati, a painter and illustrator from the Marche region of Italy who had recently moved to the outskirts of the French capital. Paris glowed at the turn of the century with all the sparkle, enthusiasm and carefree, euphoric atmosphere associated with the World's Fair,[6] symbolizing the triumph of the age of progress. It is also the time of the official triumph of Impressionism, even though academic *art pompier* was still in place, and of the late Symbolists, the Nabis and indeed the followers of Auguste Rodin, now hailed as a great master. Paris epitomized luxury and pleasure. As Balla wrote to Elisa,[7] jotting down his first impressions of the French capital by night, "Everything is flooded with light in shops with a rich abundance of fabrics, fashions, jewellery and so on. Extraordinary elegance everywhere. Certain types of lady pass you by laden with velvet, lace, furs and perfume that leave you astonished at such strange and sumptuous originality. What is really fantastic is a sort of advertising in gigantic words up on the cornices of buildings. The letters themselves are made up of electrical light bulbs and the wonderful thing is that they change colour and position all the time, so that you see all this appearance and disappearance of lights standing out against a sky that becomes as black as a grave at night, with thousands of faces passing you by all the time and shouting and the vehicles whizzing past and the surprises that every moment offers ..." No message from Paris appears, however, to reveal or suggest even the slightest interest in the painting of the period, neither French art nor that on show in the foreign pavilions of the Expo. Concentrated on his work and financial difficulties, Balla appears to have been fascinated above all by the city with its extraordinary architectural visions and phantasmagorical illuminations. One of the paintings he took back to Rome was in fact a nocturnal view of the façade of the Palais de l'Électricité, one of the greatest attractions of the period, an authentic, dazzling emblem of

4. Giacomo Balla, view of Paris from his room in a letter to his fiancée Elisa, 1900

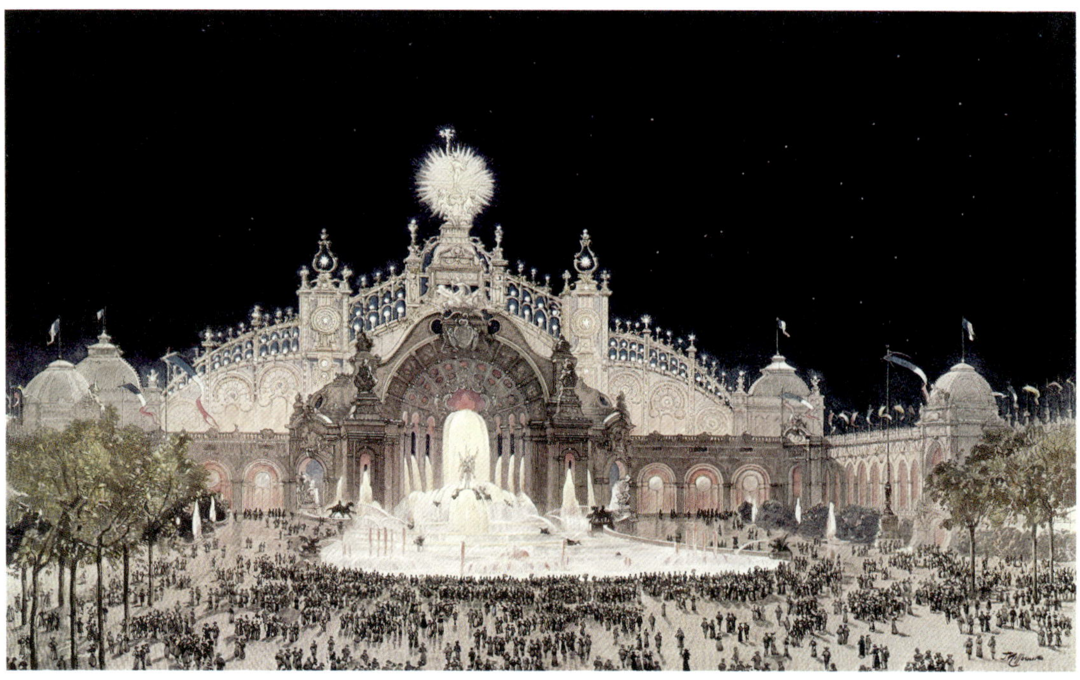

5. The Palais de l'Electricité at Paris Exposition Universelle of 1900

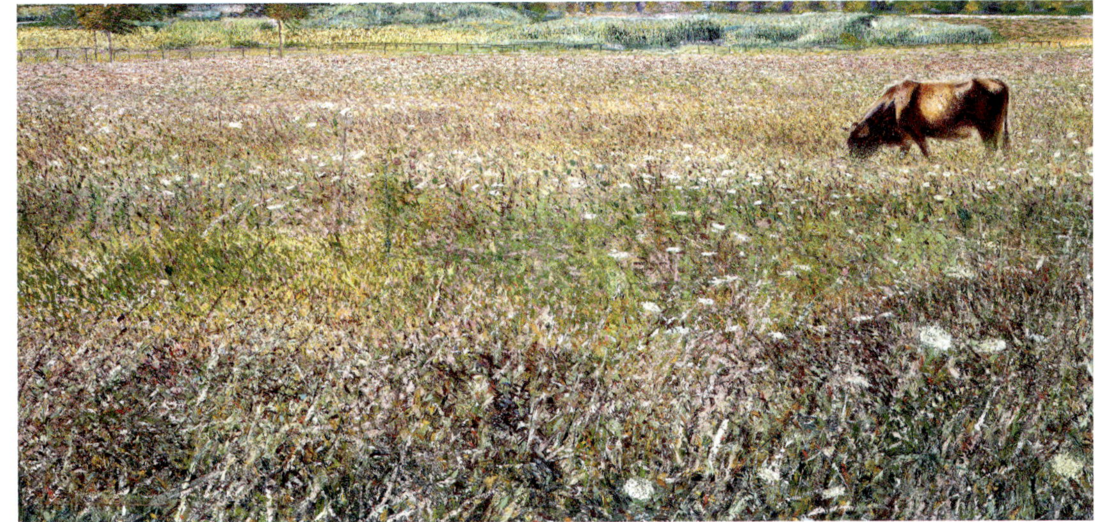

6. Umberto Boccioni
Campagna romana (*Roman Countryside*), 1903
Lugano, Museo d'arte della Svizzera italiana, collection of the City of Lugano, Chiattone donation

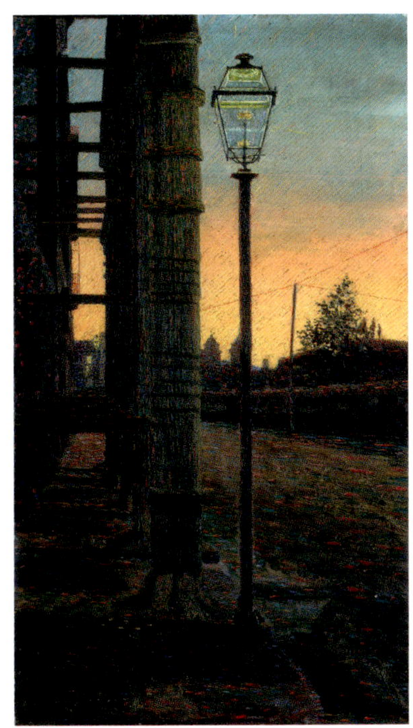

7. Gino Severini
Notturno in via di Porta Pinciana (*Nocturne in Via di Porta Pinciana*), 1903
Private collection

modernity (fig. 5). He cannot, however, have remained indifferent to the scientific breakthroughs of the time and amazing, magical inventions such as the new device to project images in motion, the mechanical stairs, the diesel engine and the huge sixty-metre-long telescope to observe the celestial vault.

The focal point of his artistic and emotional life was, however, Rome, the place where he found rules and techniques to explore in ever-greater depth. Every single detail in painting that was still realist in appearance and often featured dark hues and shadows was thus to be transformed into a radiant whole where light and colour became dynamic concatenations ready to manifest themselves beyond form. It is as though the experience of Paris and its pictorial vocabulary had reinforced his convictions. It was then these convictions, albeit enriched with what his eye drew from the art of other countries, that Balla communicated to his young pupils Boccioni[8] and Severini soon after his return to Italy (figs. 6-7). As Boccioni wrote in 1915,[9] "Balla's importance lay not in the ethical, so to speak, meaning he gave to his paintings but in the stubborn search for subjects at odds with the common appearance of paintings. He fought against the sublime with solitary, inhuman work of almost mystical severity. We young painters – Sironi, Boccioni, Severini, Costantini – were attracted to him. In order to escape from the antiquated attitude of art as it manifested itself in Rome, Balla saw no other salvation than immersion in a sort of scientific sensibility that was to lead him inevitably to the present interpretation. [...] What Balla wants is to arrive at the pure primordial element and the germ of the architectonic principle of art."

The *Lampada ad arco* is therefore the manifesto with which Balla declared his allegiance to Futurism. The style of the painting refers to 1910-11. Dated 1909,[10] it represents his complete embrace of the spirit of the new movement in a relationship of symmetrical sharing with Marinetti and his programme. Close to the solar spectrum, the light from the street lamp, in an antinomic relationship with the crescent moon in the sky, breaks up into the colours of the rainbow (fig. 8). It is as though progress and technology were able to breathe new life into the vital principle of nature through mechanical synthesis. Small curves entwine with the strokes around them to represent the electrical potential released by the electric lamp, decomposed and diffused in its primary values at high frequency. These are, however, threads of a perceptual pattern that can only be reunited in the complex definition of an idea, the higher idea that guided Balla in his art, the idea of universal energy reflected in human impulses in an astral concord of deep strength and harmony. Rooted in the temperament of his personality, this intuitive idea found only partial correspondence in science and perhaps more in the widespread esotericism of the time. Radiant vibrations, waves in the air picked up by a mind-body like abstract figures of thought-forms in motion, were the subjects then addressed by theosophists[11] and illustrated in diagrams in accordance with a synaesthetic vision of reality. Associated with this simultaneously perceptive and cognitive phenomenon was a theory of colours and their meaning also in emotive terms (fig. 9). Not imaginary forms therefore but representations of forms generated by objects or persons, perceived and reinvented by a visionary mind or artistic genius like that of Balla.

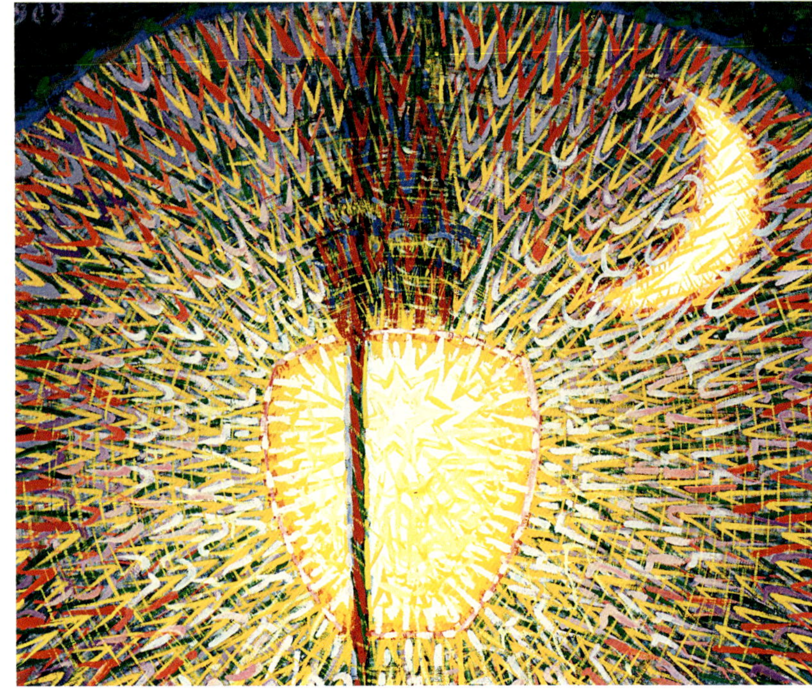

8. Giacomo Balla
Lampada ad arco (*Street Light*), detail
1910–11
New York, The Museum of Modern Art

The two long stays in Düsseldorf in 1912 were crucial to the investigation of a chromatic synthesis of the individual elements of visible light. In Germany, first in July and then again from November to late December, in a rarefied, intellectual atmosphere of shared sensibility and love for the visual and musical arts, Balla decorated the studio of the Löwenstein family's home on the Rhine.[12] These were key months both for the important cultural stimuli offered and as a long interlude allowing him to reflect on the rapid course of events that had swept him into the whirlwind of nascent Futurism in a determined attempt to identify a pathway of continuity with his previous work. The Löwenstein home in Düsseldorf offered Balla an elegant, sophisticated atmosphere and a passion for music, both the violin playing of his host and the concerts he attended (fig. 10),[13] in perfect harmony with his

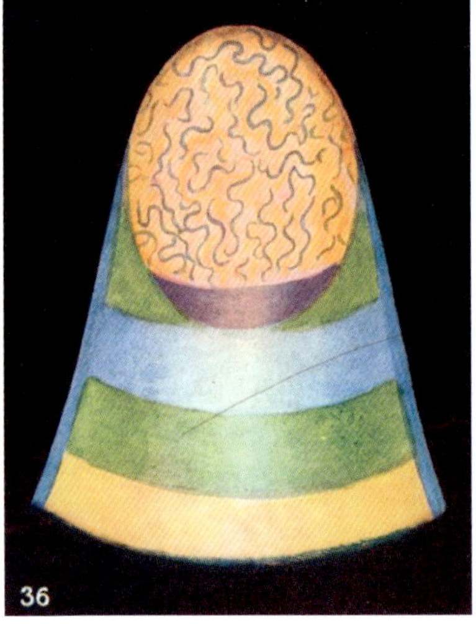

9. Table 36, *Appreciation of a Picture*, according to the emotional meaning of colours through the theosophical theories of Annie Besant and Charles W. Leadbeater, 1905

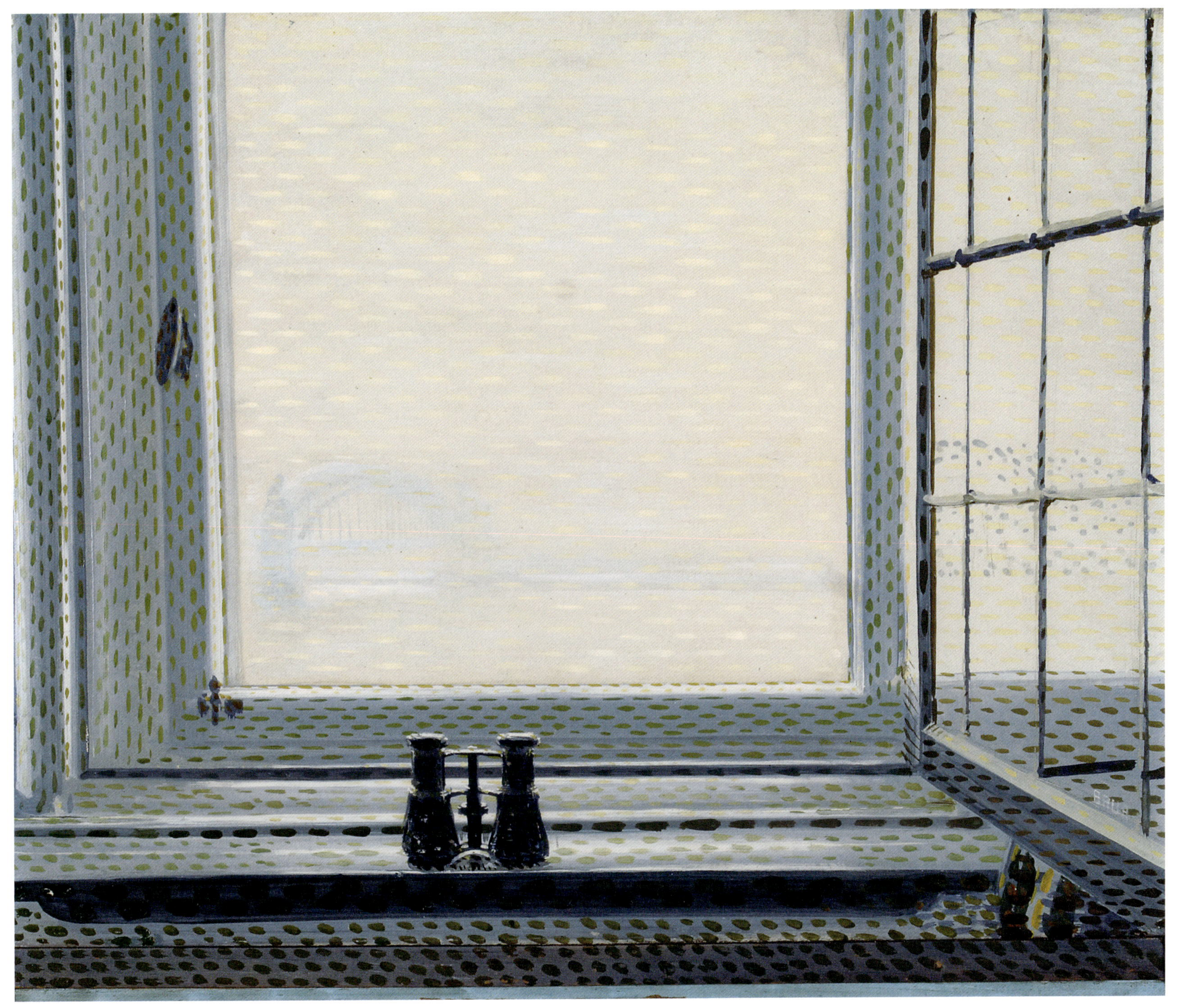

24

Finestra su Düsseldorf (Window in Düsseldorf), 1912
oil on panel, 28.5 x 35 cm

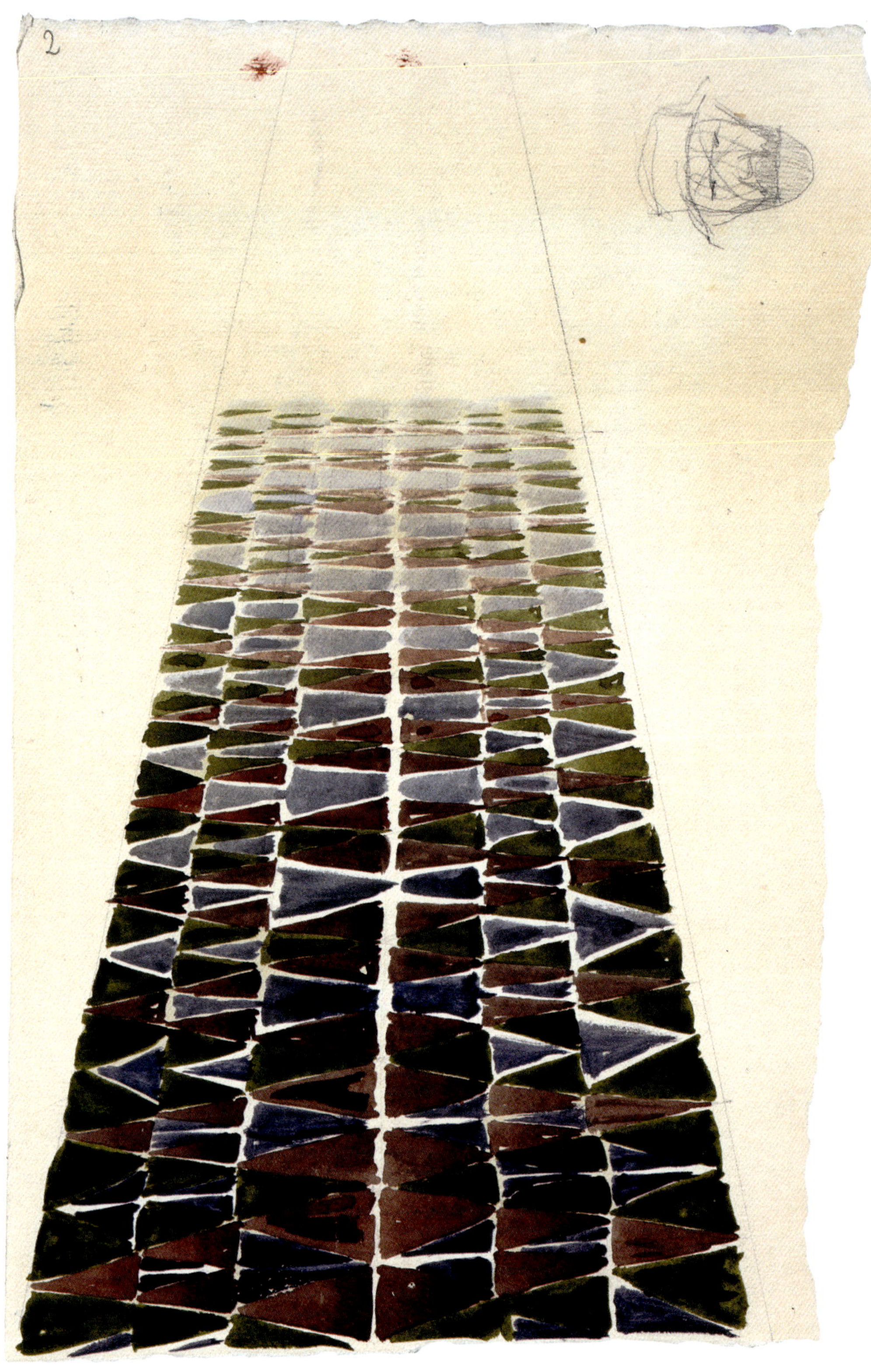

25

Studio per compenetrazione iridescente n. 9
(Study for Iridescent Interpenetration no. 9), 1912
pencil and watercolour on paper, 20.5 x 12.5 cm

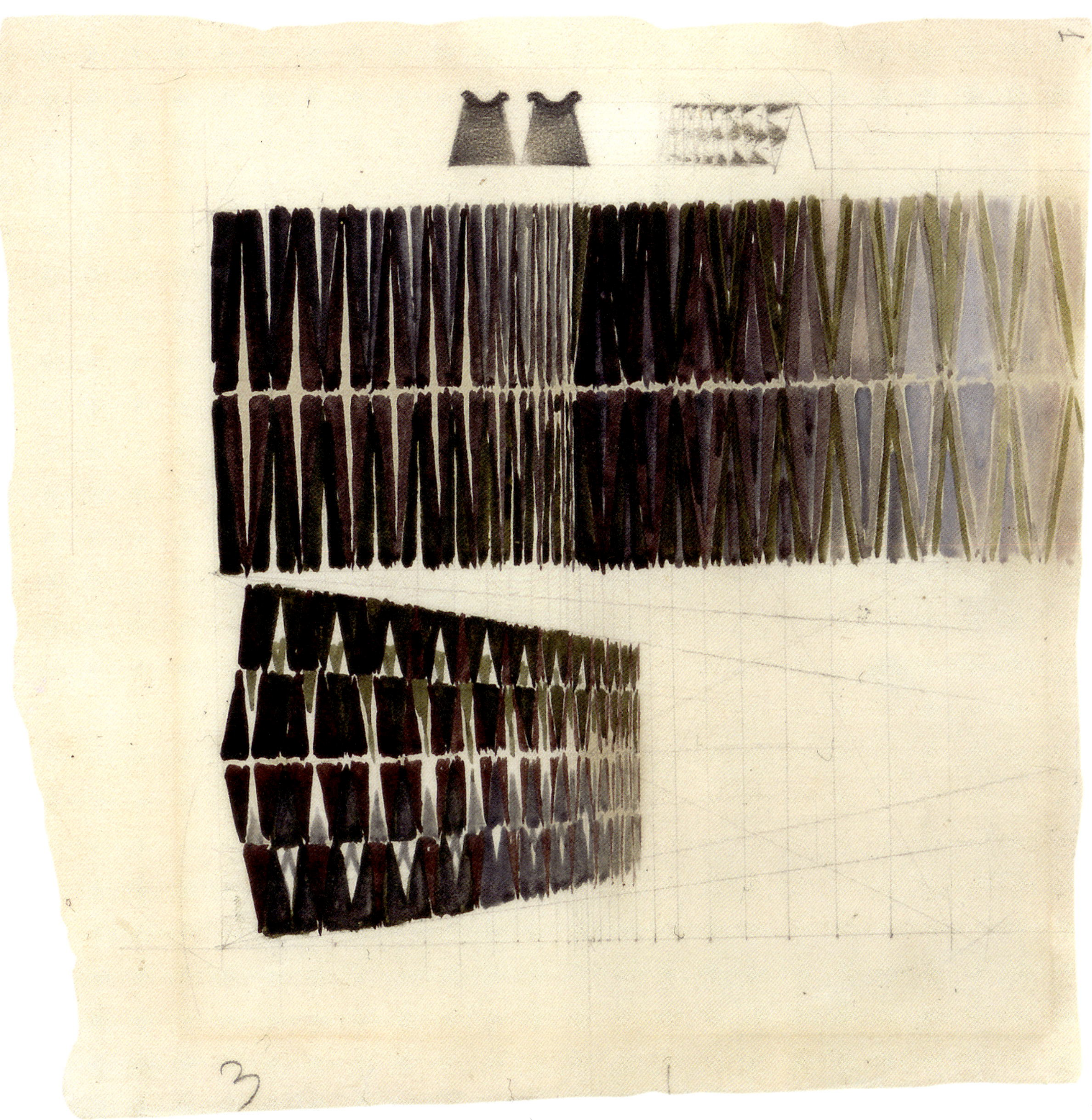

26

Studio per compenetrazione iridescente
(Study for Iridescent Interpenetration),
from the Düsseldorf notebooks, c. 1912
pencil and watercolour on paper, 20.2 x 20.1 cm

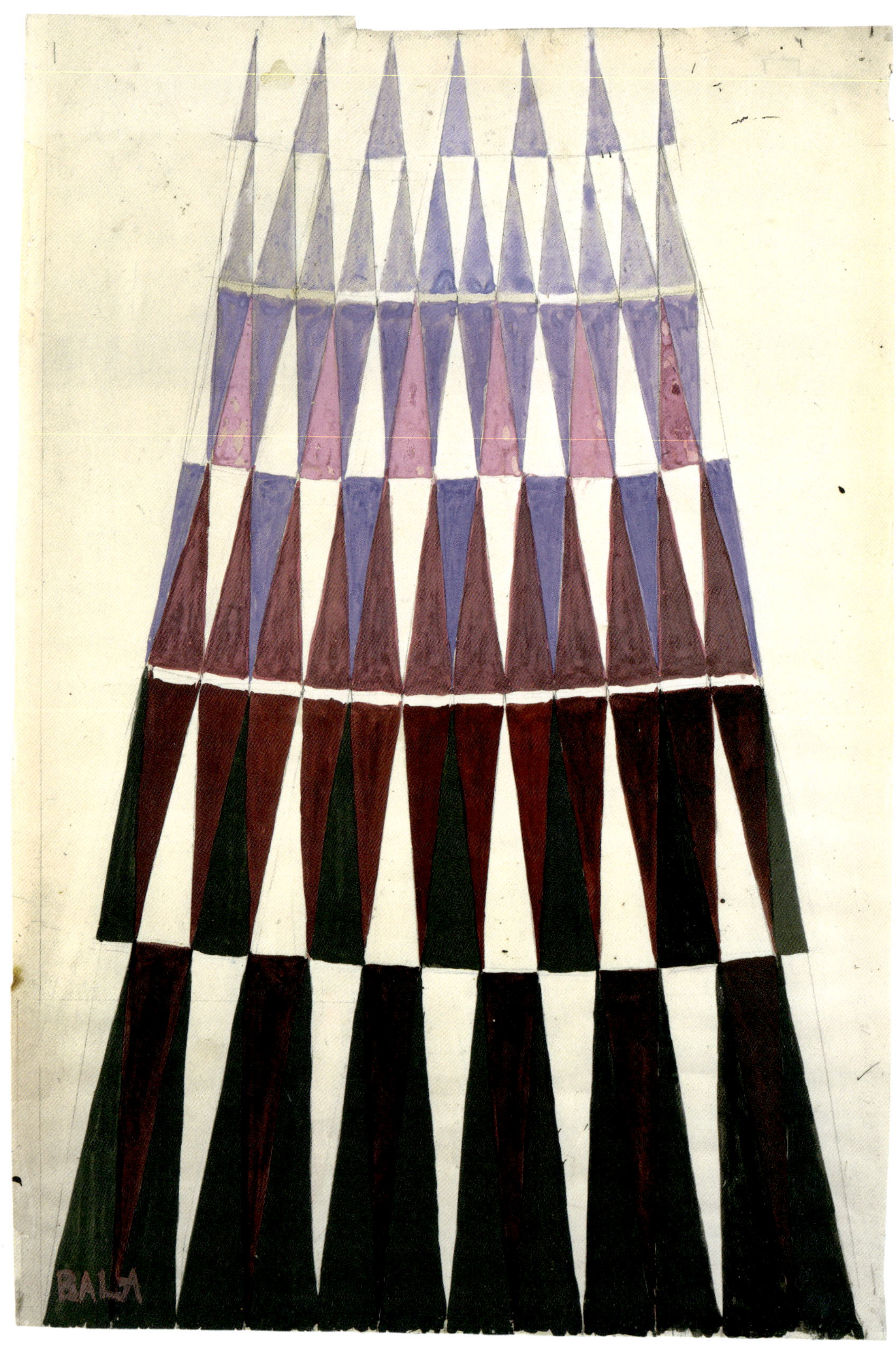

27

Compenetrazione iridescente n. 11
(Iridescent Interpenetration no. 11), c. 1912
pencil and watercolour on paper, 57.5 x 38 cm

10. Giacomo Balla
Study for La mano del violinista
(*The Hand of the Violinist*)
Private collection

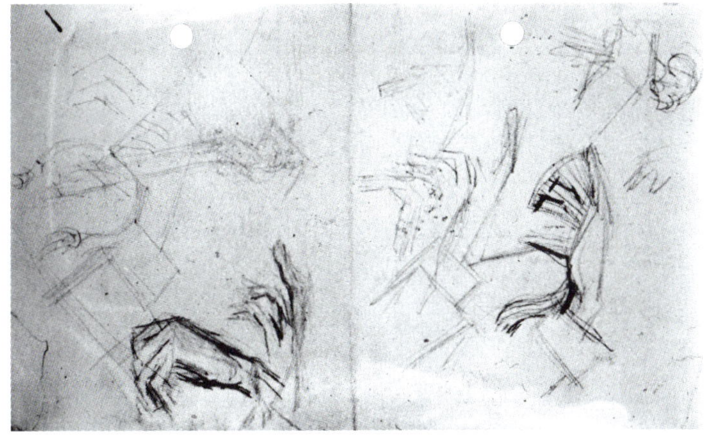

own interests, to which he devoted his free time.[14] Here he painted "a study of the hand … playing a violin but in motion with different positions and the bow passing constantly over the movements. The result was something very new …"[15] An extraordinary experiment to capture sound and movement in a frozen image by recording the succession of infinitesimal temporal fractions of an action. The reproduction in painting of the chronophotographic experiments of Eadweard Muybridge and Étienne-Jules Marey, taken up by Anton Giulio Bragaglia in 1911 in a conference and two years later in his book *Fotodinamismo futurista*, was a previously unexplored avenue. Sound, movement and light, all aspects of one vital energy. Emblematically featuring a pair of binoculars as a measure of visual unity, the *Finestra su Düsseldorf* (*Window in Düsseldorf*) (1912) is a concrete image of deep interest also in the laws of optics. In search of chromatic solutions in which "due to the quality of the light, everything becomes more veiled and mysterious, and the material less real"[16] (fig. 11). He quantifies the limits of an analysis based on the ability to observe and represent luminous stimuli, with daring contrasts in the early paintings now separated into single colours and then consolidated in revolving courses of stars and planets, where the circle frames the terms of perception in the cosmic aspects of celestial phenomena. It is as though the impulse to penetrate the deep and secret life of things through the expansion of sight were directly proportional to the search for the ungraspable truth of the universe.

11. The iron bridge over the Rhine seen in Balla's painting *Finestra su Düsseldorf* (*Window in Düsseldorf*)

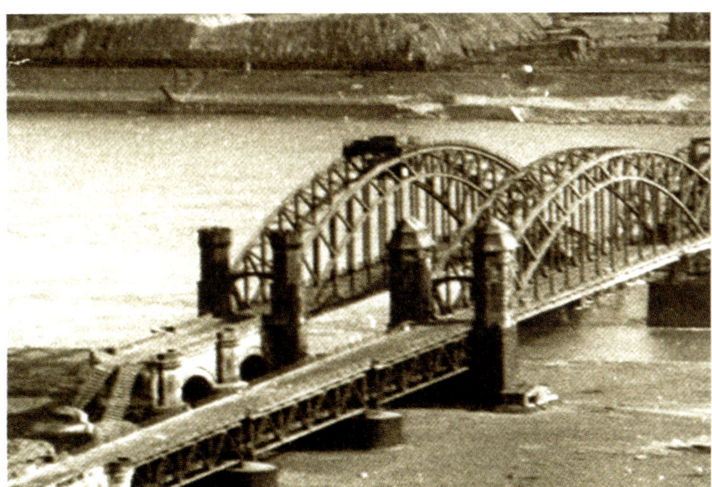

During his stays in Germany he was struck by the "beautiful coloured windows with triangles and squares of yellow and blue"[17] of the Düsseldorf railway station and repeated their geometric patterns in "endless attempts"[18] to mark the displacement of the pictorial system in the radicality of the luminous phenomenon as pure vital entity. It was not so much the motifs

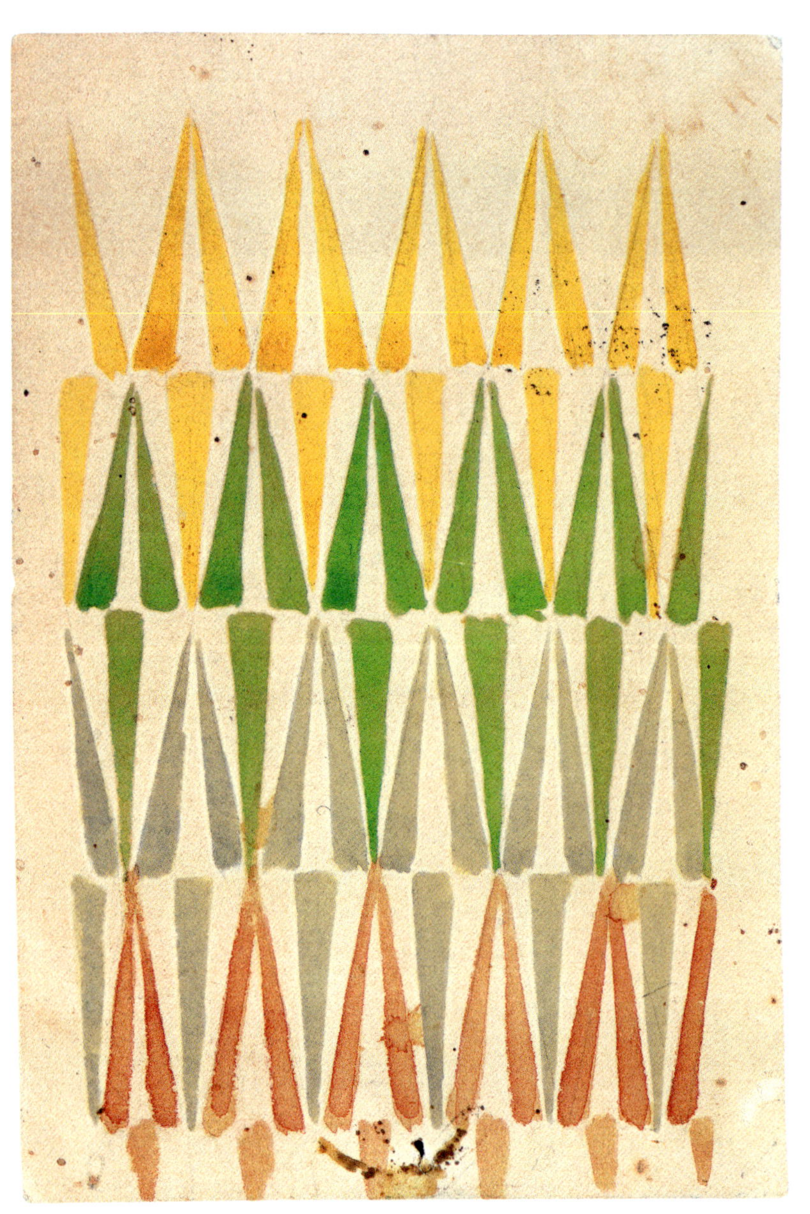

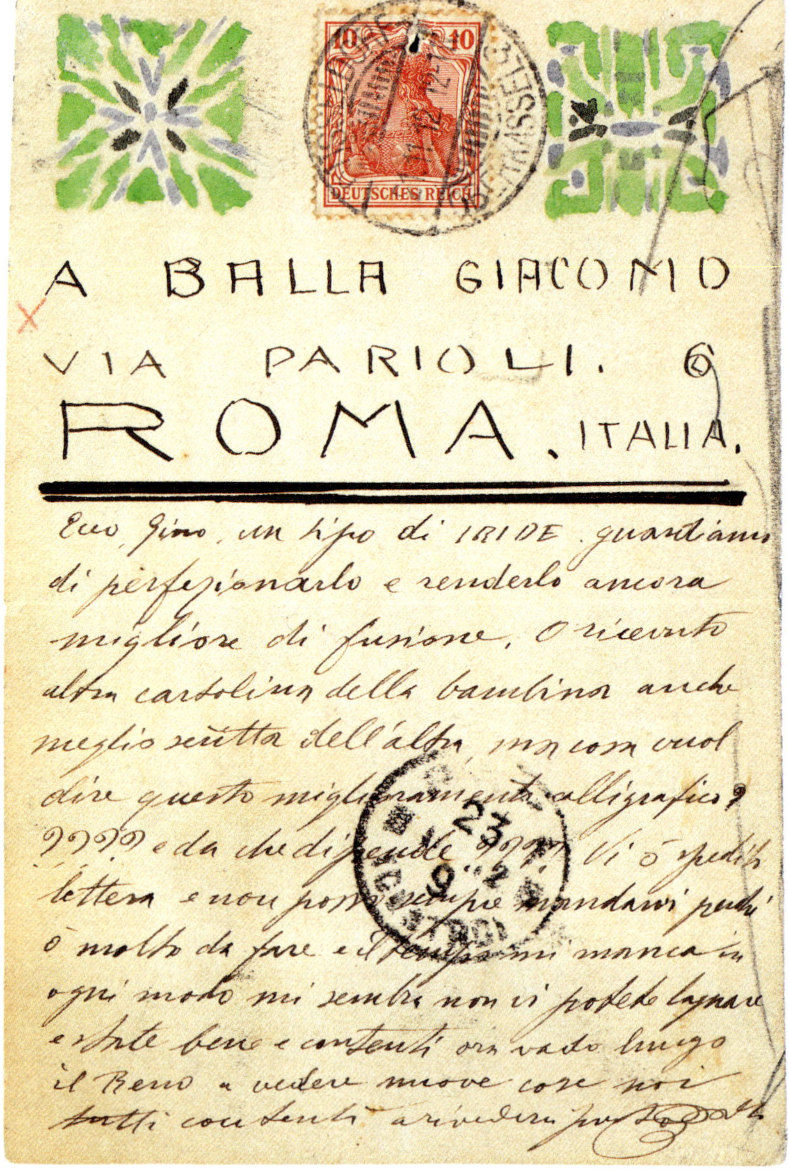

A BALLA GIACOMO
VIA PARIOLI. 6
ROMA. ITALIA.

Ecco, Gino, un tipo di IRIDE. guardiamo di perfezionarlo e renderlo ancora migliore di funzione. O ricevuto altra cartolina della bambina anche meglio scritta dell'altra, ma com vuol dire questo miglioramento calligrafico? ???? e da chi dipende ???? Vi ò spedito lettera e non posso sempre mandarvi perchè ò molto da fare e il tempo mi manca in ogni modo mi sembra non vi potete lagnare e state bene e contenti ora vado lungo il Reno a vedere nuove cose noi tutti contenti arrivederci presto

28a-b

Compenetrazione iridescente n. 1
(Iridescent Interpenetration no. 1), 1912
(postcard to Gino Galli, 11 December 1912)
watercolour on pasteboard, 14 x 9.5 cm

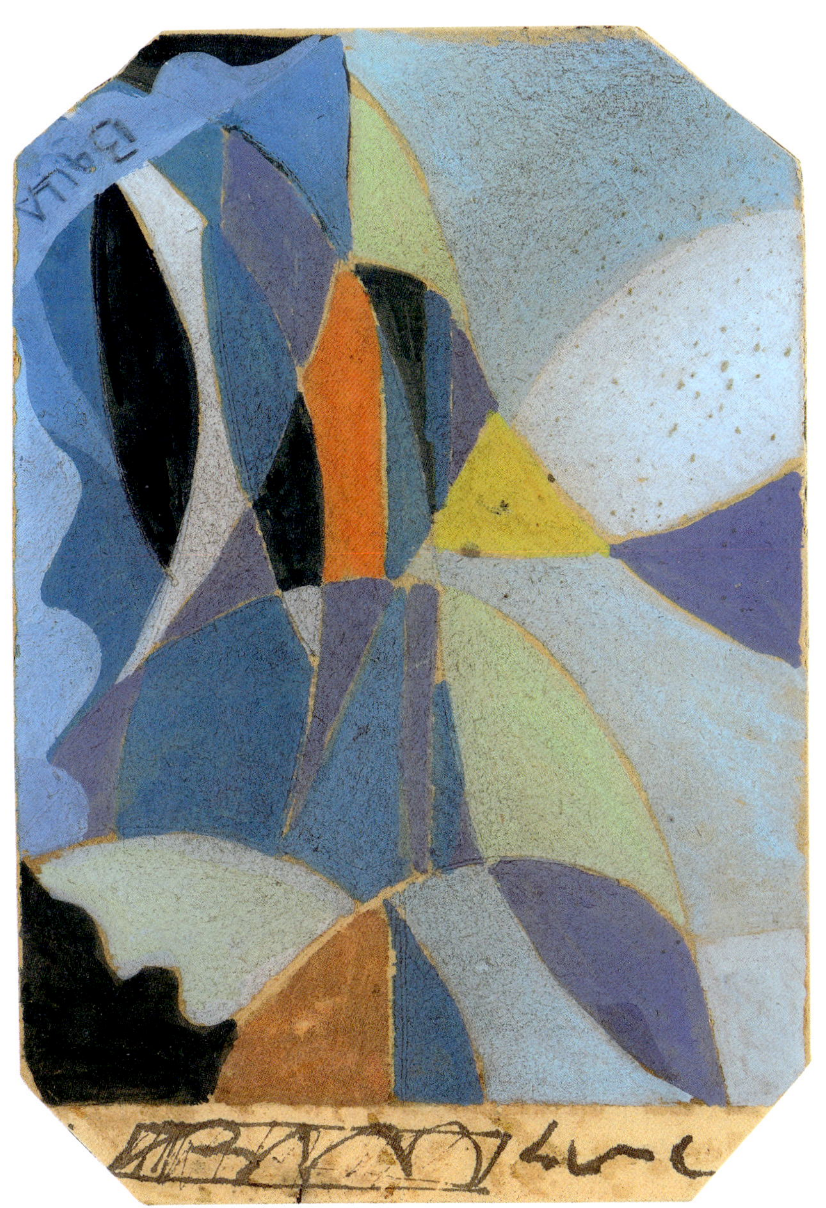

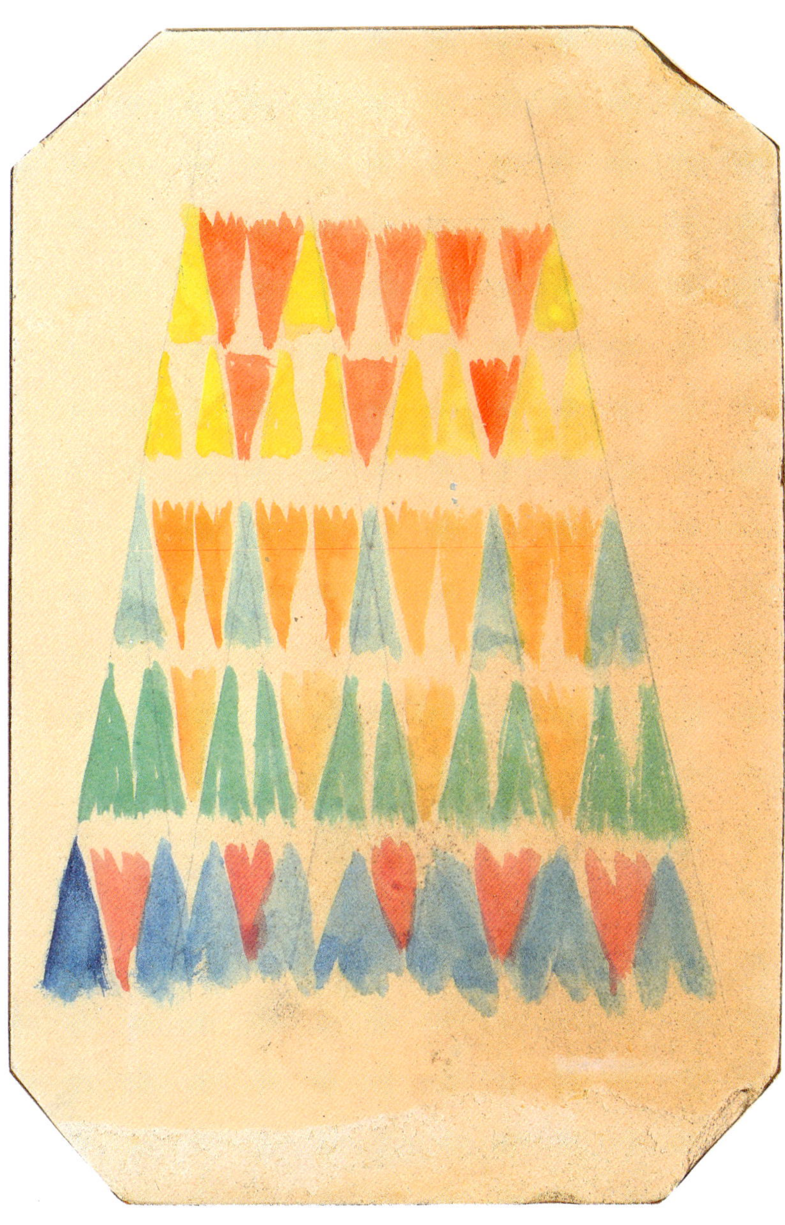

29a-b

Compenetrazioni iridescenti
(Iridescent Interpenetrations), c. 1912–14
tempera on pasteboard, 20 x 13 cm

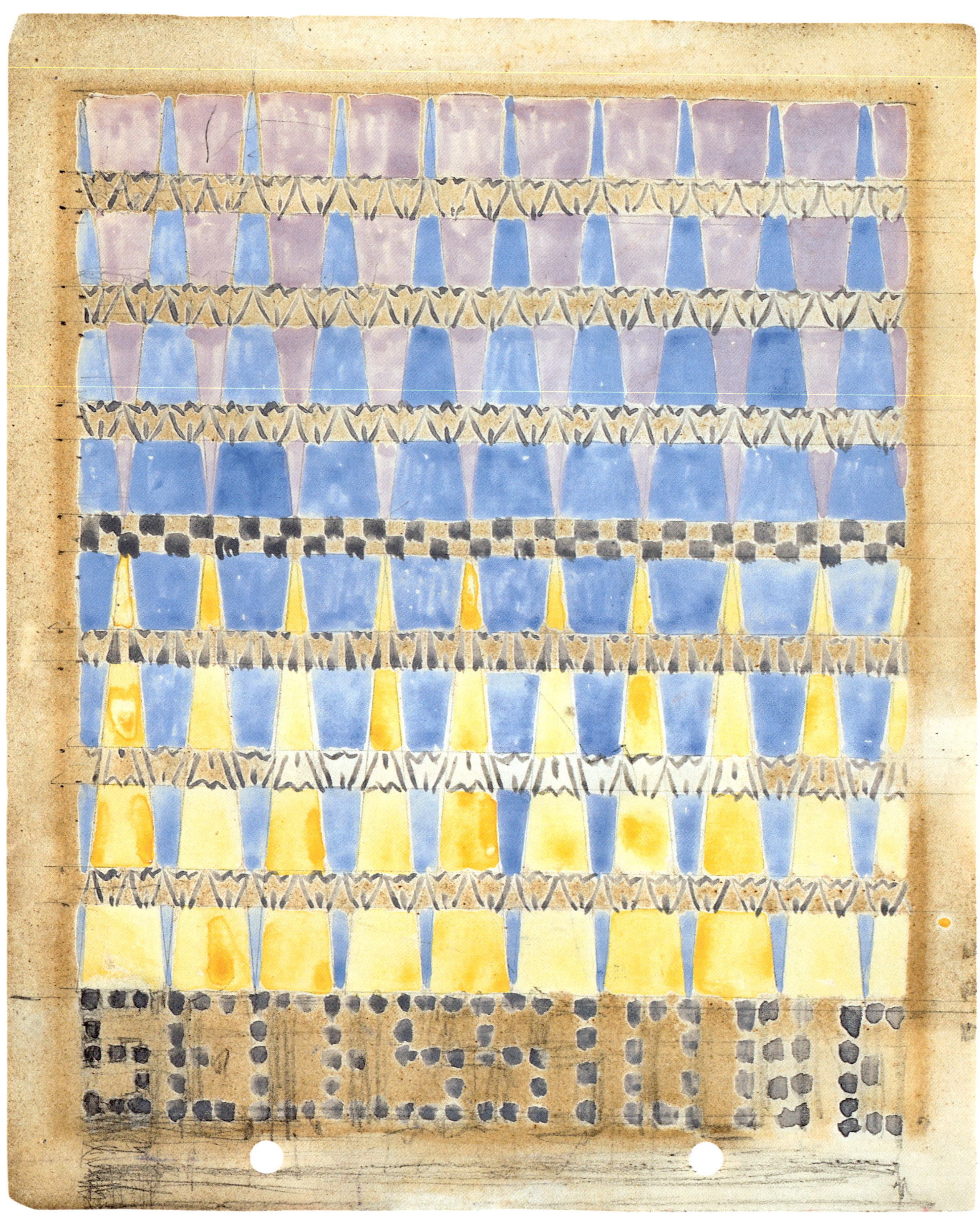

30

Studio per compenetrazione iridescente
(Studio per manifesto Secessione) (Study for Iridescent Interpenetration – Study for Secession Poster), c. 1912
pencil and watercolour on paper, 22 x 17.7 cm

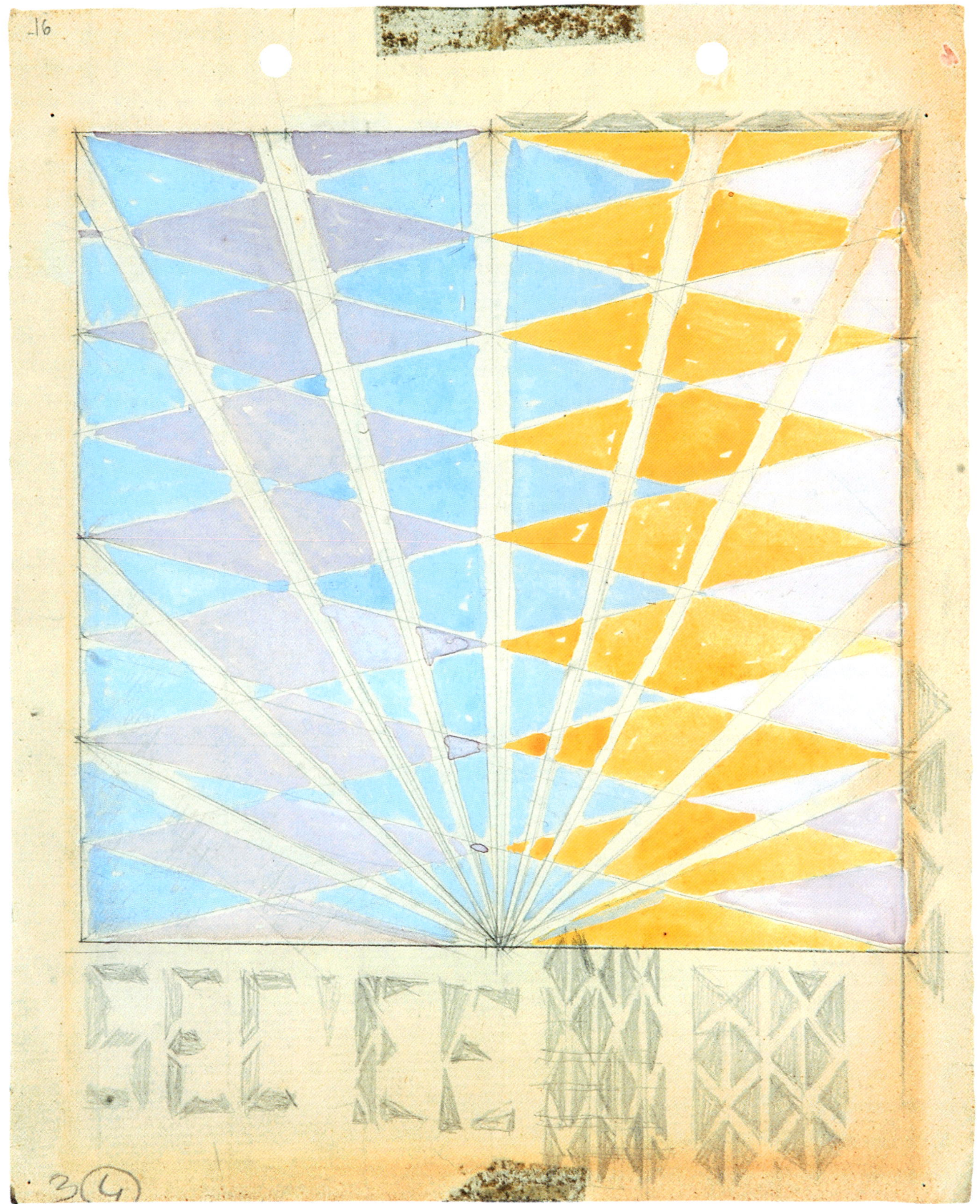

31

Studio per compenetrazione iridescente (Studio per manifesto Secessione) (Study for Iridescent Interpenetration – Study for Secession Poster), c. 1912
pencil and watercolour on paper, 22 x 17.7 cm

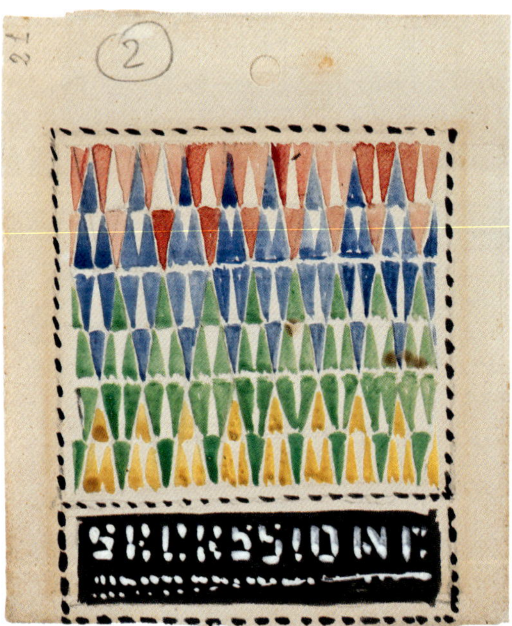

32

Studio per compenetrazione iridescente (Studio per manifesto Secessione) (Study for Iridescent Interpenetration – Study for Secession Poster), c. 1912
pencil and watercolour on paper, 11 x 9.5 cm

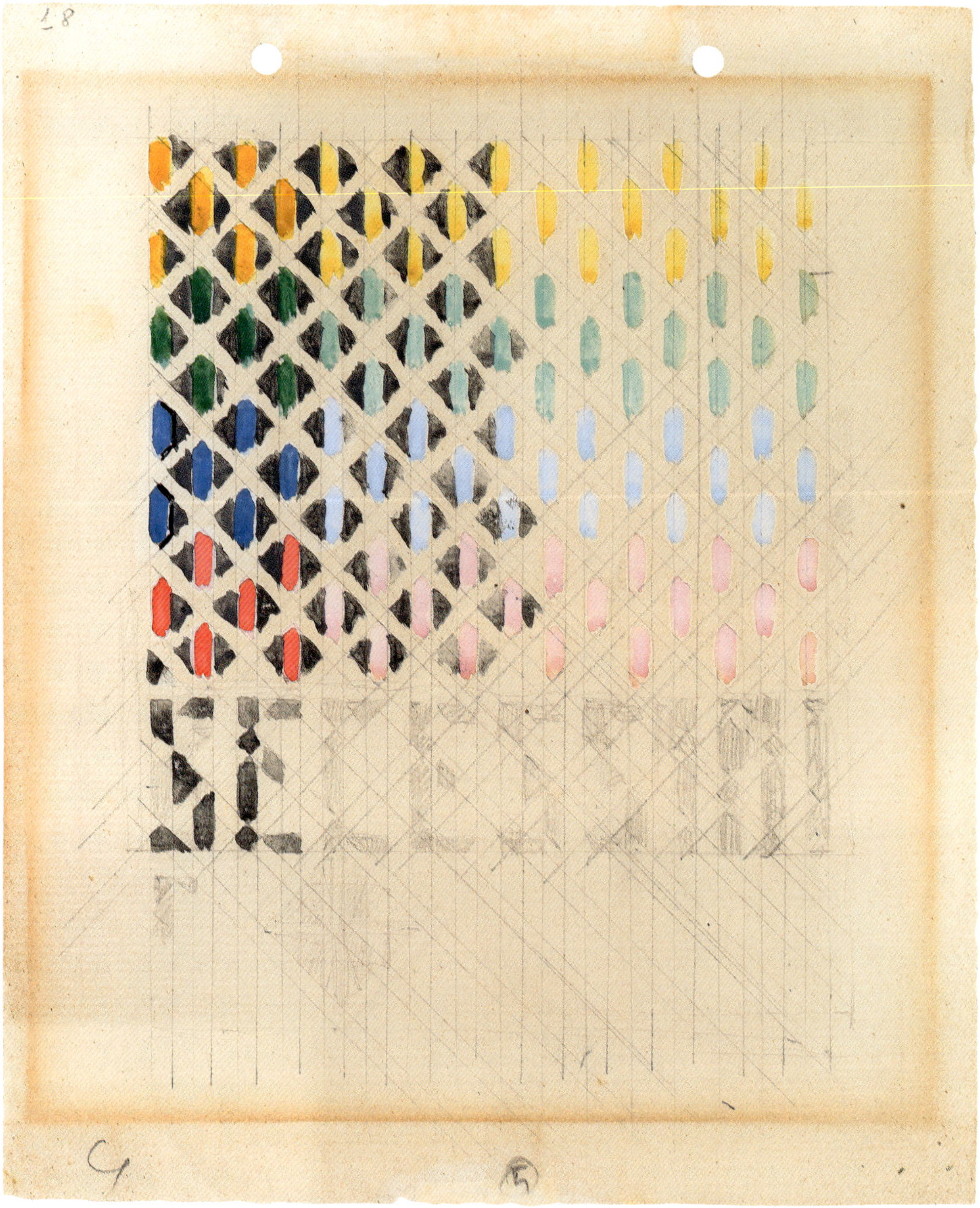

33

Studio per compenetrazione iridescente (Studio per manifesto Secessione) (Study for Iridescent Interpenetration – Study for Secession Poster), c. 1912
pencil and watercolour on paper, 22 x 17.7 cm

12. The Edvard Munch room at the Sonderbund exhibition in Cologne, 1912

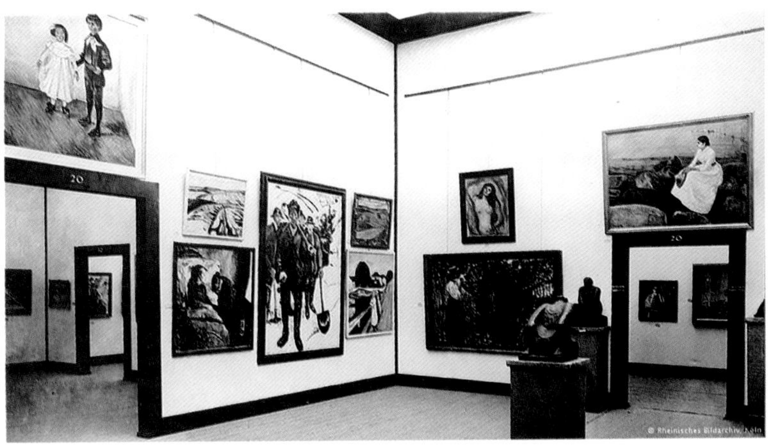

of the Secession in their decorative aspect that oriented Balla towards these choices, even if they did in part express the sense of a mechanism in action. In the early years of the 20th century, after the inebriation of an entire generation with Mitteleuropean linearity,[19] an aesthetic awareness expanded to encompass other categories gained increasing strength. The sophisticated atmosphere of the Löwenstein home, the visit to the Sonderbund in Cologne[20] (fig. 12) and the decorative elements seen during the journey amplified that awareness and expressed the new shift towards the abstract dimension already identified by Balla in his paintings at the beginning of the century. Control over a system of opposites – particular/absolute, light/shadow, objectivity/abstraction – meant mastery of reiterated speculation, the ultimate synthesis of a universal glow whose strength endures in the "voices of nature": "the iris will be able to have and give an infinity of sensations and colours through the observation of reality".[21] The decomposition of light studied by the artist during the long months of his stay in Germany does not appear to stem directly from the scientific research that enjoyed new and broad circulation at the end of the 19th century, starting with the laws of the chemist Michel-Eugène Chevreul on simultaneous contrasts.[22] Optical patterns, geometry and triangles, especially the diagrams of James Clerk Maxwell and Hermann von Helmholtz based on the examination of radiation capable of impinging upon and stimulating the optical receptors, were a great source of inspiration for numerous artists in those years. Despite the apparent similarity of forms and colours, however, what Balla developed was an exquisitely pictorial investigation of juxtapositions that simulate the chromatic timbres observed in nature. Shades of sky blue, pink and other tenuous colours capture the delicacy of shifting light, the subtlety of changing atmospheres, slight variations alluding at the same time to the nuances of slender, fragile petals. The brighter colours – reds, yellows and blues – are not perceived solely as primary elements of a spectrum and do not serve solely to develop the trans-

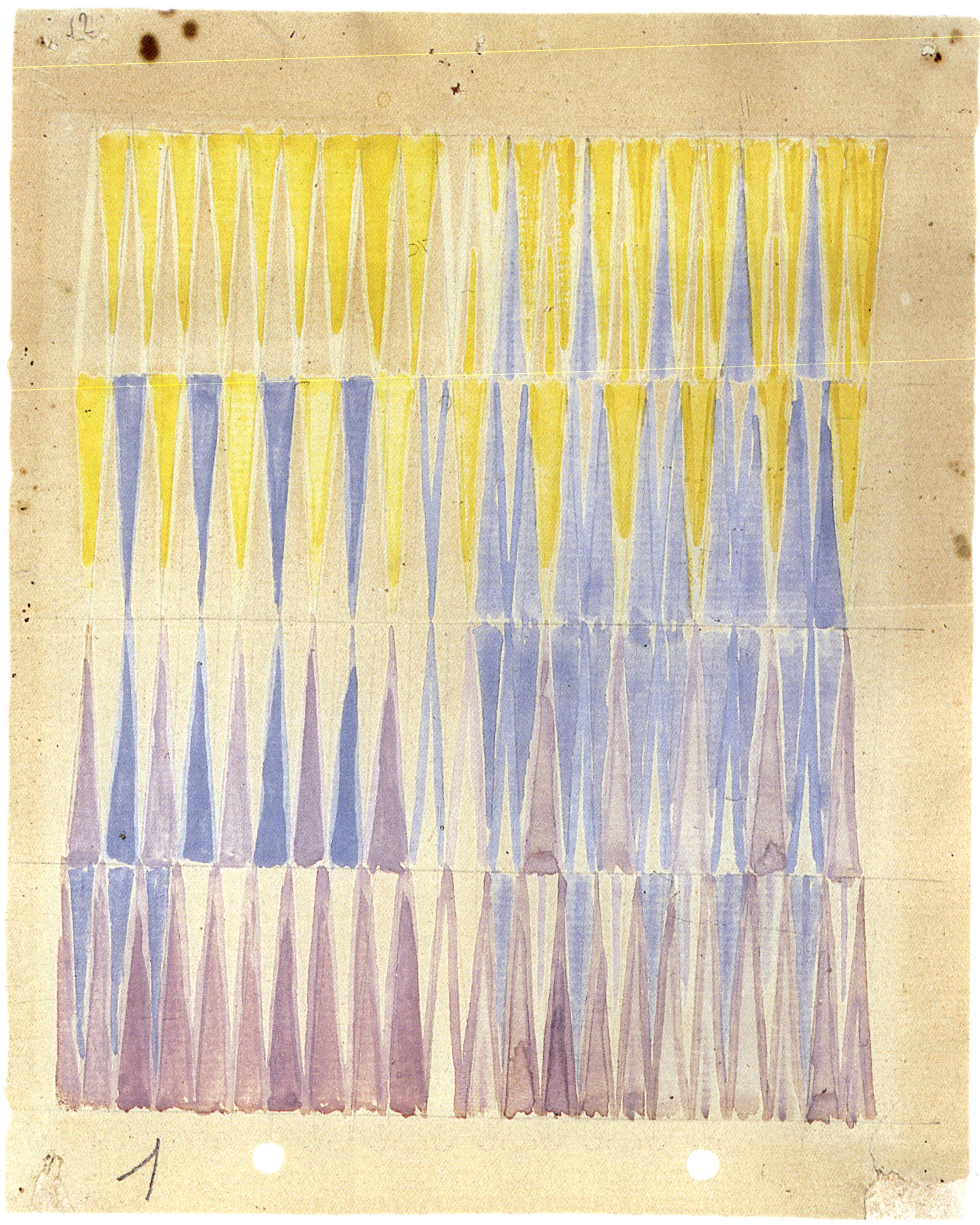

34

Studio per compenetrazione iridescente
(*Study for Iridescent Interpenetration*),
from the Düsseldorf notebooks, c. 1912
pencil and watercolour on paper, 22 x 17.7 cm

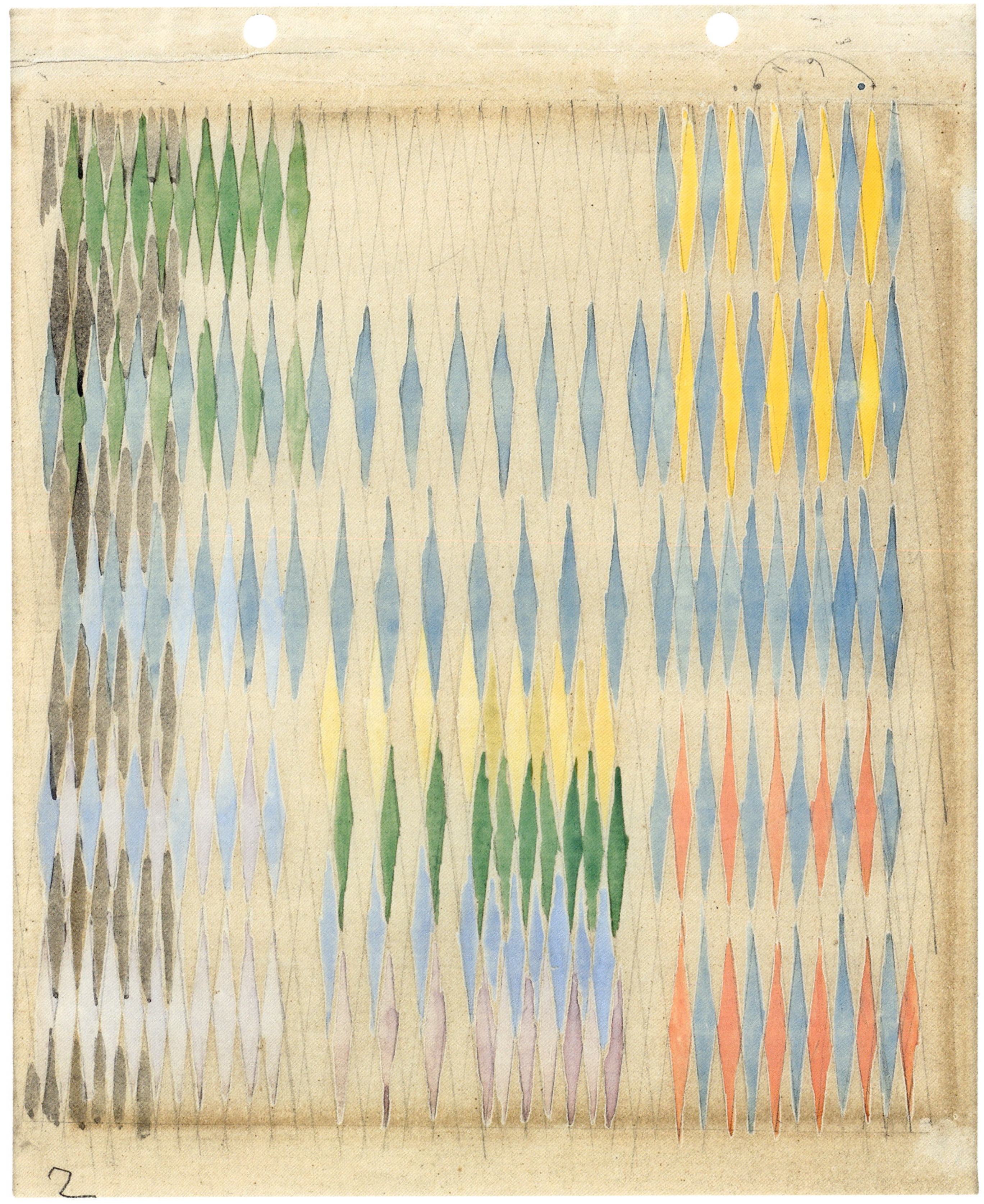

35

Studio per compenetrazione iridescente
(*Study for Iridescent Interpenetration*),
from the Düsseldorf notebooks, c. 1912
pencil and watercolour on paper, 21.9 x 17.7 cm

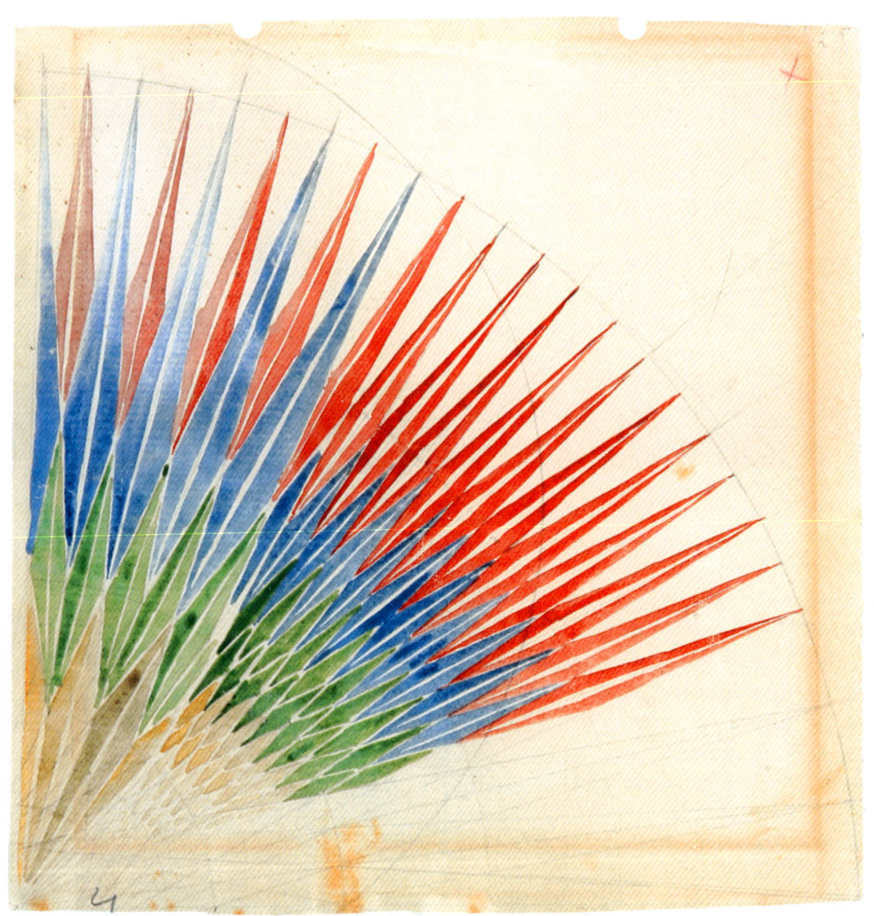

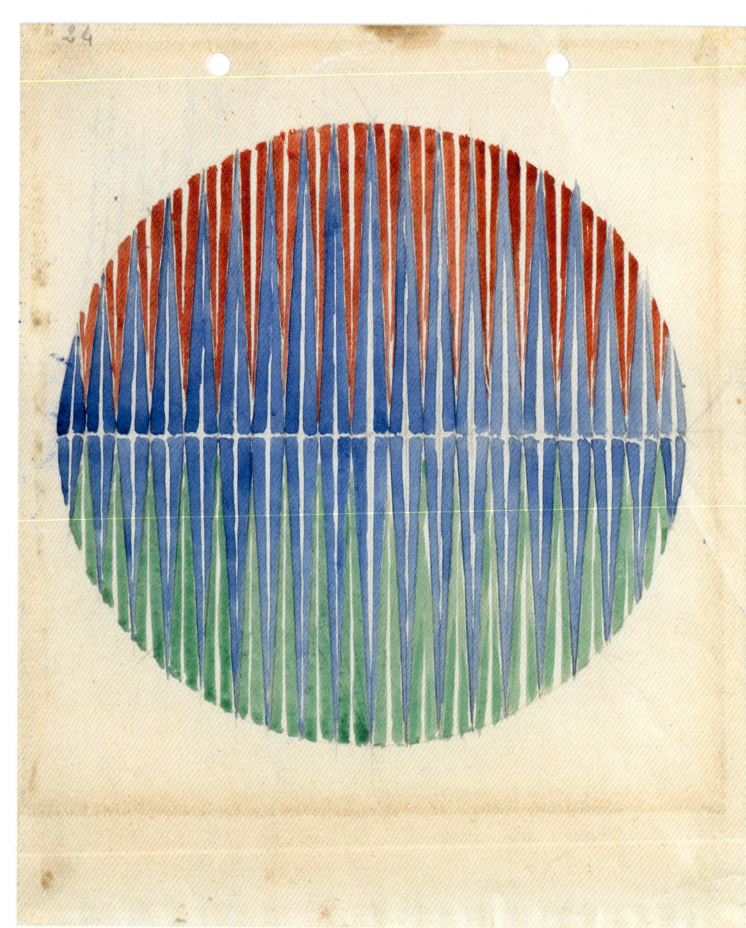

parency and luminosity of the painting (fig. 13). With an expert hand, the artist transforms them into sparkling parts of an intuitive system where the triangle encapsulates the drive for maximum elevation, the circle insists on the sphericity of the globe and other heavenly bodies (fig. 14) and the square delimits spaces whose reopening is urged by the frame itself.

Balla took notes, sketched out forms filled with watercolour and focused insistently on obtaining the "fusion" of the colours of the rainbow that he spoke of to his pupil Gino Galli.[23] What did he mean by *fusion* if not mystical, spiritual communion with the primal substance of reality? Something "very hard for those who do not study reality at great length and do not strive every day to solve all the problems of technique by themselves. Interpreting the atmosphere and giving it all its vivacity and mobility in painting does not entail the mixing of colours. [...] The result obtained on the palette then gives a low, flat, heavy tonality on the canvas. On the same canvas I juxtapose two colours, the ones that predominate in the atmosphere at that particular time. Their proximity generates vibrations. The viewer has the illusion of continuous mobility and the effect is obtained."[24]

13. Giacomo Balla
Studio per compenetrazione iridescente
(*Study for Iridescent Interpenetration*), c. 1912
Turin, GAM - Galleria Civica d'Arte Moderna e Contemporanea

14. Giacomo Balla
Studio per compenetrazione iridescente n. 2 (*Study for Iridescent Interpenetration no. 2*), c. 1914
Turin, GAM - Galleria Civica d'Arte Moderna e Contemporanea

Balla had now set off on the path identified by the analytical vision of individual particles of reality. With the utmost vitality he thus embarked on a new phase in which he developed these investigations in greater depth, taking them up again in different periods – in the years of the Great War with works inspired by the call for Italy's intervention, with the clothes, furniture and objects to which he was to devote much of his creative energy in his lifetime. His studio[25] came increasingly to constitute his world. A French journalist[26] who visited the artist between July and October 1916 had this to say: "The place is very odd and nothing like a painter's studio. It is more like being in the laboratory of a physicist or a scholar concerned with optics, as the painting on the walls represent discs, ellipses and various geometric shapes painted in beautiful, glossy colours."

[1] Lucien Corpechot, *Lettres sur la Jeune Italie*, Berger Levrault Editeurs, Nancy-Paris-Strasbourg, 1919, p. 47; now in Giacomo Balla, *Scritti futuristi*, ed. Giovanni Lista, Abscondita, Milan, 2010, p. 198.

[2] This is how he described his studies on colour in a letter to the critic Raffaele Carrieri dated 8 May 1947; see *Scritti futuristi*, op. cit., p. 123.

[3] The exhibition "Les Peintres Futuristes Italiens" was held from 5 to 24 February 1912 in the Galerie Bernheim-Jeune at Rue Richepance 15, thanks to Marinetti's contacts and his friendship with the critic Félix Fénéon, artistic director of the gallery in that period. For an excellent study of the latter, see Joan Ungersma Halperin, *Félix Fénéon: Aesthete & Anarchist in fin-de-siècle Paris*, Yale University Press, New Haven-London, 1988.

[4] An important letter from Boccioni to Severini reports what he had been told by the writer and poet Aldo Palazzeschi in a recent meeting in Florence about a conversation with Balla regarding the decision not to show his painting in Paris: "They did not want me in Paris and they were right. They are much more advanced than me, but I will work and make progress too." See *Umberto Boccioni. Gli scritti editi e inediti*, ed. Zeno Birolli, Feltrinelli, Milan, 1971, p. 364.

[5] In 1905 Gaetano Previati, for whom Boccioni professed great admiration in his notebook for 1908, published *La tecnica della pittura* (Fratelli Bocca Editori, Turin), an extraordinary treatise on painting and the individual elements involved in the creation of a work, especially colour and its components, with a view to obtaining the maximum and most lasting effects of light. A few years earlier, Paul Signac's *D'Eugène Delacroix au néo-impressionisme* (Editions de La Revue Blanche, Paris, 1899) addressed the subject of chromatic decomposition through the work of the great Romantic master, whose painting focuses on intensity of colour as against a more formal linear approach.

[6] A grand total of over 50 million visited the Expo with its architecturally imaginative pavilions along the Seine.

[7] *Con Balla*, I, op. cit., p. 70.

[8] According to Severini in *La vita di un pittore*, the discovery of Balla was due to Boccioni. This probably came about through Balla's friend Duilio Cambellotti, whose future wife was related to the family of Boccioni's father, with whom the young man was staying.

[9] See *Umberto Boccioni. Altri inediti e apparati critici*, ed. Zeno Birolli, Feltrinelli, Milan, 1972, pp. 46–48 and 90–91, an important series of notes on Balla written by Boccioni after a visit to the master's studio in 1915, in which the "plastic complexes" are mentioned as well as the last abstract works, devoted to the call for Italian intervention in the war. The notes were probably intended for an article for the magazine *Gli Avvenimenti*.

[10] The painting was bought by the New York Museum of Modern Art in April 1954. Balla, who still owned the work, wrote as follows to the museum's director about its genesis (Alfred H. Barr, Jr., *Papers*, 1,367; mf 2189: [651]): "I produced the painting of the street light during my Divisionist period (1900–10), and the glow is in fact obtained by the juxtaposition of pure colours. In addition to being original as a work of art, it is also scientific because I tried to represent light by separating its component colours … The street light painted was in Piazza Termini." As attested by numerous scholars, including De Marchis, Fagiolo dell'Arco and Lista, the painting was most probably produced in 1910–11 and constitutes a symbol of his entry into the Futurist movement.

[11] Annie Besant, C.W. Leadbeater, *Thought-forms*, Lane, New York, 1905; also available online from The Theosophical Publishing House, Adyar, Madras, India – Wheaton, Illinois, USA, http://www.anandgholap.net/Thought_Forms-AB_CWL.htm.

[12] Grethel Löwenstein (Margaretha Ehlers Cahn Speyer) had been a pupil of Balla's in the first decade of the century before getting married and moving to Monaco.

[13] For an in-depth study of Balla's relationship with music and a precise reconstruction of the Löwenstein family with the exact location of the house where Balla produced the decorations, see Giovanni Lista, "Balla e la 'musica'", in *12-29 Futur Balla*, ed. Elena Gigli, Arte Centro, Milan, 2008, pp. 9–15.

[14] Balla is shown in numerous photographs, also of later periods, strumming a musical instrument, usually a guitar. There has also been talk of him having begun to study music, which has still to be confirmed.

[15] Letter of 18 November 1912 to the family, in Maurizio Fagiolo dell'Arco, *Balla: le "compenetrazioni iridescenti"*, Bulzoni, Rome, 1970, p. 31.
[16] Letter to the family, July 1912, in *Con Balla*, op. cit., p. 264.
[17] Letter of 29 July 1912 to the family, in *Balla: le "compenetrazioni iridescenti"*, op. cit., p. 30.
[18] Postcard to Gino Galli, 21 November 1912; letter to the family, 5 December, in *Balla: le "compenetrazioni iridescenti"*, op. cit., p. 31.
[19] As Boccioni wrote in 1916, "Fifteen or twenty years ago, the young looked to Munich and Vienna as the centres of European artistic thought …" ("L'arte di Carlo Fornara", in *Gli Avvenimenti*, no. 15, 2 April), in *Umberto Boccioni. Gli scritti editi e inediti*, op cit., p. 407.
[20] This visit has been attributed with a significance stretching beyond the possible interest or "impact of abstract and expressionist works" glimpsed by Giovanni Lista (in *Balla. La modernità futurista*, Skira, Milan, 2008, p. 50). Kandinsky showed *Improvisation 21A* (Munich, Städtische Galerie im Lenbachhaus), a painting whose influence could only lie in the bold assonance of lines and colours. To judge from the letter to the family of 18 July 1912, Balla does not appear to have been particularly struck by the exhibition: "The canvases look to me like pieces of badly washed red, green or yellow rags that are supposed to represent nude fancies, poems of flowers or meadows or landscapes or portraits – paintings or attempts that cannot convince even those well accustomed to the liberal dispensation of plenary indulgence …" Fagiolo, op. cit., p. 30.
[21] Ibid., p. 31.
[22] Michel-Eugène Chevreul, *De la loi du contraste simultané des couleurs et de l'assortissement des objets colorés*, Pitois-Levrault, Paris, 1838; Michel-Eugène Chevreul, *Des couleurs et de leurs applications aux arts industriels à l'aide des cercles chromatiques*, J.B. Ballière & Fils, Paris, 1864.
[23] See note 17.
[24] This statement appeared in a long article on Balla, mostly in the form of an interview with Aymerillot, pen name of Emilio Cecchi. The article is one of a series on Roman artists in 1911, the year of Rome Expo, in *L'Alfiere*, II, 25, Rome, 24 January 1911.
[25] At Via Paisiello 29, previously Via Parioli 6.
[26] Lucien Corpechot, *Lettres sur la Jeune Italie*, op. cit., p. 43; Lista, op. cit., p. 196.

36

Studi per compenetrazioni iridescenti
(Studies for Iridescent Interpenetrations), c. 1912
pencil and watercolour on paper, 9 x 14 cm

37

Studio per compenetrazione iridescente
(Study for Iridescent Interpenetration), c. 1912
pencil and watercolour on paper, 18 x 13.3 cm

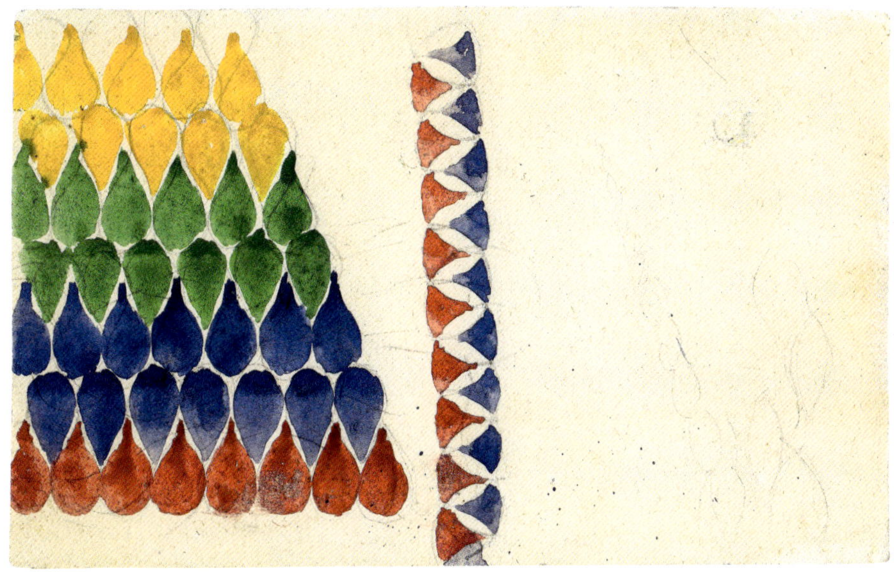

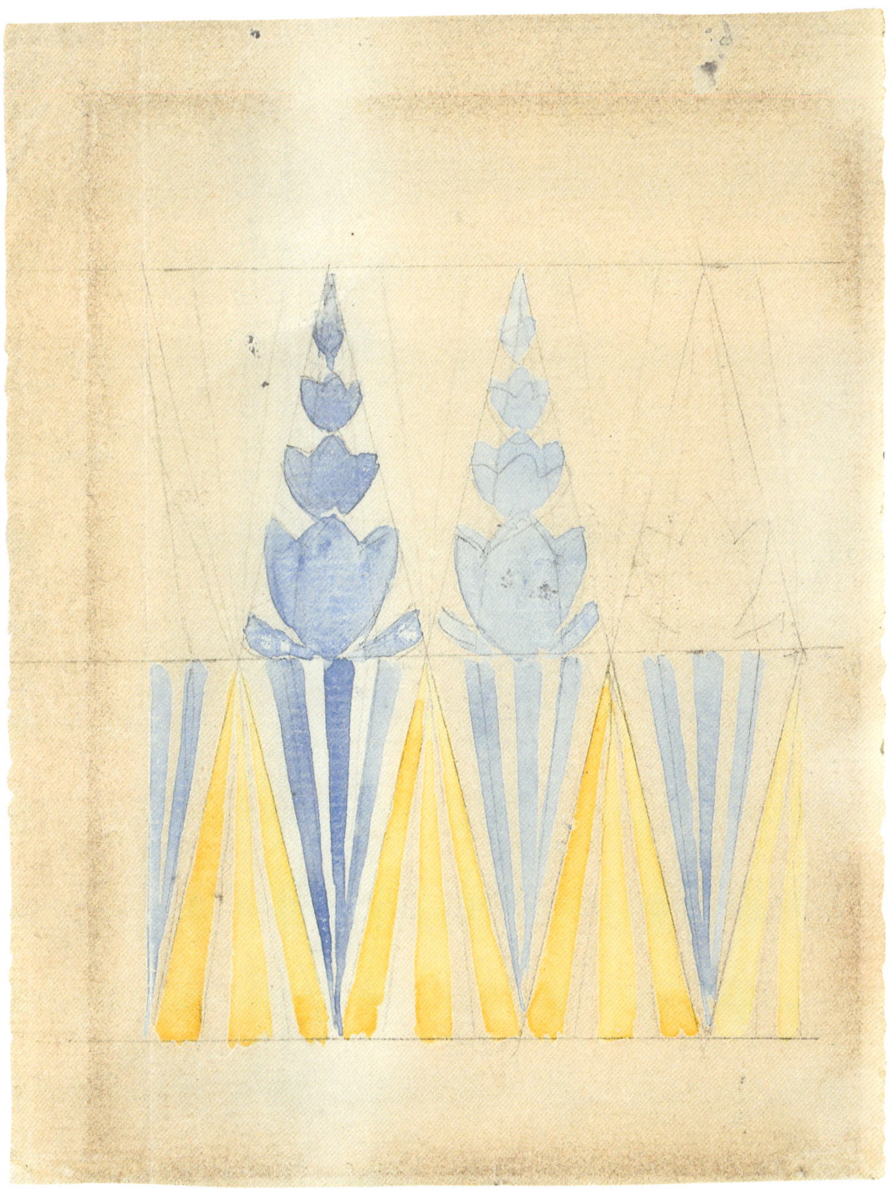

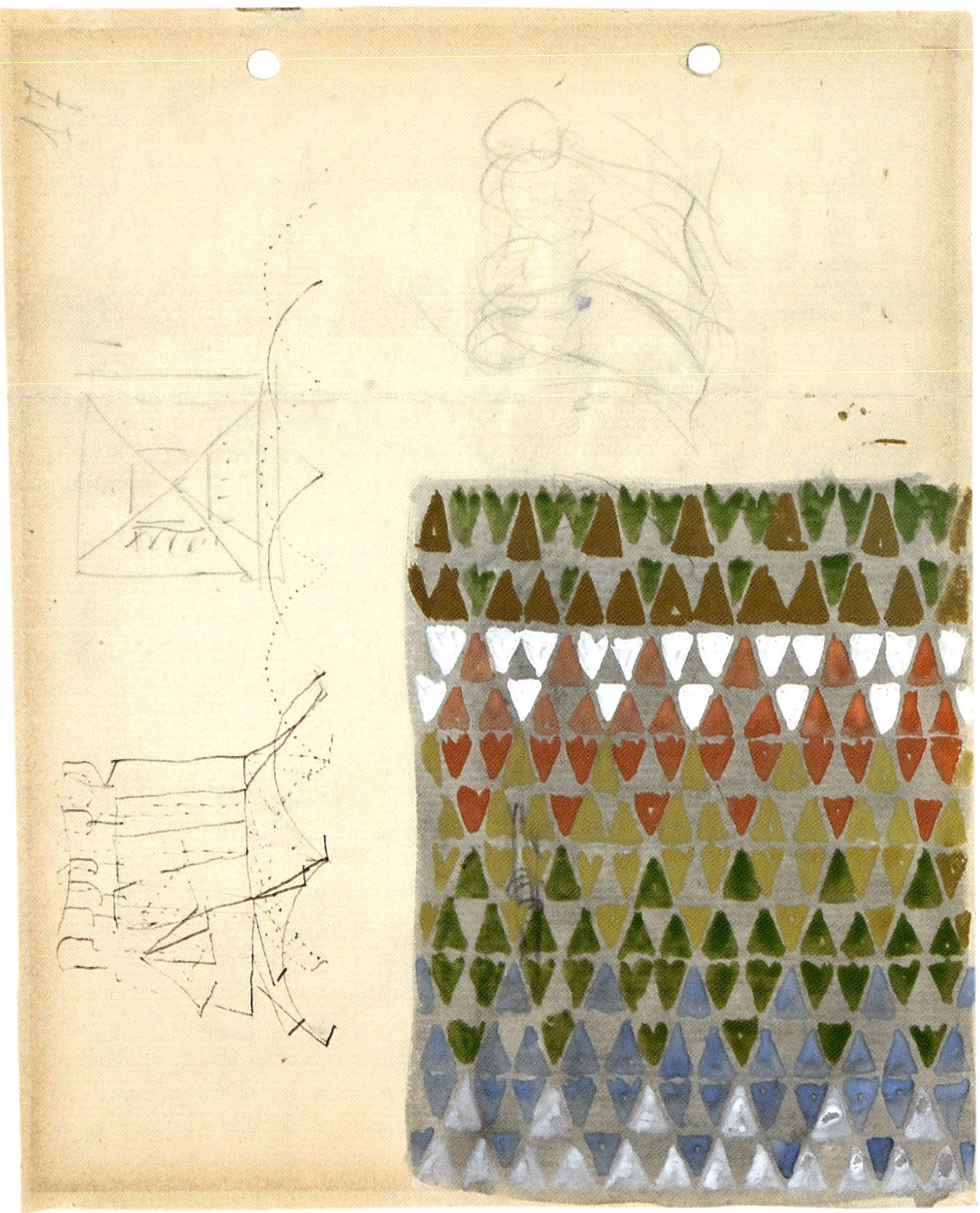

38

a) Studio per compenetrazione iridescente b) Studio per Bambina che corre sul balcone (a. Study for Iridescent Interpenetration b. Study for Girl Running on a Balcony), c. 1912
pencil, pen and watercolour on paper, 22 x 17.7 cm

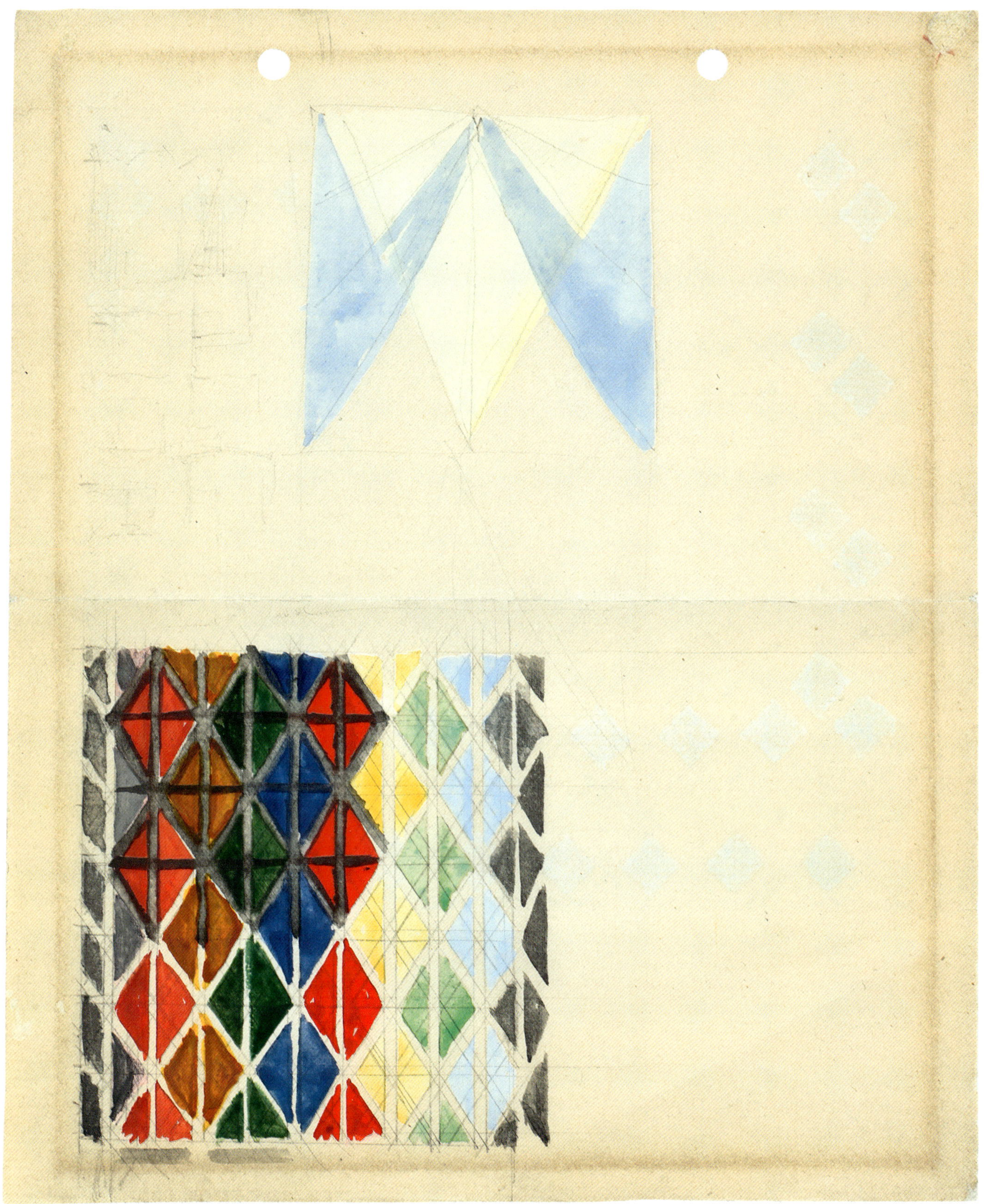

39

Studio per compenetrazione iridescente
(Study for Iridescent Interpenetration), c. 1912
pencil and watercolour on paper, 22 x 17.7 cm

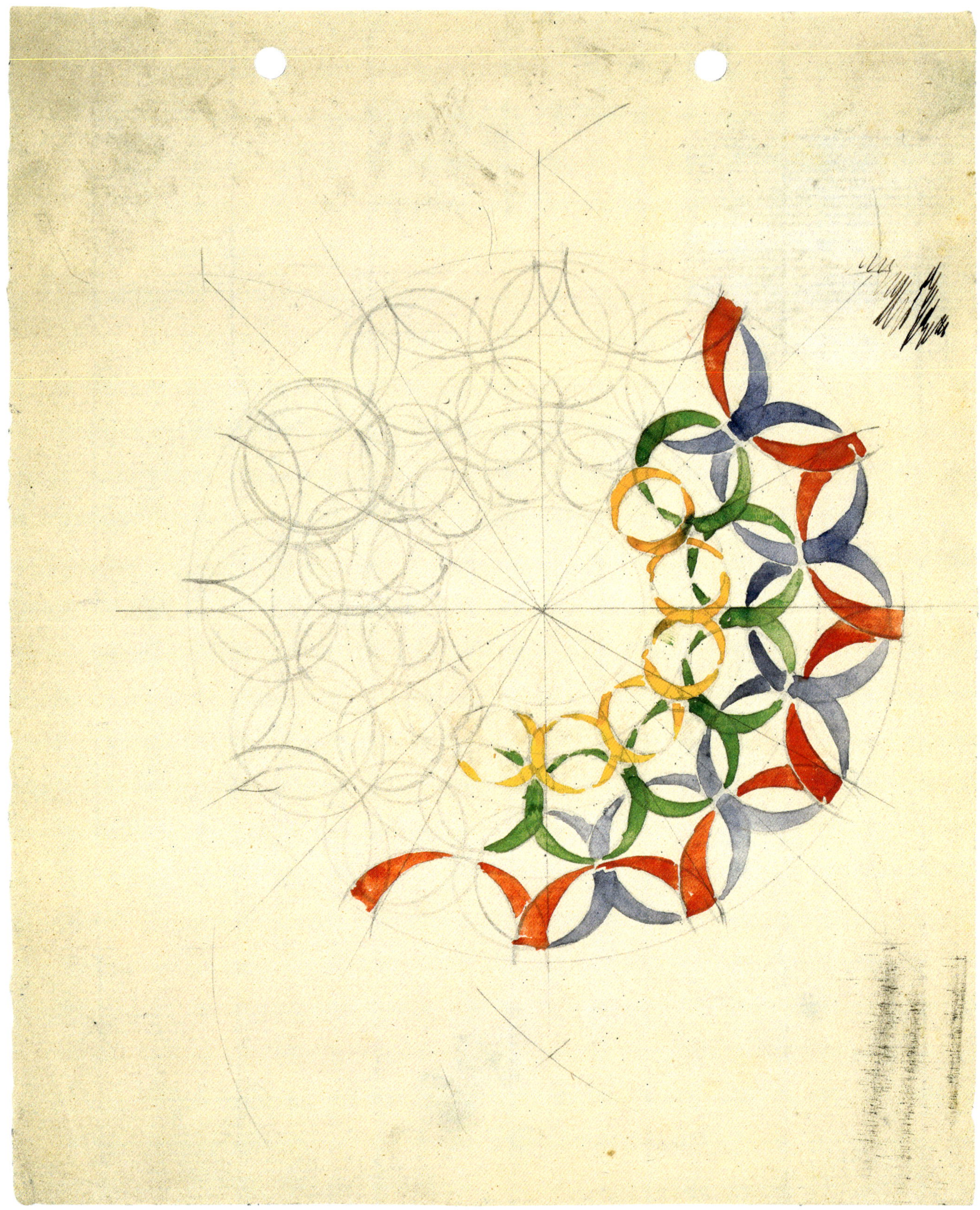

40

Studio per compenetrazione iridescente a cerchi
(Study for Iridescent Interpenetration with circles), c. 1912
pencil and watercolour on paper, 22 x 18 cm

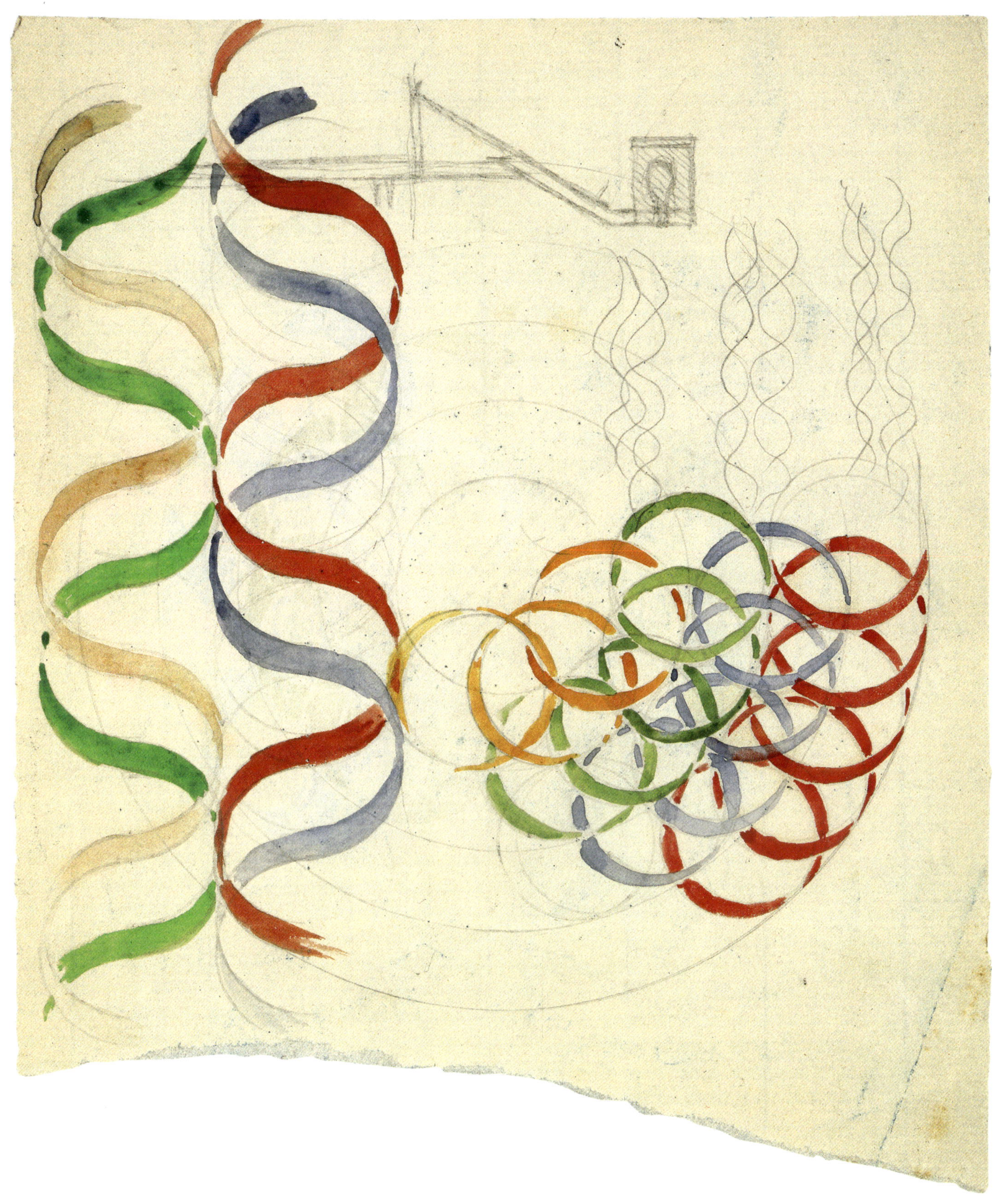

41

Studio per compenetrazione iridescente nel tondo
(Study for Iridescent Interpenetration in tondo), c. 1912
pencil and watercolour on paper, 22 x 17.7 cm

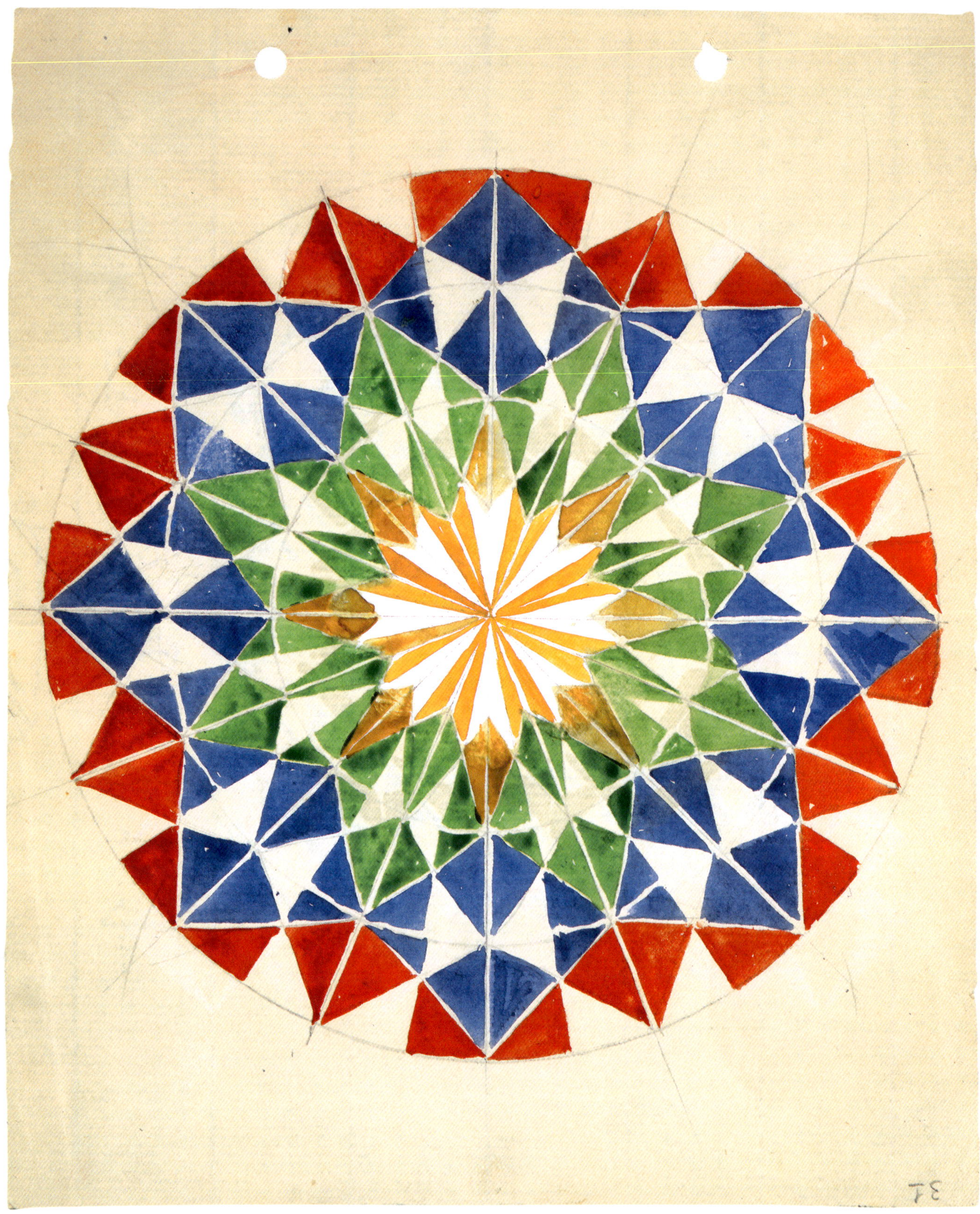

42

Studio per compenetrazione iridescente (per soffitto tondo)
(Study for Iridescent Interpenetration – for round ceiling),
c. 1912
pencil and watercolour on paper, 22 x 17.7 cm

The physics of light and the perception of colour in Giacomo Balla's oeuvre

Luca Francesco Ticini

Giacomo Balla explored new artistic frontiers in the early years of the 20th century and produced original compositions that marked a radical departure from the pictorial reproduction of reality, now regarded as superfluous "given the existence of photography and cinematography" (*Manifesto del Colore*, 1918). Leading gradually towards abstraction, the path embarked upon involved the empirical isolation, amplification and analysis of physical and above all perceptual phenomena. The most evident results of this stylistic development include the geometric compositions with broad chromatic expanses known as *Compenetrazioni iridescenti* (*Iridescent Interpenetrations*). The present study examines the relations between this type of artistic language and what is known about the physiology of colour perception, in the belief that this approach can offer an understanding of Giacomo Balla's work complementary to that of art-historical analysis.

The concept of light as expressed in scientific, religious and philosophical terms has had a dramatic and lasting impact on art over the centuries. It is therefore hardly surprising that the fascinating and mystical influences of this natural phenomenon should have still been felt even at the beginning of the 20th century by many artists, despite the scientific knowledge acquired about the physical nature of light as electromagnetic radiation and the physiology of colour perception. Their ranks include those who adopted the principles of the *Manifesto tecnico dei pittori futuristi* (1910) and described themselves somewhat immodestly as "primitives of a new sensibility" and "lords of light". A marked interest in light is already evident in the first Futurist canvas of a signatory of this manifesto, Giacomo Balla. Entitled *Lampada ad Arco* (*Street Light*) (fig. 1), it looks forward to the subsequent stylistic developments, representing the radiation from an incandescent lamp graphically in a new way as a multitude of dynamic arrows and triangles of colour. It was, however, between 1912 and 1914 that Balla's artistic experimentation with light and colour took mature and definitive shape with the *Compenetrazioni iridescenti*. We can of course agree on the fact that the radiant beauty and captivating rhythm of these compositions require no interpretation or comment other than art-historical references to point out their creative uniqueness. In my view, however, it is fascinating to examine at length the artist's masterly attempt to capture in a rare series of works what presents itself as a personal investigation of light, understood as a physical phenomenon, and proves to be an extraordinary exploration of the shifting nature of colour, understood as a perceptual phenomenon.

First of all, it is interesting to note the conceptual similarities between some *Compenetrazioni iridescenti* and the experiment on the decomposition of light carried out by the Englishman Isaac Newton in the 18th century, hailed as the father of modern science of colour. Newton's experimental approach can perhaps be identified as the archetype or even the scientific equivalent of the *Compenetrazioni*. But while Balla used the brush to decompose, as he put it, "light into its colours arranged in triangular shapes that correspond to the structure of the luminous beam", Newton brought the measurements – begun the century before by Descartes and Francesco Maria Grimaldi – to their conclusion by using a crystal prism to decompose a ray of white sunlight into what he named the "colour spectrum". The "structure of the luminous beam" of the *Compenetrazioni* recalls in some respects the classic depiction of this experiment, where triangular shapes emerge from the prism struck by the beam of white light (fig. 2). Observing the indefinite variety of intermediate shades between the colours, Newton drew a circle to define the qualitative relations between them, sorting them into complementaries and suggesting that adjacent colours developed harmonic relations equivalent to those between the seven musical notes. The exploration of these relations can be seen also in the *Compenetrazioni*, where the tonalities of iridescent luminosity and saturation interweave with one another and are juxtaposed with their complementaries (fig. 3). Subsequently, as described in his treatise *Opticks* (1704), Newton turned the colours back into white light with the aid of a convergent lens, thereby demonstrating experimentally – and for the first time in history – that colour is a property of light (fig. 4).

Balla obviously composed his intricate interpenetrations of colour when Newton's discoveries were well established as the cornerstone of scientific research into optics and light. In my opinion, the artist also delighted in using metaphorical language, with an allusion to Newton, in announcing the division of "light into its colours" (since, as we

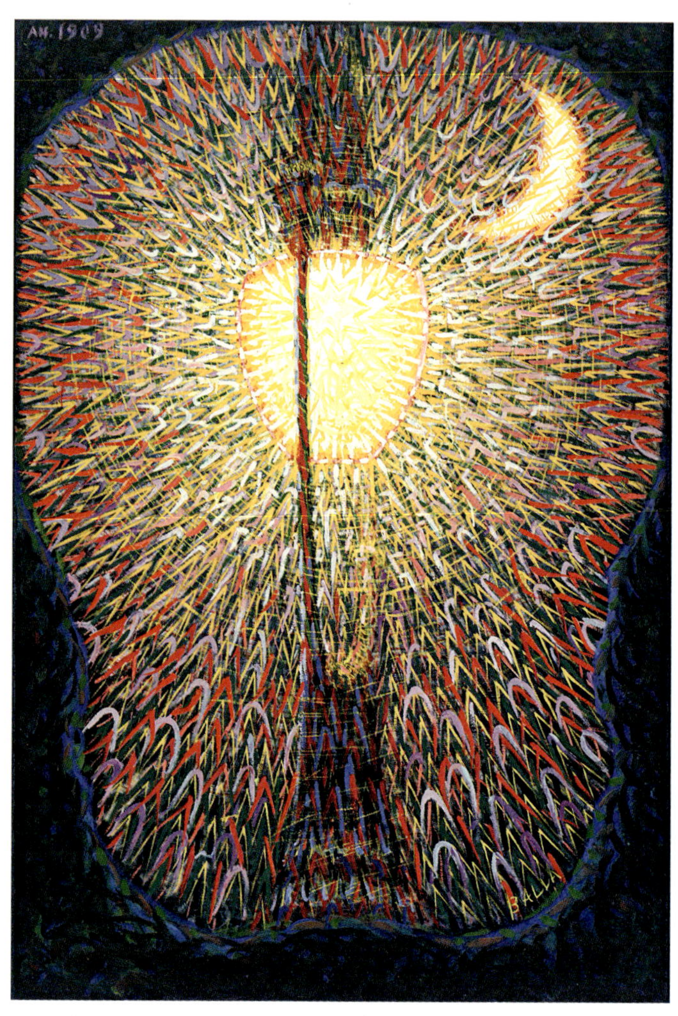

1. *Lampada ad arco* (*The Street Light*), Giacomo Balla's first Futurist work representing light, painted between 1910 and 1911
New York, The Museum of Modern Art

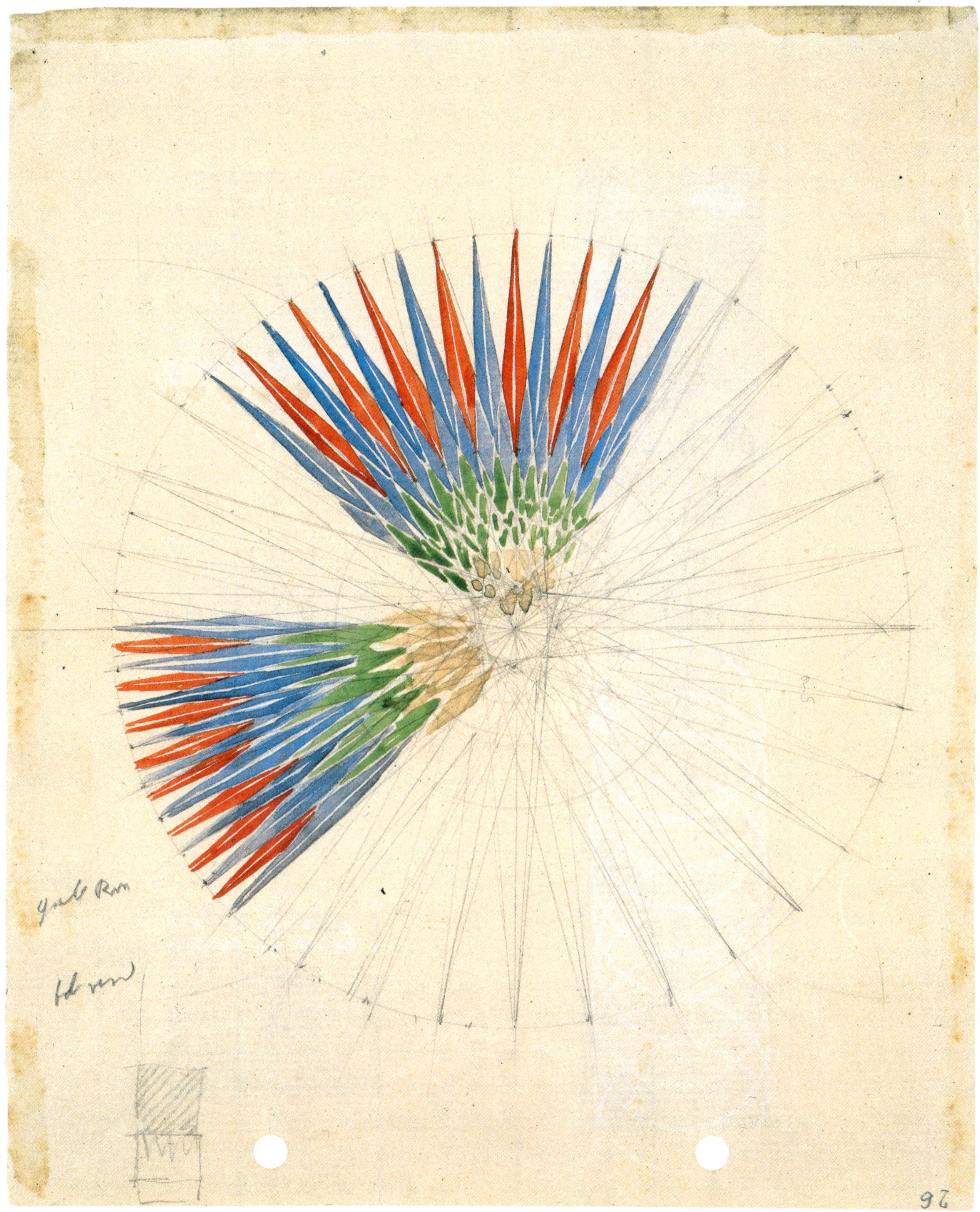

43

Studio per compenetrazione iridescente radiale nel tondo
(Study for radial Iridescent Interpenetration in tondo), c. 1912
pencil and watercolour on paper, 22 x 17.7 cm

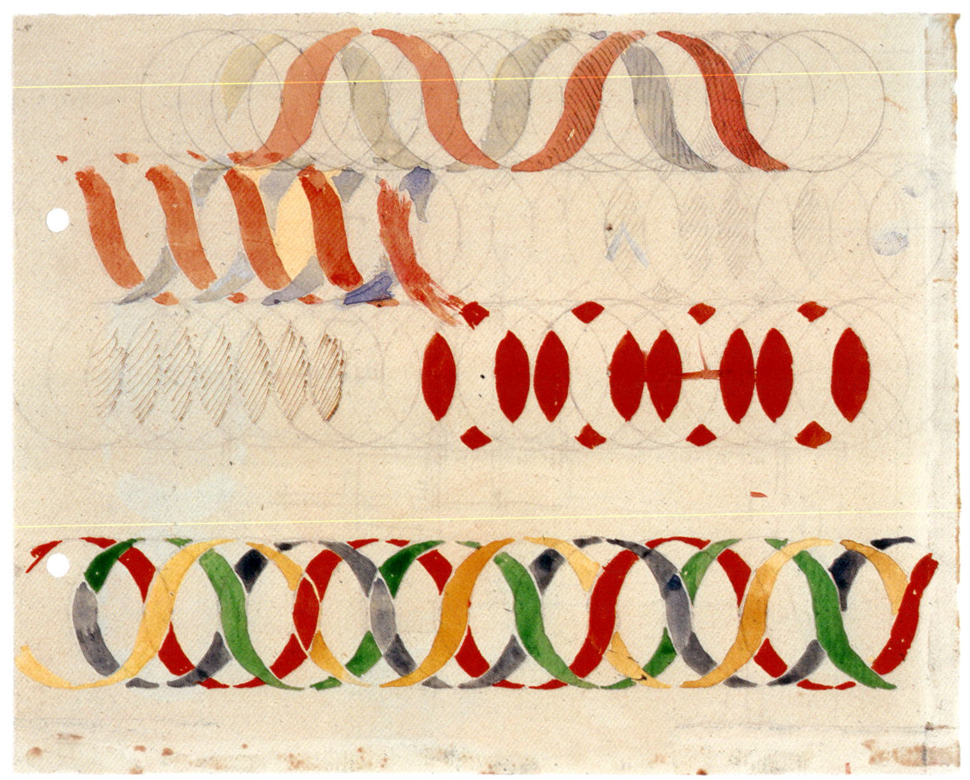

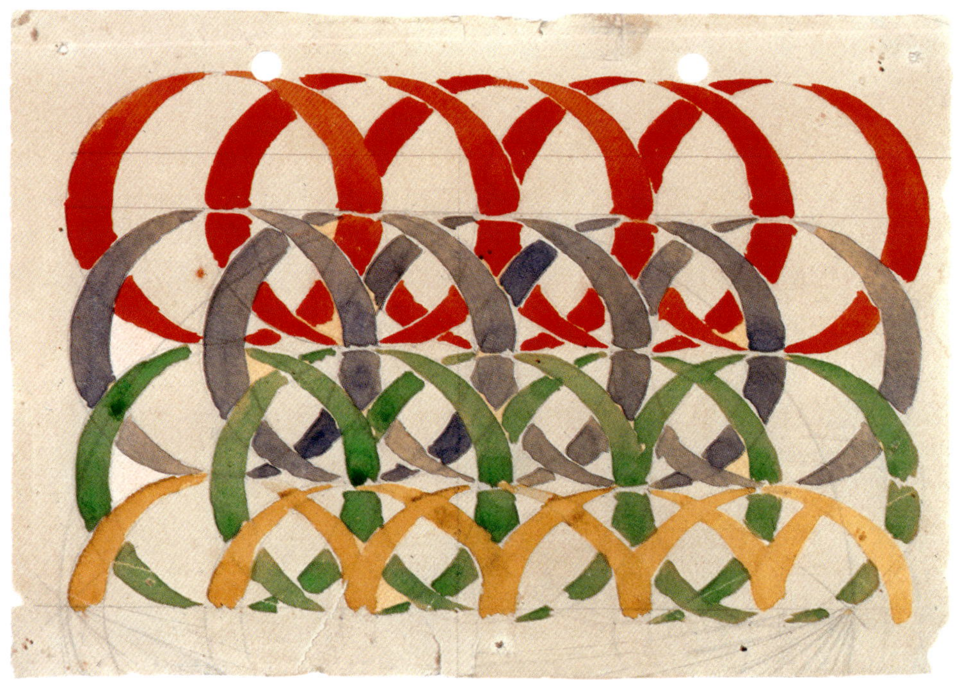

44

Studio per compenetrazione iridescente
(*Study for Iridescent Interpenetration*),
from the Düsseldorf notebooks, 1912–13
pencil and watercolour on paper, 17.7 x 21.9 cm

45

Studio per compenetrazione iridescente
(*Study for Iridescent Interpenetration*),
from the Düsseldorf notebooks, 1912–13
pencil and watercolour on paper, 12.5 x 17.7 cm

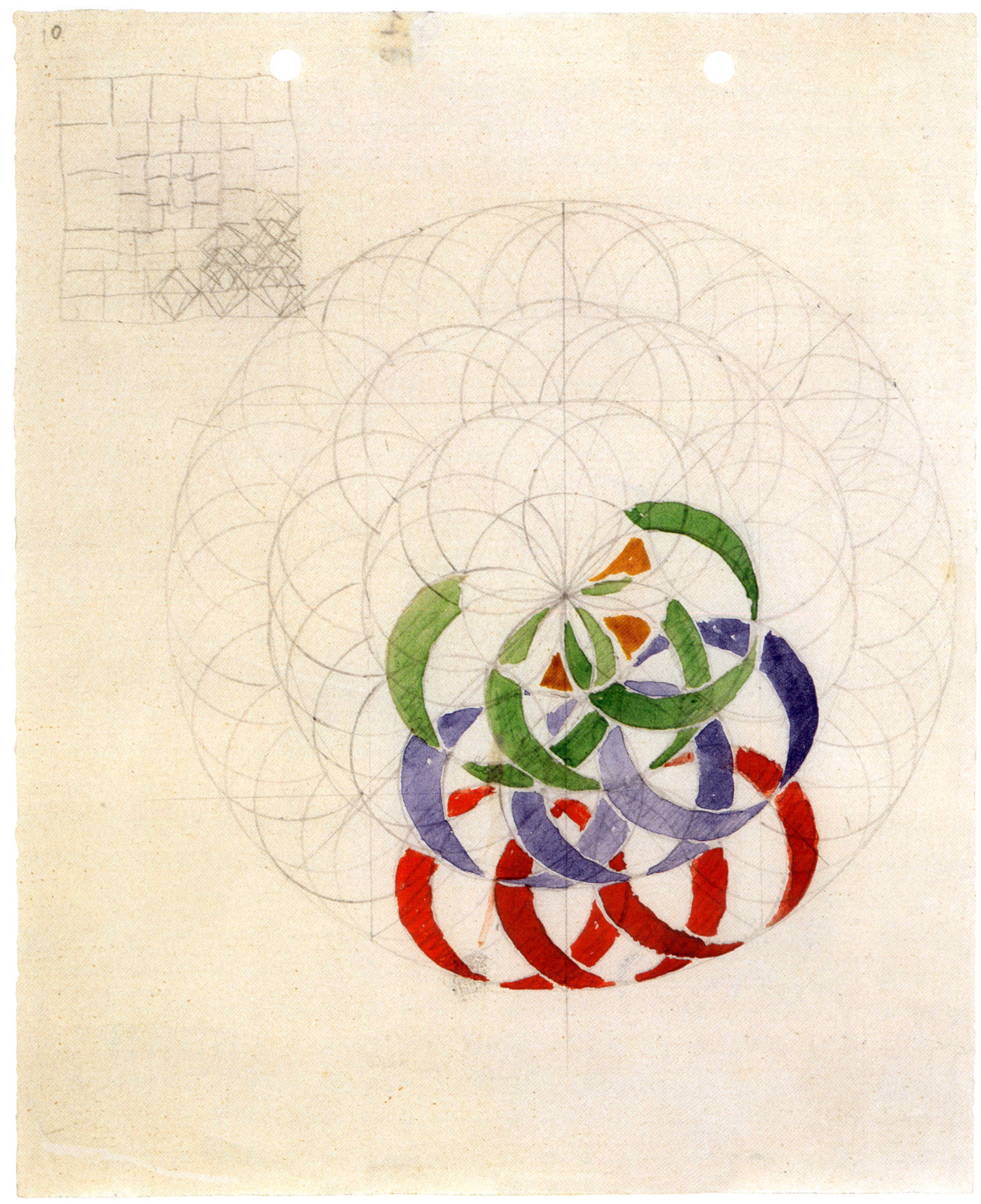

46

Studio per compenetrazione iridescente
(*Study for Iridescent Interpenetration*),
from the Düsseldorf notebooks, 1912–13
pencil and watercolour on paper, 20 x 17 cm

shall see, colour was now recognized as a perceptual rather than physical phenomenon). The conclusions drawn in Newton's *Opticks* had instead not fully convinced his contemporaries in the 18th century. At that time, the predominant view of Aristotelian origin was in fact that colour was a property of objects and light did no more than illuminate their coloured surface. In other words, every object had a certain colour even in the dark. The English physicist instead regarded colour as determined by the way in which surfaces react to light. As he wrote: "So Colours in the Object are nothing but a Disposition to reflect this or that sort of Rays more copiously than the rest." For Newton, once colour was defined as a property of light, it evidently followed that a surface could not have a colour of its own but presented a certain hue (green for example) when it reflected a particular type of light (green). Newton's ideas were even challenged by Goethe, who rejected his mechanical interpretation and accused the author of *Opticks*, perhaps wrongly, of conceiving colour as a phenomenon independent of the individual (Goethe 1810). What we actually find in Newton's words is a timid (or perhaps insufficiently appreciated) reference to colour as perception and not as a physical entity: "For the rays to speak properly are not coloured. In them there is nothing else than a certain Power and Disposition to stir up a Sensation of this or that Colour."

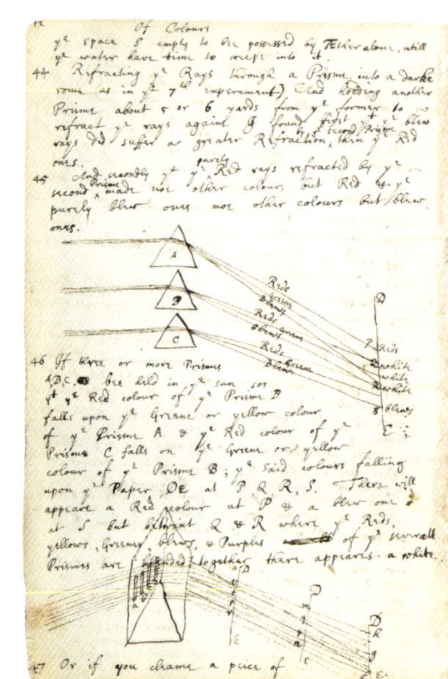

2. The decomposition of light by means of a prism as described by Newton in one of his diaries
Cambridge, Cambridge University Library

The first solid theory of colour recognizing its nature as a perceptual phenomenon did not appear until the beginning of the 19th century, when the physicist Thomas

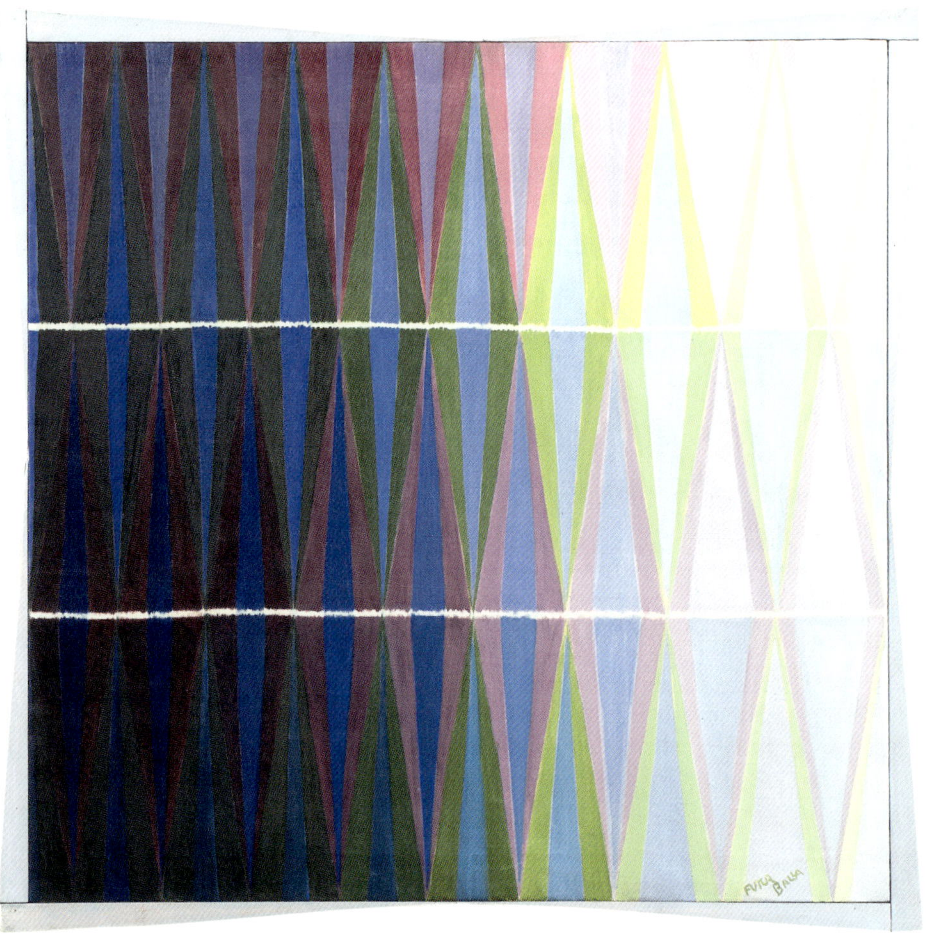

3. Giacomo Balla
Iridescent Interpenetration no. 7, c. 1912
Torino, GAM - Galleria Civica d'Arte Moderna e Contemporanea

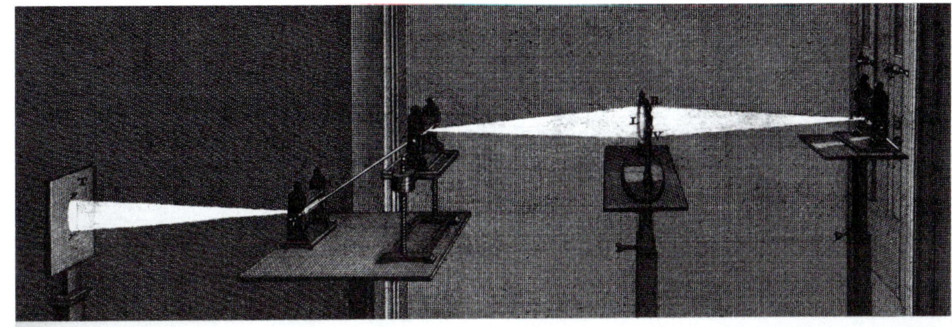

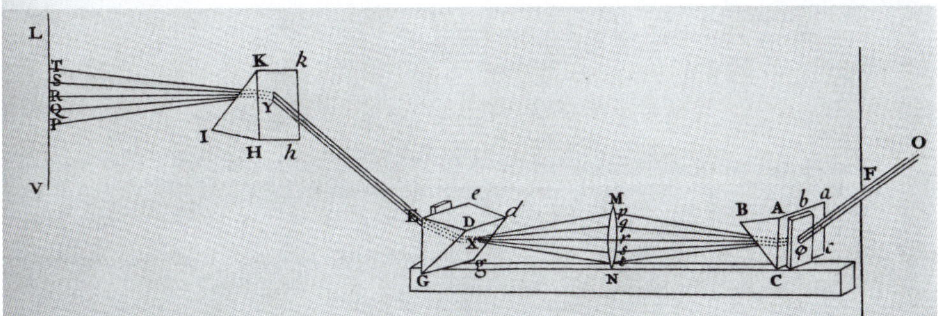

4. Newton demonstrated that colour is a property of light and not of objects by decomposing white light into a beam of colours and then turning it back into white light by means of a lens

Young posited the existence of three elementary sensations of colour. He also suggested that the sensation of shades between these colours was generated by their combination: "As it is almost impossible to conceive each sensitive point of the retina to contain an infinite number of particles, each capable of vibrating perfectly in unison with every possible undulation, it becomes necessary to suppose the number limited, for instance to three principal colours" (Young 1801), thus referring to the three primary colours. Hermann von Helmholtz then suggested in 1852, albeit with no tangible experimental evidence, the existence of three different kinds of nerves in the retina, now known as cones (fig. 5). When excited, each of these photoreceptors would generate one of Young's three primary sensations, each of them having, as we now know, maximum sensitivity in three regions of the spectrum of visible light (red, green and blue). The time was now ripe to announce that the origin of colours was to be sought "not in the nature of light, but in the constitution of man" (Maxwell 1856, 1872). The physicist James Maxwell, renowned for his equations of electromagnetism, drew on Young's idea and Helmholtz's intuition to show that the laws of colour perception must necessarily depend on the physiology of the nervous system, being determined not only by the physical nature of the events registered by the retinal receptors but also, and above all, by the physiological processes of interpretation of these signals. The science of colour was definitively established henceforth as a science of the mind.

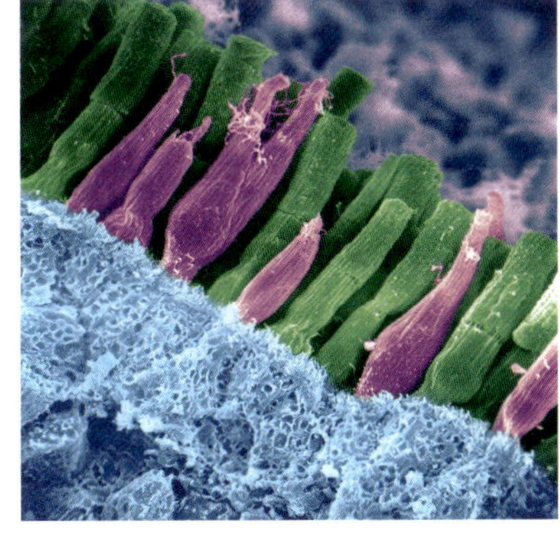

5. Electron microscope image of photoreceptors in the retina: cones and rods. It is the cones, shown in purple, that make colour perception possible

Opposite
48

Compenetrazione iridescente n. 10
(Iridescent Interpenetration no. 10), c. 1912–13
pencil and watercolour on paper, 50 x 32 cm

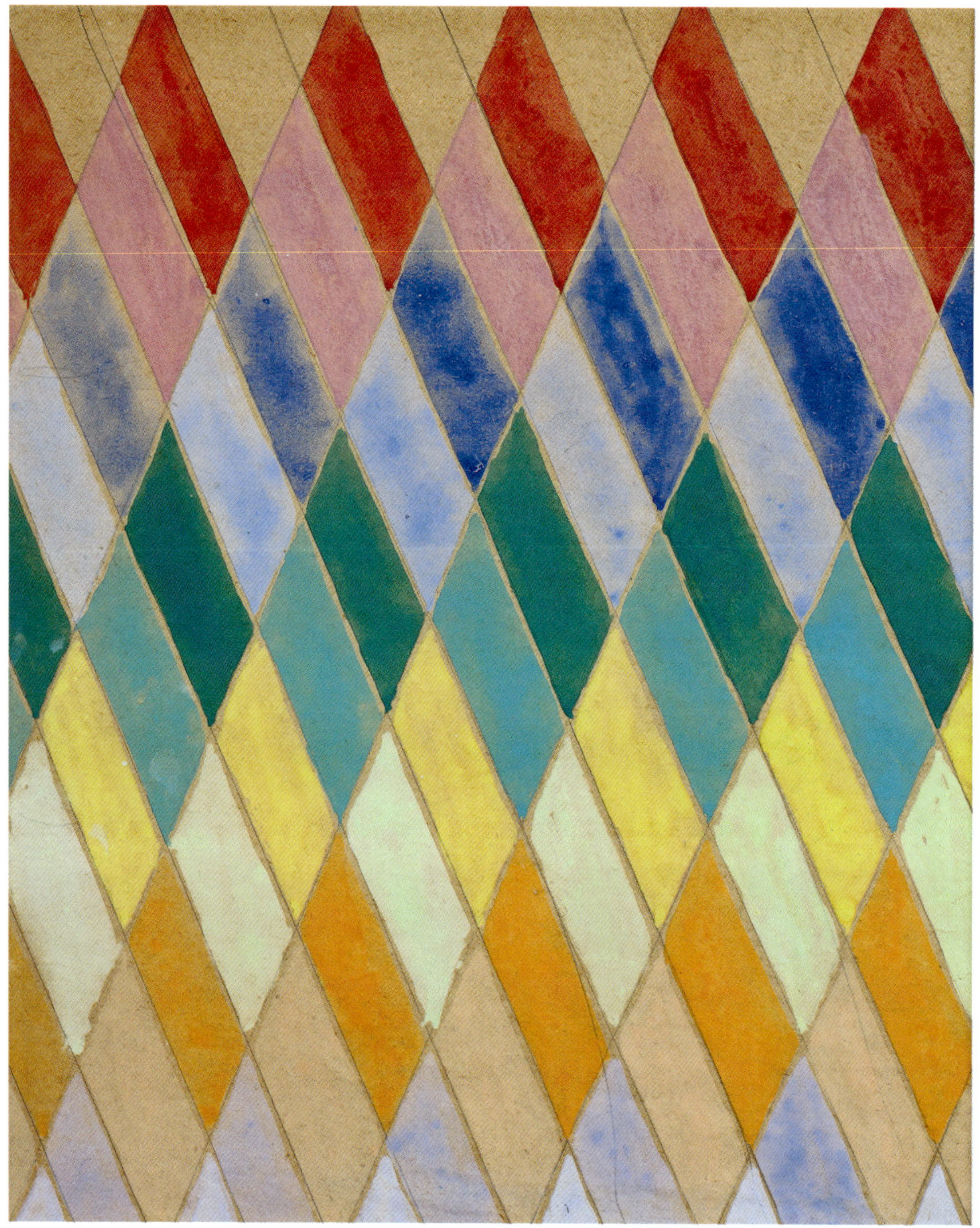

47

Compenetrazione iridescente – studio
(Iridescent Interpenetration – Study), c. 1912
watercolour and pencil on paper, 24 x 18.5 cm

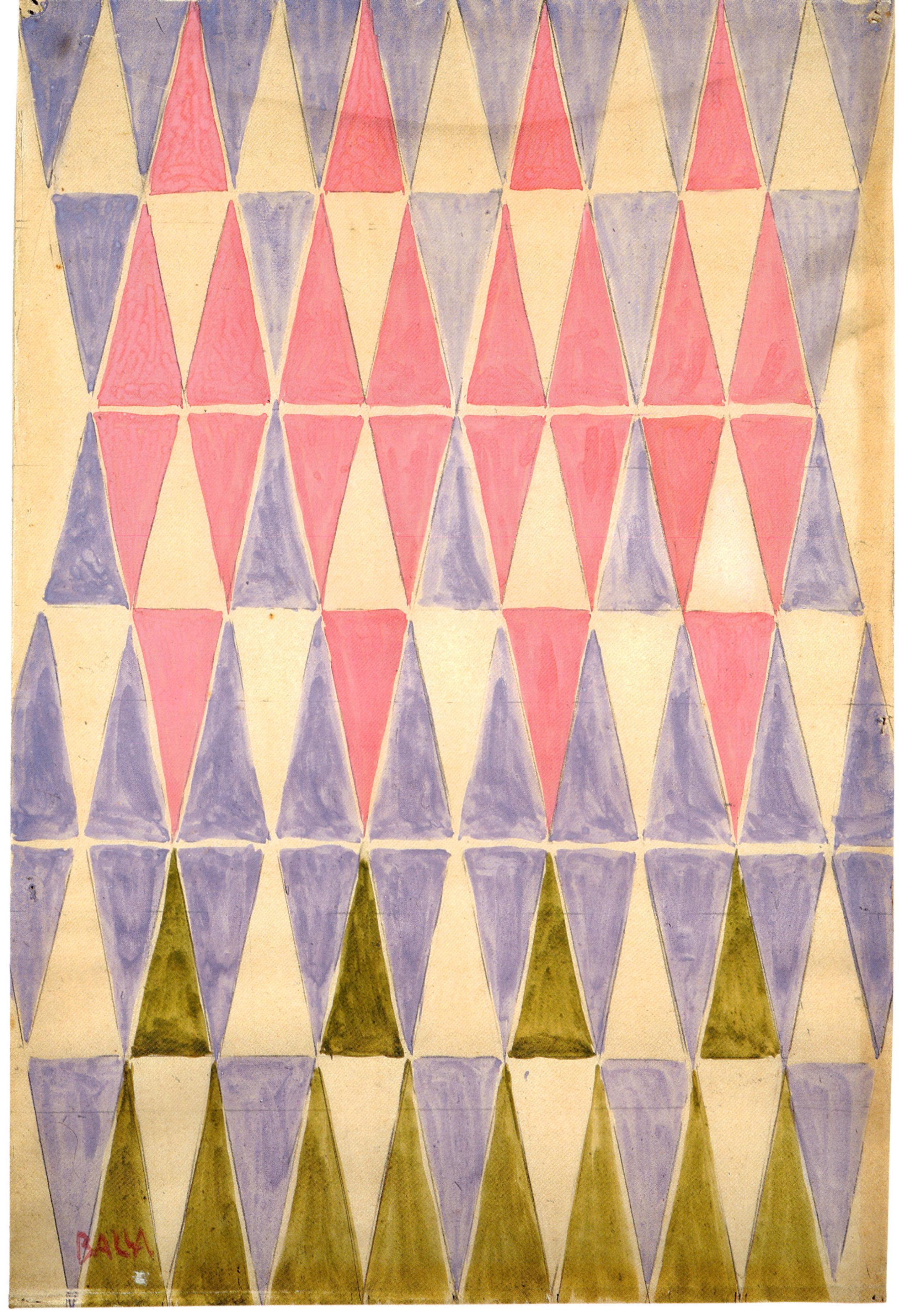
BALLA

Opposite
50

Compenetrazione iridescente n. 1
(Iridescent Interpenetration no. 1), 1912–14
oil and wax crayon on canvas, 99 x 59 cm

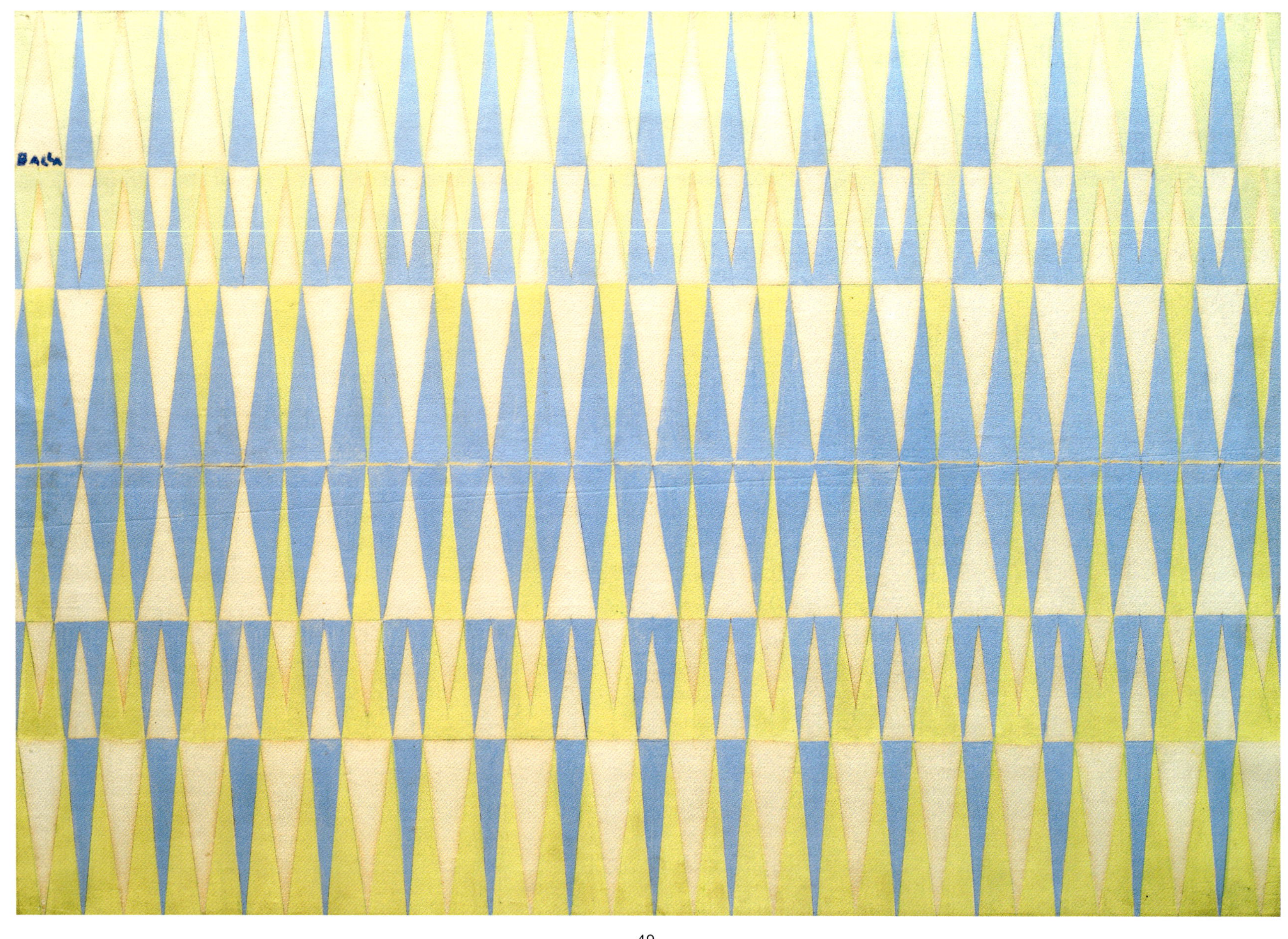

49

Compenetrazione iridescente n. 4
(Studio della luce) (Iridescent Interpenetration no. 4 –
Study of Light), 1912–13
oil and pencil on paper mounted on canvas, 55 x 76 cm

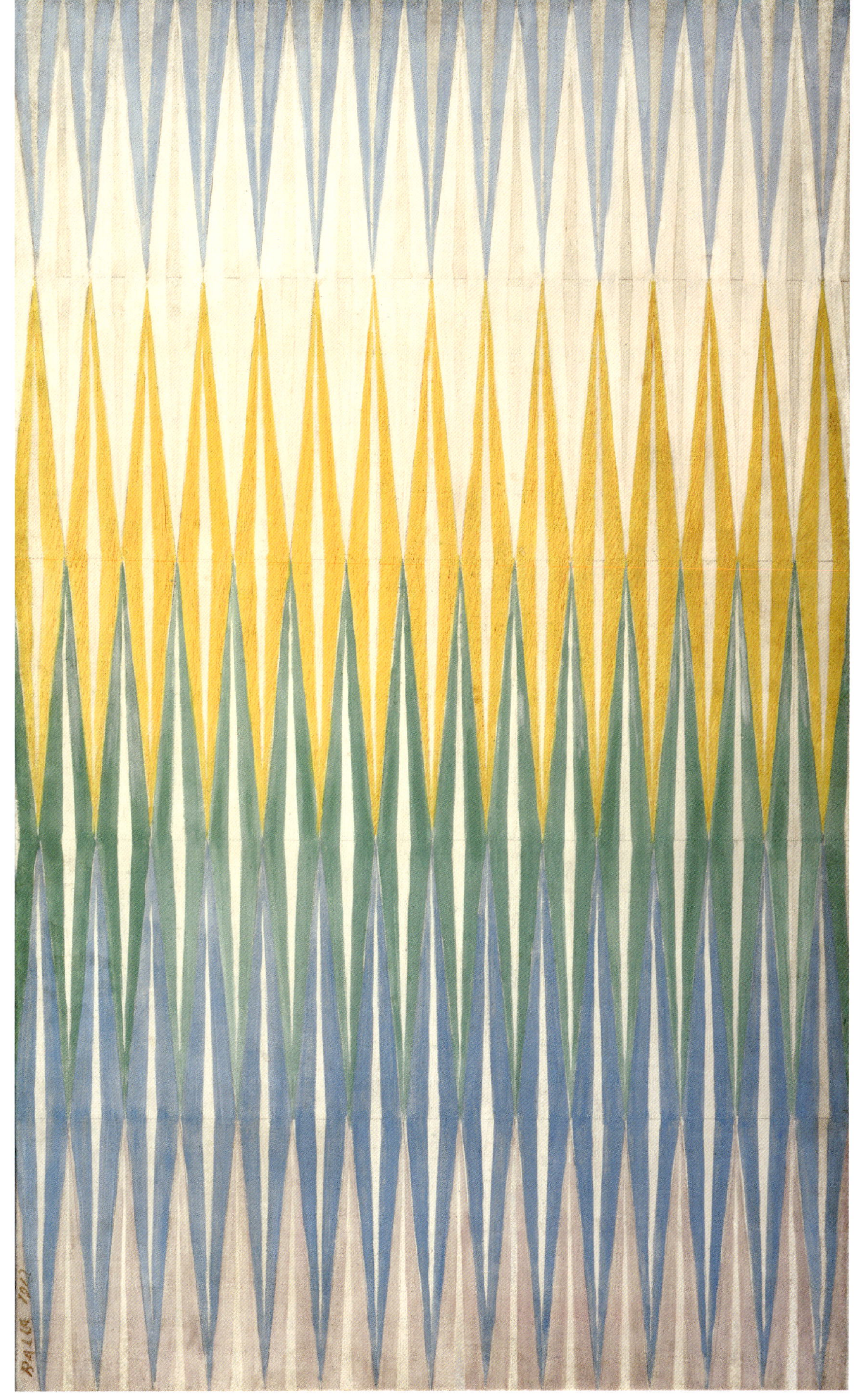

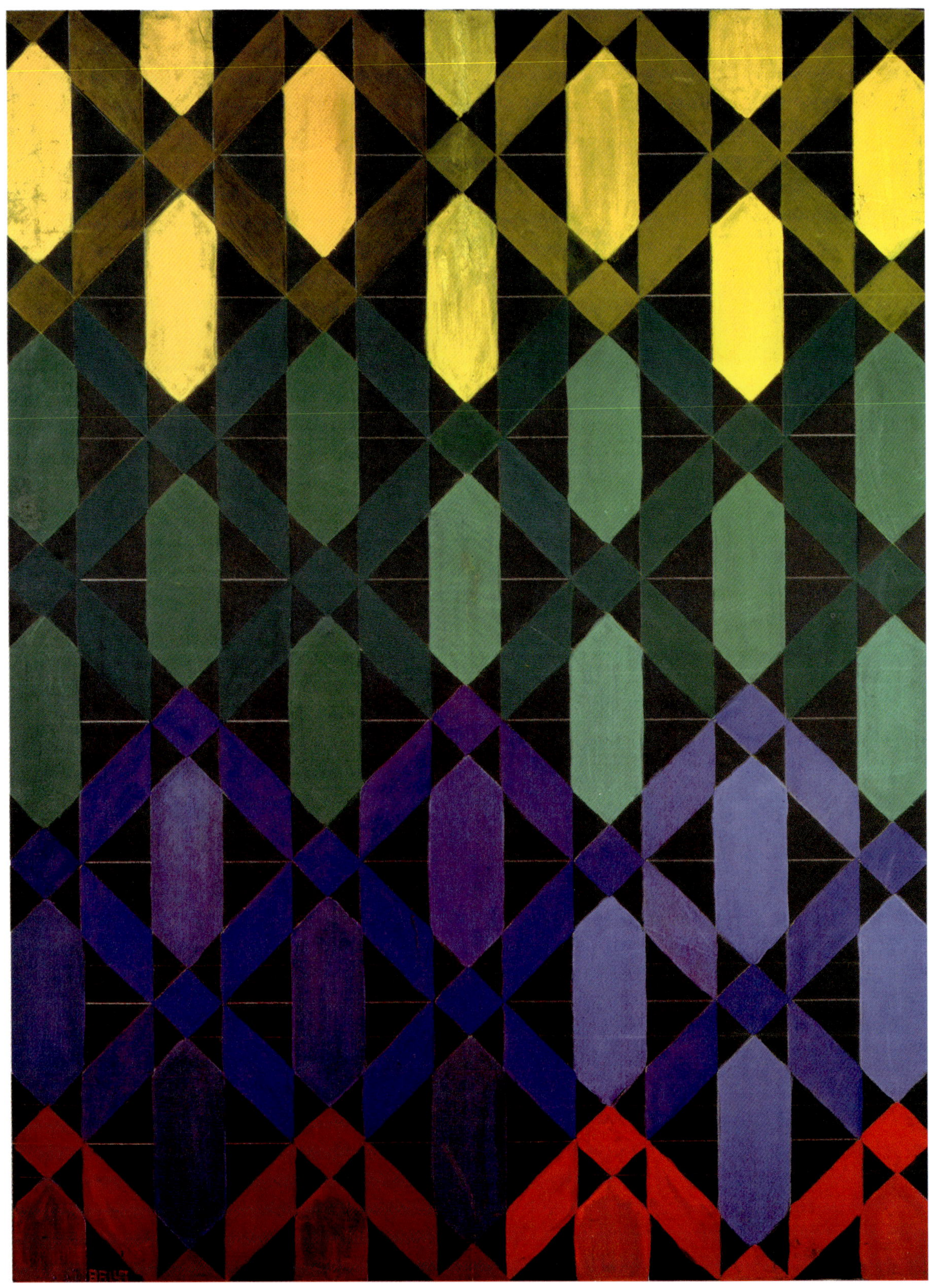

51

Compenetrazione iridescente n. 13
(Iridescent Interpenetration no. 13), c. 1913–14
tempera on paper mounted on canvas, 94 x 72 cm

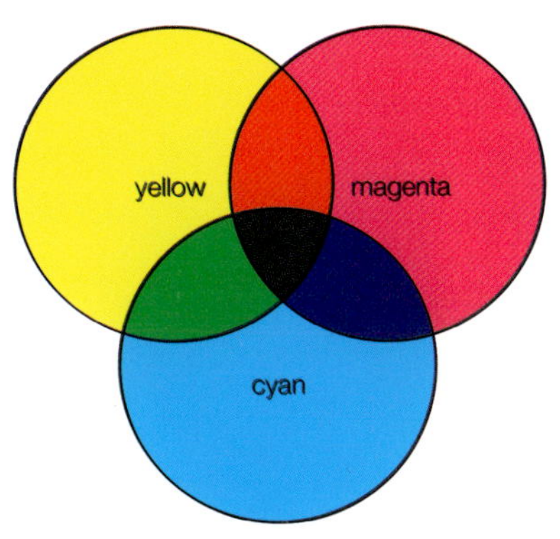

6. The mixing of colours on the palette generates a greyish hue through the phenomenon of subtractive synthesis

As it is known, the development of scientific knowledge on the acquisition of colours at the retinal level, albeit still limited in many respects, was to influence the movement of Pointillism in France and, in some ways, the development of the Italian Divisionism in the second half of the 19th century. Often erroneously lumped together, these two approaches are actually based on practically opposite physiological principles. Pointillism involved decomposition of the image into minuscule dots of "pure" colour arranged so as to be melded in the viewer's eye by the retina into homogenous shades and tonalities when the work was observed from a certain distance. Georges Seurat realized that the technique of what he originally called *peinture optique*, based on an optical mixing of colour, made it possible to enhance the brightness of colours as though the painting itself emanated light instead of reflecting it. The primary concern of Seurat and the artists who followed in his footsteps was to avoid the mixing of pigments on the canvas, something advised against also in antiquity and described as "deflowering" and "death" by Aristotle. In actual fact, the combination of different pigments, as often observed on the artist's palette, prompts the subtractive synthesis of colour with the result of generating tonalities that lose saturation or intensity and tend towards brownish or grey (Ball 2003; fig. 6). This happens because the colour obtained from the combination of two pigments reflects only the part of the light or electromagnetic spectrum that both are capable of reflecting, while the light reflected by each of them on its own is lost, subtracted from sight. Despite the numerous preparatory studies, the scientific application of *peinture optique* did not produce the results hoped for. The brilliance to which Pointillism aspired depended in actual fact on the purity of colours and the size of the dots painted on the canvas, but Seurat had paid little attention to these two factors, thus decreeing its failure, so to speak, as an orthodox application of the results of scientific research on colour. It did, however, create paintings of enhanced compositional exuberance.

Divisionism in Italy took a different path that diverged from Pointillism's empirical investigation of light and colour in the greater freedom of its interpretation of scientific results. The Italian artists took care to avoid representation of the Pointillist type by developing a technique based on fragmented filaments (not dots), often overlapping on the canvas. The filaments then became large patches of colour that were certainly not susceptible of retinal fusion but endowed the painting with diffuse and often artificial light. This accentuation of colour naturally evolved towards the simplification of forms and thus a decrease in the representational character of the paintings.

Balla's artistic effort in this direction, tending towards abstraction, was born with the accentuation of colour in the Divisionist canvases and arrived in the *Compenetrazioni* at the complete isolation of colour from everything that is not colour. The question is why the artist embarked on this path and arrived at this goal. An answer in physiological terms will require a brief outline of how the human brain processes the visible world and especially colour. The research in electrophysiology and neuroimaging of the last few decades has shown that the signals from the retina, the point where Pointillism stopped, are transmitted along a complex neural pathway involving numerous cerebral structures. One of these is the comparatively small visual area number 4 or V4 (Zeki et al. 1991; Bartels & Zeki 2000; Zeki 2003). Clinical studies have shown over the years how essential this area is to the perception of colour, dramatic proof being provided by the fact that a lesion to it causes achromatopsia or colour blindness, plunging the victims of this type of trauma into a world dominated from monotonous shades of grey (Zeki 1990, 1993). This implies that V4 is a cerebral area functionally and anatomically distinguished from the others, because the brain processes visual stimuli through separation in not only spatial but also temporal terms. In other words, before being perceived as part of a single visible entity, the shape, colour and motion of an object (for example a black dog walking on the pavement) are processed separately in different areas of the brain (fig. 7). Psychophysical experiments have even demonstrated that the perception of the colour and the movement of an object are temporally distinct, the former taking place some hundredths of a second before the latter (Moutoussis & Zeki 1997). These minute differences cannot be noticed in everyday life.

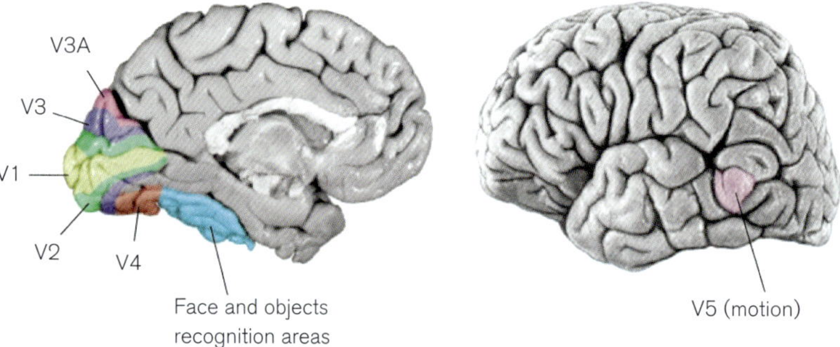

7. Representation of the anatomical position of V4, the area responsible for colour perception, in red together with other areas of the visual brain, including those required for the perception of faces and objects (in blue) and movement (in pink) (from Zeki 2003)

This separation of the visual signal and its perception, known as the "functional specialization" of the brain, underlies a physiological phenomenon that may have interesting implications for art. The well-known neuroscientist Semir Zeki has indeed suggested that the creative act of an artist, who separates and isolates one perceptual phenomenon from another, sometimes accentuating colour and sometimes movement, is directly related to this functional specialization (Zeki 1999a). In other words, this would be the neurophysiological reason for Balla's ability to isolate and accentuate colour in the *Compenetrazioni iridescenti* or separate movement from colour in *Linee di velocità* (*Lines of Speed*) (Zeki & Lamb 1994; Ticini 2009): by maximizing the activity of the neurons in V4, where colour is represented, and decreasing the stimulation of the areas dedicated to the perception of form and movement at the same time.

Other artists have produced representations that are conceptually not dissimilar to Balla's, such as Kasimir Malevich's squares of colour. In my view, however, the peculiarity of the *Compenetrazioni* lies in the simultaneous representation in a single work both of the physical nature of light and of investigation into the perceptual phenomenon of colour. Observation of these facetted chromatic compositions suffices to show that Balla's decision to represent the beams of light as "triangular shapes", in which I detect a reference to Newton, is perfectly correct in the study of the complicated relationship between colours (fig. 8).

The science of colours is enriched by complex phenomena that still await clarification. The *Compenetrazioni*, for example, demonstrate that the perception of the colour of each of their elements cannot be predicted by Young's three principal colours, i.e. solely from the existence of the three types of cones of the retina. The colour of each surface depends significantly in fact on the context in which it is placed. Attention should be drawn in this connection to chromatic contrast (already observed by Leonardo da Vinci) and colour constancy. The former indicates that when an object is placed on a coloured background, its perceived colour will tend to assume a tonality on Newton's circle of colours opposite (complementary) to that of the background. The later indicates that an object preserves its colour in every condition of light. Phenomena of this kind are readily identifiable in the *Compenetrazioni*, where a yellow triangle is always yellow (colour constancy) but will tend towards reddish when placed alongside a green and towards greenish alongside a red (chromatic contrast). If it is instead placed beside another triangle that is also yellow but of different saturation (or intensity), it will appear to be of the same colour but less saturated, greyish. Less present in Balla's work is the phenomenon known as

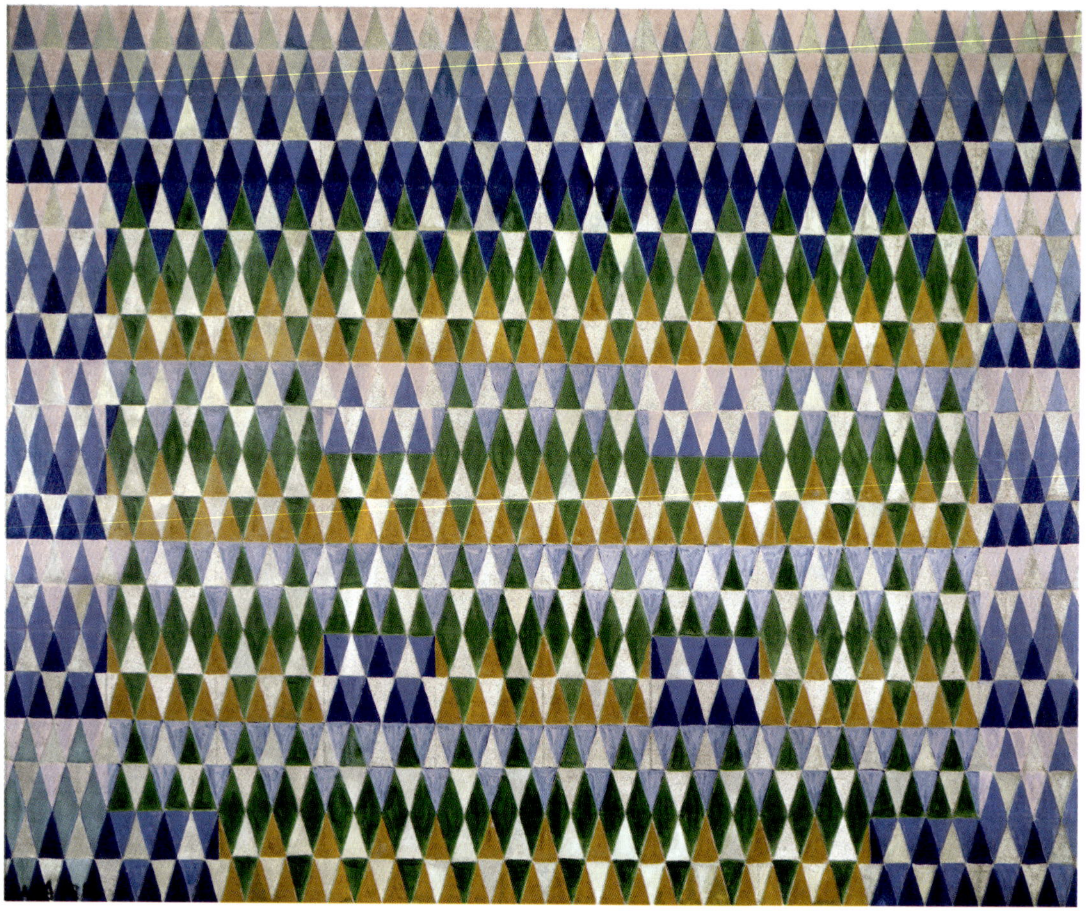

8. Giacomo Balla
Compenetrazione iridescente n. 5 (Eucaliptus) (Iridescent Interpenetration no. 5 - Eucaliptus), 1914
Private collection

chromatic assimilation, which takes place when a pattern of coloured lines is placed on a background of another colour. In this case, the tonality of the pattern tends not towards the complementary colour but towards that of the background. For example, a red pattern will tend towards blue on a blue background.

One of the oldest ancient demonstrations of chromatic contrast is that of coloured shadows, as described by Goethe among others (Goethe 1810). The experiment can be outlined as follows. When a white screen is illuminated by two different sources of light, one red and one white for example, it appears pink. When an object is placed between these lights and the screen, it casts two different shadows on the pink background, one when it blocks the white light and one when it blocks the red. The first is perceived as a saturated shade of red because the red light is observed striking the pink background. The second, caused by blocking the red light, in instead greenish as the result of the white light on pink (green being the complementary colour to the background in this case; Lotto & Purves 2002) (fig. 9). The exhaustive description of chromatic contrast published by the chemist Michel-Eugène Chévreul in a study of complementary colours had a considerable influence on artists (Chévreul 1839). He was in fact the first to provide art with an empirical method for the application of colour as well as complex and rigorous wheel of colours illustrating the relations between them. Chévreul had the opportunity to develop his research in this field in greater depth when Louis XVIII placed him in charge of the Gobelins tapestry works in Paris, where he was required in particular to study (and obviously remedy) the chromatic dullness of yarn. He realized that this aesthetic problem was not due to the quality of the dye used but rather to the combination of colours in the weaving process, and showed that when complementary colours were placed side by side, they appeared brighter close up but confused at a distance and generated an impression of greyness (merging on the retina in a process similar to the additive synthesis that Pointillism sought to avoid). Chévreul's work provided scientific proof that pure colours do not exist, only perceived colours do. This important discovery underlies Delacroix's assertion, "I can paint you the skin of Venus with mud, provided you let me surround it as I will."

The second phenomenon of importance here is colour constancy (Zeki 1999b). Measurement of the light reflected by a white sheet of paper at midday and sunset with a photometer would show that it differs with the time of day, as the white sheet will in fact reflect more red light at sunset. Nevertheless, the colour perceived will remain white. It is therefore clear from everyday experience that the colour of the paper (and any other surface) remains the same, albeit with variations in saturation and brightness, despite drastic change in the ambient light. We have only a limited understanding of why that happens at present and of the neural processes responsible for colour constancy. In any case, we do know that it is an efficient biological mechanism providing information on the physical properties of a surface despite constant change in the light it reflects. As an example to help show the biological significance of colour constancy, let us imagine that the brain judged the ripeness of a tomato solely on the light reflected by its surface. In this case, an unripe tomato that looks green at noon would appear red at sunset and therefore be considered eatable. The brain instead makes us independent of the contin-

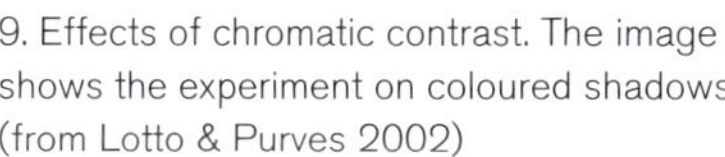
9. Effects of chromatic contrast. The image shows the experiment on coloured shadows (from Lotto & Purves 2002)

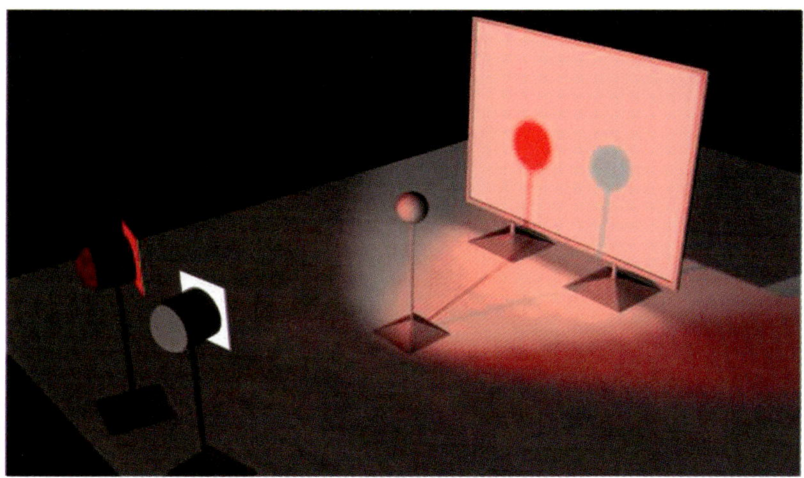

uous change in light. Some studies suggest that its computations consist in determining the relation between the light reflected by the surface observed and its context. Since this relation is always the same (the nature of surfaces does not change as a result of change in the incident light), the brain can evaluate the nature of the surface, i.e. its efficiency in reflecting a certain wavelength of light. Edwin H. Land, the inventor of the Polaroid, put forward the retinex (retina-and-cortex) theory to explain colour constancy (Land 1977). He performed an experiment in which two identical panels were covered in differently coloured sheets of paper to form a pattern similar to a painting by Mondrian (fig. 10). Three spotlights of different wavelength – long (red), medium (green) and short (blue) – were placed in front of each panel and a photometer was used to measure the light reaching the observer's eye from every area of the "Mondrians". During the experiment, the spotlights were adjusted so that a white area of the "Mondrian" on the left reflected the same light as a green area of the one on the right. In the experimental conditions, even though the two areas reflected the same light and the same triad of long, medium and short waves reached the retina, the areas on the left and right continued to be perceived respectively as white and green. This confirms that colour is not determined by incident or reflected light but rather it is an interpretation of the quality of the surface of an object generated by the retina and the brain.

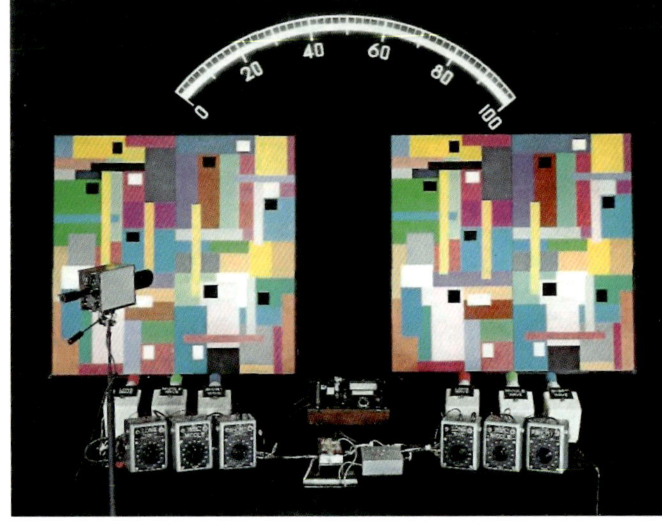

10. The experimental apparatus used by Land to demonstrate colour constancy (from Land 1977)

To conclude, Balla's artistic work and in particular his development towards the abstraction of the *Compenetrazioni* is addressed here from an unusual viewpoint. An albeit superficial analysis of his work is used to illustrate some general points about light and colour, and about how the visual information from the painting is integrated by the retina and processed further by the cerebral cortex, emphasizing in particular the critical role of the V4 area. While this kind of contribution obviously cannot help to explain the aesthetic experience of viewing Balla's work, a relationship is indicated between the physical nature of light, the physiology of colour perception and visual art. This suggests that Balla's artistic experiments can be regarded, in one way or another, as an interesting study of the human brain (Zeki 1999a, b; Ticini 2003, 2004, 2010; Agudio & Ticini 2012).

Bibliography

Ball, P. (2003), *Bright Earth: Art and the Invention of Color*, University of Chicago Press.

Bartels, A., Zeki, S. (2000), "The architecture of the colour centre in the human visual brain: new results and a review", *European Journal of Neuroscience*, 12(1), pp. 172–93.

Chevreul, E. (1839), *De la loi du contraste simultané des couleurs et de l'assortiment des objets colorés*, Chez Pitois-Levrault.

Goethe, J. W. von (1810), *Die Farbenlehre*.

Helmholtz, H.V. (1852), "Über die Theorie der zusammengesetzten Farben", *Annalen der Physik*, 163(9), pp. 45–66.

Land, E. H. (1977), "The Retinex Theory of Color Vision", *Scientific American*, 237 (6), 1977, pp. 108-128.

Lotto, R.B., Purves, D. (2002), "The empirical basis of color perception", *Consciousness and Cognition*, 11(4), 609–29.

Maxwell, J.C. (1872), "On colour vision", *Proc. R. Instn Gt Br.*, 6, pp. 260–71.

Maxwell, J.C. (1856), "Theory of the perception of colours", *Trans. R. Scottish Soc. Arts*, 4, pp. 394–400.

Moutoussis, K., Zeki, S. (1997), "A direct demonstration of perceptual asynchrony in vision", *Proceedings of the Royal Society of London, Series B: Biological Sciences*, 264 (1380), pp. 393–99.

Newton, I. (1704), *Opticks: or a treatise of the reflexions, refractions, inflexions and colours of light*.

Ticini L.F. (2003), "Cervello pittore", *StileArte*, 68, pp. 6–7.

Ticini L.F. (2004), "Arte e cervello", *StileArte*, 79, pp. 38–39.

Ticini L.F. (2009), "Eppur si muove", *StileArte*, 128, pp. 70–73.

Ticini L.F. (2010), "Cervello d'artista", *StileArte*, 134, pp. 44–47.

Ticini L.F., Agudio E., (2012), "Neuroestetica: Canaletto e la resa della realtà. Una questione di cervello", *Art e dossier*, 292, pp. 48–53.

Young, T. (1801), "The Bakerian Lecture: On the Mechanism of the Eye", *Philosophical Transactions of the Royal Society of London*, 91, pp. 23–88.

Zeki, S. (1990), "A century of cerebral achromatopsia", *Brain*, 113 (6), pp. 1721–77.

Zeki, S. (1993), *A Vision of the Brain*, Blackwell Scientific Publ.

Zeki, S. (1999a), *Inner Vision: An Exploration of Art and the Brain*, Oxford University Press, Oxford.

Zeki, S. (1999b), "Splendours and miseries of the brain", *Philosophical Transactions of the Royal Society of London, Series B: Biological Sciences*, 354 (1392), pp. 2053–65.

Zeki, S. (2003), "Improbable areas in the visual brain", *Trends in Neurosciences*, 26 (1), pp. 23–26.

Zeki, S., Lamb, M. (1994), "The neurology of kinetic art", *Brain*, 117 (3), pp. 607–36.

Zeki, S., Watson, J.D., Lueck, C.J., Friston, K.J., Kennard, C., Frackowiak, R.S. (1991), "A direct demonstration of functional specialization in human visual cortex", *The Journal of Neuroscience*, 11(3), pp. 641–49.

SPEED

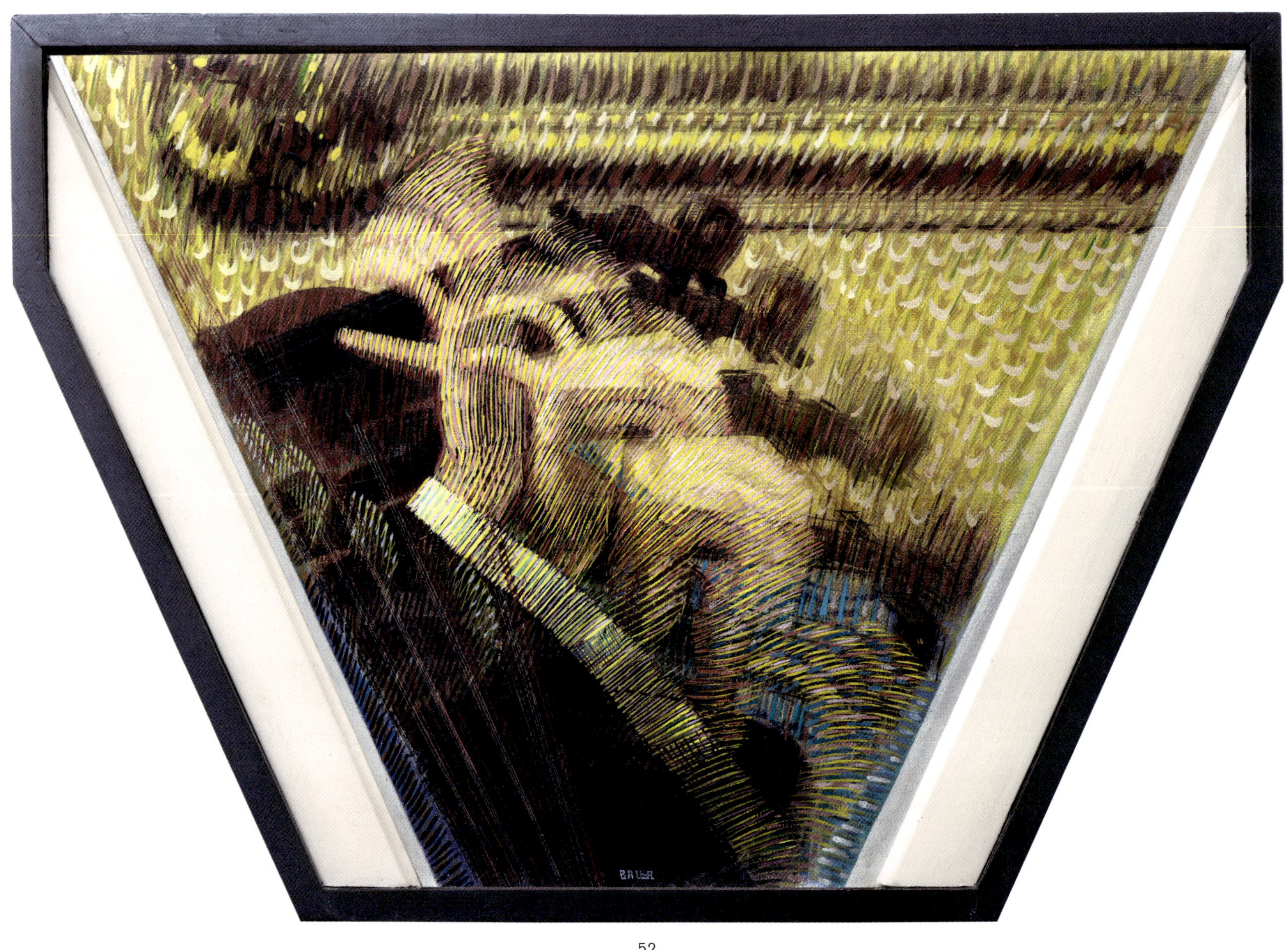

52

La mano del violinista – Ritmi d'archetto
(The Hand of the Violinist – The Rhythms of the Bow), 1912
oil on canvas, 52 x 75.2 cm

Speed

Ester Coen

Light, the expression of truth, in accordance with the laws of the universe and the scientific hypotheses of the age. To start by breaking down simple appearances and arrive at the essence of a pure pantheistic ideal, this was Balla's true aspiration. His ideas were very close to the gnoseological problems and the different sciences, not excluding the esoteric and theosophical ones, in the conception of a universal metaphysics in the very logic of an objective matter fragmented and divided to the point of dissolving into abstract, subjective substance, as he wrote to Boccioni in 1914[1] (fig. 1). It is indeed Boccioni that makes it possible to follow Balla through the striving that led the artist to reinvent himself with "the strength and power of his love for art"[2] in those few months and rediscover the true nature of his work. Boccioni went with Marinetti to Rome "the day before Christmas Eve" in 1912, shortly after his master's return from Düsseldorf. As he wrote to his friend Severini, also Balla's pupil and a signatory of Futurist manifestos, "We are famous in Rome! Balla has astounded us. In addition to launching a Futurist campaign with all the tenacity you can imagine, he has embarked on a complete transformation. He has begun four paintings of movement, still realistic but incredibly advanced and very strange in comparison with a year ago … He spent two months in Germany and must have seen things with intelligence. He admires us and is in complete agreement with our ideas. Though still too photographic and episodic, he is 42 years old with a practically intact, virgin will. Marinetti and I were moved at the sight of his courageous evolution, the kind of heroism you seldom see."[3] Boccioni therefore saw the works in Balla's studio, admired his tenacity, found the impetus with which he threw himself into this new "wonderful" adventure and praised the heroic humility of his allegiance to Futurist ideas in a spirit of respectful, admiring indulgence towards his young pupils. Though judging him "too photographic and episodic", Boccioni displayed great admiration for the spontaneity and sincerity with which Balla advanced into the unknown territories of experimental art. The four paintings that Boccioni found to be still episodic – meaning fragmentary and broken down into short

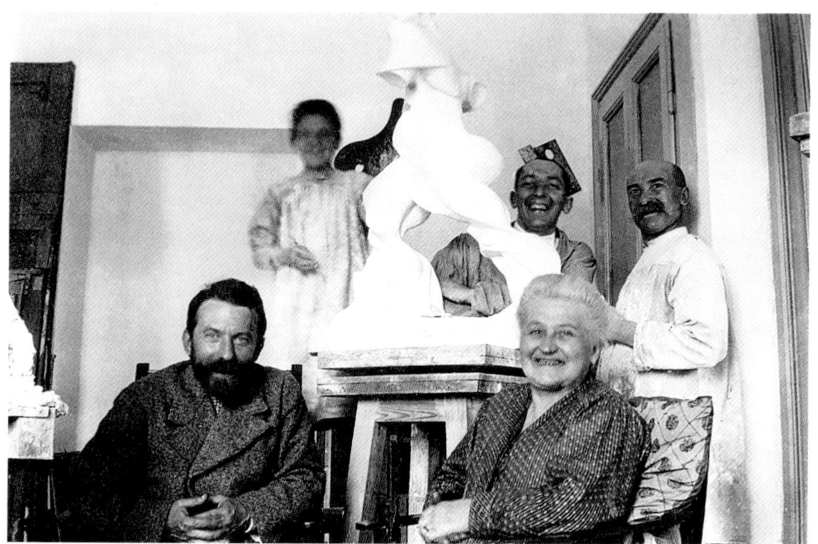

1. Boccioni in his studio in Milan with his mother and Balla, early 1913

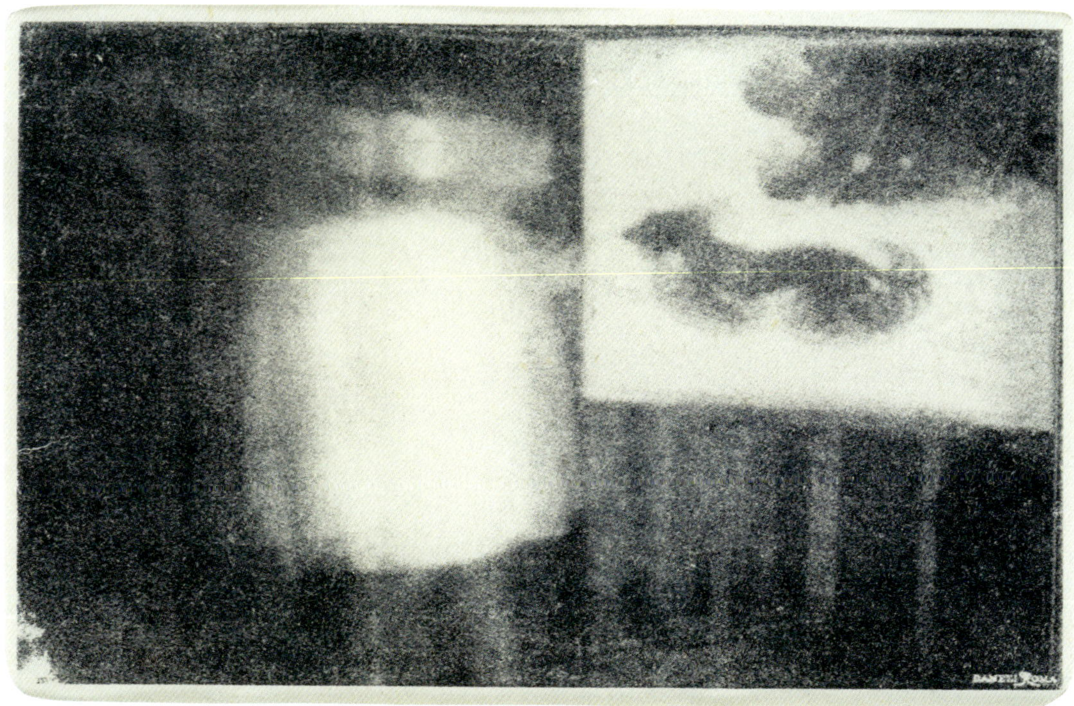

53

Anton Giulio Bragaglia
Giacomo Balla davanti a Dinamismo di un cane al guinzaglio
(Giacomo Balla in front of Dynamism of a Dog on a Leash),
c. 1912–13
postcard, 9 x 13.5 cm

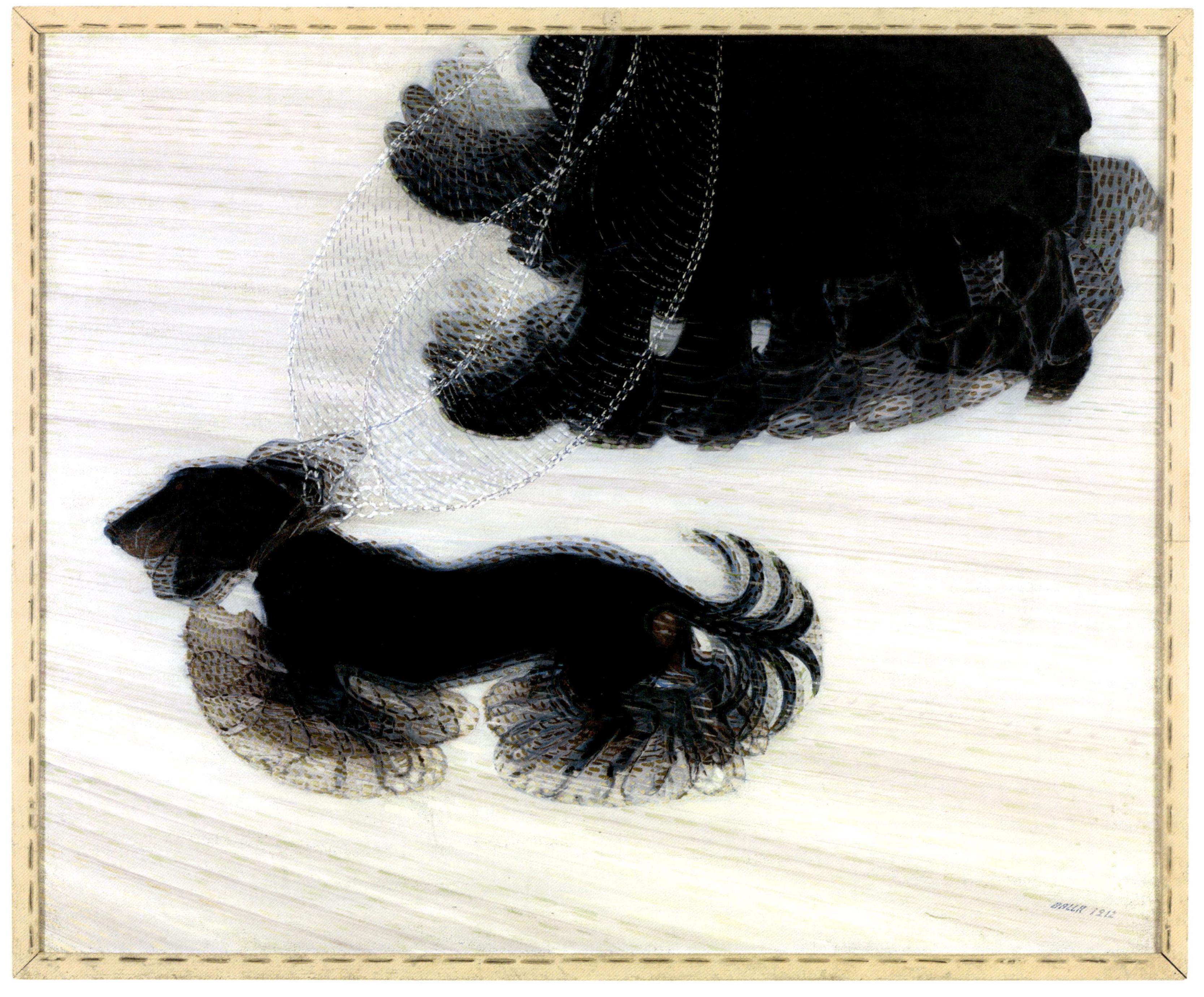

54

Dinamismo di un cane al guinzaglio
(Dynamism of a Dog on a Leash), 1912
oil on canvas, 89.85 x 109.85 cm

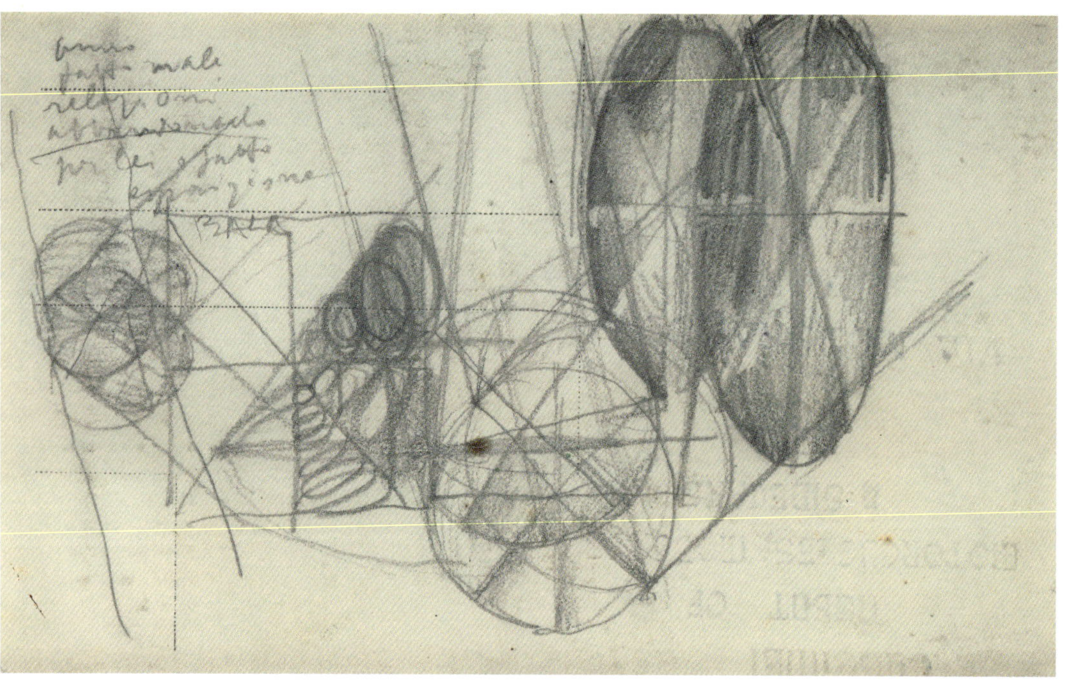

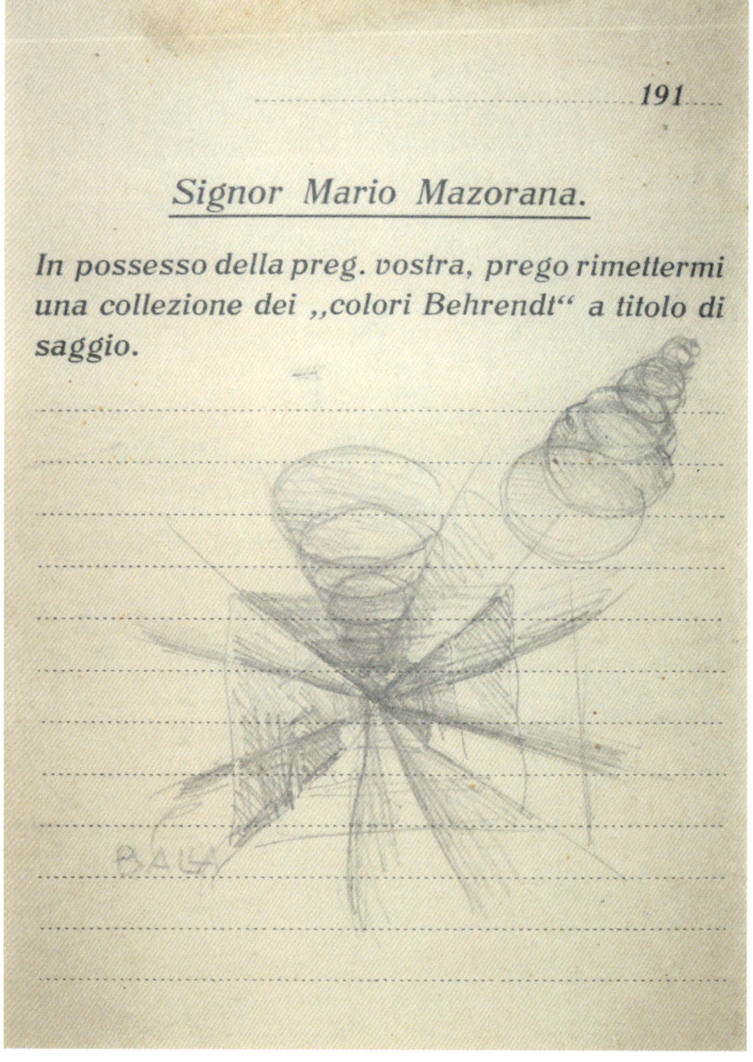

191

Signor Mario Mazorana.

In possesso della preg. vostra, prego rimettermi una collezione dei „colori Behrendt“ a titolo di saggio.

55

Studio di volumi (Study of Volumes), 1912
pencil on pasteboard, c. 8.5 x 14 cm

56

Studio di volumi (Study of Volumes), 1912
pencil on pasteboard, 14 x 9 cm

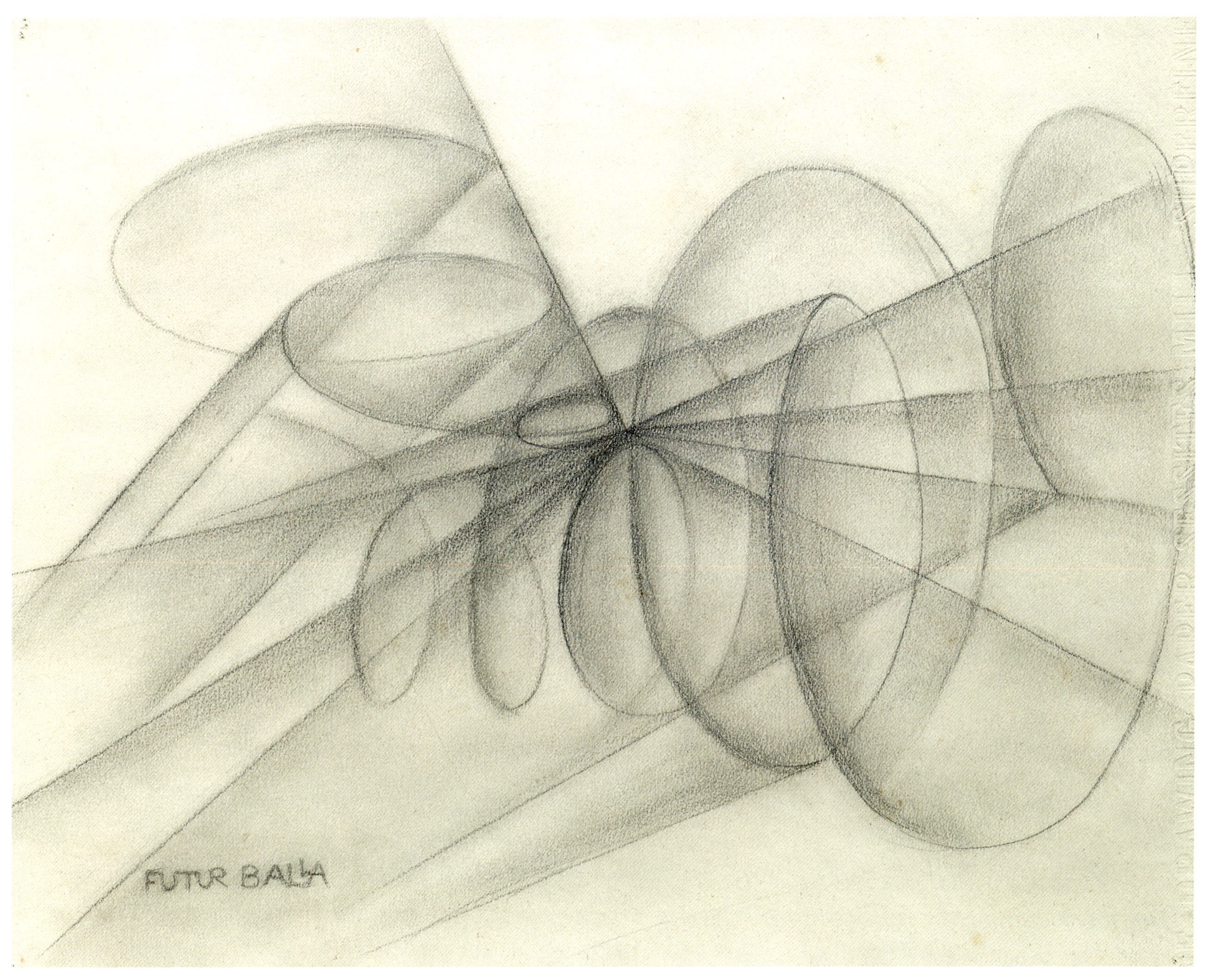

57

Studio di volumi (Study of Volumes), 1912–13
pencil on paper, 30.2 x 37 cm

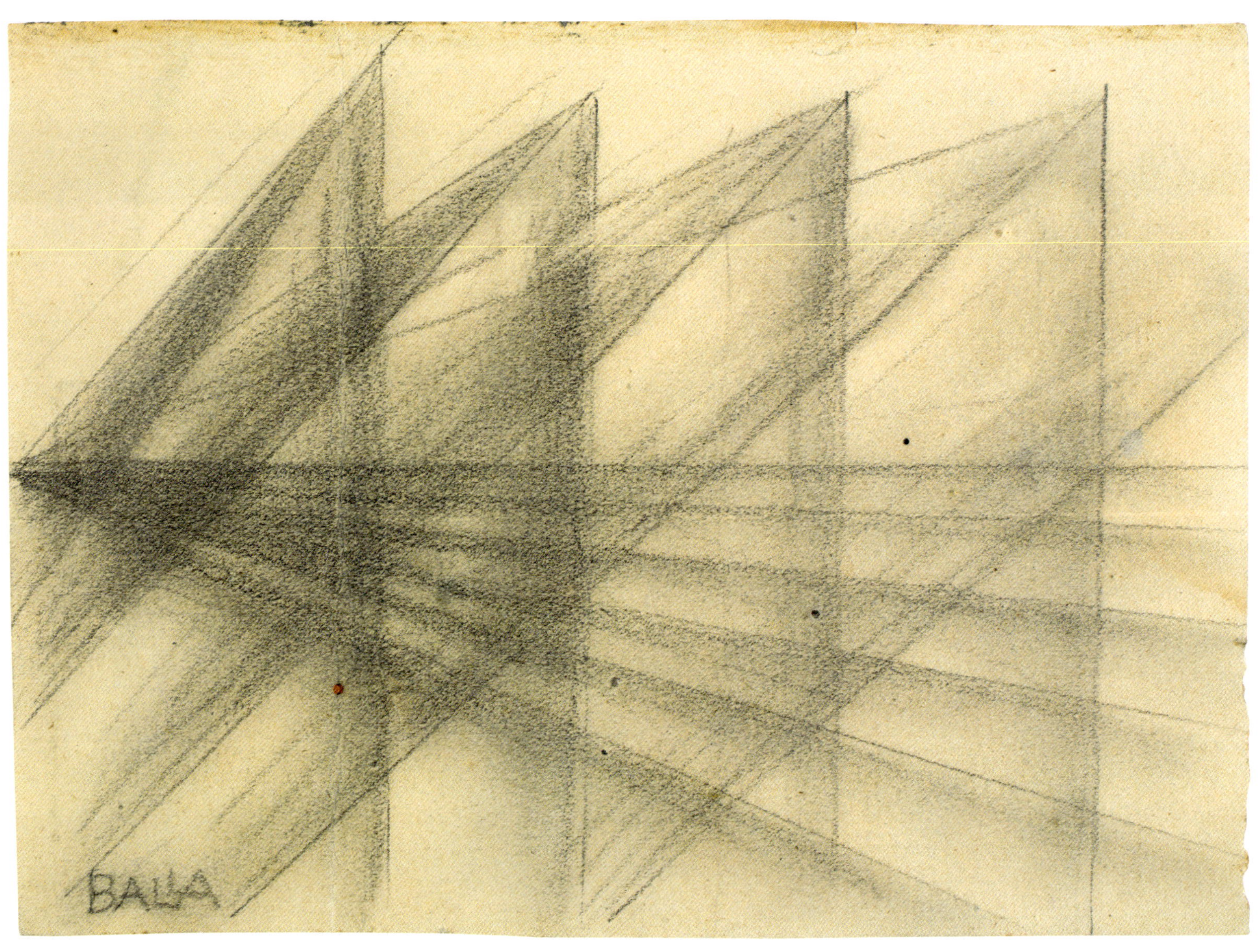

58

Compenetrazione – spazio (Interpenetration – Space), 1913
pencil on paper, 15 x 20.5 cm

2. Giacomo Balla
Velocità d'automobile + luce + rumore
(*Automobile Speed + Light + Noise*), 1913
Zurich, Kunsthaus Zürich

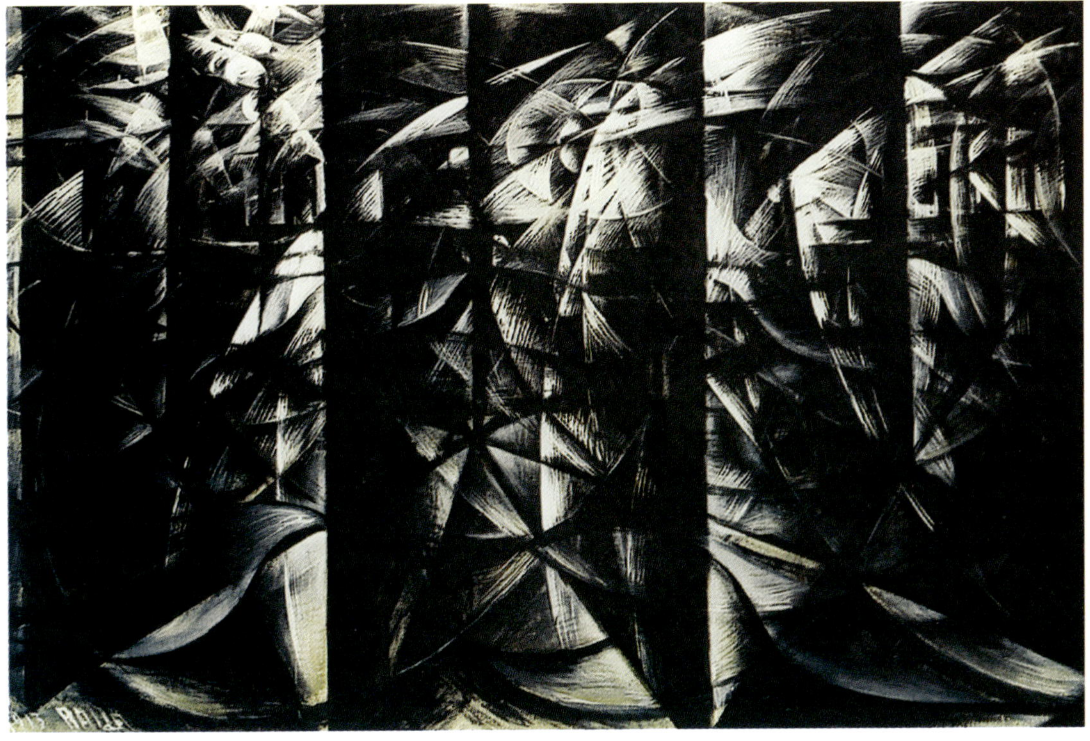

sequences – were not yet nor indeed could be the dynamic studies on the movement of automobiles (fig. 2). This series constitutes in fact material for a formally different analysis with respect to the rhythm and motion produced by a single action, as in the *Dinamismo di un cane al guinzaglio* (*Dynamism of a Dog on a Leash*), *La mano del violinista* (*The Hand of the Violinist*) and the *Bambina che corre sul balcone* (*Girl Running on a Balcony*). Here Balla tests the possibility of expressing in a single representation the mobility of an act in a fraction of non-frozen time (figs. 3-4). They are extraordinary works even though partly divergent from the credo of the young Futurists and above all Boccioni, the group's theoretician and impassioned champion of the synthetic complexity of the artwork in a

3. Giacomo Balla
Bambina che corre sul balcone
(*Girl Running on a Balcony*), study, 1912
Private collection

4. Giacomo Balla
Bambina che corre sul balcone
(*Girl Running on a Balcony*), study, 1912
Private collection

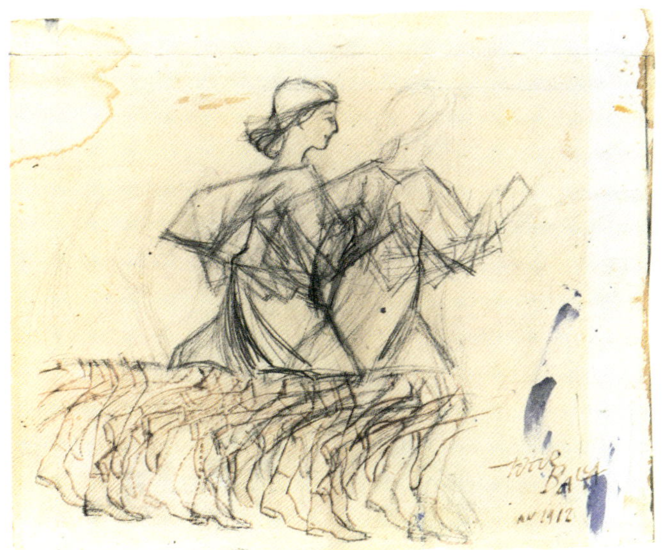

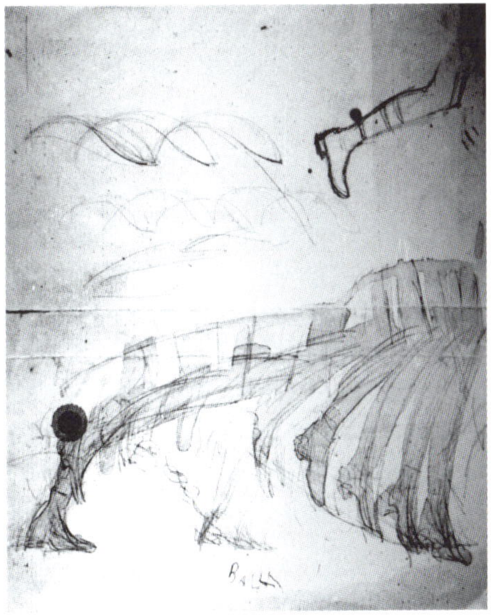

sweeping, rotating, circular dimension. Boccioni sought in dynamism the possibility of a transposition of vital energy in image, as stated in his *Pittura Scultura Futuriste*[4]: "the lyrical conception of forms interpreted in the infinite manifestation of their relativity between absolute motion and relative motion, between environment and object, until the apparition of a whole: environment + object. This is the creation of a new form that yields the relativity between weight and expansion, between motion of rotation and motion of revolution. In short, it is life itself grasped in the form that life creates in its endless happening. This happening, as now appears clear to me, is not captured through the repetition of legs, arms, figures, as many have stupidly supposed, but attained through the intuitive search for the sole form capable of giving continuity in space."[5] (fig. 5)

The ardour in these words reflects the aspiration to translate into theory and practice the visual experiments that followed the meeting with Filippo Tommaso Marinetti in 1910. And while it is not always easy to trace the principles of the new architecture of Futurist thought back to the direct sources of the readings and axioms from which they stem, it is quite impossible not to stress the powerful impact of the ideas of philosophy, science and above all modern physics on the creative imagination of an entire generation then entering the world of art and culture. With a sensational shift in perspective, the field of human experience expanded to encompass the abstract, incorporeal territories of the mind, and the fascinating hypothesis of a new entity bound up with spatiotemporal simultaneity took shape increasingly in the sphere of intuition. As Marinetti emphatically proclaimed in the first Futurist manifesto of February 1909, "Time and Space died yesterday. We are already living in the absolute, as we have already created eternal, omnipresent speed."[6] The impassioned, intuitive literary paraphrase of disturbing scientific breakthroughs perceived by a purely humanistic eye became the basis for the construction of a new aesthetic vision around speed and dynamism, fascinating concepts that incite action rather than simple observation, that call for the artist's total involvement in the corporeality of the act and, at the same time, fantasize of projection into the abysses of the indistinguishable.

"Space no longer exists: the street pavement, soaked by rain beneath the glare of electric lamps, becomes immensely deep and gapes to the very centre of the earth. Thousands of miles divide us from the sun;

5. Umberto Boccioni
Dinamismo di un corpo umano
(*Dynamism of a Human Body*), 1913
Milan, Museo del Novecento

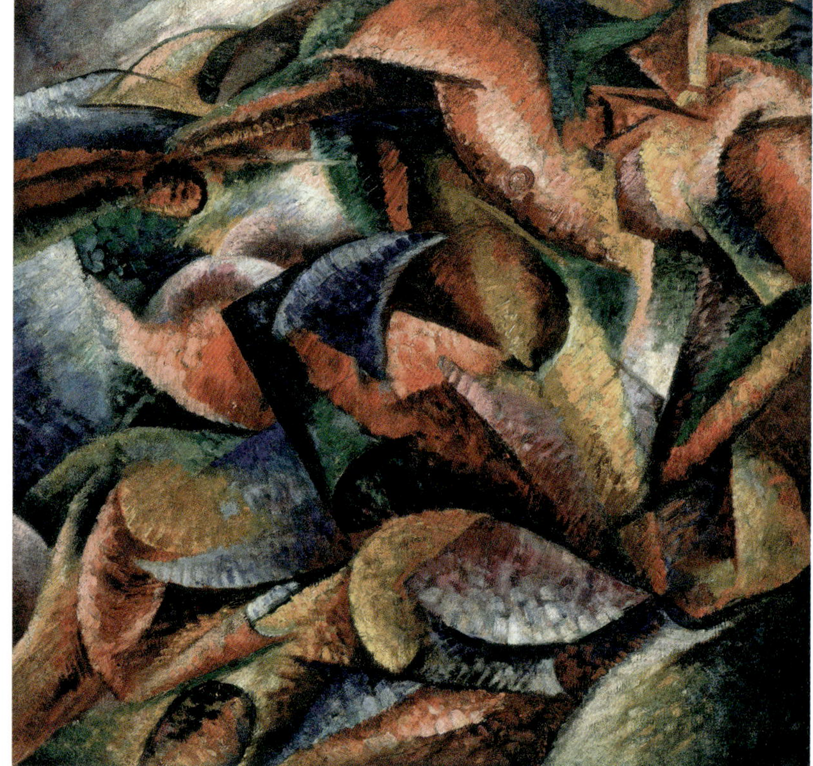

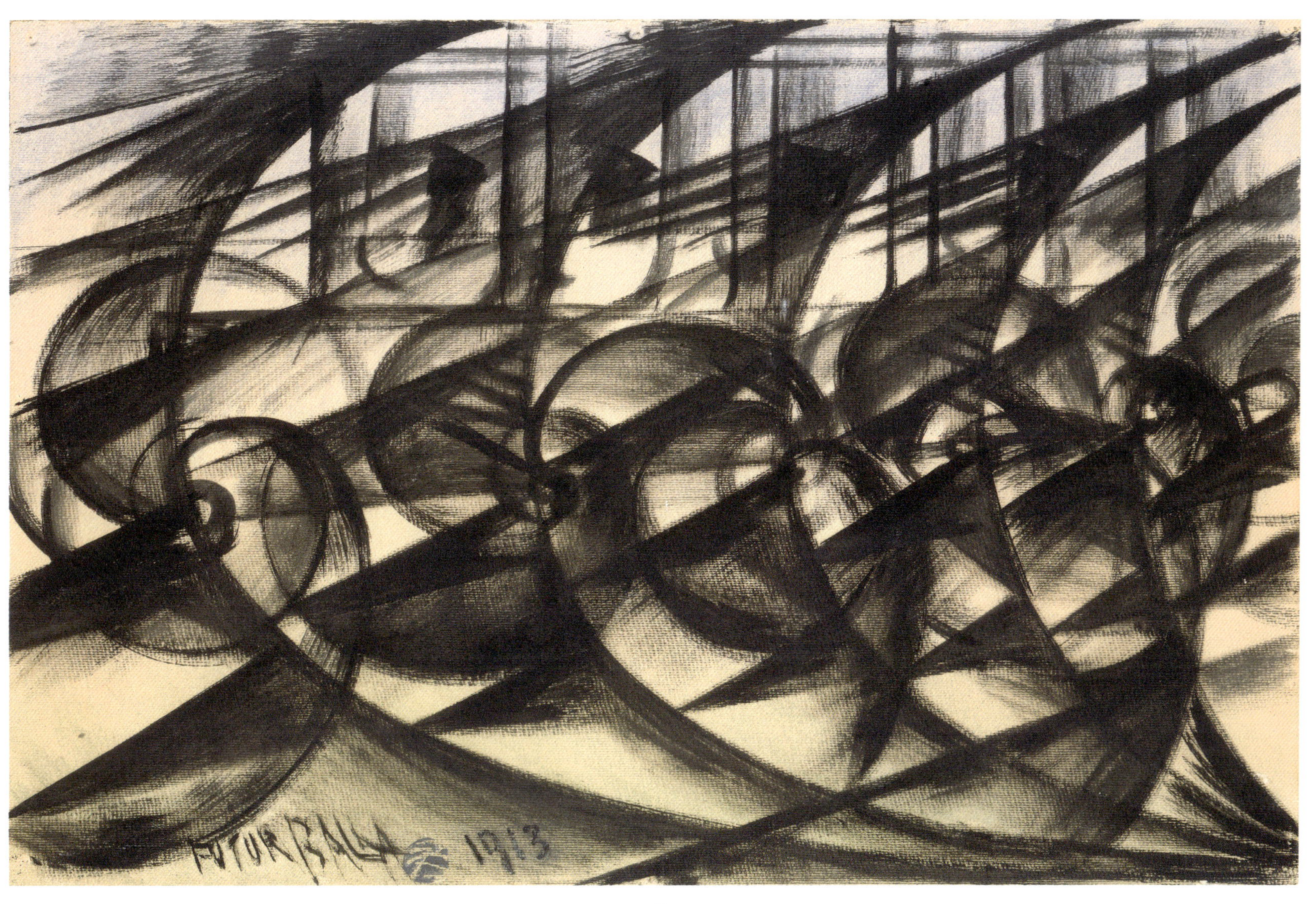

59

Auto in corsa (studio). Velocità astratta
(Speeding Car – Study. Abstract Speed), 1913
gouache and watercolour on paper mounted on canvas,
67.5 x 99.6 cm

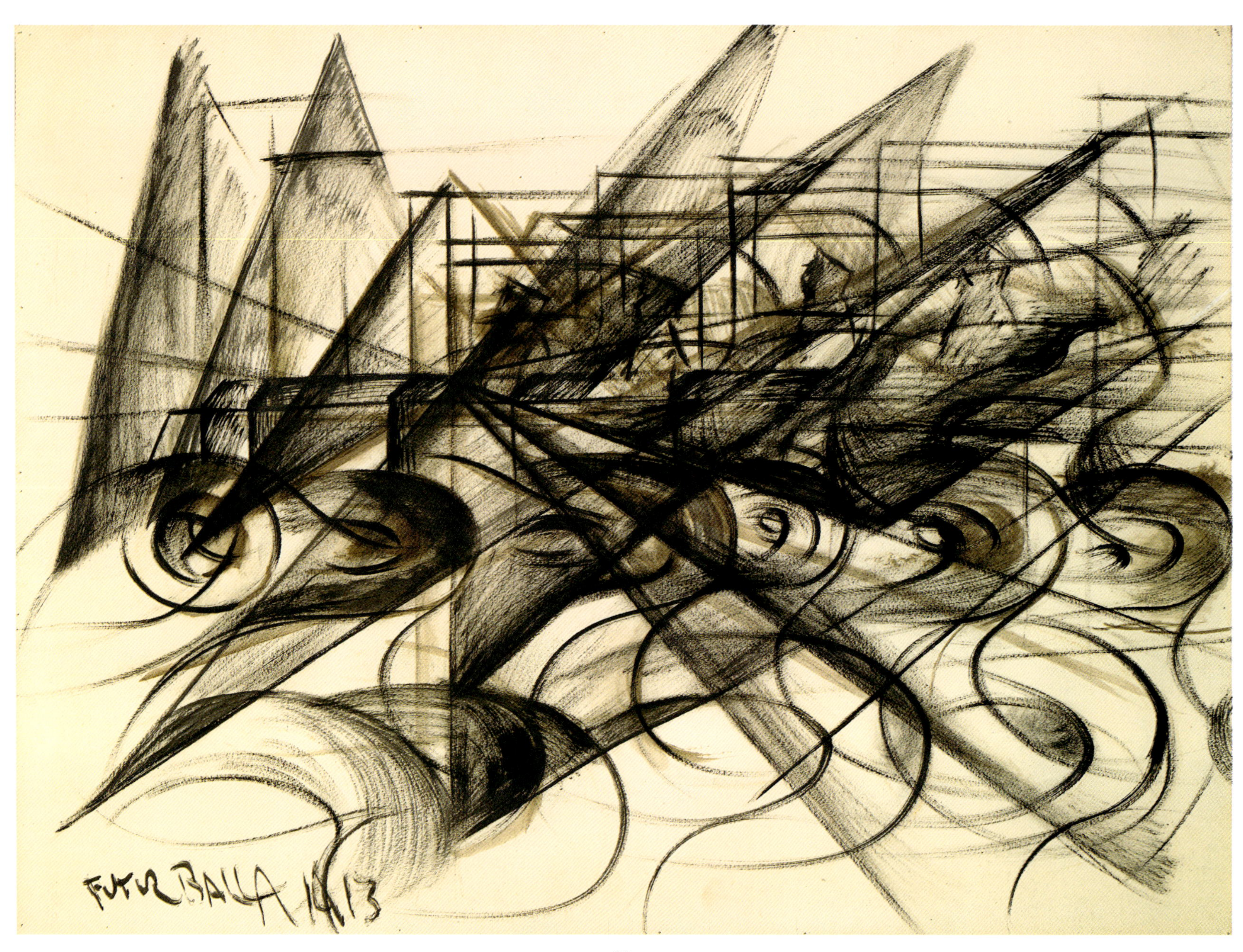

60

Automobile + velocità + luce (Car + Speed + Light), 1913
watercolour and sepia on paper, 67 x 88.5 cm

6. Étienne-Jules Marey
Uomo che cammina (*Man Walking*), 1890–91
chronophotograph

7. Étienne-Jules Marey
Sviluppo lineare di uomo in corsa con strisce bianche e nere (*Linear Development of Man Running with Black and White Stripes*), c. 1882, from "La station physiologique de Paris", in *La Nature*, 11 (2), 1883, p. 277

yet the house in front of us fits into the solar disk. [...] The sixteen people around you in a rolling motor bus are in turn and at the same time one, ten, four, three; they are motionless and they change places; they come and go, bound into the street, are suddenly swallowed up by the sunshine, then come back and sit before you, like persistent symbols of universal vibration. [...] The construction of pictures has hitherto been foolishly traditional. Painters have shown us the objects and the people placed before us. We shall henceforward put the spectator in the centre of the picture."[7]

These words are from the second manifesto that Balla signed, carried away by almost childlike passion, as though he glimpsed the beginning of rebirth in them. As though he had grasped the truly revolutionary spirit of the assertions and felt that the time had come to detach the image definitively from its outline, as he had already attempted in 1905 with *La pazza*, one of the figures in the polyptych *I viventi*. And as he was to attempt again in the three new major paintings with the aim of attaining fusion between the elements of the painting and reality. In the *Dinamismo di un cane al guinzaglio* the border of the sketch-like outline seems to repeat the sound of the heels on the ground in the alternation peculiar to the gait. In *La mano del violinista* the frame contains a further division. Inside the rectangular space marked out, an isosceles trapezium turned upside-down with the short side as its base expands the acoustic resonance of the vibrations of the bow on the strings of the instrument, synchronized in a pre-established temporal sequence. In *Bambina che corre sul balcone* the steps of his daughter Luce along a horizontal axis are cadenced in accordance with schematic diagrams of progressive movement along a spatial line that continues beyond the frame. Balla unquestionably knew the work of Marey (figs. 6-7) and his truly scientific view of the more empirical experiments of his contemporary Muybridge (figs. 8-9). Movements in sequence of every kind – often recorded by the former with the aid of a rifle equipped with viewfinder and lens of his own invention (fig. 10) – prompted painstaking examination of the relationship between the object and its condition in space in a time susceptible of capture on film. Chronophotography, the stroboscope and the kinetoscope,[8]

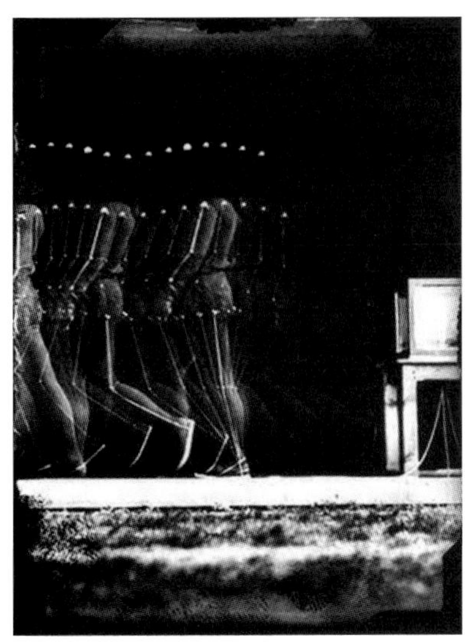

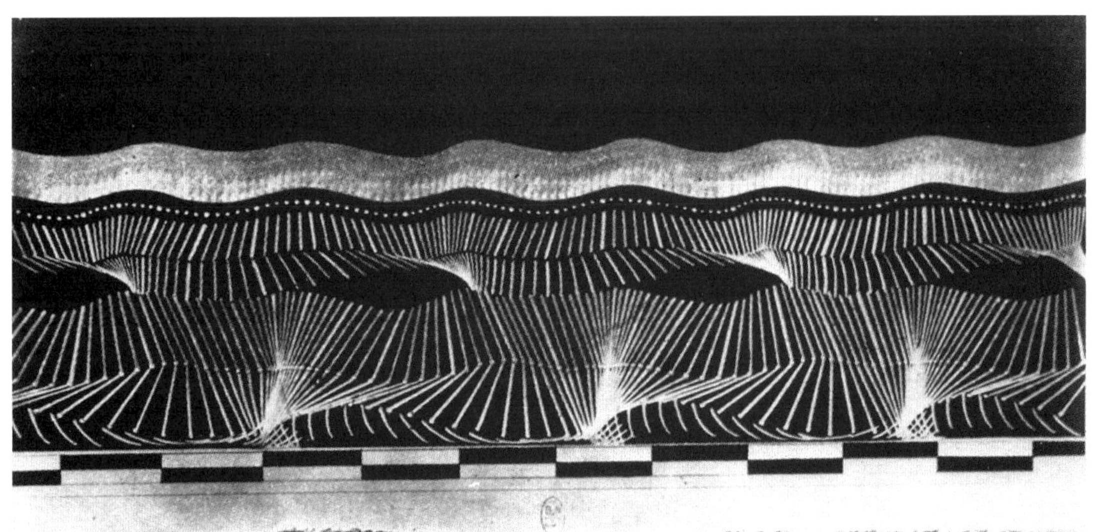

61

Espansione dinamica + velocità
(Dynamic Expansion + Speed), 1913
paint on paper mounted on canvas, 65.6 x 108.5 cm

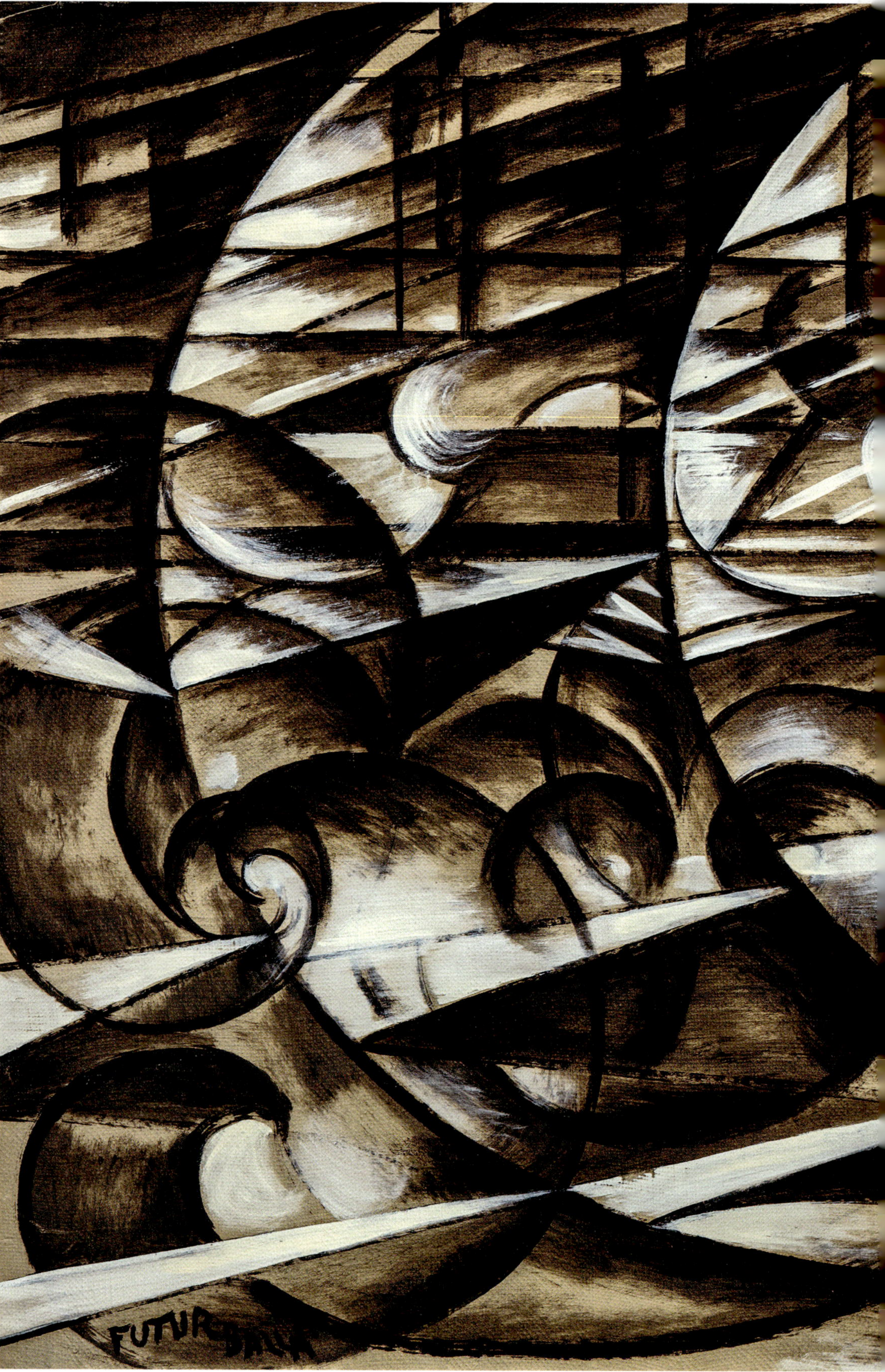

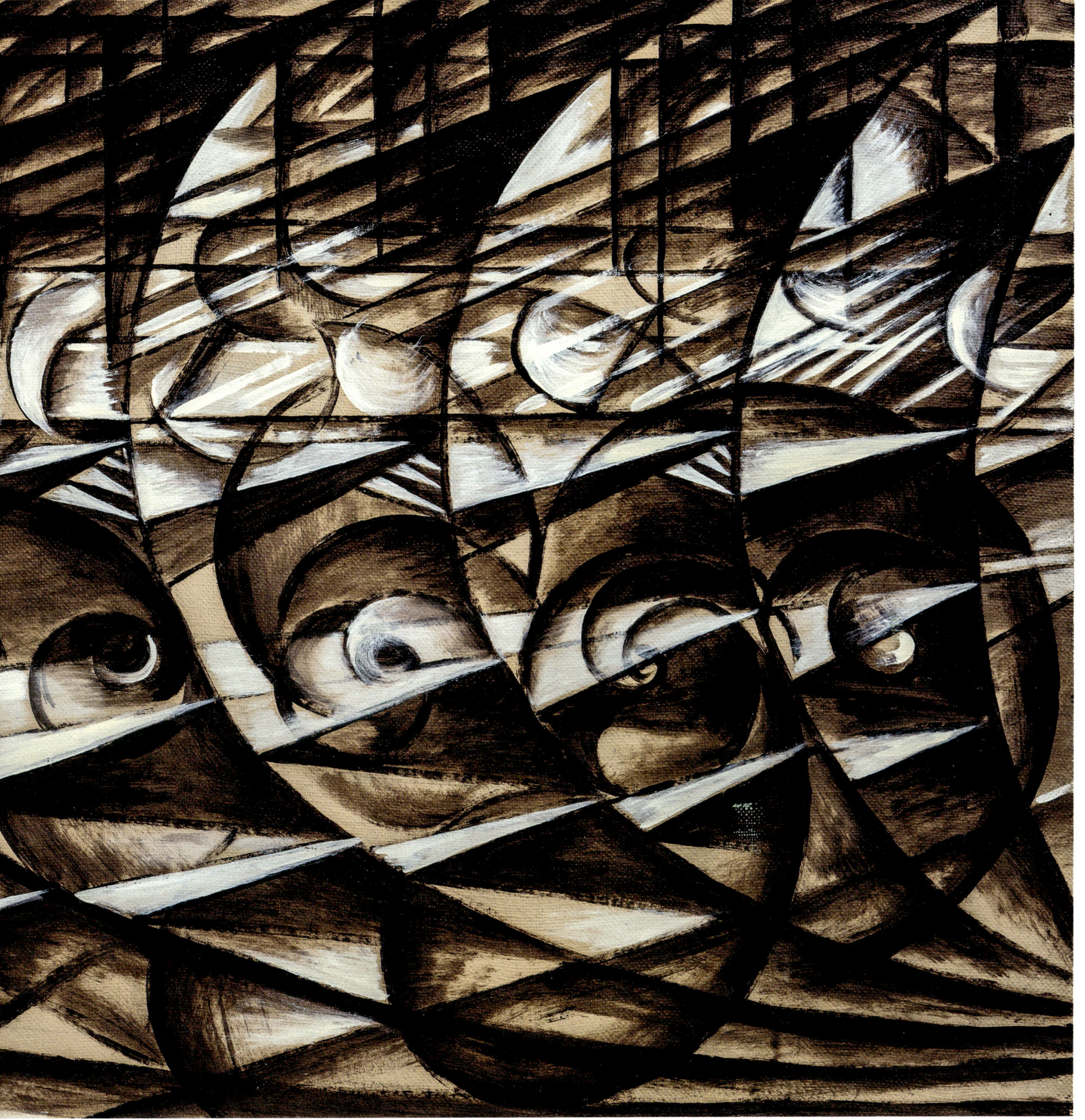

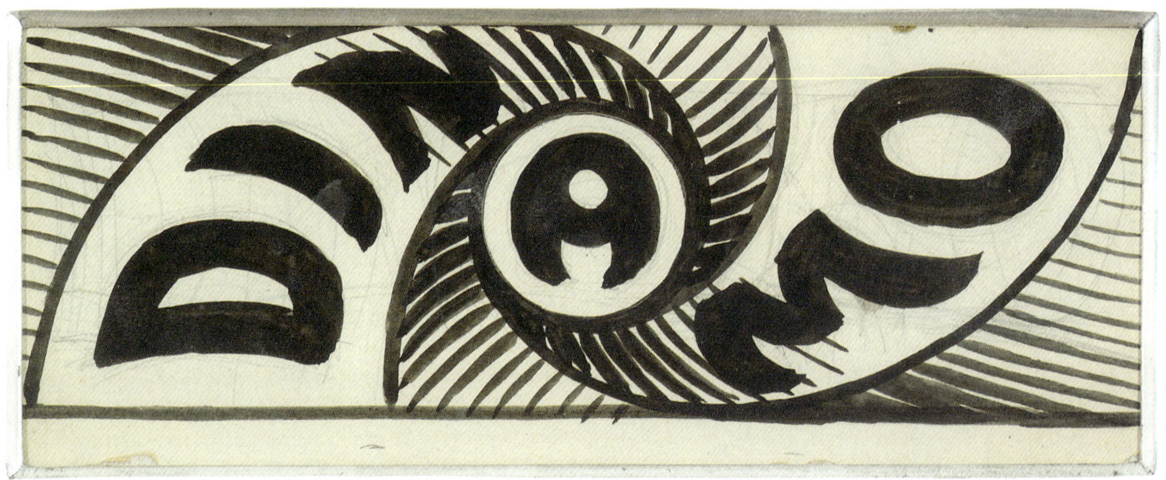

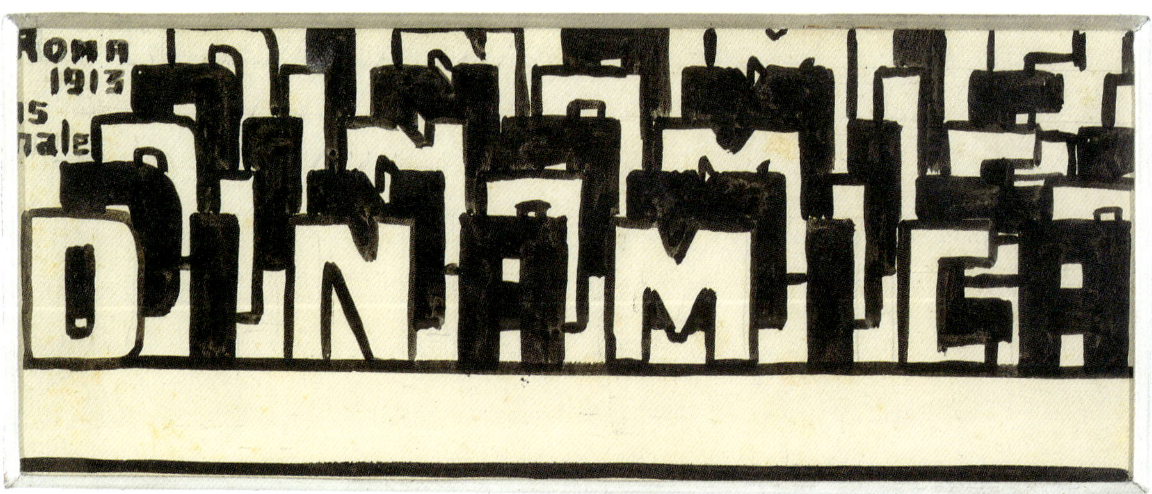

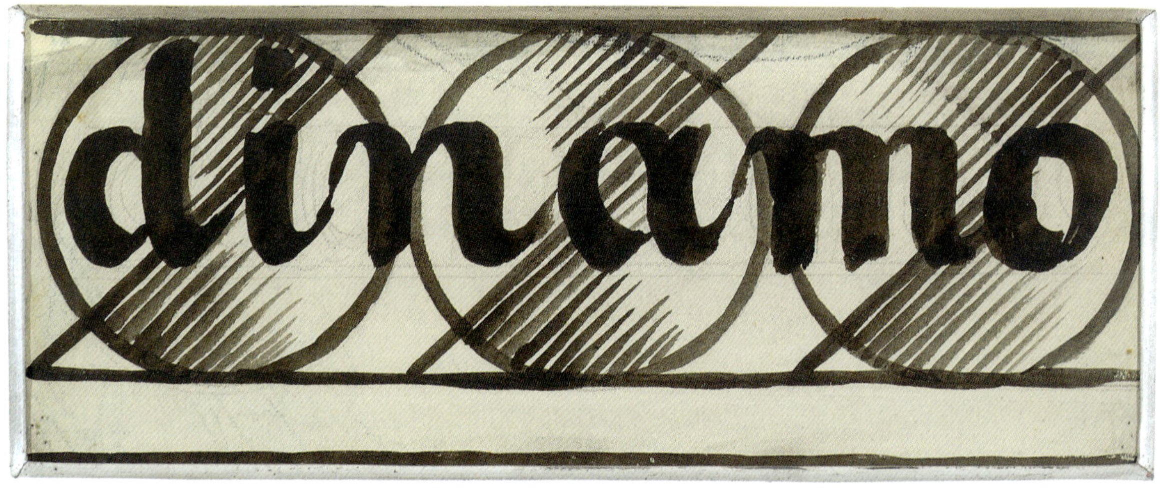

62

Studi per Dinamo – Dinamica
(Studies for Dynamo – Dynamics), 1913
India ink on paper, 12.5 x 30 cm; 12 x 30 cm ; 12.5 x 30 cm

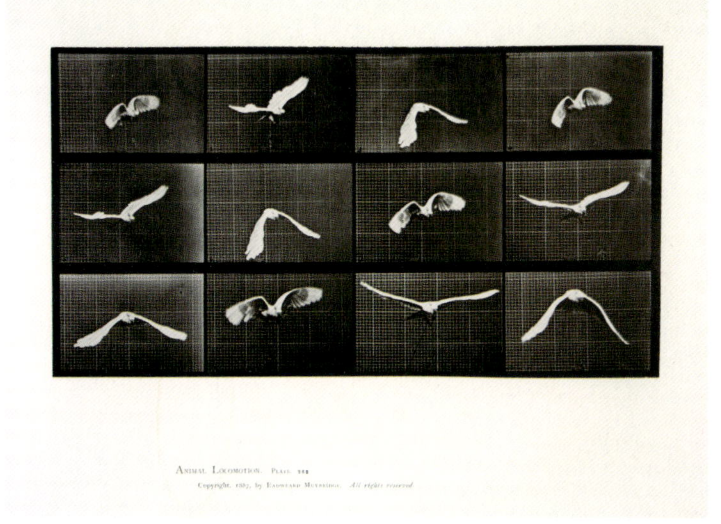

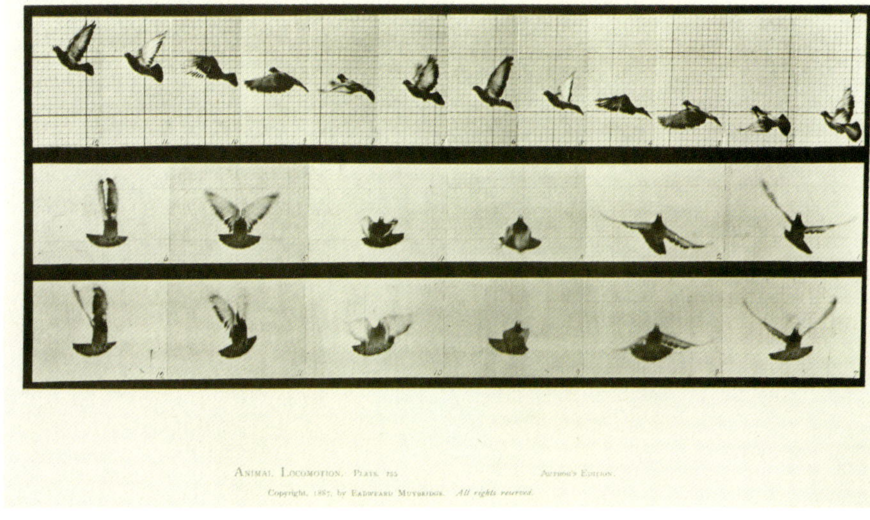

8. Eadweard Muybridge
Sequenza di uccelli in volo (*Sequence of Birds in Flight*), 1883–86 chronophotograph

9. Eadweard Muybridge
Birds in Flight, from *Animal Locomotion: an electro-photographic investigation of consecutive phases of animal movements, 1872-1885*, University of Pennsylvania, Philadelphia 1872–85, XI, pl. 755, 1887

the first experiments and equipment for the projection of images in motion, means making it possible to expand or contract the field of vision, pick out, isolate and repeat a detail and moreover – for a painter – to experiment with transparency and superimposition, to imagine a dimension of the imperceptible, of another visibility. Is this not perhaps one of the reasons why Balla described himself as an "intuitive transcendental man" with a "green, violet-facetted" chromatic timbre and semicircular flaws in a summary, pared-down linear form?

Balla thus appears to have followed two paths with perseverance in this particular year of frenzied and impetuous experimentation. On the one hand, the dissection of phenomena in ever greater depth all the way to their essence led him to reproduce the patterns published in the sphere of photographic research, which we can see underlying the *Bambina che corre sul balcone*, especially if the chromatic dimension is disregarded. A certain number of sketches, including the study on a sheet in the *Compenetrazioni* notebook, attests to his stubborn determination to allow the expression of the constituent principles of Futurism to emerge, combining the ideas about movement with those on energy and light, the primary source and absolute synthesis of spiritual purity. On the other, this subjective, subjective-abstract, subjective-mnemonic, "intuitive transcendental" entity represents the imperceptible substructure of a simple but at the same time complex mind, of a spirit that transforms emotions and feelings into images, that traces being and becoming back to a single principle. The two aspects overlap to create a highly singular coincidence of place between conscious and unconscious in figuration initially distinguished by the imprint of reality, which appeared in the works of the following years with a different and apparently opposite significance. Ghosts of what once was, of what is past, the memory of love and the furrows of sorrow are traces of

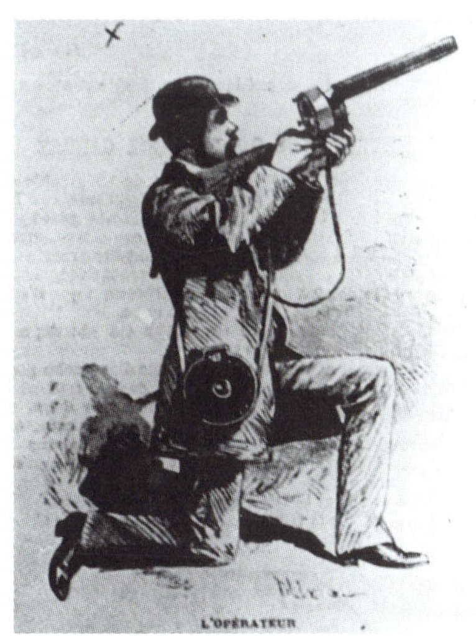

10. Étienne-Jules Marey with his chronophotographic gun in Naples in 1882

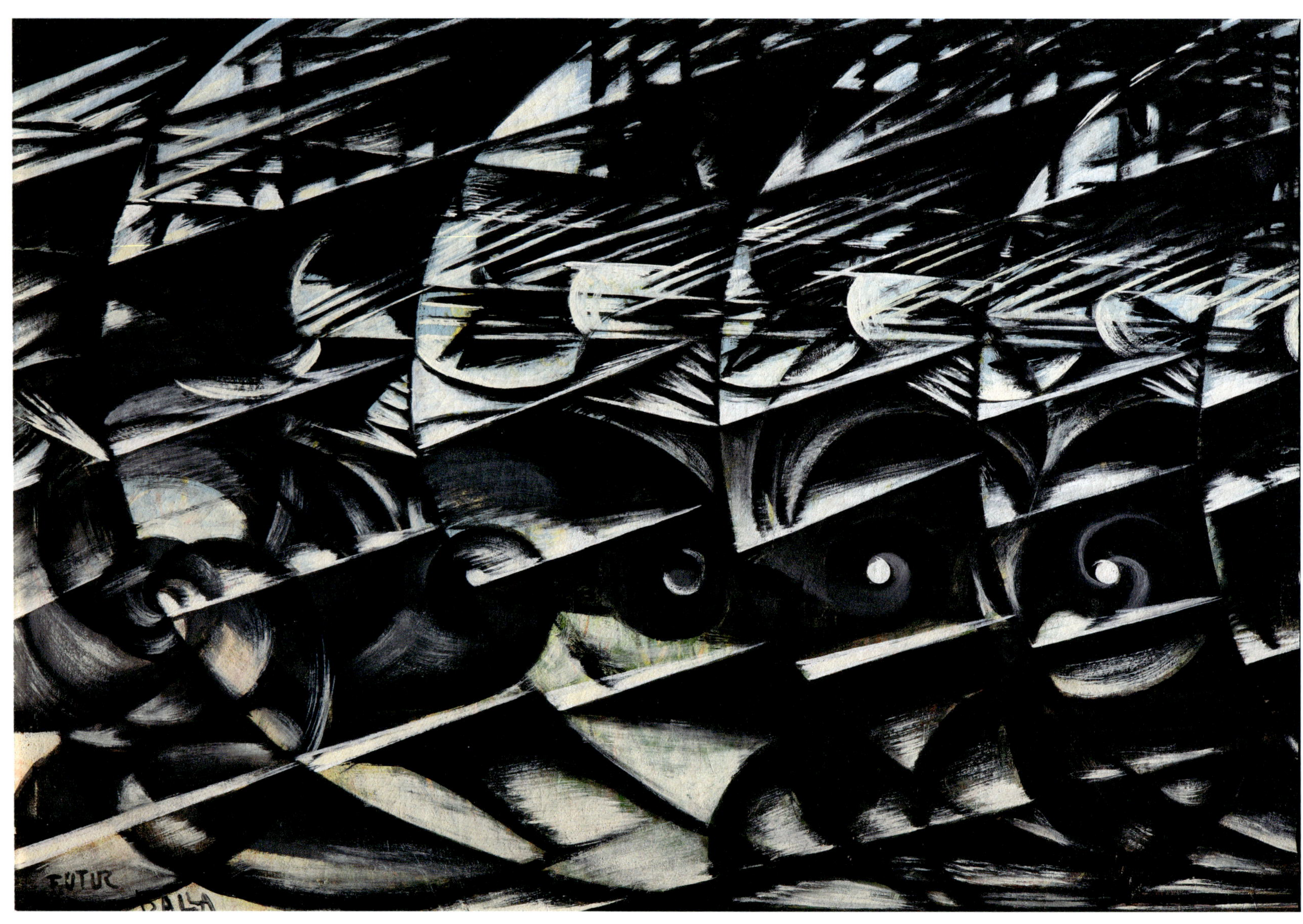

63

Velocità astratta (Abstract Speed), 1913
oil on canvas, 78 x 108 cm

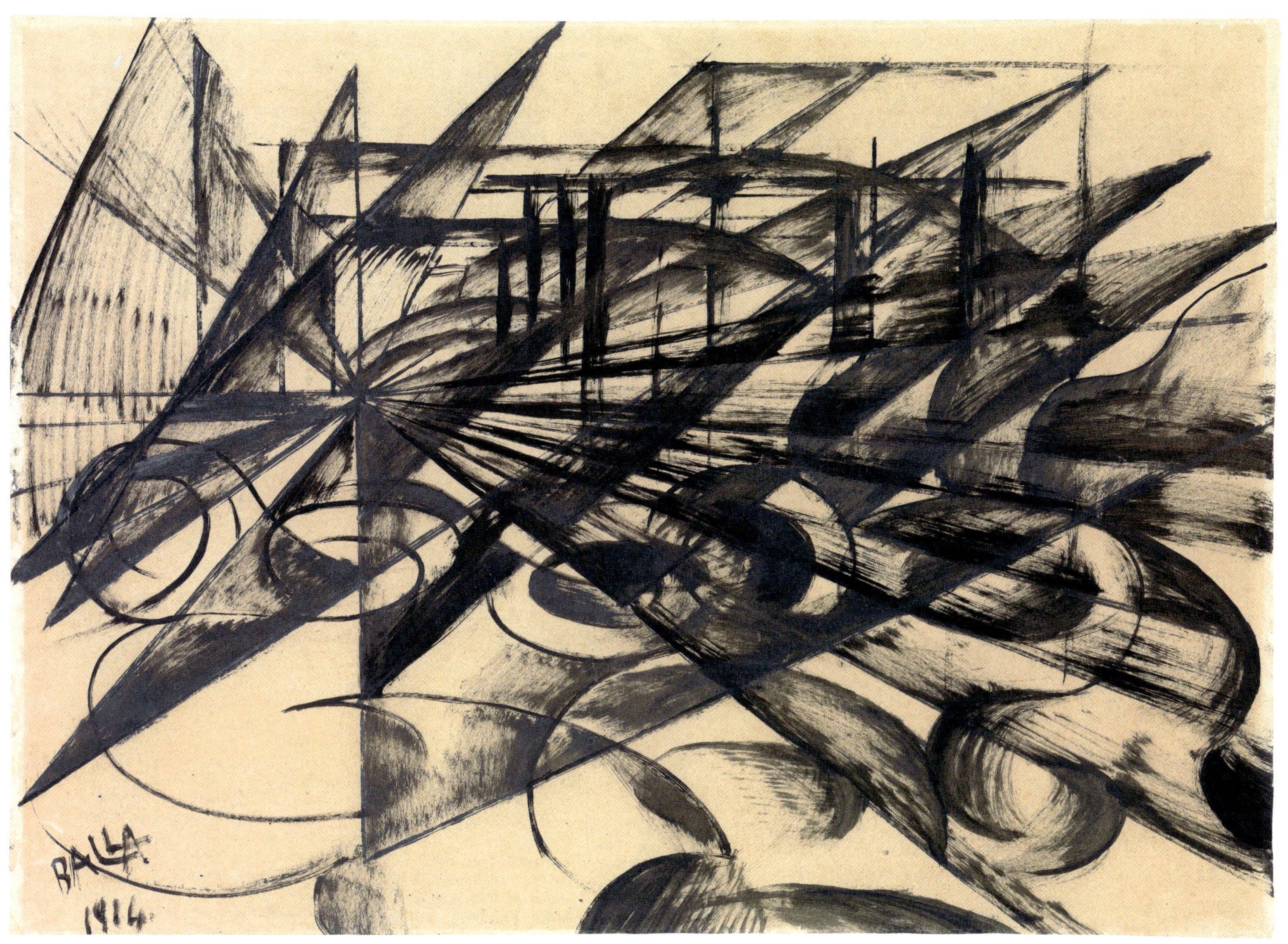

64

Automobile in corsa (Speeding Automobile), 1914
tempera and India ink on paper mounted on canvas,
53.8 x 73.3 cm

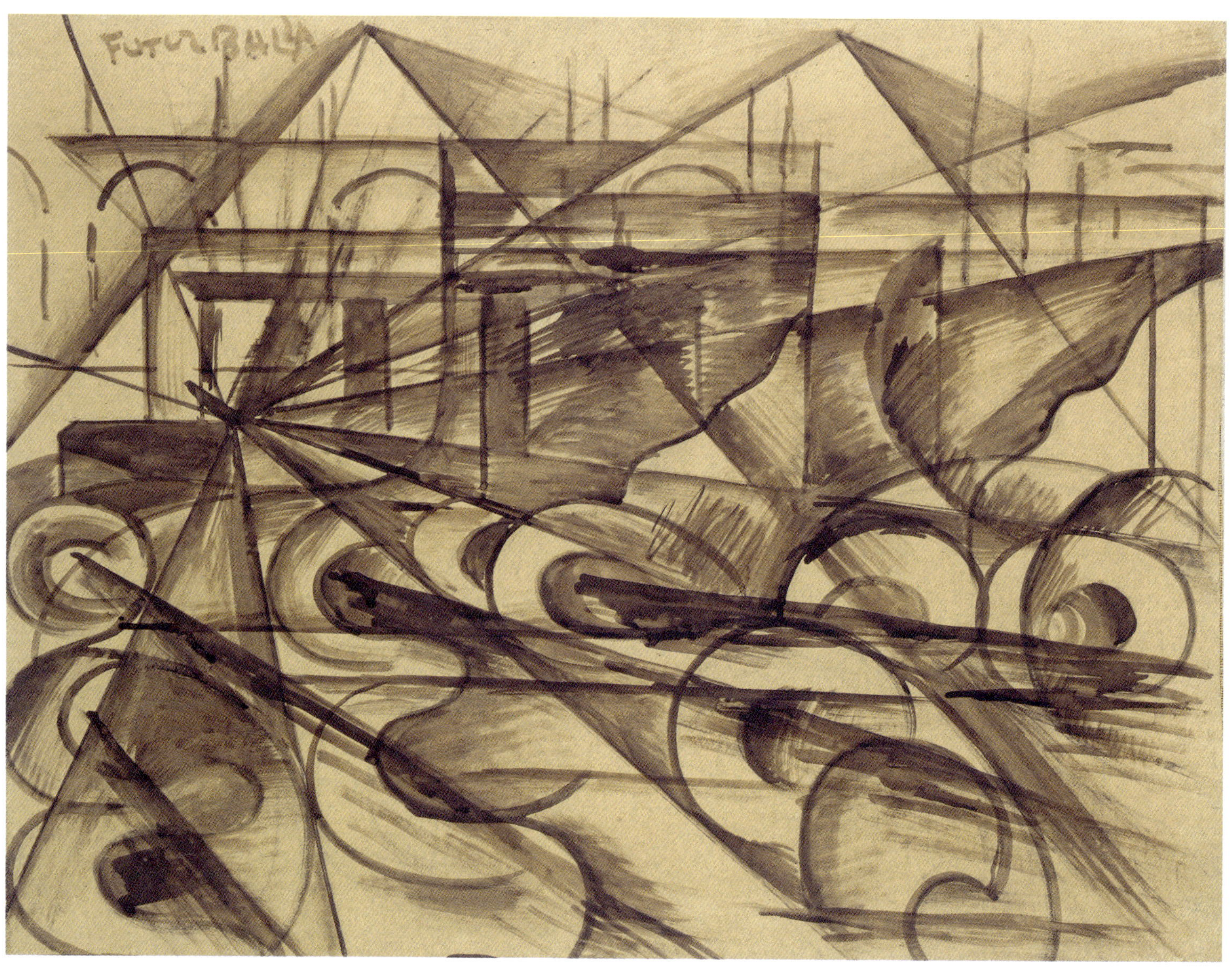

65

Velocità d'automobile (velocità n. 1)
(Automobile Speed – Speed no. 1), 1913
ink wash on mounted paper, 46.5 x 60 cm

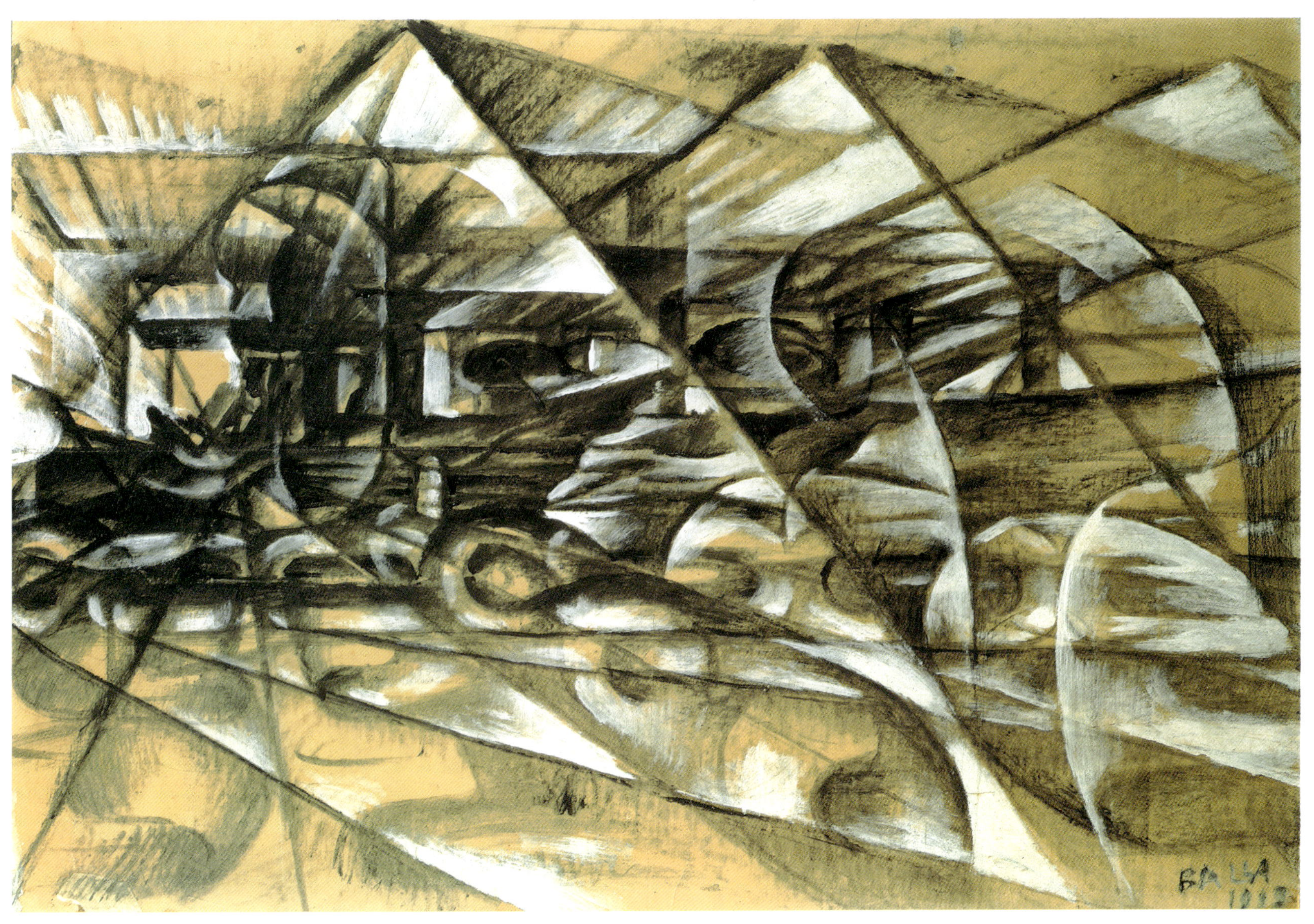

66

Velocità di automobile (Automobile Speed), 1913
oil on paper mounted on cardboard, 64.7 x 93.8 cm

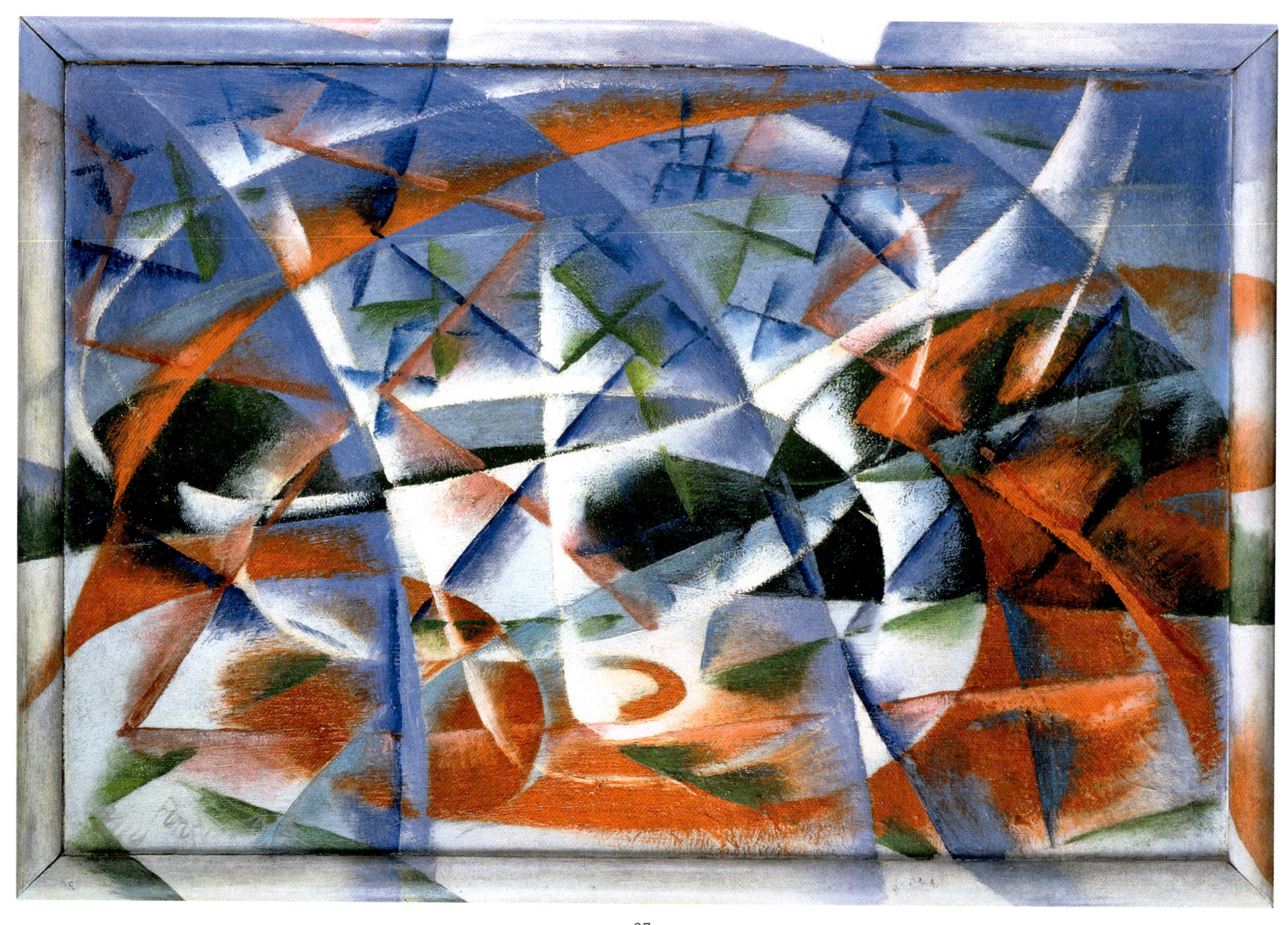

67

Velocità astratta + rumore (Abstract Speed + Sound),
1913–14
oil on board, 54.5 x 76.5 cm

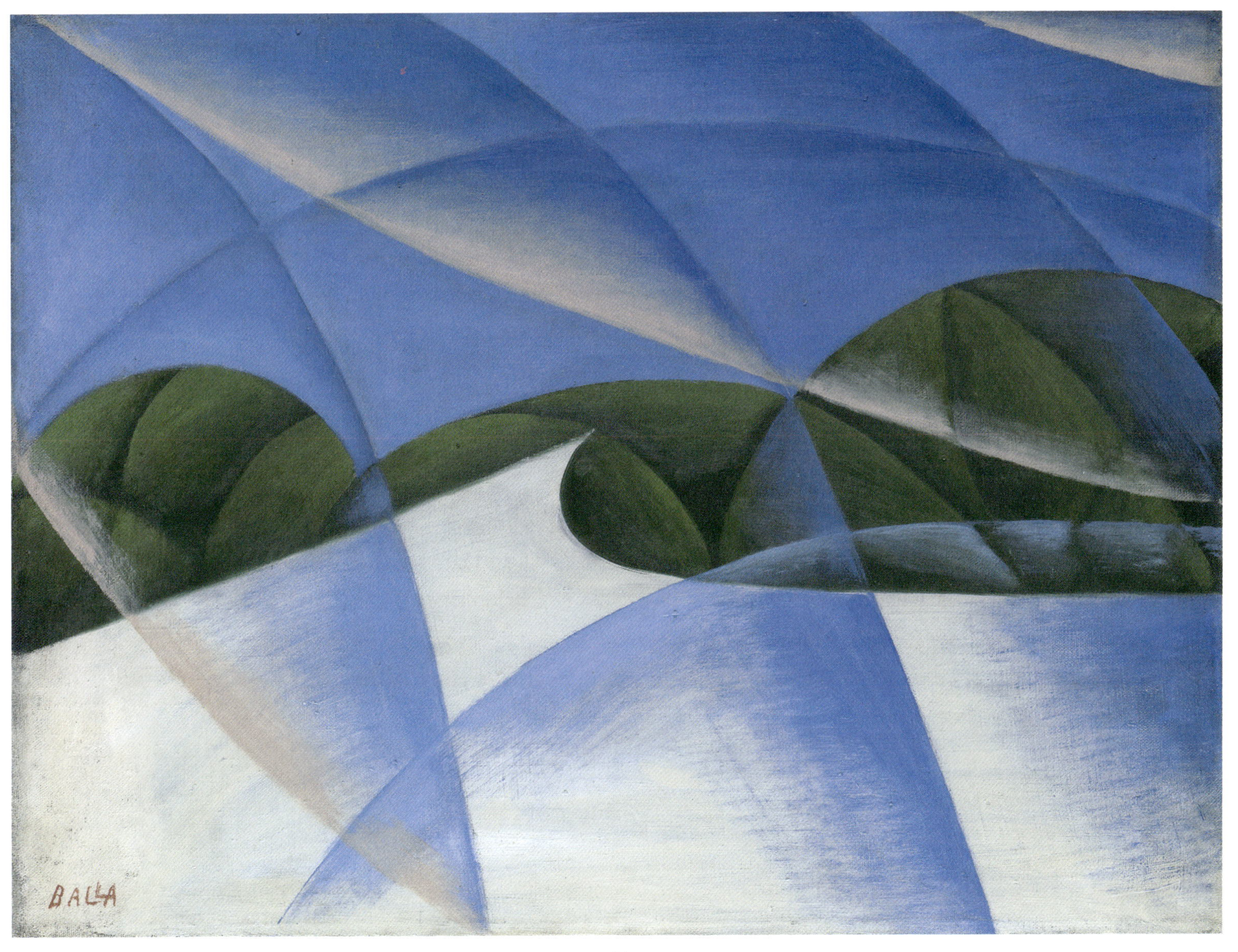

68

Velocità astratta – L'auto è passata
(Abstract Speed – The Car Has Passed), 1913
oil on canvas, 50.2 x 65.4 cm

a passage, an apparition. The not immediately perceptible psychic dimension is the measure of an impulse towards every form of the universe governed by instinctive curiosity about the systematic nature of scientific thought and its laws. Among the philosophical schools of a scientific cast, opposed to the Kantian approach, the anti-dogmatic epistemological investigations of Ernst Mach into the theoretical foundations of physics were crucial in those years in the formulation of a concept of abstraction. Fundamental theses that underpinned Albert Einstein's speculations on relativity, the subject of impassioned debate on the relationship between philosophy and science, of arguments involving disciplines of every kind. As Robert Musil, the future "man without qualities", wrote in 1908 in his doctorate thesis on Mach's theories, "The multiple application in the most general way possible of the laws of nature to factual, concrete cases becomes possible only by means of the abstraction, simplification, schematization and idealization of facts and the mental decomposition of the same into simple elements that can be used to reconstruct and recompose the given facts mentally with sufficient precision. These elements of idealized, elementary facts, which are never perfectly encountered in reality, are the uniform and uniformly accelerated motion of mass, the stationary (immutable) electrical and thermal current, the current of uniformly increasing and decreasing intensity, and so on."[9] How then could the echoes, albeit simplified and popularized, of scientific-gnoseological studies, arguments and demonstrations fail to arouse interest and the desire for knowledge if the ramifications of these ideas extended in that precise period even to everyday life and politics, dragging into the debate also a figure like Lenin at the height of his ideological fervour?

The theoretical formulations of Albert Einstein had unquestionably revolutionized knowledge about the nature of the universe as from 1905. In an attempt to understand and interpret the objective phenomena of reality not simply through the cold, empirical exposition of abstract data, ruling out the idea of empty space, Einstein hypothesized a space capable of interaction with matter. But while his discovery turned the understanding of space and time upside-down, other inventions also had an incredible impact on the culture of the period: the research on electromagnetic and radio waves, the discovery of X rays (Wilhelm Röntgen) and the radioactivity of uranium (Henri Becquerel), the investigation of the atom and its composition (Ernest Rutherford) and the work on energy (Max Planck). This radical change altered the very way of referring to objective reality in terms that are also obviously philosophical, as demonstrated by Edmund Husserl's phenomenology and Henri Bergson's work on perception and memory. The customary schemata were jettisoned along with merely intellectual methods.

11. Giacomo Balla
Velocità astratta (*Abstract Speed*), 1913
Turin, Pinacoteca Giovanni e Marella Agnelli

12. Giacomo Balla
Marcia su Roma (*The March on Rome*)
(painting on the back of *Velocità astratta*, 1913), 1931–32
Turin, Pinacoteca Giovanni e Marella Agnelli

While Balla never really got to grips with these theses, he did perceive their revolutionary importance and entered an extraordinarily fascinating universe by virtue of his spontaneous inclination, the attraction he felt for the exact and esoteric sciences, his intuitive grasp of the phenomena of reality and the assimilated thrust of Futurism. Light and movement became the expression of an overall analysis and unique synthesis: "Going beyond the cinematic form too, I embarked on idealist and abstract painting."[10] From pure experience in an ascending trajectory, 1913 saw the commencement of a series of works in which Balla, taking into account the suggestions of Boccioni and Marinetti, began to break away from an idea of fragmented temporality to involve all the surrounding reality in his act and the action of the subject (figs. 11-12). The compositional framework of the first depictions of speeding automobiles thus insists on the form of the elements from which the motion derives, capturing its essential lines and properties. Filtering the image of its corporeality – the automobile chassis and wheel, then the silhouette of a swallow in flight – to the point of complete distillation was a process carried out in successive stages. In a succession of sequences (studies, sketches and paintings), not the simple repetition of an iconographic model but a serial process capable of penetrating the intrinsic meaning of a primary motion so as to capture the very nature of the dynamic form and rise from the simple detail to the divine and absolute intuition of the universe. The reduction of the surface into geometric lines, diagonals, curves and patterns now cadenced an infinitely multiplied space. The diffraction of light, acoustic resonances and the reflection of volumes towards synthetic lines propagating abstract quantities of energy spread the roar of the mechanical movement of the automobile or the beating of swallows' wings to the point of registering and monitoring a visual vocabulary of wedge-shaped, triangular, arched signs. Vibrant lengths of horizontal, vertical, undulatory development were cap-

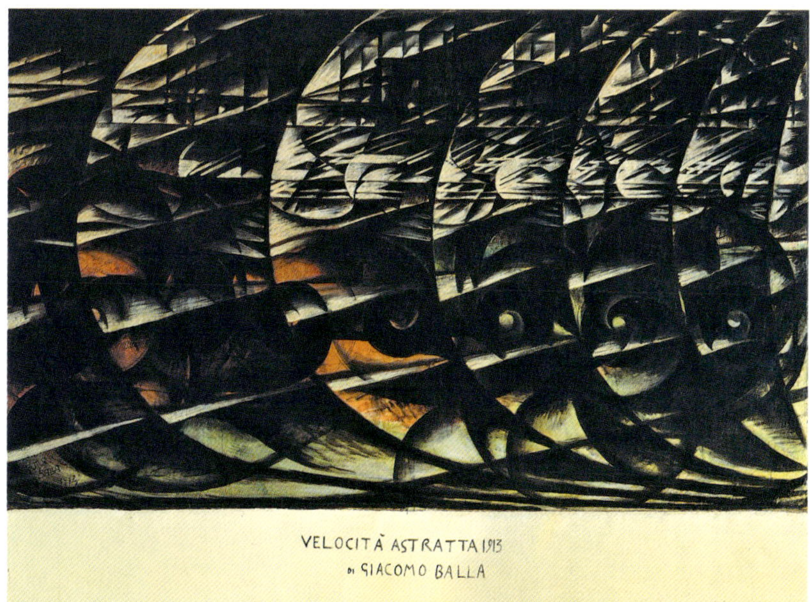

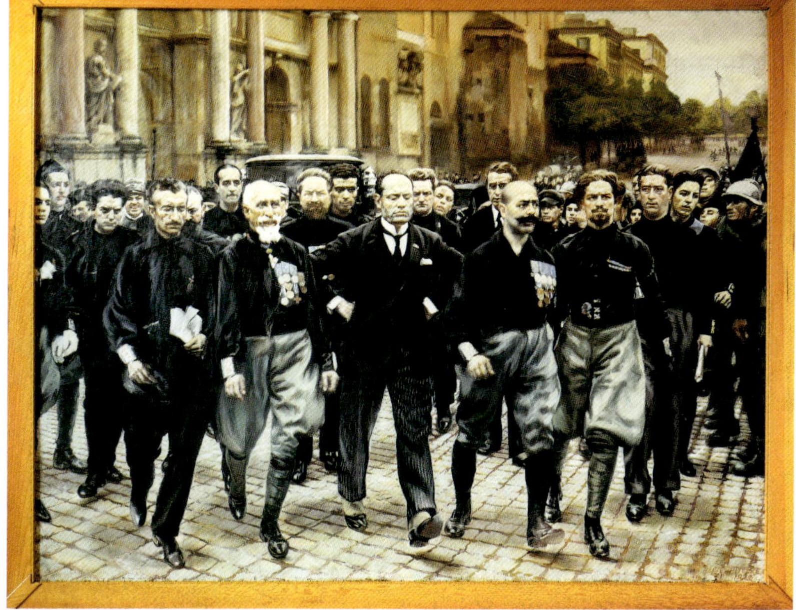

tured on surfaces of paper or canvas, reverberating in the depth of the visual space in an expansion of diffuse energy.

Balla's analyses of photography, light, kinetics and the representation of movement did not lead, however, to a simple linear-progressive multiplication of states of motion. The idea of time as the persistence of changing things, rhythmic spatial succession and image of numerical intervals. In the wake of thought rooted – albeit instinctively – in the becoming of nature to the thought of cyclicity measurable in mathematical quantities susceptible of translation on canvas in sharply defined forms and rhythms, where light is a physical entity but above all the immutable truth of a cosmogony fraught with mystery. The study of the luminous reflections, isolated in the structure of the rigidly two-dimensional plane, was thus an investigation into the decomposition of colour but also a parameter of an eternal dimension. A point of force bringing all the tensions and lines into equilibrium, an impulse for movements that intersect without opposing one another. An essential characteristic also of compositions striving for ever-greater formal reduction: the sense of reality is never refuted, nor are the traces of nature or cosmic temporality eliminated. The image represents the isolated and infinitesimal fragment of a mobile universe and becomes the visible translation of a concept connected with the objectification of the cognitive act. Not reduction but rather the trace of a passage developed in the succession and pauses of bodies or objects divided to the point of being lost in the glare of light in a stylistic dynamism generated by a singular mystical sensibility.

If the experiment drove the Futurists towards the threshold of the impossible, the subject of the succession of movements in space captured the attention of Marcel Duchamp, fervent admirer among other things of Balla's work, especially the *Dinamismo di un cane al guinzaglio*.[11] And the Futurists' beloved conflict between the figurative representation of motion and the resistance of a stationary, two-dimensional surface was something Duchamp resolved only after breaking away from the fixity of the support. As from the *Nude Descending a Staircase* (1912) (fig. 13), he abandoned canvas with an apparently Dadaist gesture and succeeded in transforming dynamic representation into a tangible object. The vision of "instantaneous rest" of the *Bicycle Wheel* (1913) thus contains the idea of the de-multiplication of a form made up of multiple radiuses.

13. Marcel Duchamp
Nude Descending a Staircase No.2
Philadelphia, Philadelphia Museum of Art

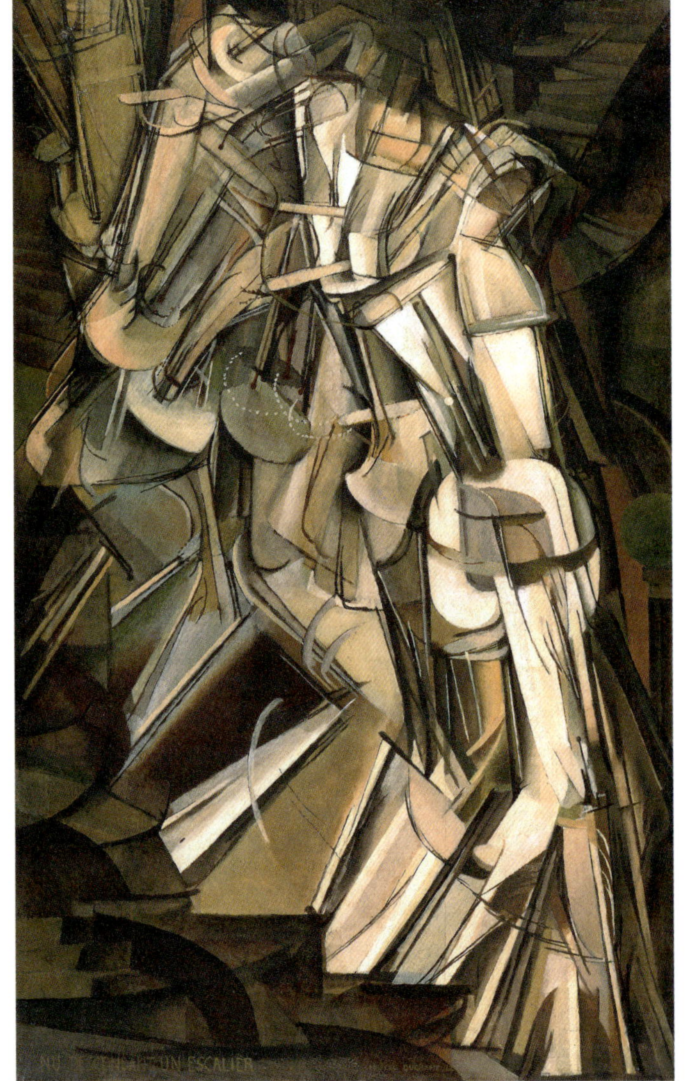

14. Giacomo Balla
Velocità d'automobile (*Automobile Speed*), 1913
New York, The Museum of Modern Art

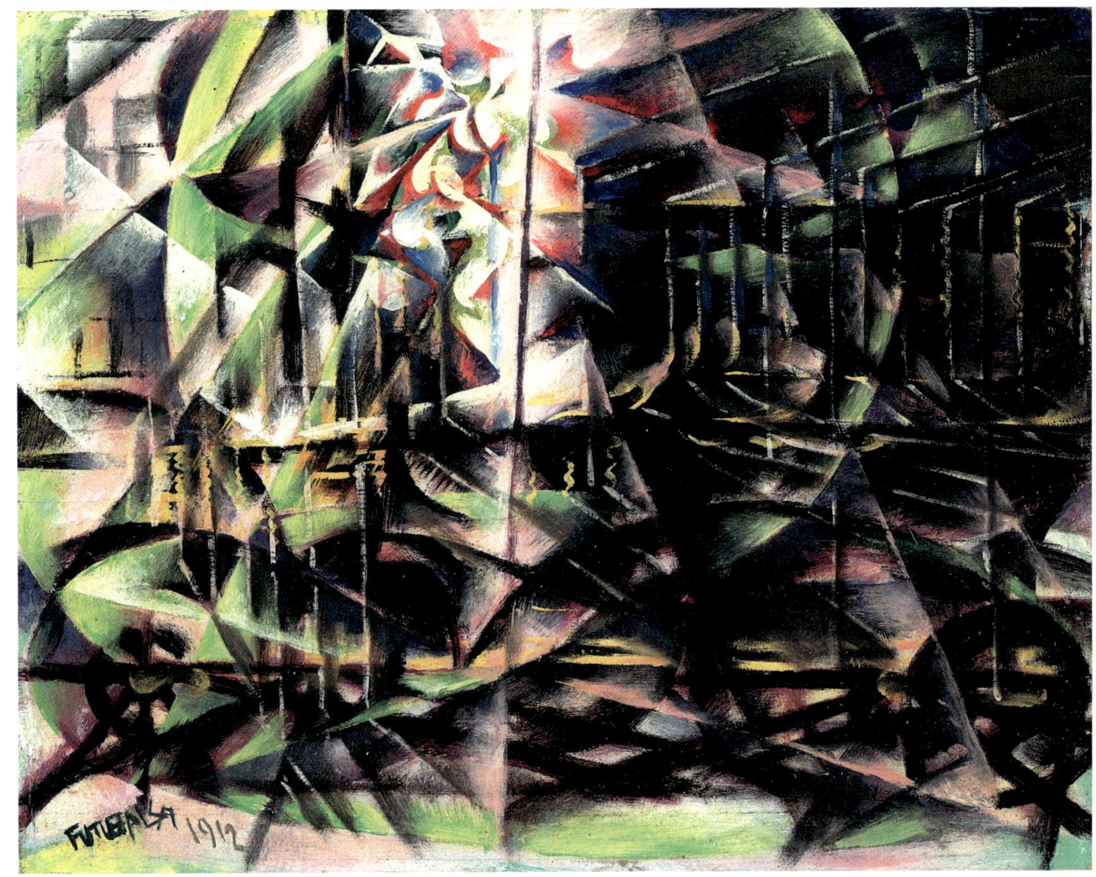

The idea of a set of n + 1 dimensions also lies, however, within that logic. And if the thickness of the wheel conceptually represents the structure of the painting, the dynamic unity is grounded on the idea of frequency. In the succession of motion, the spokes revolving at speed are no longer perceivable and the circular surface becomes a compact area where the line of the radius itself appears to be located on all the points of the circumference simultaneously. In the wake of research into the representation of dynamic motion, the artifice of painting was by now definitively superseded. Duchamp defeated it with an object that simulates its own artifice, thus eliminating the possibility of presenting a form in motion on canvas.

This was not, however, Balla's aim. He was still totally immersed in an aesthetic idea and a morality bound up with the concept of representation. Capturing sounds, colours and lines in motion as a synaesthetic verification of painting, the depiction of new wholes and representation of the world. A world constructed by means of selective vision that identifies the primary causes of sensible reality like a powerful lens aimed at the intersections, the spatial grafts, the apparition of the image in the spectral interval of the visible. The emblematic vision of the infinitesimal, molecular perception of the cosmos, a vision en-

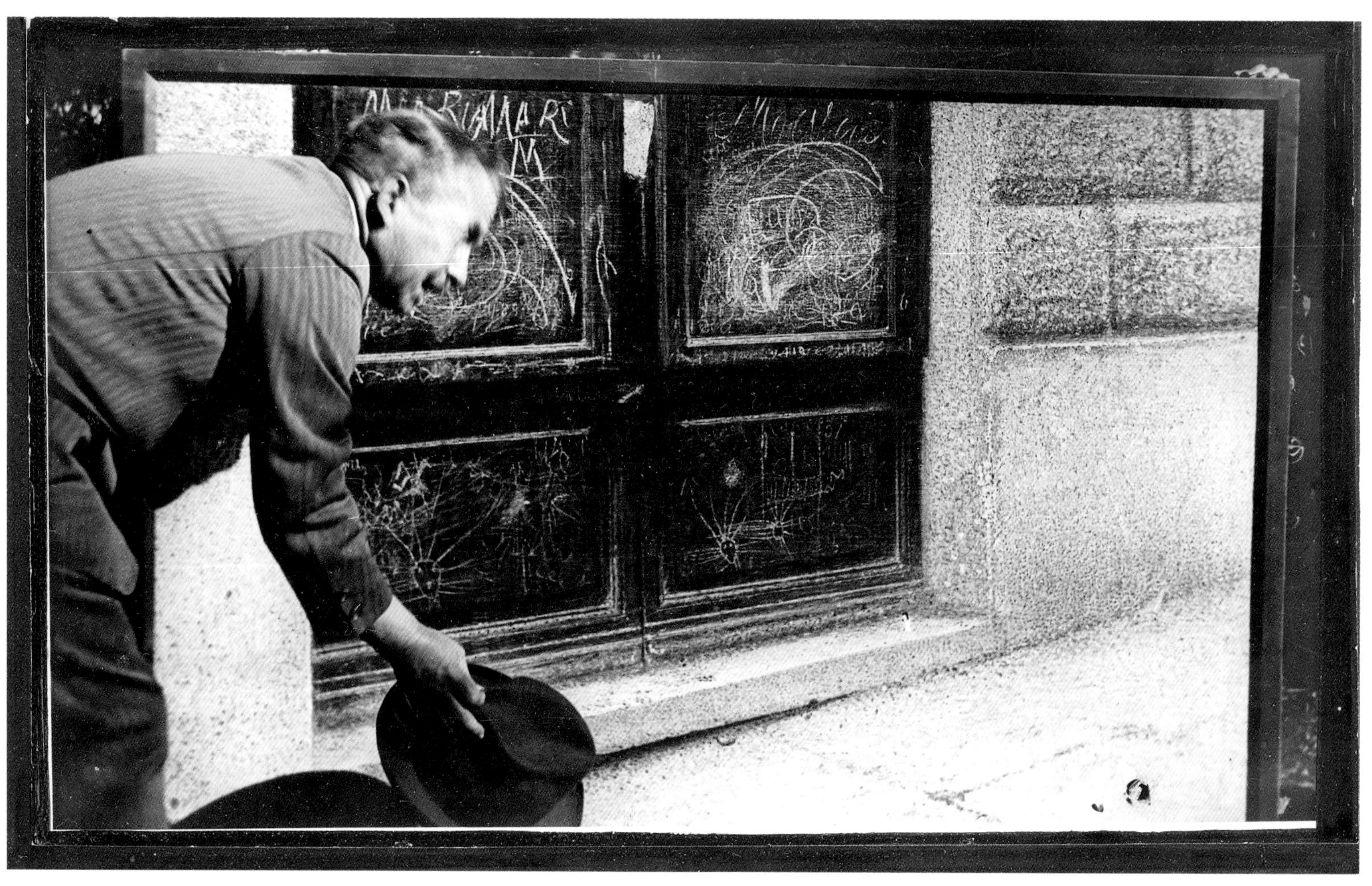

69

Antonio Fornari
Giacomo Balla davanti a Fallimento
(Giacomo Balla in front of Bankruptcy), c. 1919
photographic print, 13 x 20 cm

larged by the lenses of the binoculars already placed on the window sill in Düsseldorf, which delimits the boundaries of an investigation capable of representing luminous impulses and stimuli, of separating the colours of the prismatic spectrum while rhythmically developing the concept of extension in space. Through this diaphragm Balla perceives the meaning of a quantitative dimension, the signs of a close-up transparency where the extremes of the imperceptible and the sensible are still filtered through the artifice of painting (fig. 14).

"*The Works of the Late Balla Are on Sale Here* … Freed from the burden of experience, fame and all his works, restored to virginity, imbued with faith, as fresh as the freshest daisy, happy and freshly laundered, he began in the middle of a huge, empty, snow white room to draw on sheets of paper the first lines of a speeding automobile, initially objective and later synthetic, thc basic foundations of his thought forms."[12] Quoting himself just over a decade after putting all his works of the first period on sale, Balla relived the moment of that simulated and symbolic but very real death.[13] The thought-forms, as he himself called them, were now the echo of images projected and cadenced by the intensity of the waves, emissions and forms of bundles of acoustic transmissions reworked by the brain in visual form through the artist's hand. With the doggedness of a mechanical engineer, one who has observed mechanical and animal dynamism with photographic attention and succeeded in melding in a single representation sound and its peaks, light and its wavelengths and chromatic correspondences in a fascinating array of intersecting analogies. Propagating abstract quantities of energy, synthetic lines now scored the canvas to capture trajectories and parabolas, as in *Volo di rondini* (*Linee andamentali + successioni dinamiche*) (*Flight of Swallows – Paths of Movement + Dynamic Sequences*) (1913). The window, the pane, the gutter and the swallows, all dissected and reworked in the succession of a movement in which even the inanimate elements are infused with energy. Patterns comparable to interpretive models of the physical world but which, unlike other models of abstraction, echo even in the utmost simplification of planes and areas of colour the throb of a higher belief born out of the forms of nature and disseminated through correspondences of sound and light to the point of materialization in "plastic complexes for a Futurist reconstruction of the universe" (1915). Balla's painting was to explode once again from that moment on in the dynamic joy of the states of mind of a universe reinvented in "glowing", "fragrant", "noisy" colours. What prevented him from slipping into empty ornamentalism was the bastion of reality, the beginning and end of painting that was to become figurative once more at the end of the 1920s. Before returning to figuration, however, Balla was to penetrate the mysteries of the universe, extracting numbers and punctuation marks, hermetic figures to be interpreted only by members of a small circle of initiates and visionaries. As he stated in 1911, "I have enjoyed myself for a long time producing impressions of the sky, astronomical paintings. I live up here, almost cut off from Rome, studying by day Villa Borghese, whose spirit I seem to feel vibrate in mine at night in the sky. The constellations have thus taken on for me not only a very marked appearance but also a particular spirit that I understand as full of enchantment and would like to express as best I can on canvas. It is a difficult task but there is too much poetry in the eternal motion of those worlds not to tempt an artist."[14]

[1] See note 8, part I.

[2] Boccioni to Gino Severini, [Milan], 1 January 1913, in *Umberto Boccioni. Gli scritti editi e inediti*, op. cit., pp. 363–64 (where the date is erroneously given as 11 January).

[3] Ibid.

[4] Edizioni futuriste di "Poesia", Milan, 1914.

[5] "Dinamismo", in *Pittura Scultura Futuriste*, Edizioni Futuriste di "Poesia"; now in *Umberto Boccioni – Gli scritti editi e inediti*, op. cit., p. 149.

[6] *Archivi del futurismo*, ed. Maria Drudi Gambillo and Teresa Fiori, 1, De Luca, Rome, 1958–1962, pp. 17–19.

[7] *La Pittura Futurista. Manifesto tecnico* (11 April 1910); now in *Archivi del futurismo*, op. cit., pp. 65–67.

[8] For Balla's prior acquaintance with these new devices at the Paris Expo on 1900, see Giovanni Lista, *La modernità futurista*, op. cit., pp. 42–45.

[9] Robert Musil defended his thesis on the challenge to the foundations of scientific knowledge at the University of Berlin in March 1908. His first novel, *Die Verwirrungen des Zöglings Törleß*, had been published two years earlier.

[10] Enrico Santamaria, "Conversando con Giacomo Balla", in *Griffa*, anno I, no. 10, 15 August 1920; now in *Scritti futuristi*, op. cit., p. 201.

[11] Duchamp attempted unsuccessfully to persuade Katherine Dreier to buy it (but had more success with Malevich's *Knife Grinder*). The painting was bought by the philanthropist and collector Anson Conger Goodyear, founder and first president of the New York Museum of Modern Art from 1929 to 1939. During this decade, probably also on the advice of the museum's director Alfred Barr, Goodyear purchased Balla's *Dinamismo di un cane al guinzaglio*, which he bequeathed to the Albright-Knox Art Gallery in Buffalo, his hometown. The bequest was transformed into a gift in 1964 by his son George.

[12] "Demolizione della casa di Balla", a long note on his career until 1926, the year in which he was forced to leave the house in the Parioli district, in *Balla: le "compenetrazioni iridescenti"*, op. cit., p. 33.

[13] So real that his wife turned to the mayor Nathan in desperation for help to prevent what the family considered an act of madness.

[14] From an interview with Balla by Aymerillot in *L'Alfiere*, II, 15, Rome, 24 January 1911; now in *Scritti futuristi*, op. cit., p. 194.

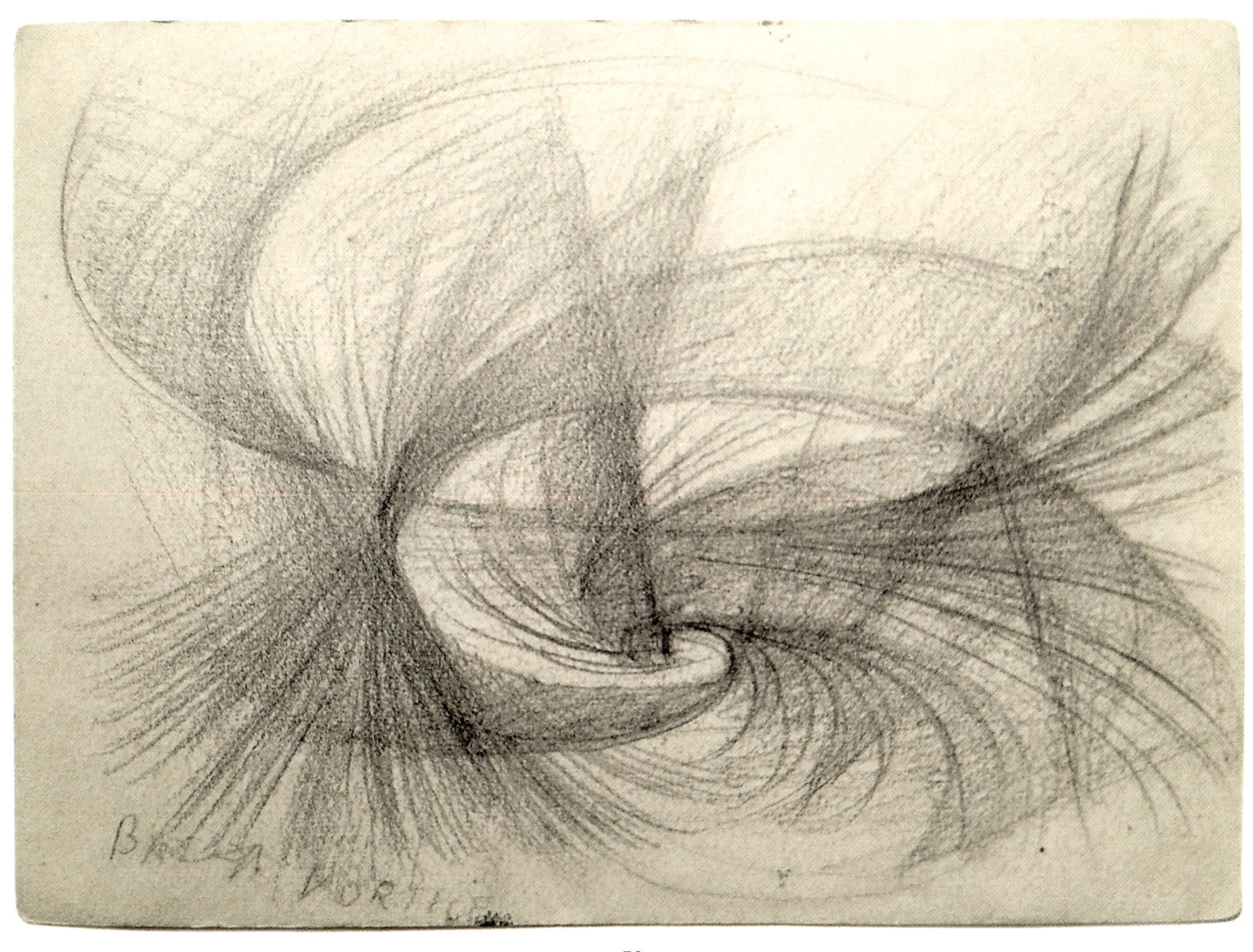

70

Vortice (Vortex), c. 1913
pencil on paper, 13 x 17.7 cm

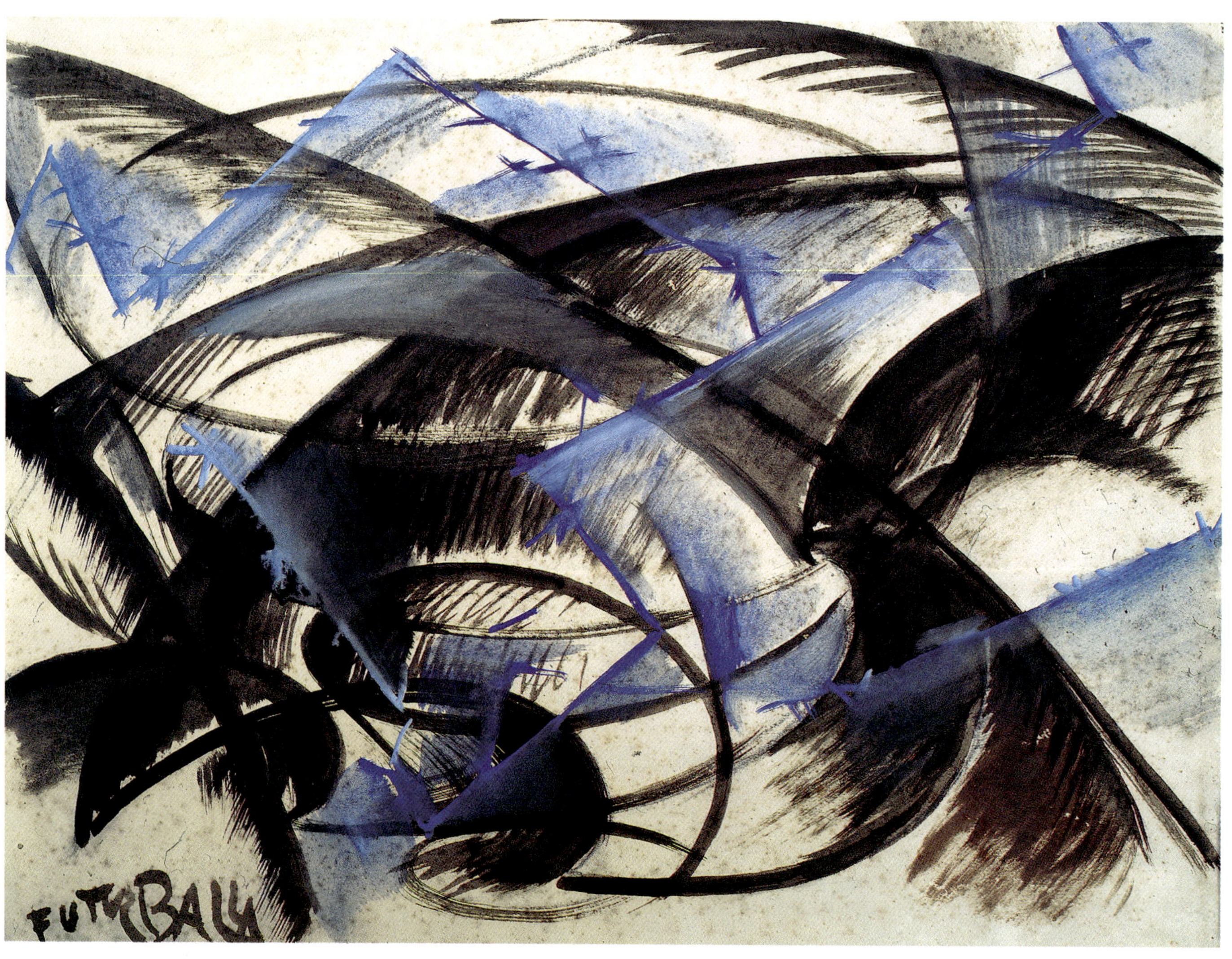

71

Linee di velocità astratta (Lines of Abstract Speed), 1914
tempera and watercolour on paper, 43 x 55.5 cm

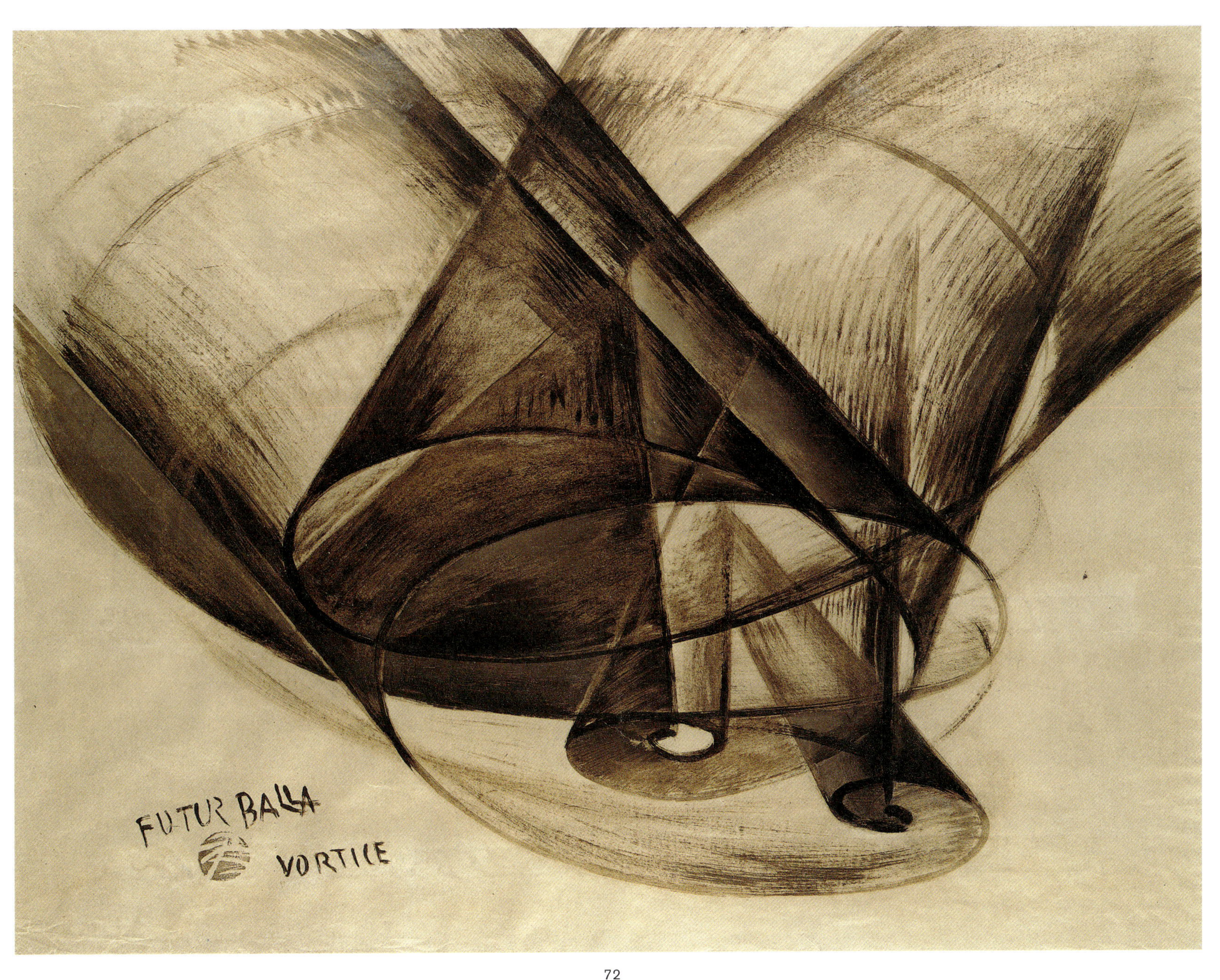

72

Vortice (Vortex), 1914
oil on paper, 65 x 83 cm

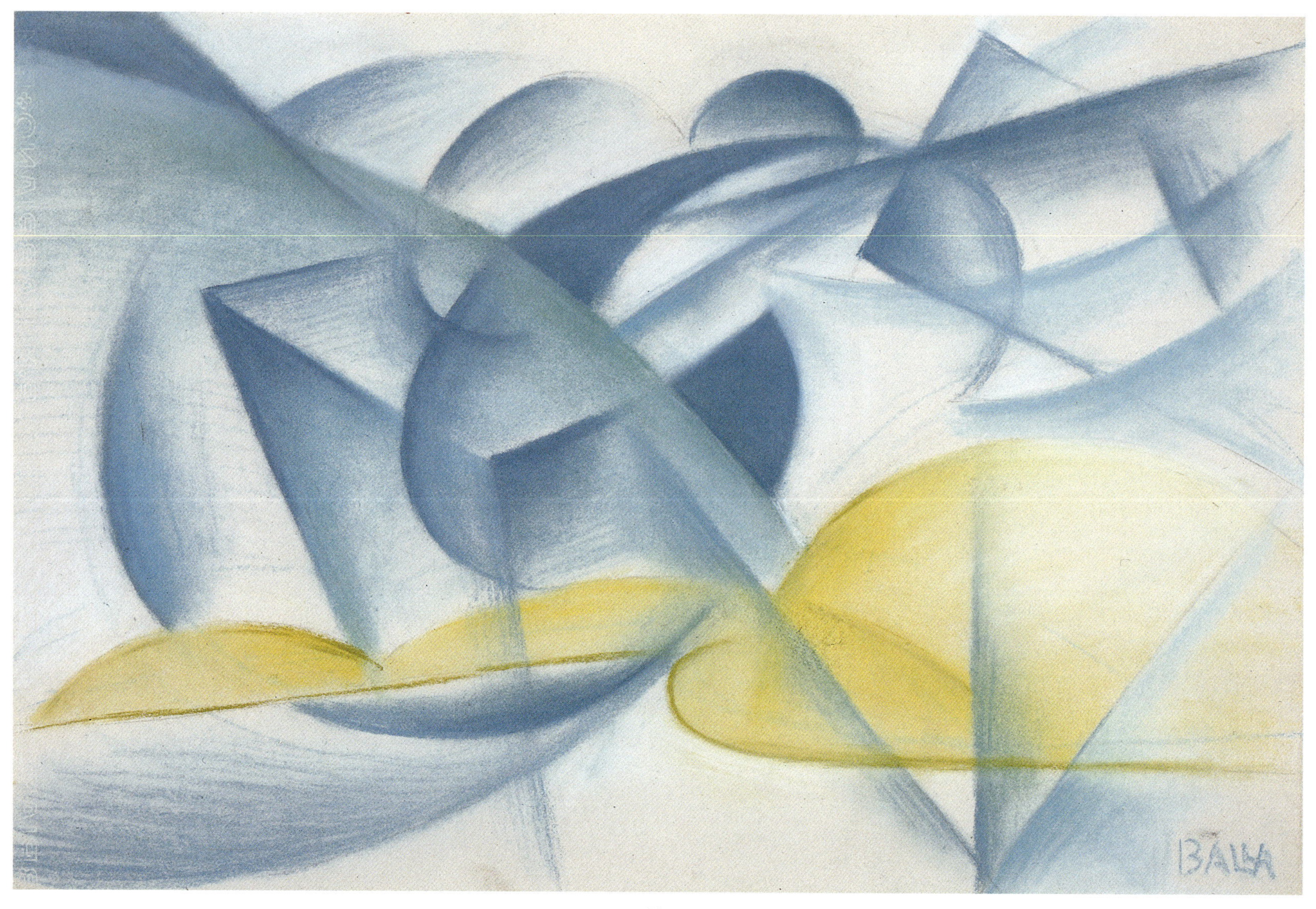

73

Linea di velocità dell'aereo Caproni
(Speed Line of the Caproni Aircraft), 1915
crayon on paper, 40 x 57.5 cm

Reconstructions of the Universe: Balla, Mercury, Einstein

Vincenzo Barone

"We Futurists, Balla and Depero, seek to realize this total fusion in order to reconstruct the universe by making it more joyful, in other words by an integral re-creation. We will give skeleton and flesh to the invisible, the impalpable, the imponderable and the imperceptible. We will find abstract equivalents for all the forms and elements of the universe, and then will combine them according to the caprice of our inspiration, to shape plastic complexes which we will set in motion." The intent expressed in such peremptory terms in the manifesto *Ricostruzione futurista dell'universo* (11 March 1915) (fig. 1) had begun to take shape over the previous years and in particular a few months earlier, at the end of 1914, when Balla produced a dozen paintings and drawings of a celestial phenomenon he had witnessed, namely the transit of the planet Mercury across the Sun late in the morning of 7 November 1914.

Though still in a phase of transition and bearing the signs of the author's Divisionist past, *Mercurio transita davanti al sole* (*Mercury Passing in Front of the Sun*) fully achieves the fusion of "conception and sensation" that Boccioni[1] regarded as the hallmark of Futurist painting. The work constitutes a major milestone on Balla's artistic path, a synthesis of the key themes of previous years as expressed in the series of *Compenetrazioni iridescenti* (*Iridescent Interpenetrations*) and *Velocità astratte* (*Abstract Speeds*). It is, however, the subject of *Mercurio* that concerns us here. Balla's daughter Elica tells us that he took a keen interest in observation of the heavens and popularizing works of astronomy (Schiaparelli and Flammarion being his favourite authors). As she wrote, "The first things he taught me were about astronomy, even before painting. He showed me the steady light of the planets, Venus, Mars, Jupiter and Saturn, constellations like Ursa Major and Ursa Minor, which are useful to find the north star, the wonderful constellation of Orion, Cassiopea, Scorpius, and the brightest suns, like Rigel, Sirius and Arcturus [...] He was fascinated by the mystery of light and life in the starry universe and said that there must be other inhabited worlds because light is the same throughout the universe."[2] Filippo Tommaso Marinetti also remembers his friend "late at night, lying in the Roman countryside, face upwards [...] talking to the constellations, trying to grasp their untranslatable formulae and splendour."[3] As Balla

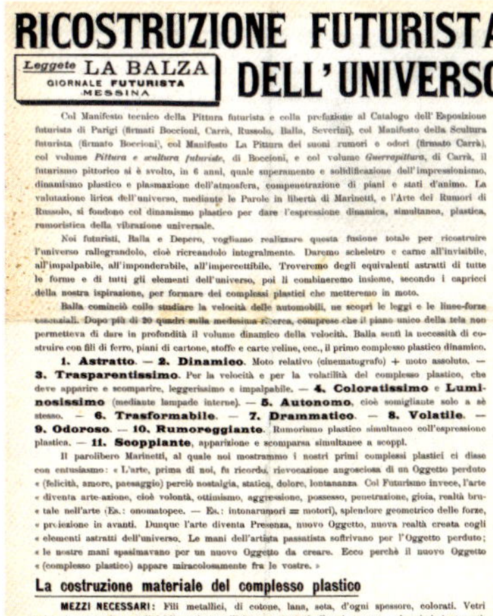
RICOSTRUZIONE FUTURISTA DELL'UNIVERSO

Leggete LA BALZA
GIORNALE FUTURISTA
MESSINA

Col Manifesto tecnico della Pittura futurista e colla prefazione al Catalogo dell'Esposizione futurista di Parigi (firmati Boccioni, Carrà, Russolo, Balla, Severini), col Manifesto della Scultura futurista (firmato Boccioni), col Manifesto La Pittura dei suoni rumori e odori (firmato Carrà), col volume *Pittura e scultura futuriste*, di Boccioni, e col volume *Guerrapittura*, di Carrà, il futurismo pittorico si è svolto, in 6 anni, quale superamento e solidificazione dell'impressionismo, dinamismo plastico e plasmazione dell'atmosfera, compenetrazione di piani e stati d'animo. La valutazione lirica dell'universo, mediante le Parole in libertà di Marinetti, e l'Arte dei Rumori di Russolo, si fondono col dinamismo plastico per dare l'espressione dinamica, simultanea, plastica, rumoristica della vibrazione universale.

Noi futuristi, Balla e Depero, vogliamo realizzare questa fusione totale per ricostruire l'universo rallegrandolo, cioè ricreandolo integralmente. Daremo scheletro e carne all'invisibile, all'impalpabile, all'imponderabile, all'impercettibile. Troveremo degli equivalenti astratti di tutte le forme e di tutti gli elementi dell'universo, poi li combineremo insieme, secondo i capricci della nostra ispirazione, per formare dei complessi plastici che metteremo in moto.

Balla cominciò collo studiare la velocità delle automobili, ne scoprì le leggi e le linee-forze essenziali. Dopo più di 20 quadri sulla medesima ricerca, comprese che il piano unico della tela non permetteva di dare in profondità il volume dinamico della velocità. Balla sentì la necessità di costruire con fili di ferro, piani di cartone, stoffe e carte veline, ecc., il primo complesso plastico dinamico.

1. Astratto. — **2. Dinamico**. Moto relativo (cinematografo) + moto assoluto. — **3. Trasparentissimo**. Per la velocità e per la volatilità del complesso plastico, che deve apparire e scomparire, leggerissimo e impalpabile. — **4. Coloratissimo** e **Luminosissimo** (mediante lampade interne). — **5. Autonomo**, cioè somigliante solo a sè stesso. — **6. Trasformabile**. — **7. Drammatico**. — **8. Volatile**. — **9. Odoroso**. — **10. Rumoreggiante**. Rumorismo plastico simultaneo coll'espressione plastica. — **11. Scoppiante**, apparizione e scomparsa simultanee a scoppi.

Il parolibero Marinetti, al quale noi mostrammo i nostri primi complessi plastici ci disse con entusiasmo: « L'arte, prima di noi, fu ricordo, rievocazione angosciosa di un Oggetto perduto « (felicità, amore, paesaggio) perciò nostalgia, statica, dolore, lontananza. Col Futurismo invece, l'arte « diventa arte-azione, cioè volontà, ottimismo, aggressione, possesso, penetrazione, gioia, realtà bru- « tale nell'arte (Es.: onomatopee. — Es.: intonarumori = motori), splendore geometrico delle forze, « proiezione in avanti. Dunque l'arte diventa Presenza, nuovo Oggetto, nuova realtà creata cogli « elementi astratti dell'universo. Le mani dell'artista passatista soffrivano per l'Oggetto perduto; « le nostre mani spasimavano per un nuovo Oggetto da creare. Ecco perchè il nuovo Oggetto « (complesso plastico) appare miracolosamente fra le vostre. »

La costruzione materiale del complesso plastico

MEZZI NECESSARI: Fili metallici, di cotone, lana, seta, d'ogni spessore, colorati. Vetri colorati, carteveline, celluloidi, reti metalliche, trasparenti d'ogni genere, coloratissimi, tessuti,

1. Giacomo Balla and Fortunato Depero, *Ricostruzione futurista dell'universo*, flyer, 11 March 1915

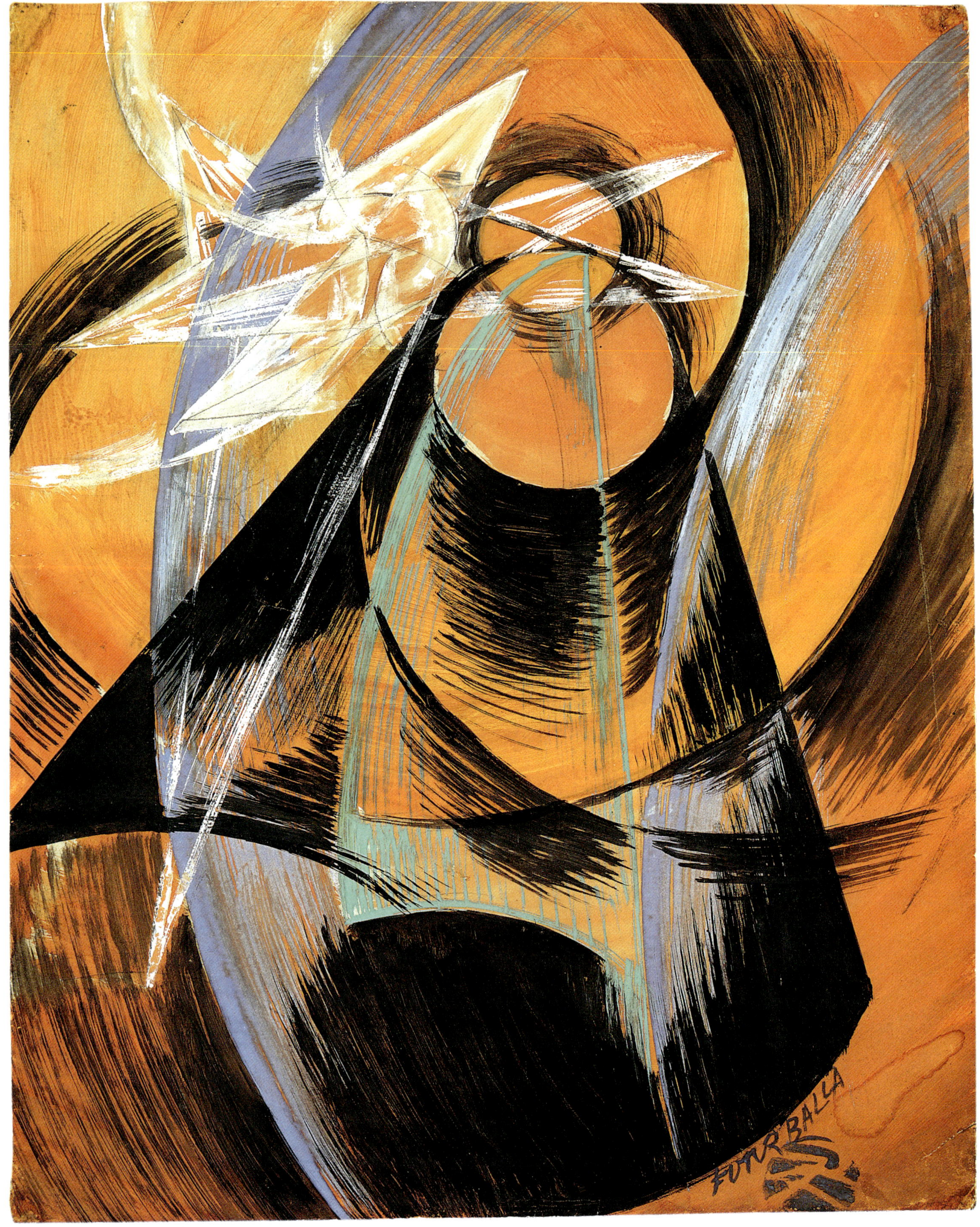
FUTUR BALLA

Opposite
74

Mercurio passa davanti al sole
(Mercury Passing in Front of the Sun), 1914
tempera on paper mounted on canvas, 45 x 35.7 cm

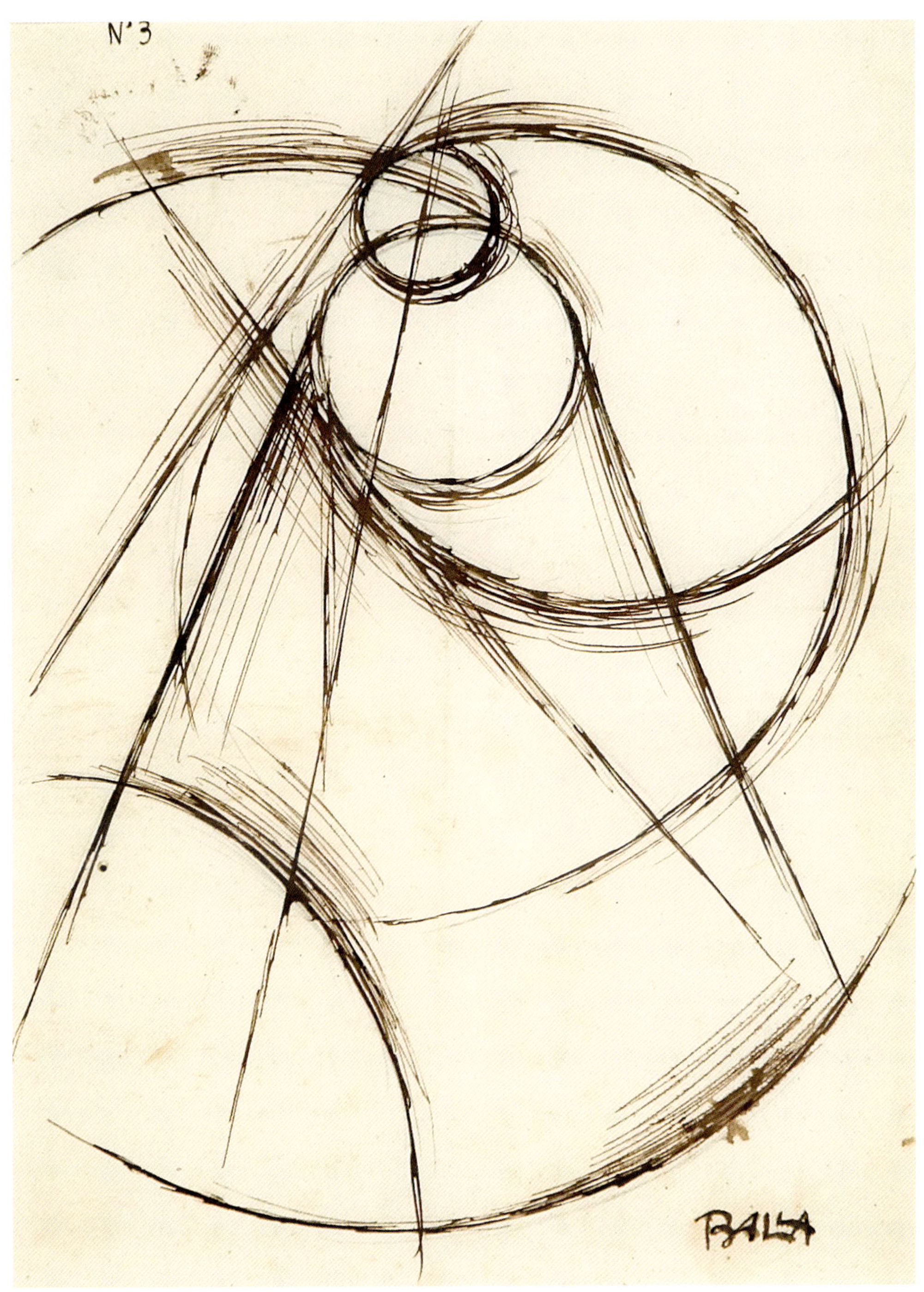

75

Mercurio passa davanti al sole
(Mercury Passing in Front of the Sun), c. 1914
ink on paper, 27 x 19.4 cm

himself said in an interview with a Roman journalist in 1911, "I have enjoyed myself for a long time producing impressions of the sky, astronomical paintings. I live up here, almost cut off from Rome, studying by day Villa Borghese, whose spirit I seem to feel vibrate in mine at night in the sky. The constellations have thus taken on for me not only a very marked appearance but also a particular spirit that I understand as full of enchantment and would like to express as best as I can on canvas. It is a difficult task but there is too much poetry in the eternal motion of those worlds not to tempt an artist."[4]

While a constellation like Orion, which Balla depicted in 1910, is a static subject, the transit of Mercury is, in line with the purest Futurist spirit, a genuinely dynamic phenomenon as well as one of the rare astronomical phenomena in which the motion of a celestial body is directly and immediately perceptible. Mercury crosses the face of the Sun in the space of a few hours and its transit can be observed by means of a small telescope (like the one at the disposal of Balla and his friend De Paolis, an engineer and astrophile who joined him in his observations), using a filter or projecting the image onto a screen. Elica Balla describes the painting as follows: "There is the yellow Sun inside the eyepiece with the black disk of Mercury passing in front of it, the impression of the Sun outside the eyepiece, movement in the mysterious green lines that specify the relationship between the instrument and the star under observation"[5] (figs. 2a-c). The dark tube of the telescope is clearly delineated in some versions of the work, while in others – like the one in the Peggy Guggenheim Gianni Mattioli Collection, probably the last in the series[6] – there is greater emphasis on the green lines, possibly recalling the dark filter used for the observation. The lines of white light also evolve from one version to another. The rays from the upper left corner in the Philadelphia Museum of Art version become the sparkling of a lens in those of the Centre Pompidou and the Mumok in Vienna and a fragmented star-shaped tangle in Venice the most complex one from the Mattioli collection. What the expert eye notes above all is, however, the black dot of Mercury, whose size and position appear to correspond completely to photographs of the transit in 1914. As Balla was to say in one of his last interviews, art is the "science of reality"[7] (figs. 3-4).

Mercury passes in front of the Sun when it is in inferior conjunction (between the Earth and the Sun) and its orbit crosses the plane of the ecliptic (the terrestrial orbit), which occurs every seven to eight years on average – and therefore about thirteen times a century[8] – at the beginning of May or November. The event was first observed in the 17th century. Though known since the antiquity, Mercury is in fact hard to observe because it always appears in close proximity to the Sun, which makes it impossible to see except

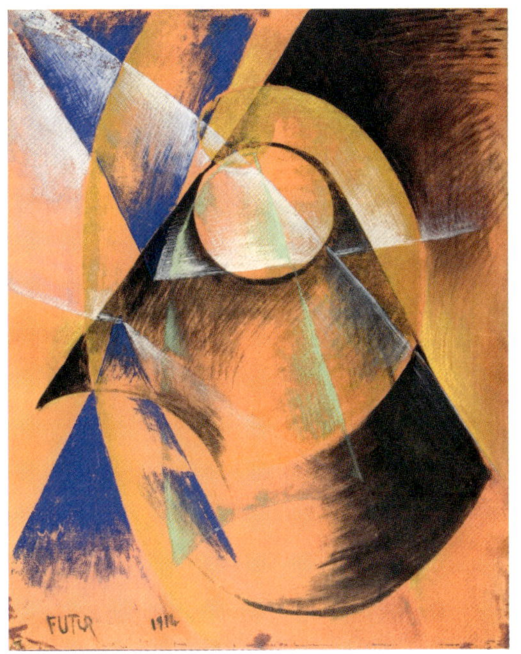

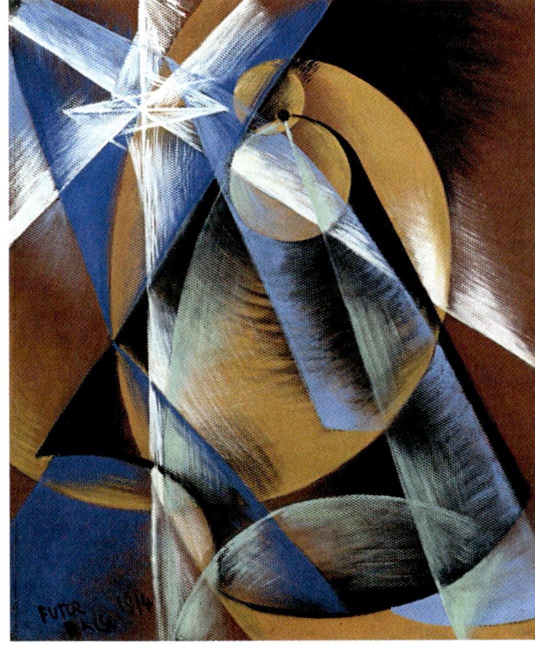

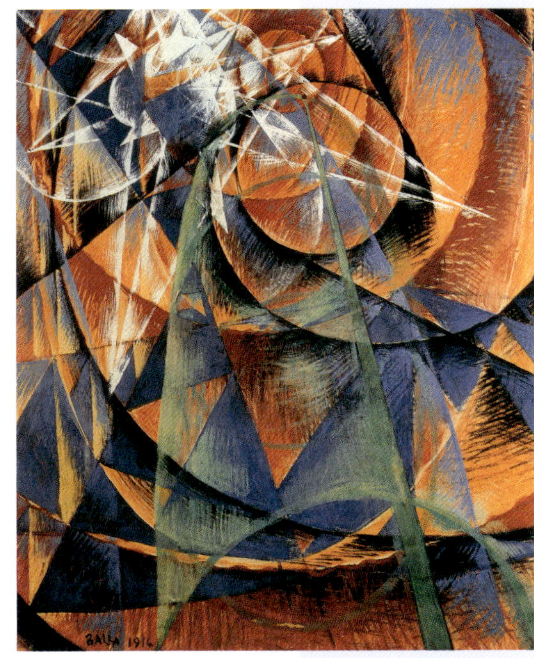

2. Giacomo Balla
Mercurio passa davanti al Sole
(*Mercury Passing in Front of the Sun*), 1914
a) Philadelphia, The Philadelphia Museum of Art
b) Paris, Musée National d'Art Moderne, Centre Georges Pompidou
c) Mattioli Collection

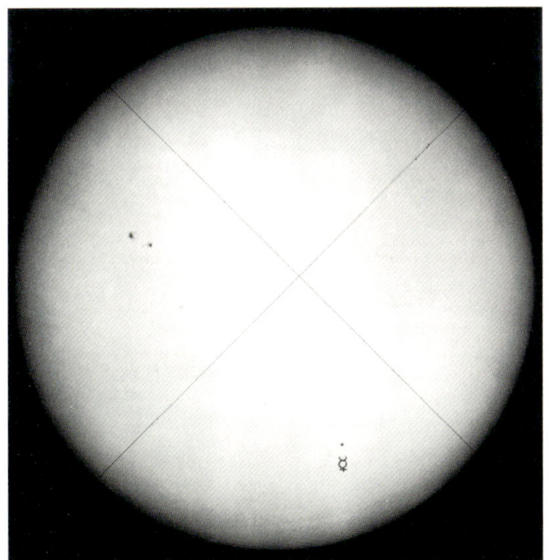

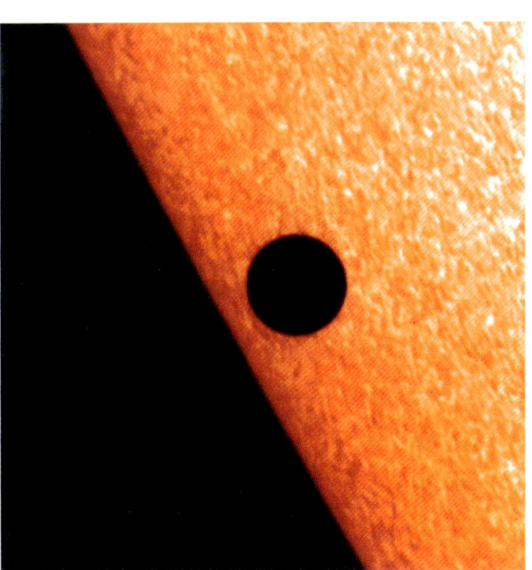

3. The transit of Mercury across the Sun of 7 November 1914 as captured by the four-inch photoheliograph of the Greenwich Observatory

4. The transit of Mercury across the Sun of 8 November 2006 as seen through the Hinode solar optical telescope

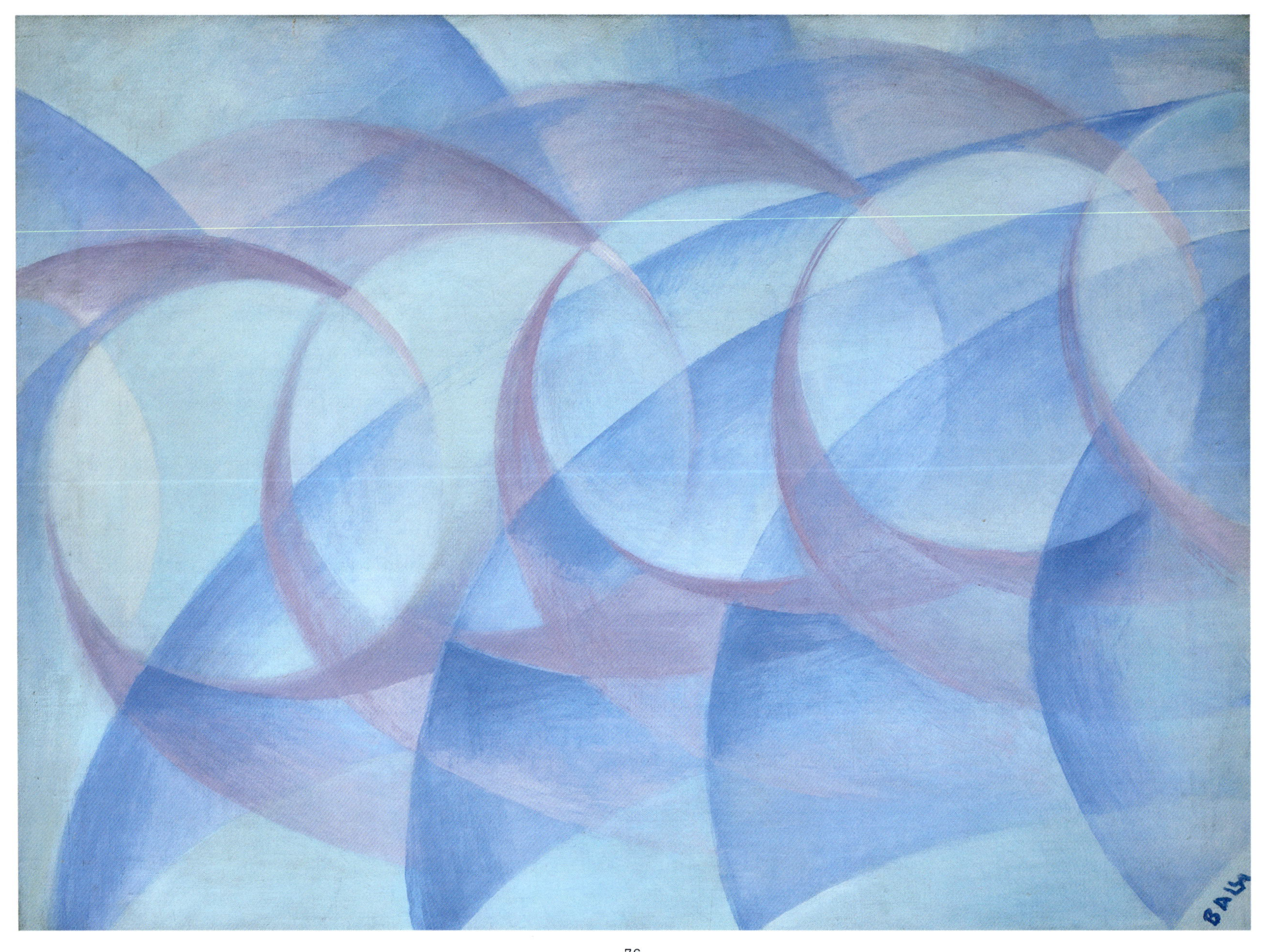

76

Orbite celesti (Celestial Orbits), 1913
oil on canvas, 60 x 80 cm

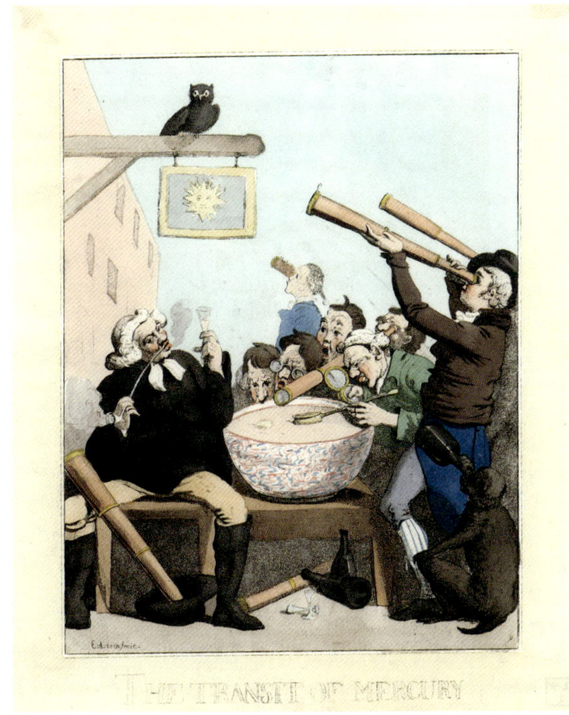

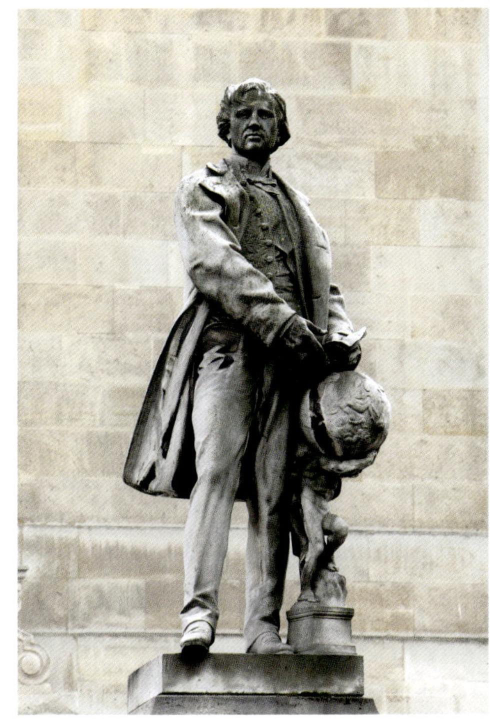

5. John Eckstein
The Transit of Mercury of 7 May 1799
Yale University, The Lewis Walpole Library

6. Henri Chapu
Statue of Urbain-Joseph Le Verrier, 1880
Paris, Observatoire de Paris

during a short period before sunrise or after sunset. Galileo observed the phases of Venus in 1610 but was unable to do likewise for Mercury. As he wrote in the *Dialogo sopra i due massimi sistemi del mondo* (1632), "Its disc is so small and its brilliance so lively that the power of the telescope is not sufficient to strip off its hair so that it may appear completely shorn."[9] Someone did, however, find a way to see Mercury "completely shorn" even before the *Dialogo* went to print. On 7 November 1631, as predicted in Kepler's *Tabulae Rudolphinae* (1627), the planet appeared as a clearly distinct black dot moving across the face of the Sun for a few hours and was observed with a Galilean telescope by Pierre Gassendi. To his great surprise, Gassendi discovered that Mercury was much smaller – about ten times – than previously thought.[10] He gave the news in the form of a letter entitled *Mercurius in sole visus et Venus invisa* (1632)[11] dispatched immediately to Galileo, who replied that he was not at all surprised, having believed for a long time that Mercury was "*incredibiliter minoris*" than all the other planets. The transit of 1631 not only revealed the smallness of Mercury, convincing astronomers of the need to take the new telescopic observations into serious consideration, but also supplied important information about the planet's orbit. Among the subsequent transits (fig. 5), particular importance attaches to the one in 1677, observed from the island of Saint Helena by Edmond Halley (famous for having predicted the return of the comet that bears his name), who suggested that the difference in the apparent position of Mercury (or Venus) recorded by observers in distant points of the world could be used to determine the distance between our planet and the Sun. Halley's idea prompted the English Navy to organize various expeditions around the world during the 18th century to record the transits of Mercury and Venus. It was on one of these, in 1769, that the renowned Captain Cook observed the transit of Mercury from a place in New Zealand that now bears the name Mercury Bay.

Historically speaking, the most important scientific consequence of the study of the transit of Mercury was the discovery in 1859 by the great French astronomer Urbain-Joseph Le Verrier of a phenomenon that was to play a key part in the development of contemporary science, namely the perihelion precession of Mercury (fig. 6). Le Verrier had become famous some years earlier, in 1846, for predicting the existence of Neptune, the eighth planet of the solar system. This was an authentic triumph of the Newtonian theory and mathematics because Le Verrier framed the hypothesis that anomalies found in the orbit of Uranus were due to perturbations caused by the presence of another planet and went on to calculate the precise position and motion of this new celestial body, which was then discovered just where he predicted it. Mercury too had an odd orbit that could not be explained solely in terms of the gravitational attraction of the Sun. Astronomical observations showed that its orbital axis revolved slowly (fig. 7) with a consequent precession of the perihelion (the point of the orbit at which the planet is closest to the Sun) of 565 arcseconds[12] per century (a very small angle corresponding more or less to a quarter of the apparent diameter of the Moon). This was thought to be caused by the gravitational pull of other planets. Le Verrier demonstrated that this was not enough to account for the entire phenomenon, as there remained a gap of 38 arcseconds (subsequently corrected to 43), which Newton's theory could not explain in terms of the gravity of the known celestial bodies.

Le Verrier put forward a solution similar to the one that had led to the discovery of Neptune, suggesting that the perihelion precession of Mercury was due to the presence of another planet between Mercury and the Sun, to which he gave the name Vulcan. An astronomer amateur named Edmond-Modeste Lescarbault claimed to have observed the transit of this planet across the Sun, but this proved some time later to have been a mistake, probably a sighting of a small sunspot.[13] Vulcan does not in fact exist and its spectre disappeared from circulation after haunting the skies of astronomy for a few years. The hypothesis gradually adopted to account for the precession was put forward by the German astronomer Hugo von Seeliger, who suggested that the phenom-

7. Perihelion shift of Mercury (effect accentuated considerably for the sake of clarity)

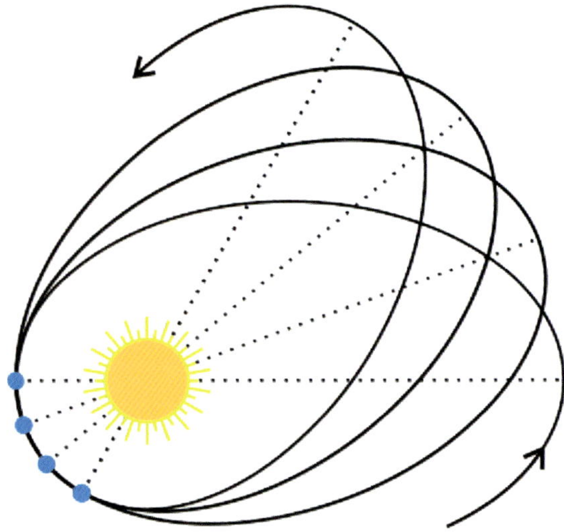

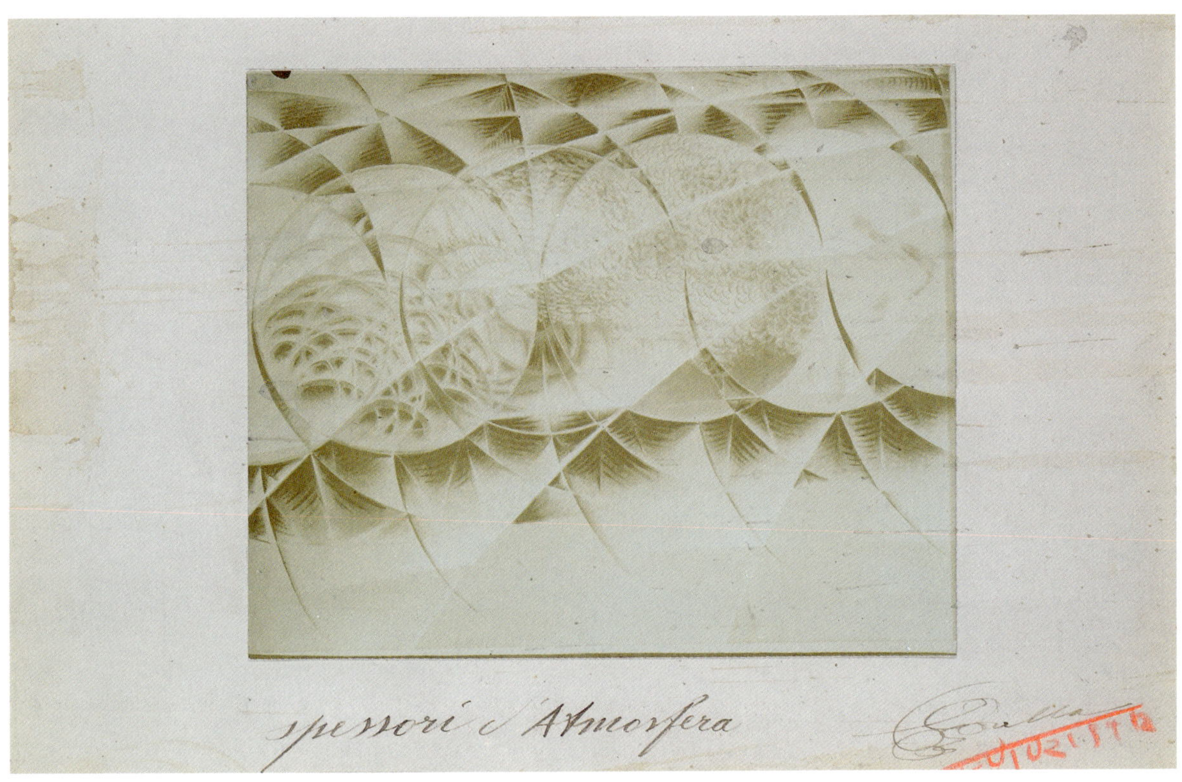

77

Alessandro Dell'Otti
Spessori d'atmosfera (Atmospheric Thicknesses), 1913
original photographic print of Balla's lost work
with autograph signature,
12 x 14.5 cm

78

Studio per Volo di rondini
(Study for Flight of Swallows), c. 1912
pencil on paper, 22.4 x 24.3 cm

79)

Studio per Volo di rondini
(Study for Flight of Swallows), c. 1912
pencil on paper, 30.8 x 31 cm

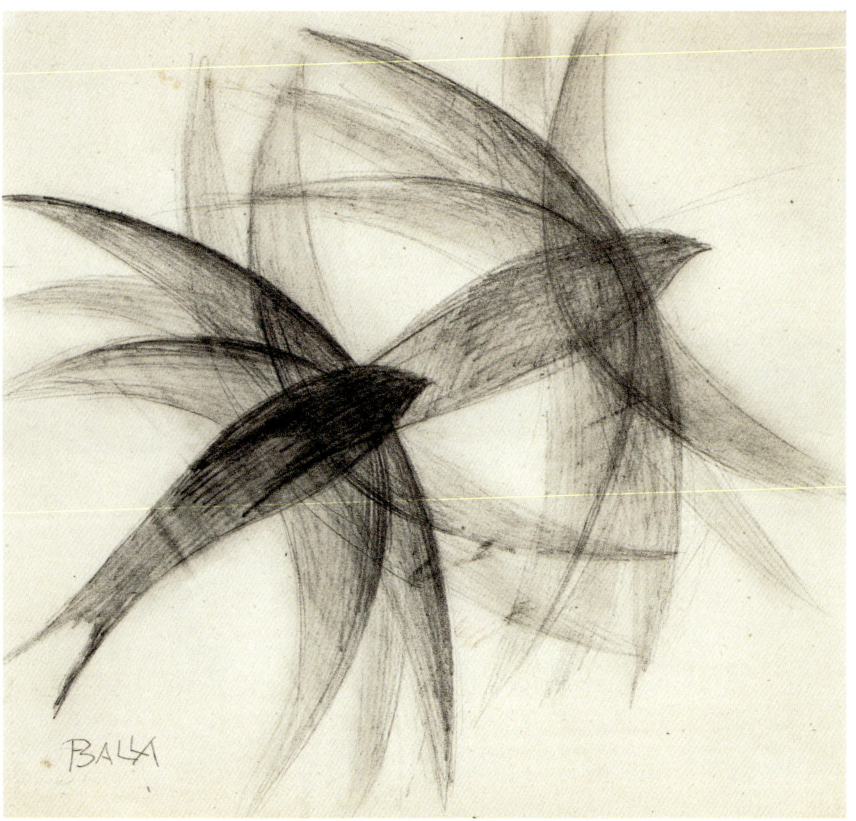

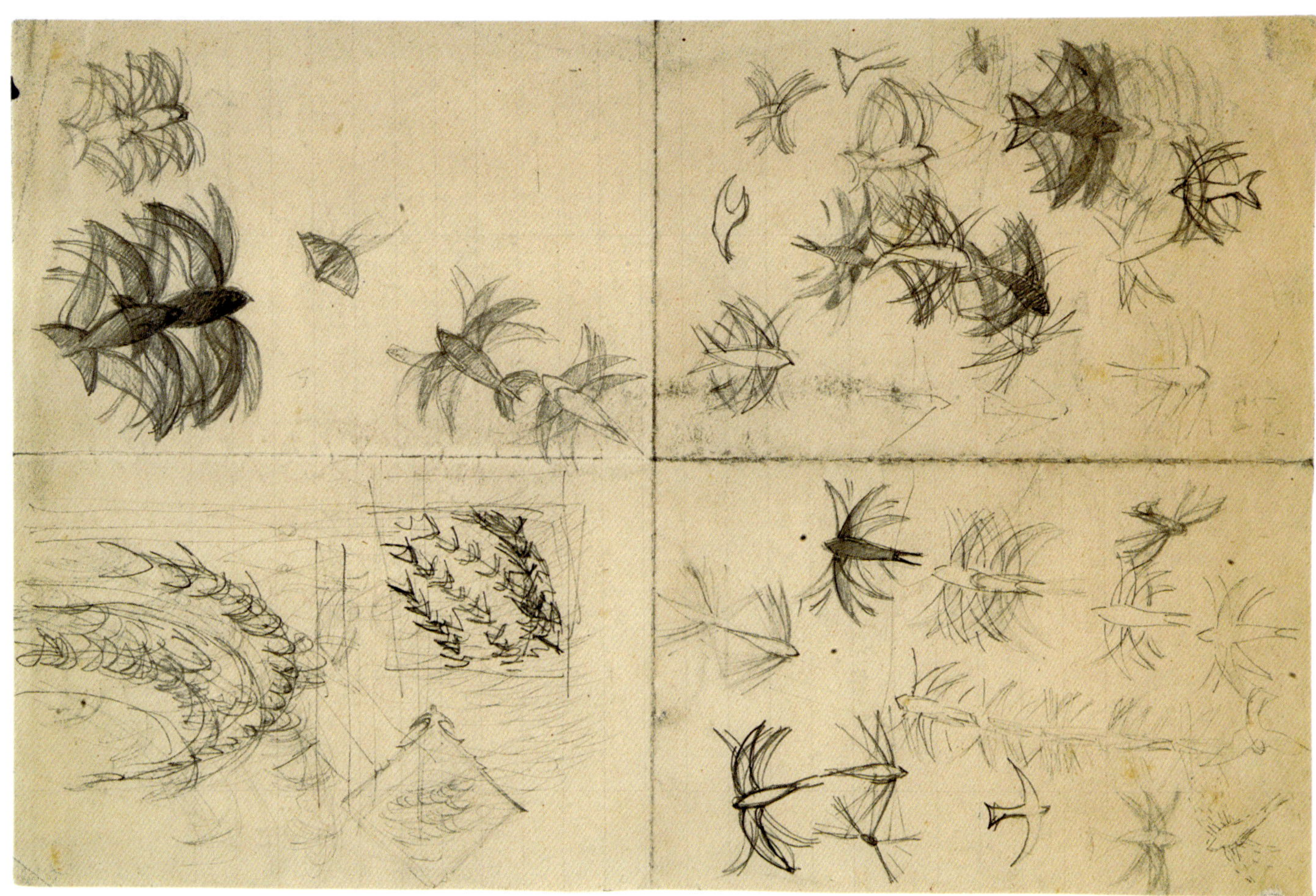

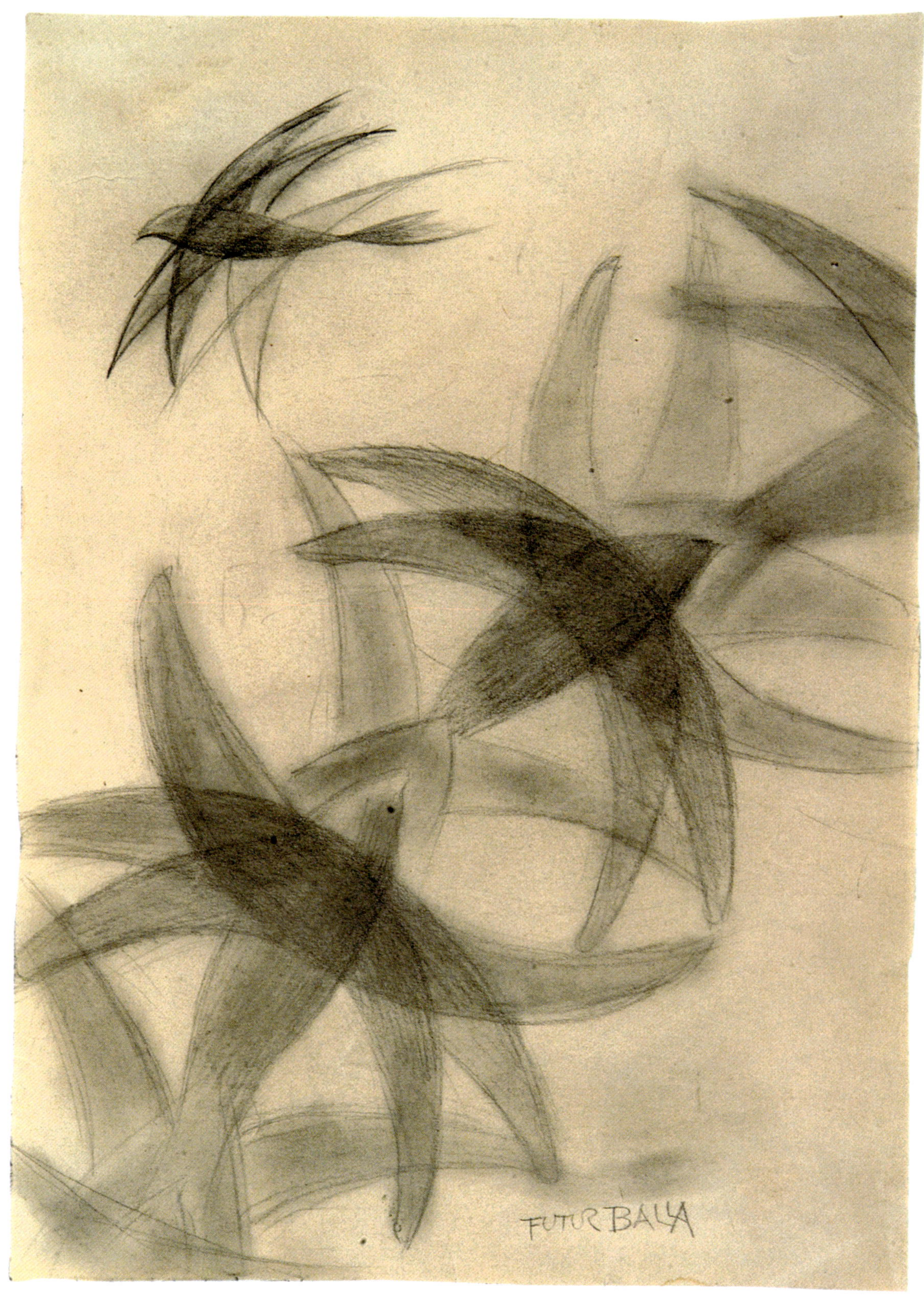

80

Studio per Volo di rondini (Study for Flight of Swallows),
c. 1912
pencil on ivory paper, 28.4 x 20.1 cm

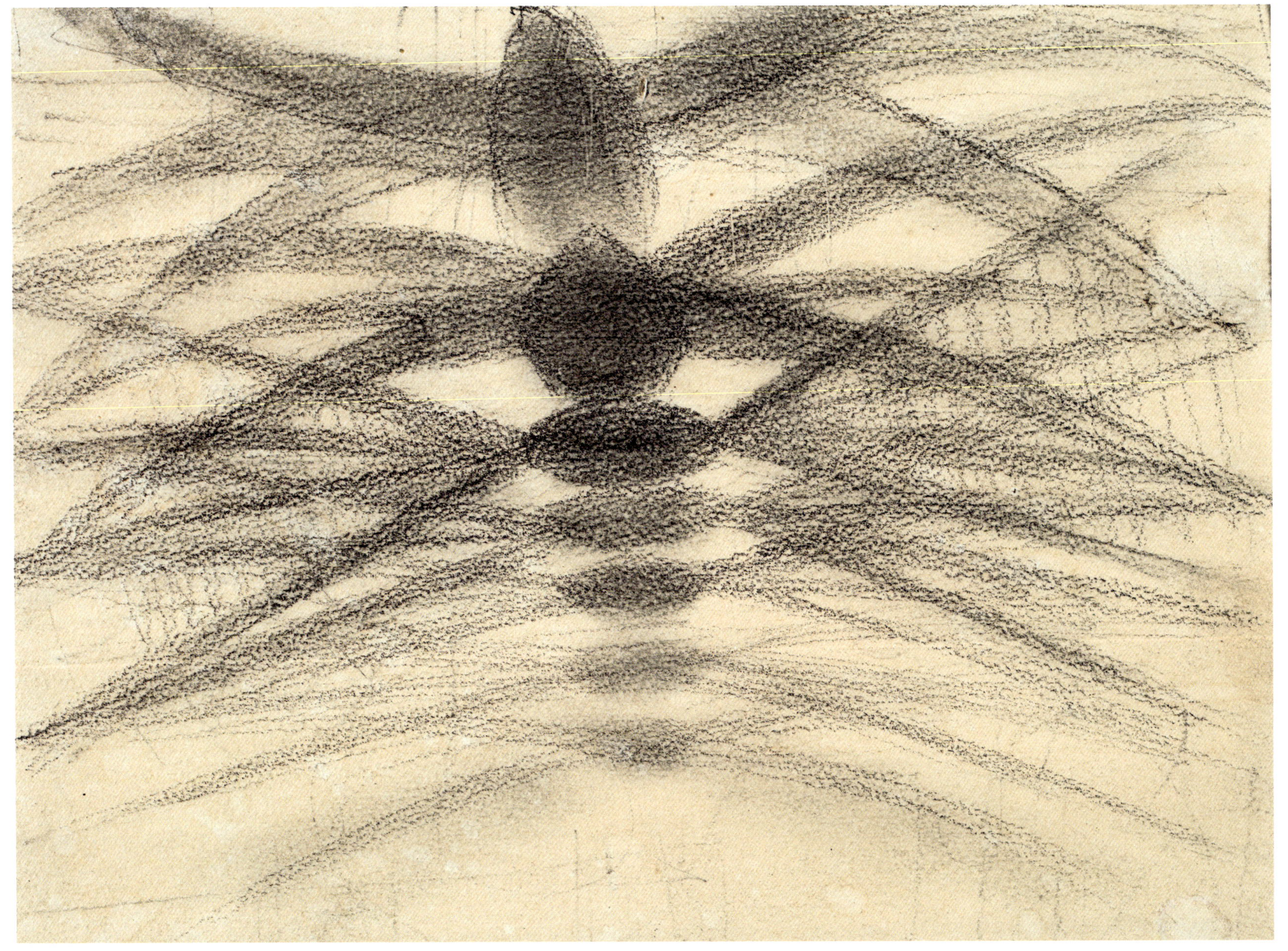

81

Studio per Volo di rondini
(Study for Flight of Swallows), c. 1912
pencil on ivory paper, 16.3 x 21.5 cm

Opposite
82

Studio per Volo di rondini
(Study for Flight of Swallows), c. 1912
pencil on paper, 11.4 x 17.1 cm

83

Studio per Volo di rondini
(Study for Flight of Swallows), c. 1912
pencil on paper, 15.4 x 21.6 cm

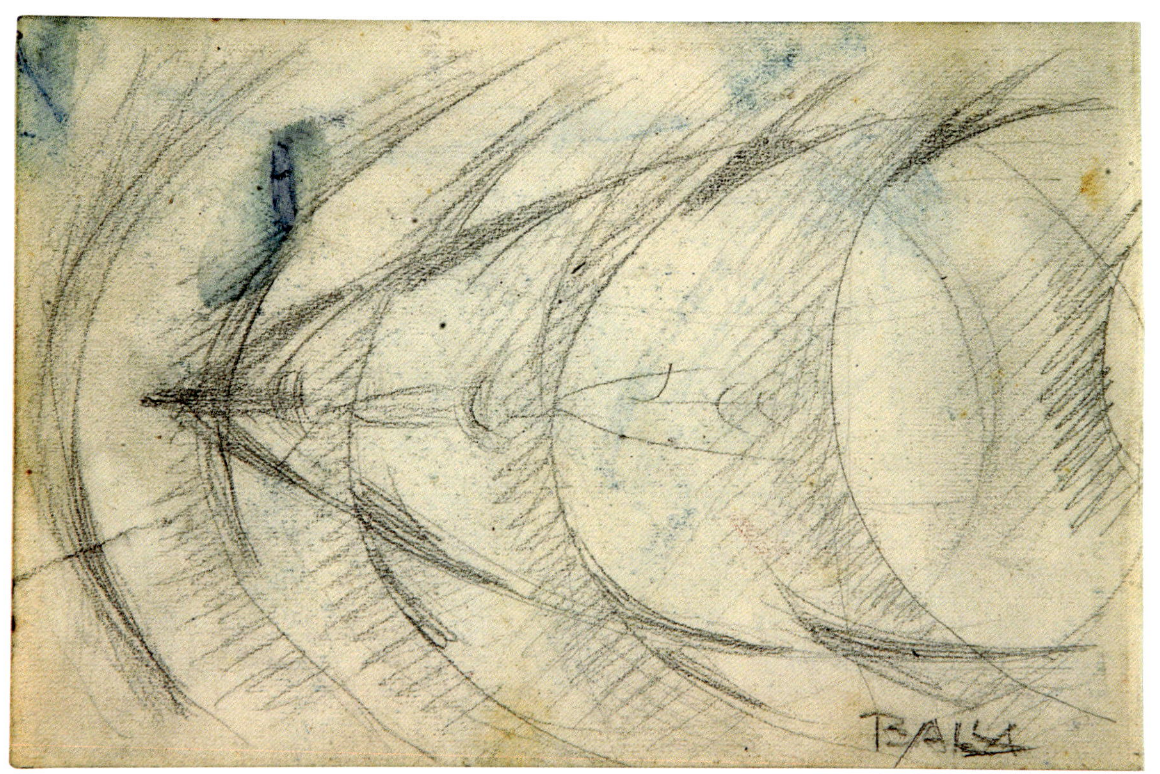
BALLA

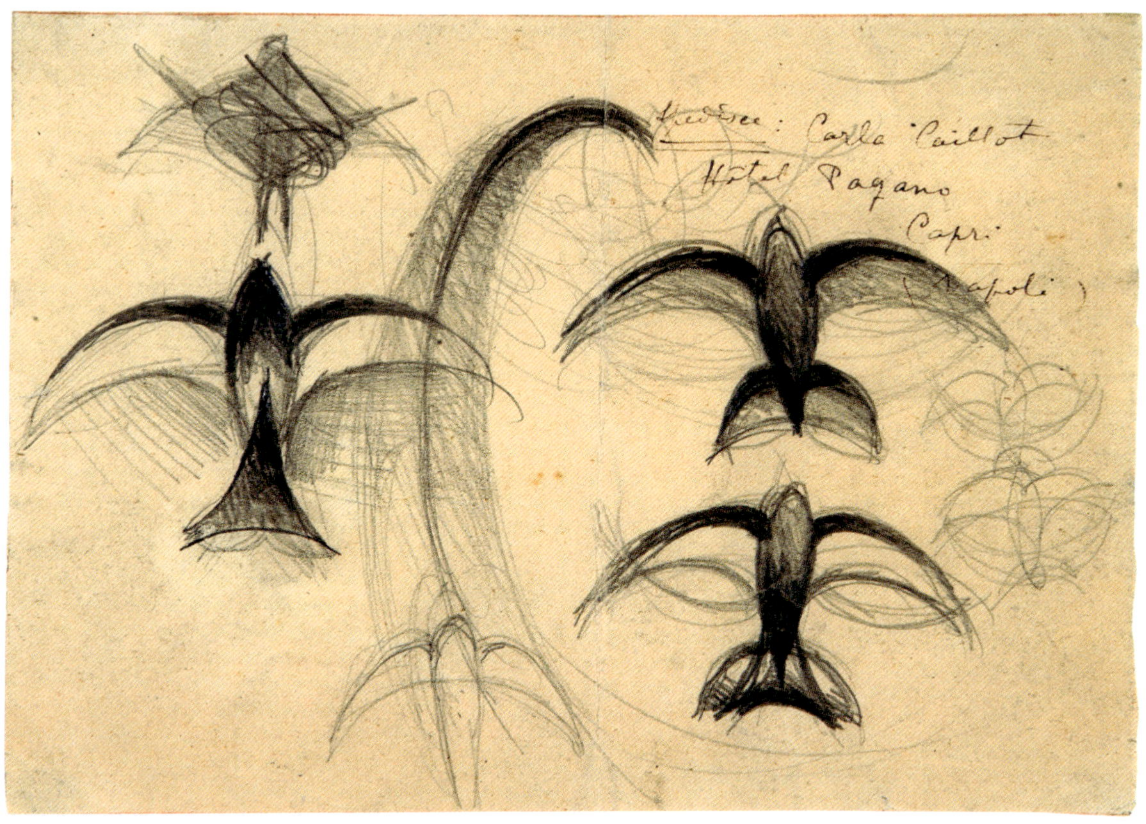
Hôtel Pagano
Capri

enon was not due to a compact body but to a region of dispersed matter between Mercury and the Sun. Many doubts still lingered, however, and the opinion of scholars at the turn of the century was summed up by the renowned astronomer Giovanni Schiaparelli in 1889: "Mercury is the only planet whose orbit has so far proved impossible to explain in terms of the laws of universal gravitation and whose theory, though developed by the acute intellect of a Le Verrier, still presents marked discrepancies with the observations."[14] With his series of works of 1914, Balla thus came unwittingly to observe and depict a crucial phenomenon that would soon bring the entire Newtonian conceptual framework tumbling down and open the way to one of the great scientific and philosophical revolutions of the 20th century.

Just a few months after the manifesto signed by Balla and Depero, physics presented its own manifesto for the reconstruction of the universe, namely the general theory of relativity (fig. 8). This was the work of Albert Einstein, a genius born in Ulm in 1879, who had unified space and time with special relativity in 1905 (the year in which he also made fundamental contributions to atomic and quantum physics) and then gone on to search for a more general theory capable of encompassing gravity too.[15] As we shall see, he too encountered Mercury on the way.

The initial relativity of 1905 was based on a principle of invariance (or symmetry), according to which the laws of physics are the same in all reference frames in uniform motion with respect to one another. The restriction of the principle solely to observers in uniform motion and the impossibility of accounting for gravitational phenomena had prompted Einstein to seek a generalization of the theory to all reference frames (the principle of general invariance). The path to discovery was long and hard, characterized by strokes of genius but also failures. The crucial intuition came around 1912, when Einstein realized that the gravity is related to the geometry of spacetime. The following year, in collaboration with his old fellow student Marcel Grossmann, who had suggested the mathematical instruments required (Riemannian geometry and the tensor calculus developed at the beginning of the century by the Italians Gregorio Ricci Curbastro and Tullio Levi-Civita), he developed an initial and still imperfect form of the new theory, which did not, however, meet the requirement of general invariance. In the autumn of 1915, after two more years of meagre progress, the mists cleared and Einstein was able to construct the definitive version of general relativity in a few weeks. He presented the theory to the Prussian Academy of Sciences in a series of weekly communications on the four Thursdays of November 1915 and then published a more detailed exposition in a long article entitled "Die Grundlage der allgemeinen Relativitätstheorie" (*Annalen der Physik*, 11 May 1916).[16] The vision of the universe

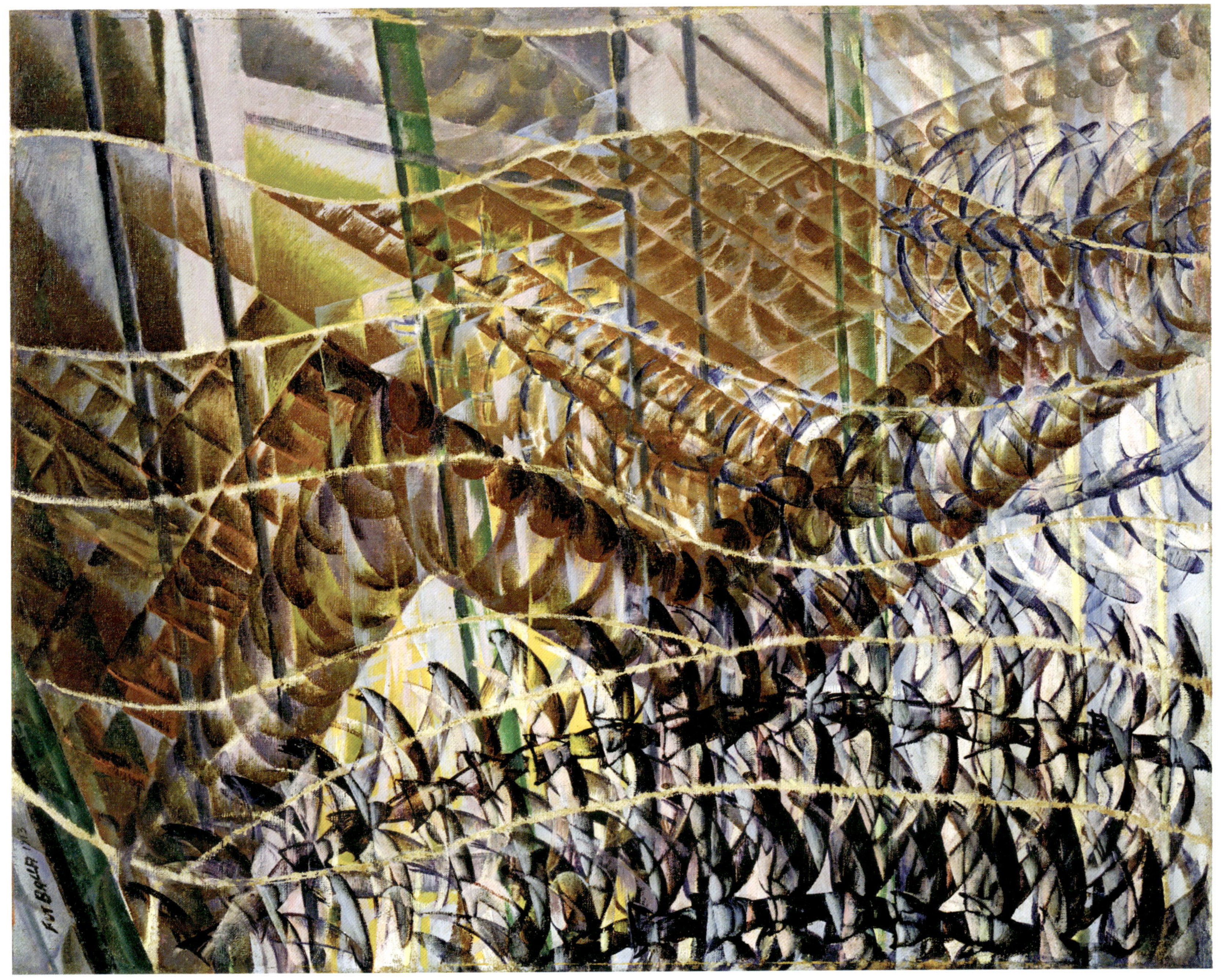

84

Volo di rondini (Linee andamentali + successioni dinamiche) (Flight of Swallows – Paths of Movement + Dynamic Sequences), 1913
oil on canvas, 96.8 x 120 cm

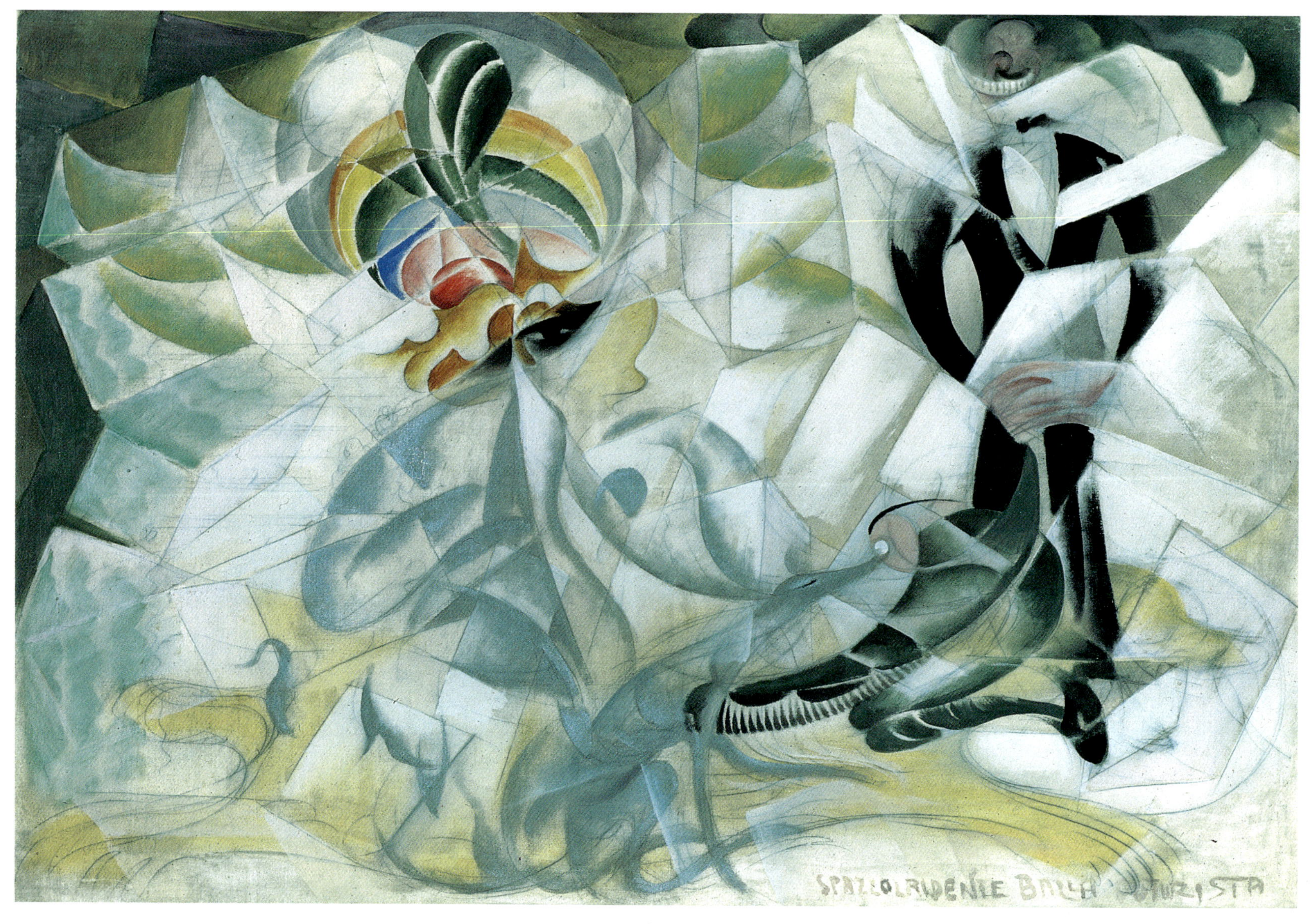

85

Spazzolridente (The Laughing Sweeper), 1918
oil on canvas, 70 x 100 cm

that emerged was astonishing. Spacetime is not something static, a sort of set backdrop to events, as in the special relativity of 1905, but a dynamic entity, an authentic physical field that interacts with everything inside it, matter and light. The fundamental equation of general relativity (fig. 9), rightly regarded as one of the greatest in physics, relates two quantities: on the one hand, the curvature of spacetime; on the other, the density of matter and energy. In the presence of mass and sources of energy, spacetime is distorted like the surface of a rubber mat and a particle or a beam of light moves along a curved trajectory. As the physicist John Archibald Wheeler put it, "Matter tells spacetime how to curve; spacetime tells matter how to move".

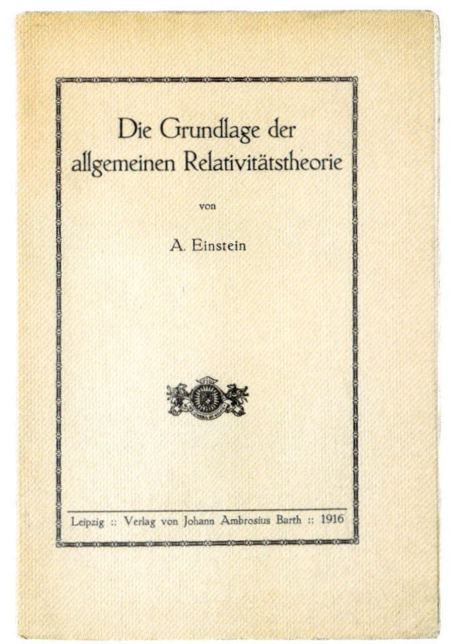

8. Albert Einstein, *Die Grundlage der allgemeinen Relativitätstheorie* (*The Foundation of the General Theory of Relativity*), Leipzig, 1916

Which brings us to Mercury. Having already expressed the hope that the new theory of gravitation would explain the perihelion precession of Mercury in 1907 in a letter to his friend Conrad Habicht, Einstein found the first empirical confirmation of general relativity precisely in the perihelion motion of this small planet. At the end of 1915, having completed his general relativity theory, he calculated the effect in a matter of days. David Hilbert, the greatest mathematician of the age, who was grappling with the same problem, complimented him on his speed in a letter of congratulations, saying that if he could calculate as quickly, the electron would have to capitulate in his equations and the hydrogen atom would have to apologise for not radiating.[17] (Hilbert erroneously thought that the equations of general relativity also described the atomic structure.) Einstein's speed was actually due to the fact that a couple of years before, with the aid of his close friend Michele Besso, an Italian-Swiss engineer, he had already attempted a similar calculation within the framework of the imperfect theory then available to him. The details of this previous attempt are known from a manuscript discovered in 1988 consisting of 52 pages, some written by Einstein and some by Besso.[18] The two friends worked on the problem in June 1913. Einstein established the framework, obtaining the expression of the gravitational field of the Sun from the equations of the theory developed together with Grossmann. Besso wrote the equation of the motion of the perihelion of Mercury and they both proceeded to solve it. The result was disappointing, as the theory predicted a shift of only 18 arcseconds, much less than the one

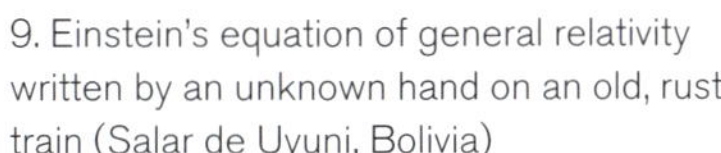
9. Einstein's equation of general relativity written by an unknown hand on an old, rusty train (Salar de Uyuni, Bolivia)

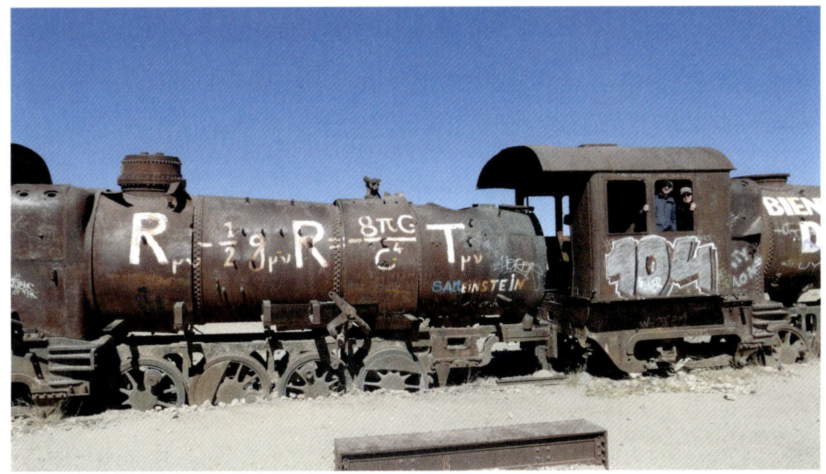

observed. The two friends' work was interrupted by Besso's departure and resumed briefly in August the same year before being finally set aside. The Dutch physicist Johannes Droste obtained their result independently and published it at the end of 1914. Even though the prediction was evidently at variance with the astronomical data, Einstein continued to believe that the theory of 1913 was correct until late in the summer of 1915, when he noted other serious flaws in the formulation that finally led him to jettison it and embark on what was to prove the right path. On redoing the calculations within the framework of general relativity, Einstein saw that the value of the shift of Mercury in 1913 had to be corrected of a factor of 12/5, thus becoming 43 arcseconds, in perfect agreement with the astronomical measurements. Beside himself with joy and excitement, as he later recalled, he wrote to Arnold Sommerfeld about the great satisfaction the result of the perihelion motion of Mercury had given him and observed that the astronomers' "pedantic accuracy", which he tended to mock in private, had been a great help in this case.[19]

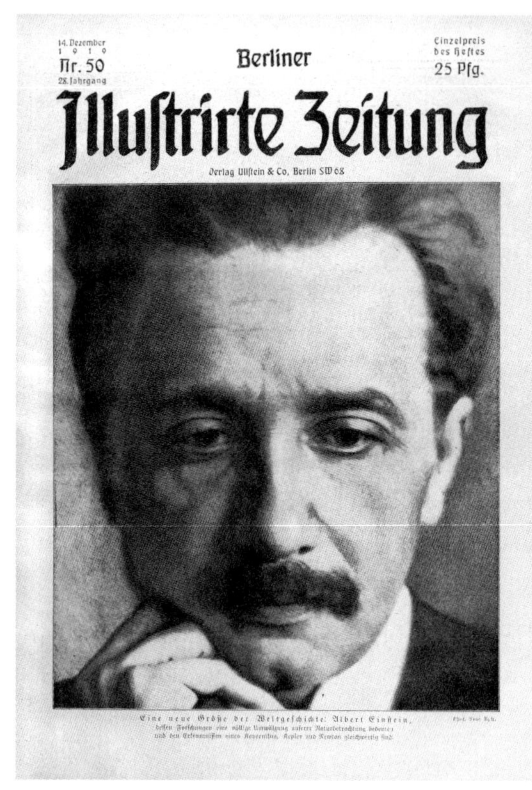

10. *Berliner Illustrierte Zeitung*, 14 December 1919

General relativity was not confined to the solution of an old riddle but also predicted sensational new phenomena, one of these being the bending of starlight by solar gravity. By curving the space around it, the Sun caused rays of light passing near its surface to deviate by a small angle, for which Einstein calculated a value of 1.7 arcseconds. He suggested that this could be tested by observing the apparent position of the stars around the Sun during a total eclipse, when the solar light that would otherwise made them impossible to see is screened by the Moon. The test was performed during the solar eclipse of 1919, visible in the equatorial part of the Atlantic, and the result predicted was obtained by two British expeditions organized by the astrophysicist Arthur Eddington at Sobral in Brazil and the Portuguese island of Príncipe off the African coast. The deflection measured corresponded to the prediction based on general relativity. The announcement of the results, made on the evening of 6 November 1919 at the Royal Society in London and trumpeted in the days to follow by newspapers all over the world with sensationalistic headlines about a scientific revolution and the bending of light, made Einstein a worldwide celebrity. His ideas began to circulate, with all the imaginable distortion and misunderstanding, in the intellectual community and the general public (fig. 10).

The perihelion precession of Mercury and the deflection of starlight constituted the sole corroboration of general relativity for decades until after Einstein's death in 1955. The theory predicted other effects of great conceptual importance but of very small magnitude and therefore hard to observe. It was not until 1960 that confirmation was obtained of one particularly intriguing element, namely the change in frequency – i.e. colour – of light in a gravitational field (a ray of light tends towards the blue on "falling" from a certain height and towards red on "ascending"). The availability of atomic clocks as from the 1970s then made it possible to measure another mind-boggling effect of relativity, namely gravitational time dilation. A clock set at sea level on the Earth, where the gravity is stronger, runs more slowly than one set at some altitude, where the gravity is weaker. The phenomenon was observed at first over distances of a few kilometres (between clocks on the ground and clocks on mountain tops or aeroplanes in flight), but the latest atomic clocks – accurate to within less than one thousandth of a billionth of a second a day – can detect the gravitational slowing down of time over a few decimetres, in practical terms, between a clock on the floor and one on a coffee table. In the field of astrophysics, the deflection of light is the cause of the spectacular phenomenon of gravitational lenses: galaxies or clusters of galaxies that distort the path of light from distant sources, thus producing effects like the multiplication of the image of the source or the formation of arches and rings (fig. 11).

In this discussion of two almost contemporary reconstructions of the universe, the artistic vision of the Futurists and the scientific theory of relativity, we have so far ducked a question that must be addressed here in the conclusion, if only out of natural curiosity. Is there any connection between them? An affirmative answer was given in the 1940s by the historian of architecture Sigfried Giedion in *Space, Time and Architecture*, one of the classics of 20th-century art criticism. According to Giedion, Cubist and Futurist painters developed the artistic equivalent of spacetime in their search for ways to express purely contemporary feelings in the first two decades of the century.[20] In particular, he drew a parallel between two passages. One is from Marinetti's *Manifesto of Futurism*, published in *Le Figaro* on 20 February 1909: "Time and Space died yesterday. We already live in the absolute

11. An Einstein ring seen through the Hubble Space Telescope: a glowing red galaxy gravitationally distorts the image of a more distant blue galaxy so as to form a ring

12. Simulated image of the fusion of two black holes

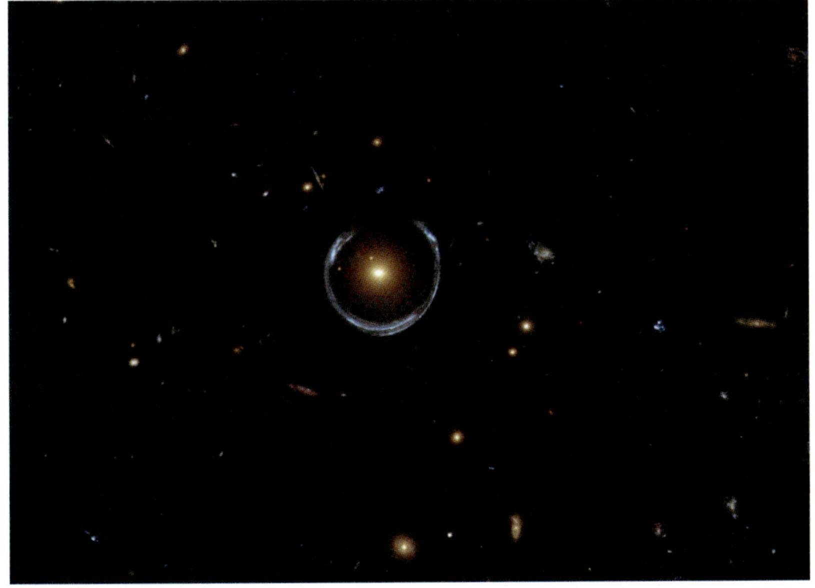

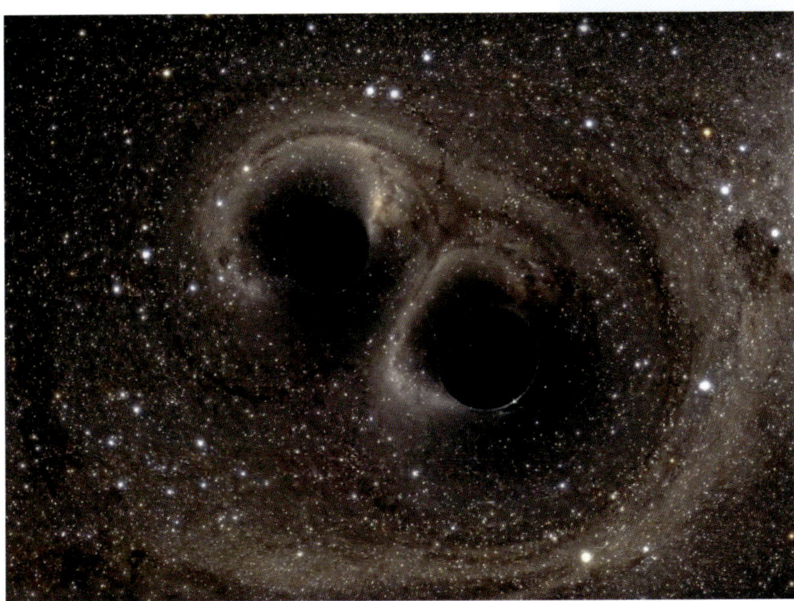

because we have created eternal, omnipresent speed." The other is from a lecture delivered by the mathematician and physicist Hermann Minkowski, one of the first to address relativity, on 21 September 1908 at a meeting of German scientists and physicians: "Space in itself and time in itself are doomed to vanish like mere shadows and only a kind of union of the two will retain independent reality." With a paradoxical reversal of terms, Minkowski then went on to add that spacetime was to be understood rather as an absolute world. It is, however, impossible that Marinetti had any knowledge of Minkowski's lecture – which is moreover highly technical – or of Einstein's theory, known at the time only to a handful of specialists. The similarities between the two texts are therefore coincidental, and indeed only apparent if we consider the real meaning of the words. Nor are we really convinced by those who, like the art critic Paul Laporte, deny any causal relationship between the artistic avant-garde and modern physics but nevertheless assert the existence of a direct link between the two in the sense that, starting "from the same roots", artists and scientists were "forced to move in the same direction by the internal logic of the situation".[21] In 1945 Laporte put the question to Einstein, who denied any conceptual affinity between Cubism and relativity, and confined himself to indicating the common attempt to introduce a principle of order into the complexity of perceptions as the only generic element of similarity between art and science.[22]

It was in the 1920s, after the sensation caused by the confirmation of the deflection of starlight, that relativity made its entrance into the broader cultural debate. The great linguist Roman Jakobson, who witnessed the blossoming of Russian Futurism, recalled outlining the theory to Mayakovsky, who was so impressed as to be obsessed for a time with the idea of sending Einstein a telegram "to the science of the future from the art of the future."[23] The answer to our question may lie simply in these words. The path of an art that looks to the future and seeks indeed to construct it by rethinking the universe will necessarily cross that of science, the other form of human creativity programmatically intent on superseding itself and constructing new worlds.

Within the sphere of the Italian Futurist movement, an implicit but unmistakeable reference to Einstein's scientific ideas appeared very late on in Marinetti's manifesto *La matematica futurista immaginativa qualitativa* (1940), written in collaboration with Marcello Puma, a former pupil of Guido Castelnuovo, one of the greatest Italian experts on Einstein's work. "Mathematicians, we urge you to love new geometries and gravitational fields created by masses moving at sidereal speed."[24] In this exhortation, Marinetti's febrile imagination appears to have been right on target. On 14 September 2015, the first gravitational wave, a ripple in spacetime caused by the collision of two black holes orbiting one another at speeds close to that of light itself, was picked up by two gigantic detectors after a journey taking 1.3 billion years (fig. 12). The existence of such waves was the last of Einstein's predictions still awaiting definitive confirmation, and nobody could have imagined a better way to celebrate the centenary of general relativity. The discovery inaugurates a new way of looking at the heavens and a new field, gravitational astronomy, that will in future enable us to obtain information on extreme astrophysical phenomena and perhaps even the first instants of life of the universe. Who knows what extraordinary ideas Giacomo Balla would have drawn from all this.

[1] G. Bartorelli, *Numeri innamorati. Sintesi e dinamiche del secondo futurismo*, Testo & Immagine, Turin, 2001, p. 30.

[2] E. Balla, "Giacomo Balla: un artista amico delle stelle", in *L'Astronomia*, no. 28, December 1983, p. 23.

[3] G. Vanin, "Mercurio sul Sole visto da Giacomo Balla", in *Le Stelle*, no. 154, May 2016, pp. 33–36. The article contains a description of the entire *Mercurio* series as seen through the astrophile's eyes.

[4] Interview with Aymerillot, "Il 1911 degli artisti romani: Giacomo Balla", in *L'Alfiere*, 24 January 1911; now in G. Balla, *Scritti futuristi*, ed. G. Lista, Abscondita, Milan, 2010, p. 194.

[5] E. Balla, op. cit., p. 25.

[6] For this, the most elaborate version of *Mercurio*, see *La Collezione Mattioli. Capolavori dell'avanguardia italiana*, ed. F. Fergonzi, Skira, Milan, 2003.

[7] Interview with G. Bocconetti, "Nei quadri di oggi ricordi futuristi", in *Corriere Lombardo*, 12–13 November 1951; now in Balla, *Scritti futuristi*, op. cit., p. 226.

[8] Rarer still are the solar transits of another inner planet, Venus: just eight since 1631, the last of which on 6 June 2012. The next will not take place until 2117.

[9] G. Galilei, *Dialogue concerning the two chief world systems*, The Third Day, ed. Stillman Drake, The Modern Library, New York, 2001, p. 394.

[10] A. Van Helden, "The Importance of the Transit of Mercury of 1631", in *Journal of the History of Astronomy*, 7, pp. 1–10 (1976). The apparent diameter of Mercury during transit is 10–12 arcseconds, less than one hundredth of that of the Sun.

[11] Gassendi also tried to observe the transit of Venus in 1631 but failed because it took place in Paris after sunset. The first solar transit of Venus was observed in 1639 by Jeremiah Horrocks and William Crabtree in England.

[12] An arcsecond or second of arc is 1/3600 of a degree.

[13] For Le Verrier and the supposed observation of Vulcan, see P. Bianucci, *Storia sentimentale dell'astronomia*, Longanesi, Milan, 2012, pp. 178–191. For the history of the discrepancy of perihelion of Mercury and the theories put forward to account for it until its solution by Einstein (as recounted below), see T. Levenson, *The Hunt for Vulcan*, Random House, New York, 2015.

[14] G. Schiaparelli, "Sulla rotazione e sulla costituzione fisica di Mercurio", in *Atti della Reale Accademia dei Lincei*, series 4, vol. 5, 1889, p. 283; now in *Le più belle pagine di astronomia popolare*, Hoepli, Milan, 1944, p. 185.

[15] For an introduction to the life and scientific work of Einstein, see V. Barone, *Albert Einstein. Il costruttore di universi*, Laterza, Rome-Bari, 2016.

[16] See A. Einstein, *Le due relatività*, ed. V. Barone, Bollati Boringhieri, Turin, 2015.

[17] Letter from D. Hilbert to Einstein, 19 November 1915, in A. Einstein, *Collected Papers*, vol. 8A, ed. R. Schulmann, A.J. Kox, M. Janssen, J. Illy, Princeton University Press, Princeton (NJ), 1999, p. 202.

[18] This document, which had always remained in private hands, was auctioned by Christie's in 1996. For a reproduction and commentary, see A. Einstein, *Collected Papers*, vol. 4, ed. M.J. Klein, A.J. Kox, J. Renn and R. Schulmann, Princeton University Press, Princeton (NJ), 1995, pp. 344–473 and 630–82.

[19] Letter from Einstein to A. Sommerfeld, 9 December 1915, in *Collected Papers*, vol. 8A, op. cit., p. 217.

[20] S. Giedion, *Space, Time and Architecture: The Growth of a New Tradition*, Harvard University Press, 1941.

[21] M. Schapiro, *Einstein and Cubism: Science and Art*, in *The Unity of Picasso's Art*, George Braziller, New York, 2000. This work contains a thorough examination of the supposed relations between the theory of relativity and avant-garde movements in the early 20th century.

[22] P.M. Laporte, "Cubism and Relativity (with a Letter of Albert Einstein)", in *Art Journal*, 25, no. 3, 1966, pp. 246–48.

[23] R. Jakobson, "On a Generation that Squandered its Poets", chapter 16 of *Language in Literature*, ed. Krystyna Pomorska and Stephen Rudy, the Belknap Press of Harvard University Press, Cambridge, Massachusetts - London, England, 1987.

[24] F.T. Marinetti, *La matematica futurista immaginativa qualitativa* (1940), now in *Teoria e invenzione futurista*, ed. L. De Maria, Mondadori, Milan, 2010 (I ed. 1968), p. 227.

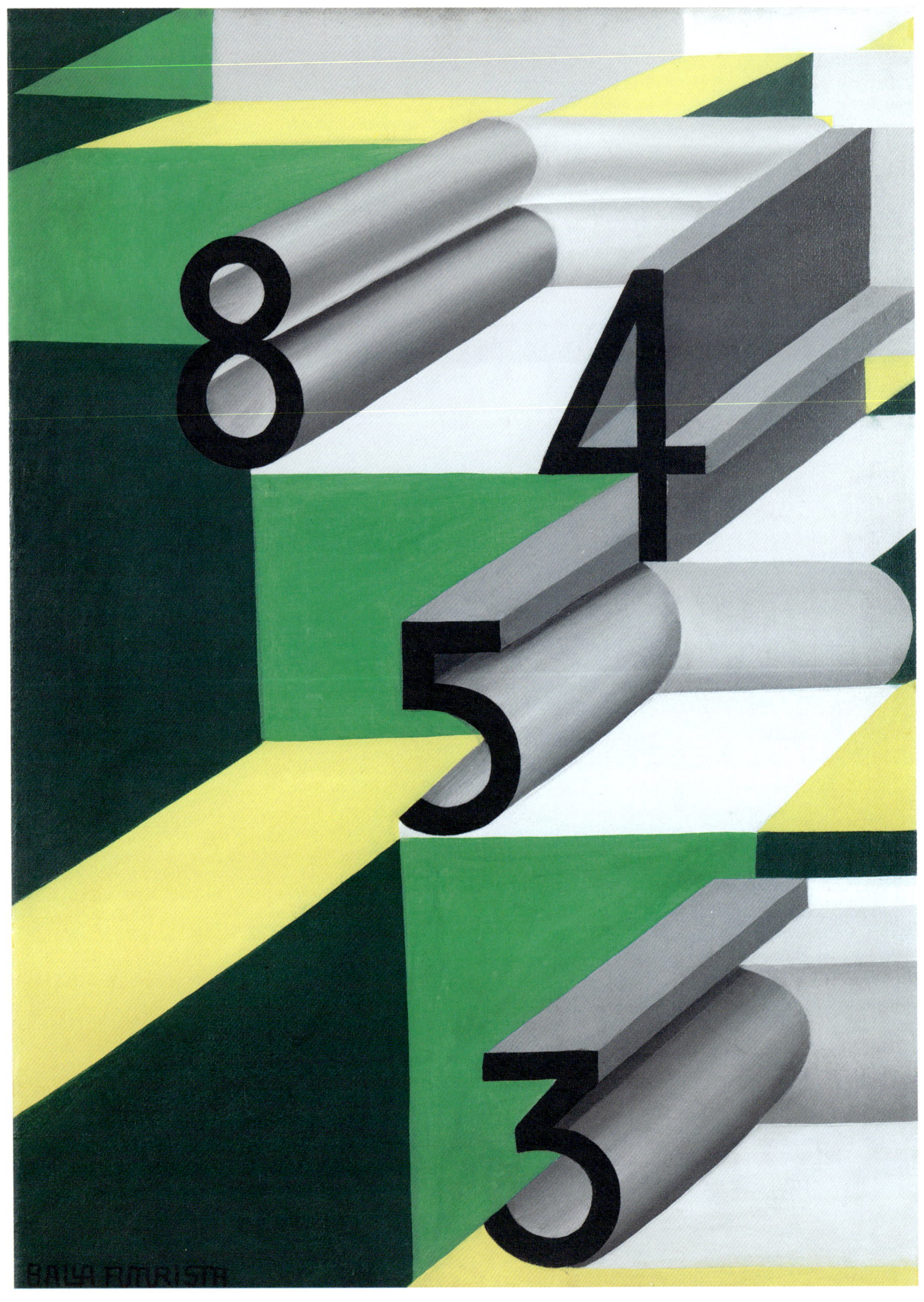

86

Numeri innamorati (Numbers in Love), 1923
oil on canvas, 77 x 55 cm

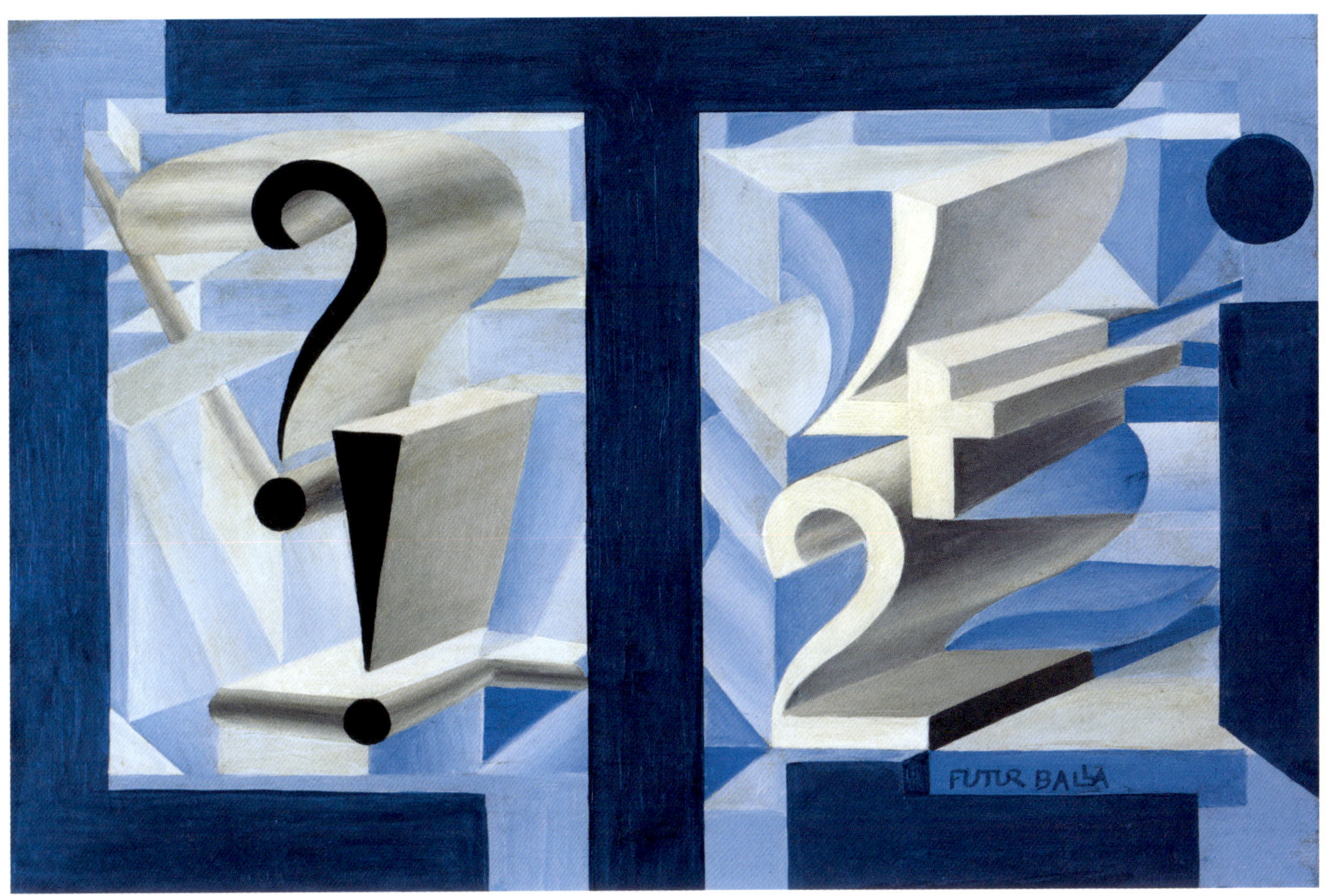

87

Bozzetto per "LTI" detto Il grande T
(Sketch for LTI or The Big T), 1923–24
enamel on hardboard, 29.5 x 44 cm

BALLA

AutoBiograf. BALLA

NEL 500 MI CHIAMAVO LEONARDO
O..... TIZIANO DOPO 4 SECOLI
DI DECADENZA ARTISTICA. SON
RIAPPARSO NEL 900 PER GRIDARE
AI MIEI PLAGIATORI CHE È ORA DI
FINIRLA CON IL PASSATO PERCHÉ
SON CAMBIATI I TEMPI. MI DISSERO
PAZZO: POVERI TONTI !!!!!!!!
Ò GIÀ CREATO UNA NUOVA SENSIBILITÀ
NELL'ARTE ESPRESSIONE DEI
TEMPI FUTURI CHE SARANNO
COLORRADIOIRIDESPLENDORIDEAL
LUMINOSISSSSSSSSSSIMIIIIII

FuturBALLA

88

Autobiografia (Autobiography), 1914
ink on paper, 18 x 14 cm

Balla

Zelda De Lillo

Giacomo Balla, the son of Luisa Giannotti and Giovanni Balla, was born in via Moncalieri on 18 July 1871 in an outlying area of Turin not far from Piazza Vittorio Emanuele. The Piedmontese city was then in a state of severe economic and social crisis, not least due to the loss of its status as the Italian capital first to Florence and finally to Rome. It is there that Balla spent his youth and witnessed the first changes in a process that was to transform Turin into the country's first industrialized hub in the space of a few decades.

Balla inherited an interest in photography and music from his father. He began to study the violin at a very early age and received his initial teaching at the San Filippo Neri choir school. An interest in painting was also soon to manifest itself. In the family, Balla liked to recall how he painted his first watercolours on the banks of the Po with a box of paints given to him for his eighth birthday by one of his mother's friends.

Balla's father died suddenly in 1879 and he was forced to attend evening classes. In 1886 his mother enrolled him at the Reale Accademia Albertina di Belle Arti. His teacher Giacomo Grosso was soon to cause an outcry at the 1895 Venice Biennial with a painting of a sensual female nude in a church.

During the years of his academic training, Balla also acquired an understanding of the new techniques of image reproduction by working first for the lithographer Pietro Cassina, the author of portraits and sightseeing views, and then for the photographer Pietro Paolo Bertieri. The latter's highly fashionable studio catered for Turin's upper classes as well as leading figures in the worlds of literature, theatre and art. It was there that Balla met the young Pellizza da Volpedo.

Those were years of positivism, socialism and scientific progress, the period in which Cesare Lombroso expounded his anthropological theories at the University of Turin.

On 29 January 1895 Balla and his mother moved to Rome, the new capital, in search of brighter prospects.

They stayed at first with Balla's uncle Gaspare Melchiorre, a royal huntsman, in the staff quarters of Palazzo Quirinale. The young Balla spent his days exploring the city, discovering its museums and monuments but also its street life. He produced numerous sketches, often caricatures, which were displayed in the windows of the shop where his mother worked for Giacomo Foà, a well-known tailor of the period. After the initial period with his uncle, Balla found lodgings in Via Montebello and then Piazza delle Terme, near the Termini railway station. In 1896 he moved into the combined apartment and studio at Via Piemonte 119 in the heart of the newly born Pinciano district.

It was in this period that he met Duilio Cambellotti, a student at the Museo Artistico Industriale, and Alessandro Marcucci, the brother of his future wife Elisa, with whom he had many social interests and passions in common. The following years saw his artistic participation in a campaign to improve the literacy of the rural population in the Pontine Marshes led by Giovanni Cena, another Piedmontese transplanted in Rome.

"It was the age of realism and psychologism, that was our creed. But we also wanted the work of art to be meaningful, to put forward an idea, to champion a cause." This is how Marcucci described the aims and hopes of those youthful years.

Balla painted *Il pertichino*, a photograph-like urban nocturne, in which he addressed the effects of artificial light for the first time. Not accepted for the 1899 Venice Biennial, the painting was shown the following year at the annual exhibition of the Società degli Amatori e Cultori in Rome.

Balla left for Paris on 2 September 1900 and remained there until March 1901 as the guest of the artist Serafino Macchiati from the Marche region of Italy, with whom he worked as an illustrator. The stay in Paris was an opportunity to witness developments on the European scene. Balla visited the major show of international painting held at the Grand Palais within the framework of the 1900 World's Fair and gained first-hand knowledge of French Pointillism as well as Impressionism and Post-Impressionism.

The city fascinated him too with its crowded boulevards and elegant buildings bathed in the intermittent glow of illuminated signs ("this appearance and disappearance of lights standing out against a sky that becomes as black as a grave at night"). This increased his interest in the effects of artificial light. It was there that he painted *Parisian Fair*.

His first successes can be dated on his return to Rome, including a prize from the General Directorate of the Antiquities and Fine Arts for *Il sentiero* (*The Path*), a work painted in Paris and shown at the exhibition of the Società degli Amatori e Cultori in 1901.

Meanwhile, Balla's home became a place where his young pupils and friends would gather to talk and exchange ideas on art. In addition to young ladies like Pierina Levi and Annie Nathan, daughter of the future mayor of Rome Ernesto Nathan, his pupils included Umberto Boccioni, Gino Severini and Mario Sironi.

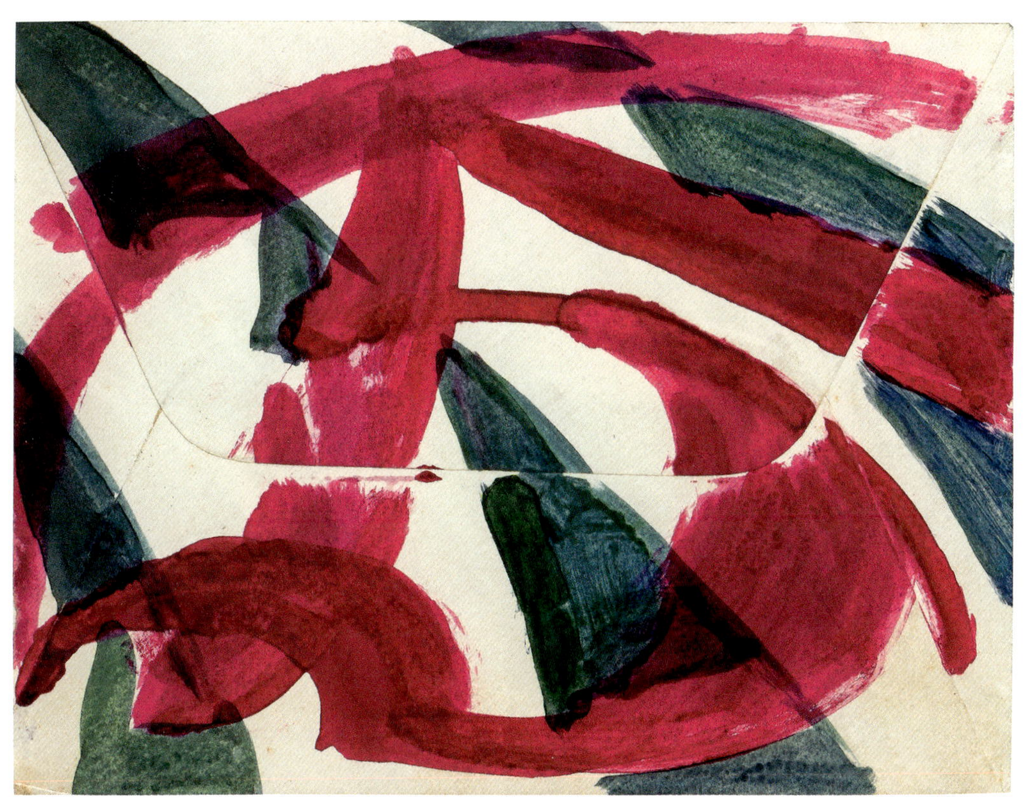

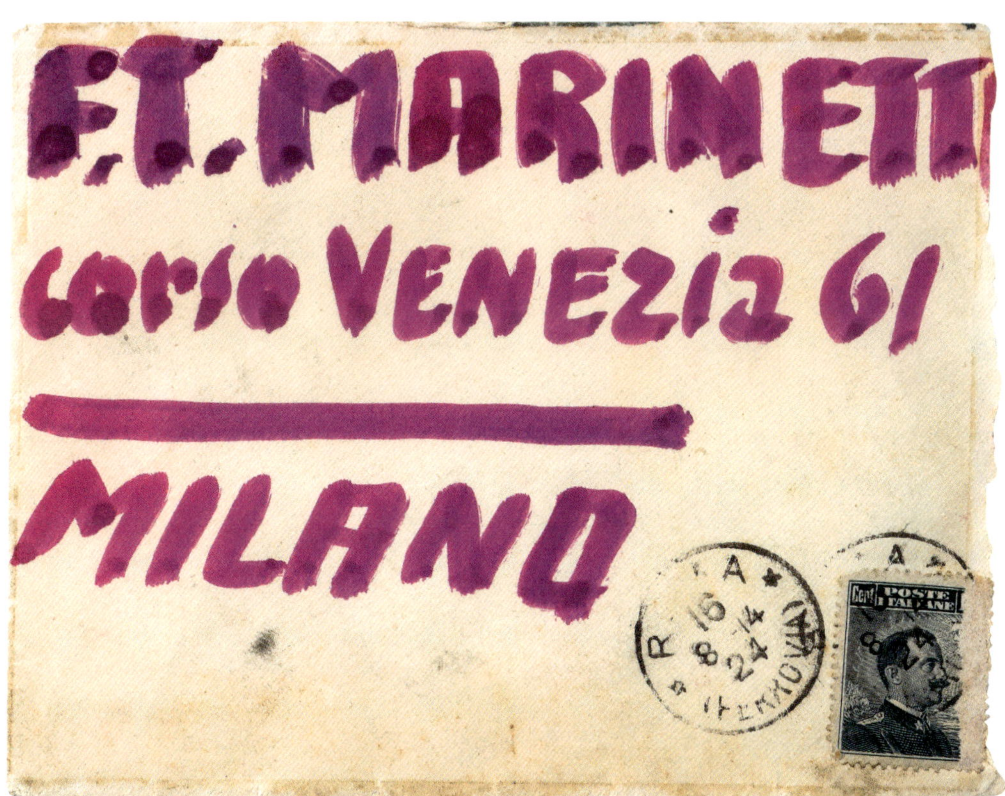

89a-b

Composizione astratta – Linee di velocità
(Abstract Composition – Lines of Speed), 1914
(letter to Filippo Tommaso Marinetti, 16 August 1914)
mixed media on paper, 11 x 13.5 cm

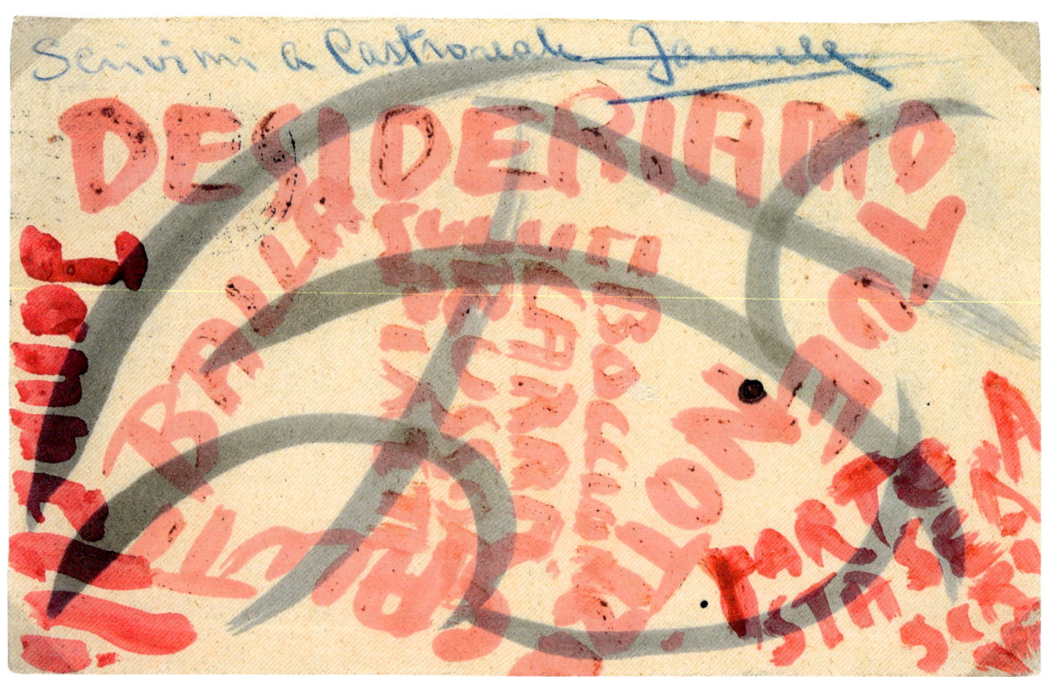

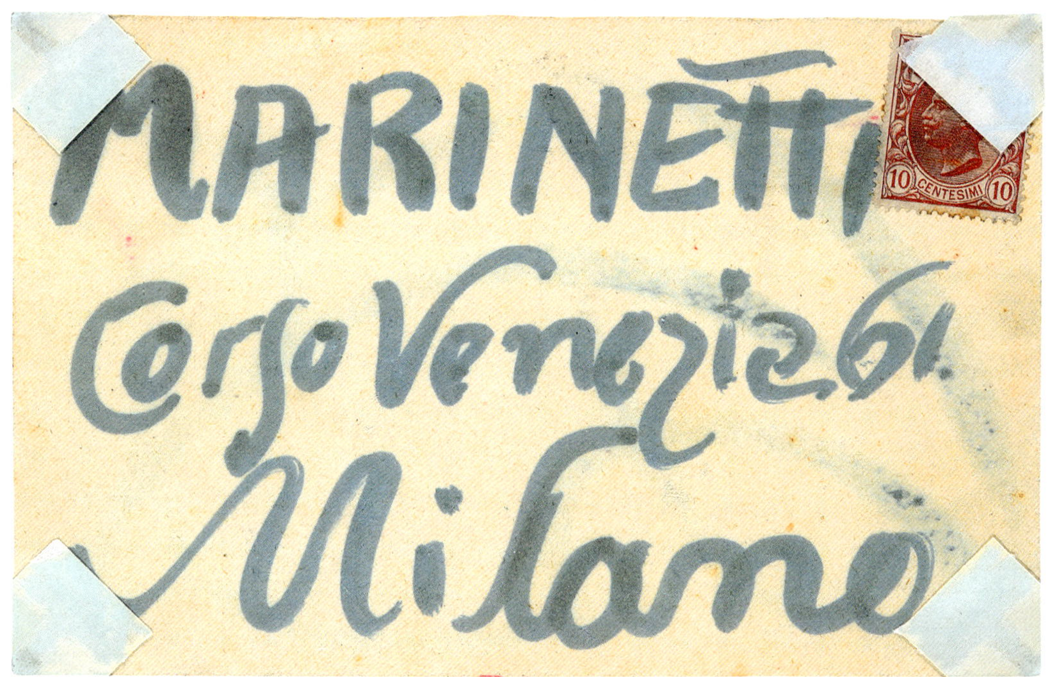

90a-b

Desideriamo tue notizie (We hope to hear from you), 1914
(postcard to Filippo Tommaso Marinetti, 1914)
watercolour on pasteboard, 9 x 14 cm

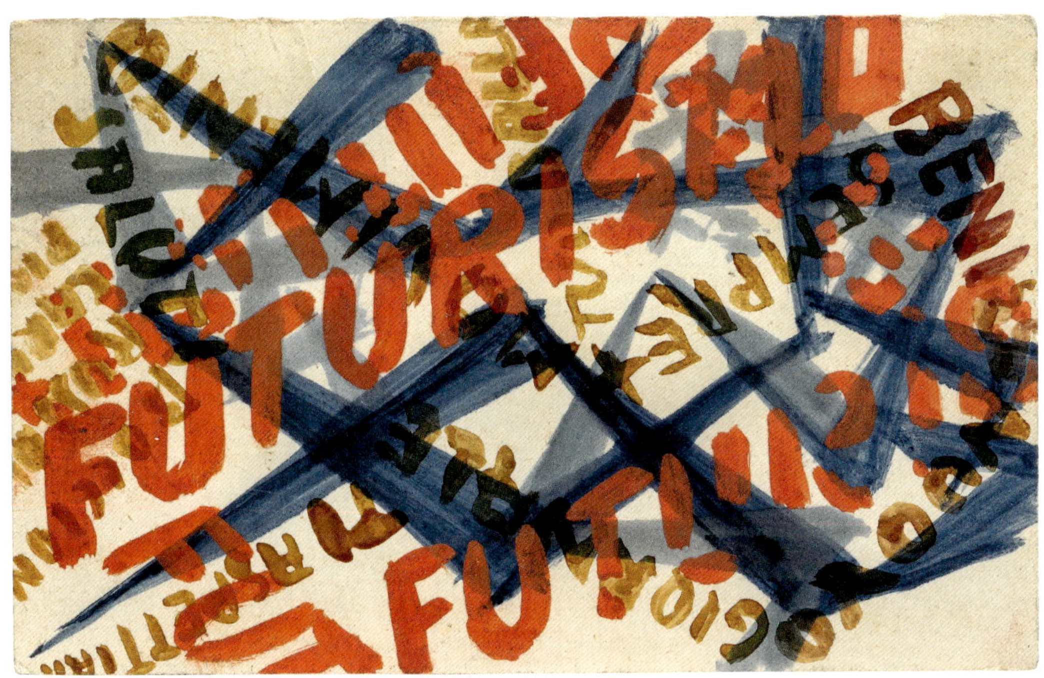

91a-b

Futurismo Futurismo (Futurism Futurism), 1914
(postcard to Filippo Tommaso Marinetti, 11 November 1914)
watercolour on paper, 9 x 14 cm

As Severini wrote in recalling the experience of those years: "Balla painted with separate and contrasting colours like the French artists. His pictorial quality was first rate, genuine ... We were very fortunate to meet such a man, whose guidance may have completely determined our careers."

Balla showed *Il sentiero* at the 1902 Turin Quadrennial, where Pellizza da Volpedo presented *Il Quarto Stato* (*The Fourth Estate*), a work epitomizing its author's social and humanitarian commitment, which received a cold and baffled reception from the critics and no official mention.

Balla also began to address subjects of a more social nature, alternating between the neutrality of an openly photographic approach in works like *Fallimento* (*Bankruptcy*) and compassionate realism, as in the first canvases of the series entitled *I viventi* (*The Living*), a major project for a polyptych "of new truth and tragically human feeling" to which Balla devoted his energies for several years. In addition to *Il contadino* (*The Farmer*), *I malati* (*The Sick*), *La pazza* (*The Mad Woman*) and *Il mendicante* (*The Beggar*), it was originally to have included many other subjects of social marginalization.

Balla married Elisa Marcucci in 1904 and they moved to an apartment in a former monastery on Via Parioli, now Via Paisiello, where they lived until 1926. It was from the long balcony that Balla observed for years the slow change of the urban outskirts and the natural scenery of Villa Borghese with "big trees all around and meadows ... in the middle of fields where they were beginning to construct some buildings, sunshine, wind, stars and swallows in the spring". The surrounding environment provided him with constant stimuli and he depicted it in countless works all through his life.

The transformation of the city skyline prompted one of the masterpieces of this period, namely *La giornata dell'operaio* (*The Worker's Day*), which presents the toil of construction through two different images of building sites. December 1904 saw the birth of his first daughter, named Lucia after his mother and later renamed Luce ("Light") during the years of Futurism.

The years before the Futurist period saw the continuation of work on *I viventi* as well as numerous commissions for portraits. Work was still a presence in paintings like *Il falegname Mariano* (*Mariano the Carpenter*), *La pialla nuova* (*The New Plane*) and the portraits of his friends Duilio Cambellotti and Giovanni Prini, immortalized in the act of artistic creation. Balla took part in numerous Italian exhibitions and showed the polyptych *I viventi* together with some views of Villa Borghese in 1909 at the Salon d'Automne in Paris. Umberto Boccioni, who also showed work there, invited him to fight for the Futurist cause shortly afterwards.

La risposta che ai
dato a Papini doveva
essere più VIOLENTA
Facendogli compren-
dere
che stringendo con tutta
la forza la materia oggettiva
nasce la reazione del
soggettivo Astratto
mio quadro Fallimento
materia oggettiva non
è pari - dica questo come
chiodo, bottiglia, mattone
ma per molti è utile
Tanti [illegible] tuo BALLA

Ill.mo Boccioni
Grazie tuo
FORMIDABILE
LIBRO PRIMO
dopo secoli di
cadavere Arte
Ora di artisti
e vivi e morti
dirci [illegible]

per sempre e parlare più di noi
sempre
Abbiamo fatto esposizione Firenze
Roma e sulla Lacerba quasi niente
invece converrebbe parlare di
ogni quadro aggiungendo Fot. o dise[illegible]
altrimenti ai pittori il giornale
pubblica [illegible] inutili
scherzetti

92a-b

Letter to Umberto Boccioni, 1914
watercolour and India ink on paper, 18 x 22 cm

Balla signed *Manifesto dei pittori futuristi* on 11 February 1910 and *La pittura futurista. Manifesto tecnico* on 11 April. His allegiance to Futurism is, however, to be regarded at first as no more than agreement with the movement's general principles, as no radical changes took place in his painting straight away. His vision was gradually ripening to take up the new challenges.

Balla's Futurist horizons began to take shape with *Lampada ad arco* (*Street Light*), which can be seen as a clear reference to Marinetti's call to murder moonlight (*Uccidiamo il chiaro di luna*) but constitutes at the same time the culmination of the work on the theme of artificial light developed since his early years in Rome.

Balla's new pupils included Gino Galli and a young lady from Vienna. She married a German lawyer named Löwenstein in 1912 and they asked Balla to go to Düsseldorf and decorate their home there.

The work is documented in some photographs of the period, which show the studio with a long frieze of the urban panorama running all the way around the room. Balla worked on this project for several months, his first stay in July 1912 being followed by another in the autumn until the end of December.

Balla often wrote to his family and his pupil Galli during those months, giving all his impressions of the German city and telling them about his new pictorial investigations. He also commented on the Sonderbund, one of the most important international exhibitions of avant-garde art, which he went to see in Cologne.

It was in the Löwenstein home that Balla painted *Finestra su Düsseldorf* (*Window in Düsseldorf*), a study of light featuring the view he saw every morning from his room, immersed in a pale glow of small bluish and yellow flecks. Light and its refraction were also addressed in a series of drawings and watercolours that finally came to be named *Compenetrazioni iridescenti* (*Iridescent Interpenetrations*) after first being referred to as "iridi": "this study will introduce other changes into painting and the iris will be able, through the observation of life, to have and give endless sensations of colour".

The persistence of this exploration is reflected in the decomposed colour of *Bambina che corre sul balcone* (*Girl Running on a Balcony*), in which Balla also addressed another important theme of the moment, namely kinetic reproduction of a body in motion. The work was shown together to *Lampada ad arco*, *La mano del violinista* (*The Hand of the Violinist*; painted in Düsseldorf) and *Dinamismo di un cane al guinzaglio* (*Dynamism of a Dog on a Leash*) in the Futurist group exhibition at the Teatro Costanzi, Rome, in February 1913. His first kinematic works evidently display the influence of Étienne-Jules Marey and Eadweard Muybridge, who captured the successive, sequential phases of movement by means of chronophotography at the end of the 19th century. These studies also inform the experiments on dynamism in Futurist photography carried out by the Bragaglia brothers, with whom Balla developed close relations.

The new pictorial path embarked upon came to absorb him completely, leading to the utter rejection of his previous works. This is the reason for Balla's determination to sever all ties with the past, to which end he took vigorous steps by organizing an auction in April 1913 at the Giosi gallery on Via del Babuino, advertised with a leaflet announcing his death, and proclaiming his rebirth as a Futurist.

It was his wife Elisa that managed to have the event cancelled with the aid of Nathan, the mayor of Rome and a close friend of the family.

Balla's association with the Futurists provided a powerful stimulus for progress towards a new, experimental art and prompted attention to the major international avant-garde. *Lampada ad arco* was listed among the works in the catalogues of the first Futurist exhibition in Paris at the Galerie Bernheim-Jeune (February 1912) and the Rotterdam show of May 1913, one of the many stages of the Futurist tour. In September the group took part with a selection of works in the Erster Deutscher Herbstsalon (First German Salon d'Automne) at the Galerie Der Sturm, founded by Herwarth Walden, editor of the journal of the same name. Balla was included with *La mano del violinista* and *Dinamismo di un cane al guinzaglio*. The event was of crucial importance to the Futurists, who thus exhibited work together with key figures in the modern experimental movements all over Europe.

Balla continued his work on dynamics all the way to *Volo di rondini (Linee andamentali + successioni dinamiche)* (*Flight of Swallows – Paths of Movement + Dynamic Sequences*) and the identification of abstract linear schemata.

Having freed himself from "the burden of experience", Balla began "in the middle of a huge, empty, snow white room to draw on sheets of paper the first lines of a speeding automobile, initially objective and later synthetic, the basic foundations of his thought forms: his irrefutable creations." He addressed the theme of speed in a series of works that attest to the transition from compositions still bound to the observation of life to works in which the image becomes more abstract. Motion spread from the automobile to the surrounding space to take shape in "plastic complexes". Balla showed his works on speed in the major Futurist exhibitions, including the *Lacerba* show in Florence (1913) and those held in 1914 at the Galleria Futurista Permanente Sprovieri in Rome and the Doré Gallery in London.

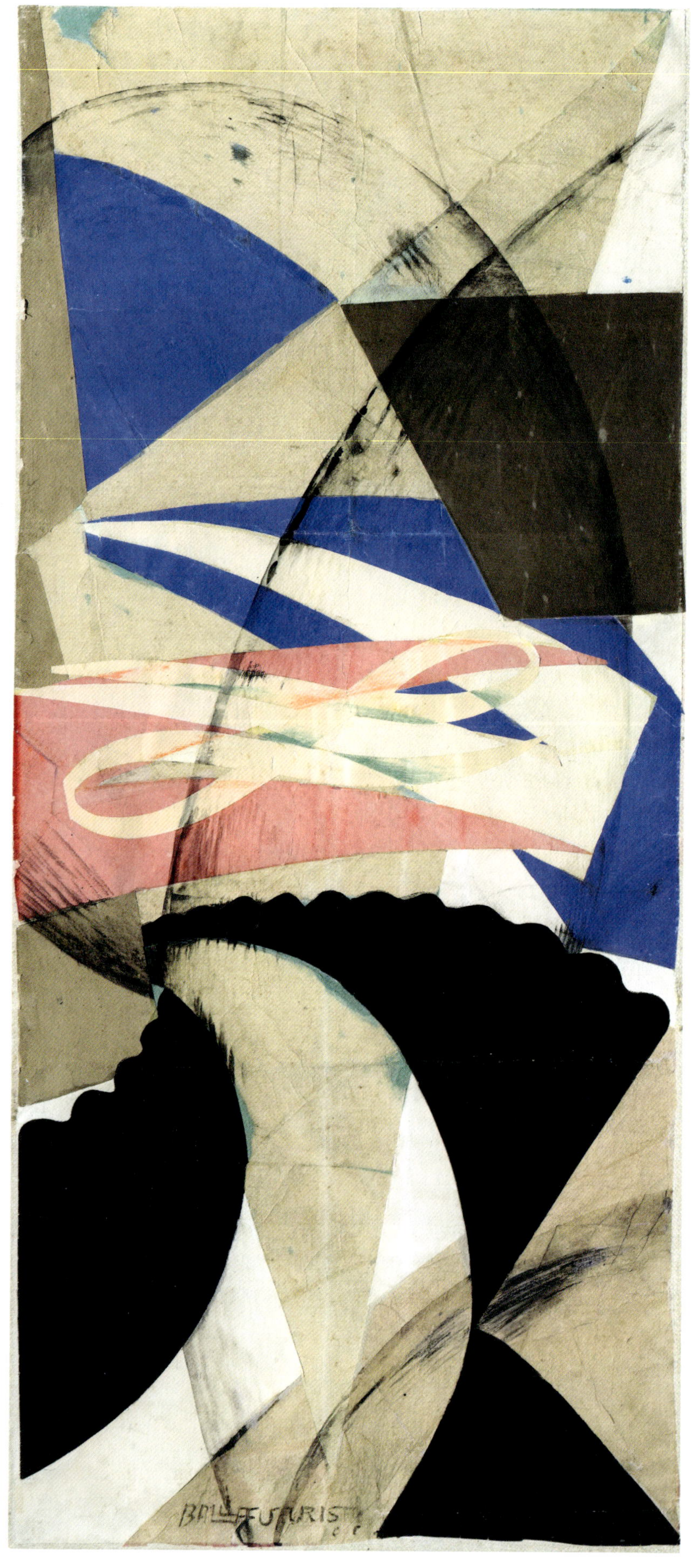

Opposite
93

Folla + Paesaggio (Crowd + Landscape), 1915
collage of painted paper and tissue paper laid down
on canvas, mounted on masonite, 152.5 x 66.7 cm

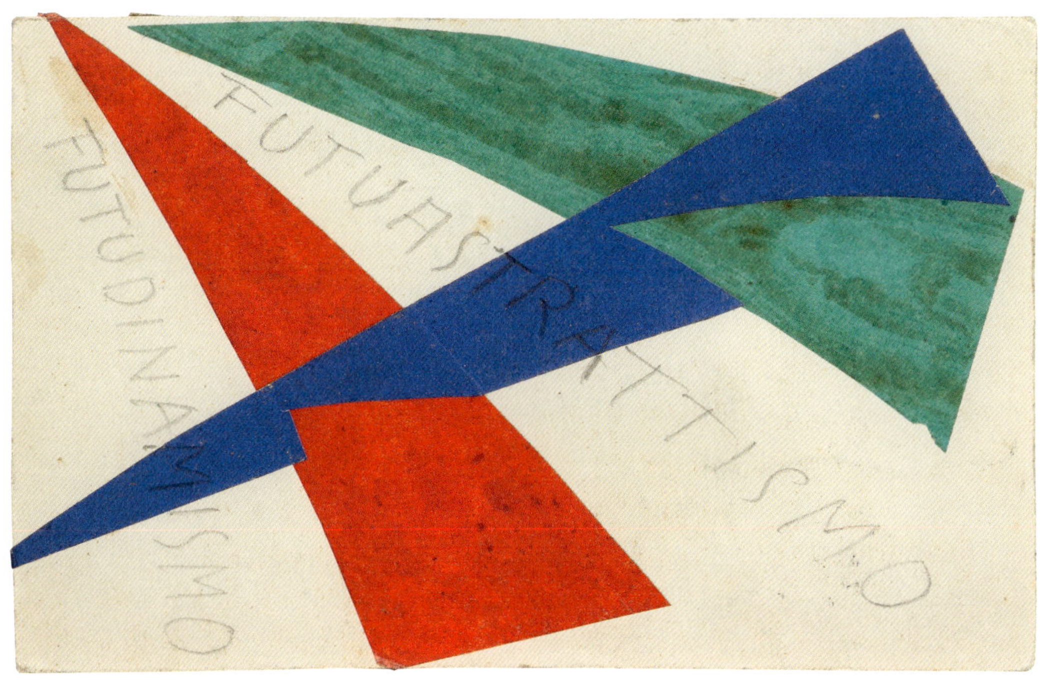

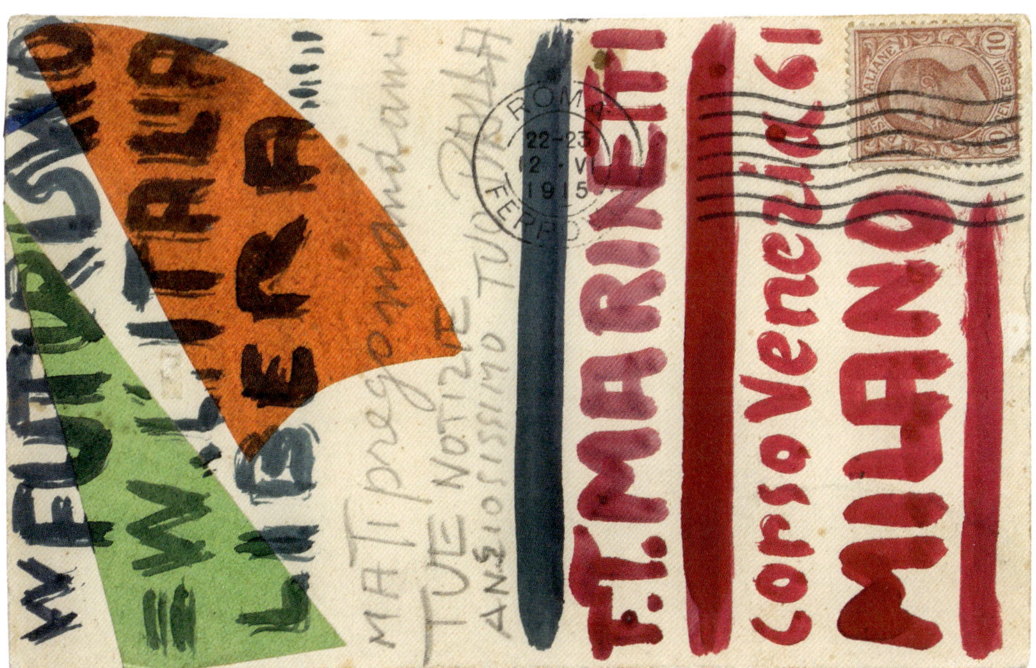

94a-b

Futuastrattismo Futudinamismo
(Futuabstractism Futudynamism), 1915
(postcard to Filippo Tomaso Marinetti, 12 June 1915)
tempera and collage on pasteboard, 8 x 14.2 cm

On the outbreak of the Great War, the Futurists called for Italy to take part and Balla took an active part in the group's tumultuous interventionist demonstrations as well as painting a series of works on war shown in 1915 at the Sala d'Arte Angelelli in Rome. It was in this general atmosphere of patriotic frenzy that he wrote the *Manifesto del vestito antineutrale* (*Manifesto of Anti-Neutral Clothing*), which appeared in September 1914.

It was for his second daughter Elica, born in October the same year, that he designed Futurist furniture in line with the principles of the *Ricostruzione futurista dell'universo* (*Futurist Reconstruction of the Universe*), a manifesto jointly authored by Balla and Fortunato Depero the following year.

The sudden deaths of Boccioni and Sant'Elia in 1916 led to a change in direction for the first wave of Futurism. The new experimental nature of the new artistic approaches of Carrà, Severini and Soffici, and Russolo's almost exclusive interest in music left Balla as the only member of the original nucleus to continue along the Futurist path as a constant point of reference in Rome for the new recruits that gave birth to the movement's second phase.

Balla's drawing *Pugno italiano di Boccioni* (*Boccioni's Italian Fist*), published shortly after his former pupil's death in the Florentine journal *L'Italia Futurista*, was subsequently developed into the sculpture of the same name, in line with the "plastic complexes" of 1915.

In 1916 Balla was among the signatories of the Futurist manifesto on cinematography and involved in the making of the film *Vita Futurista*, also as a scriptwriter.

The same period saw closer relations with esoteric circles frequented by intellectuals, aristocrats and artists of international standing. He took part in séances with his pupil Růžena Zátková and also developed his relationship with the Marchesa Luisa Casati, whom he had met through Marinetti and depicted in numerous portraits.

In the meantime, he was commissioned to produce sets for Stravinsky's *Feu d'artifice* by Sergei Diaghilev, the famous impresario of the Ballets Russes. The work was staged in April 1917 at the Teatro Costanzi in Rome in a setting of brightly coloured abstract shapes illuminated by a rhythmic sequence of lights corresponding to the movements of music. The first and only performance was a complete failure, however, as a mistake on the part of the management left the theatre and stage in utter darkness. The vigorously anti-naturalistic nature of the sets, every piece of which was later purchased by Balla for a considerable sum, is evidently reflected also in the *Forze di paesaggio* (*Landscape Forces*) series that he began to paint the same year. In these works, having abandoned the cult of modernity, the

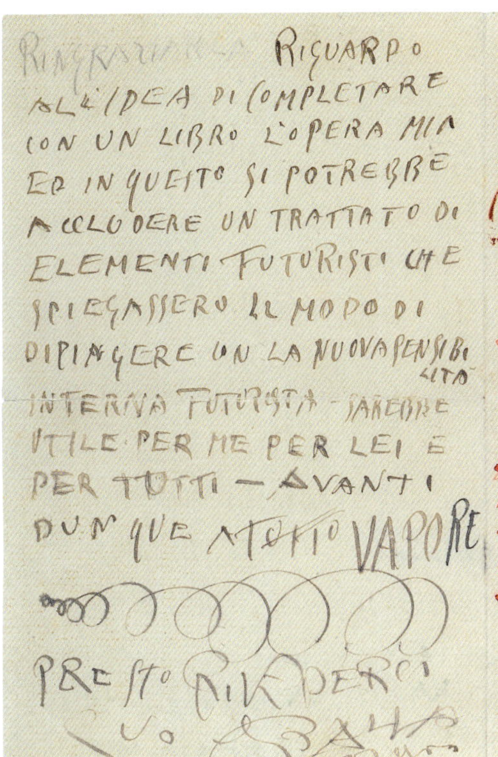

Ringraziamenti Riguardo
all'idea di completare
con un libro l'opera mia
ed in questo si potrebbe
accludere un trattato di
elementi futuristi che
spiegassero il modo di
dipingere con la nuova sensibilità
interna futurista – sarebbe
utile per me per lei e
per tutti – avanti
dunque a tutto vapore

Presto rivederci
suo Balla futurista

18.4.20

Carissimo Marchi

Balla futurista

Ritornato ora fuori per un lavoro
leggo ora suo articolo e lettera
Meravigliosissimo
Veda questo tipo di parole ornamentali
da applicarsi architettura futurista

Sopratutto vedo nel suo nuovo
tipo di critica balza fuori il
suo temperamento

che istruisce il pubblico di intellettualissime finezze da
renderlo migliore come esistenza ← certamente
fra qualche anno avremo superato le difficoltà
materiali e distrutte le contemplative passatiste
avremo così un'infinità di lavori che spiegheranno
finalmente la nuova arte futurista

Il suo articolo lo farò tirare a macchina poi leggere
e vedremo di piazzarlo molto bene anche per risultato pratico

Sono in vista diverse cose che vanno svolgendo
insieme ai cambiamenti della vita – ma per risolverli si
dovrebbero risoluzioni politiche sociali energiche
decise con qualche violenza delle forze nuove le quali
ci facessero uscire da questa [illegible] infettante
caro Marchi le sono gratissimo e non ò parole per

95a-b

Lettera metallica (Metallic Letter), 1915
(letter to Mario Broglio and Aldo Molinari, 1915)
tempera and pencil on paper, 20 x 28.5 cm

Opposite
97

Poster for the show at the Galleria Angelelli, Rome, 1915
tempera and watercolour on paper, 94 x 65 cm

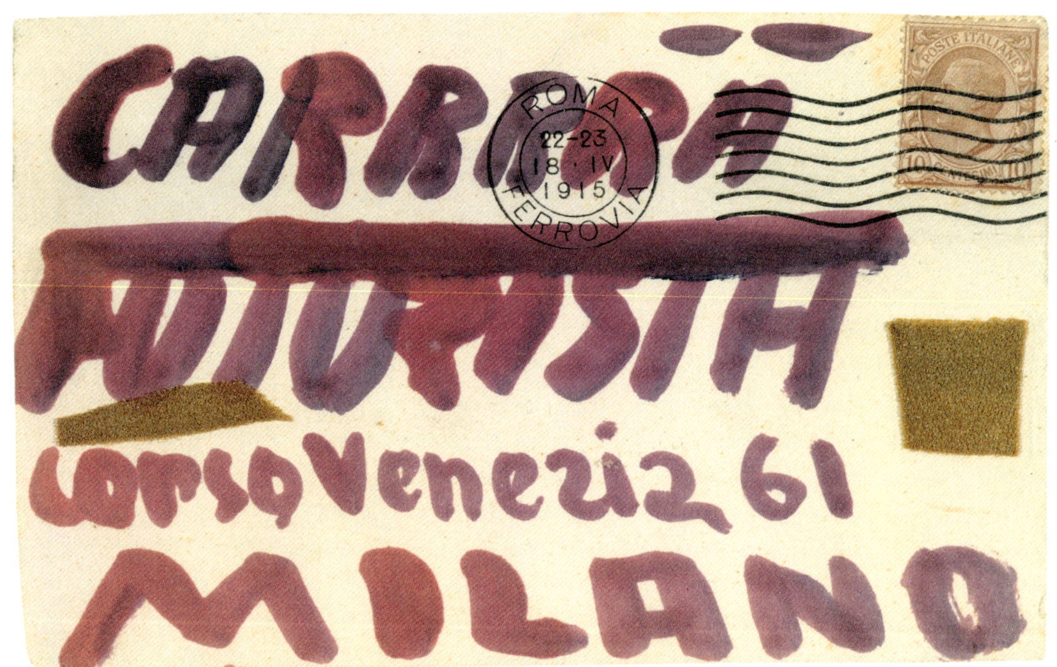

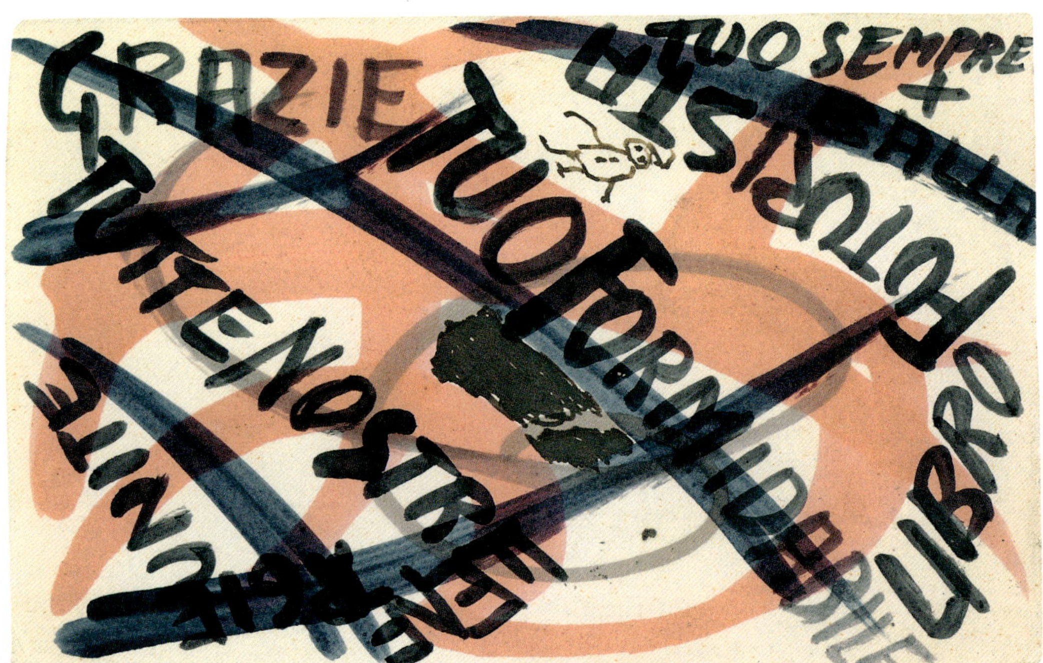

96a-b

Linee di velocità (Lines of Speed) , 1915
(postcard to Carlo Carrà, 18 April 1915)
watercolour on pasteboard, 9 x 14 cm

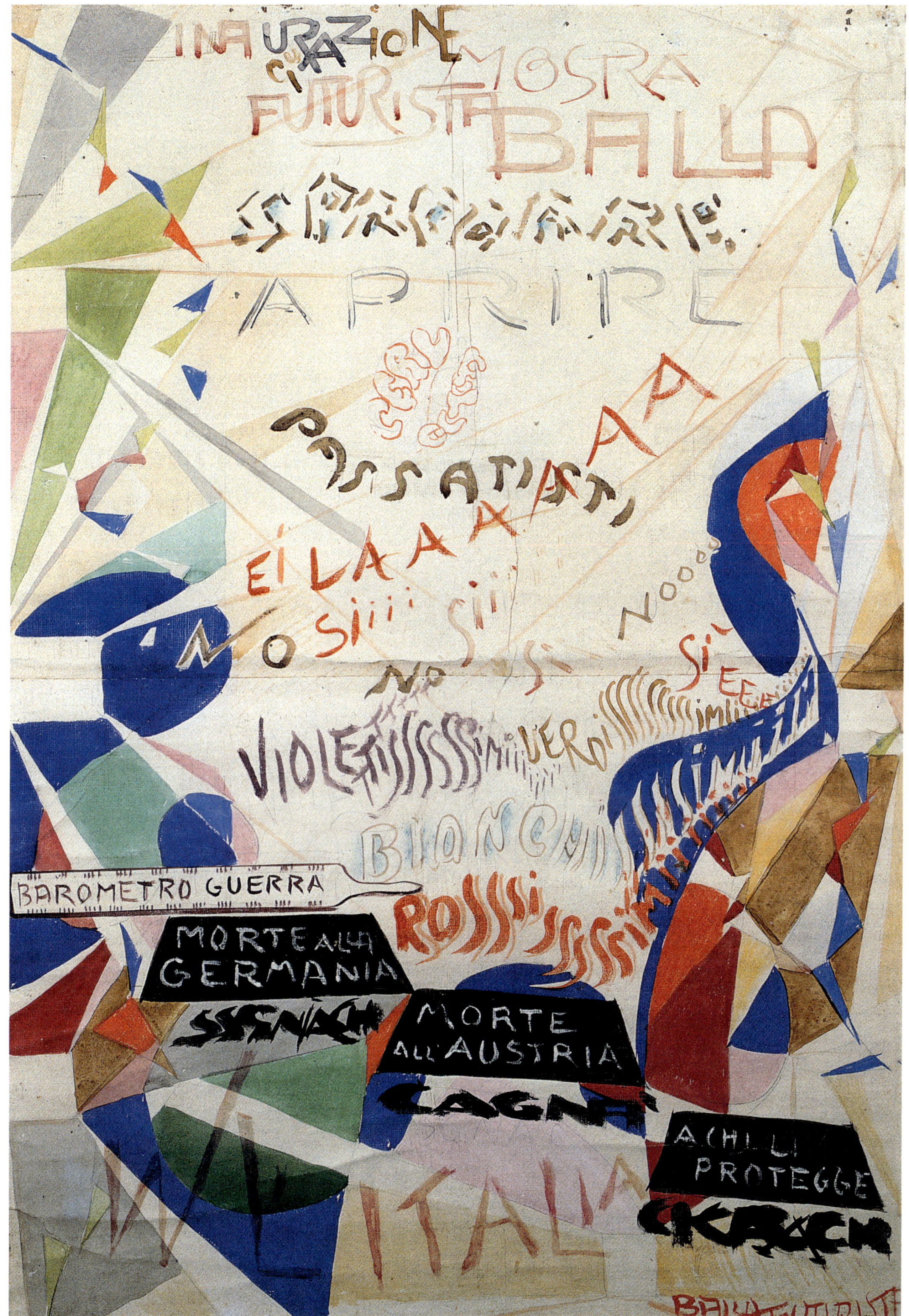
INAUGURAZIONE
MOSTRA FUTURISTA
BALLA
APRIRE
PASSATISTI
BAROMETRO GUERRA
MORTE ALLA GERMANIA
MORTE ALL'AUSTRIA
CAGNA
ACHILLI PROTEGGE
ITALIA
BALLA FUTURISTA

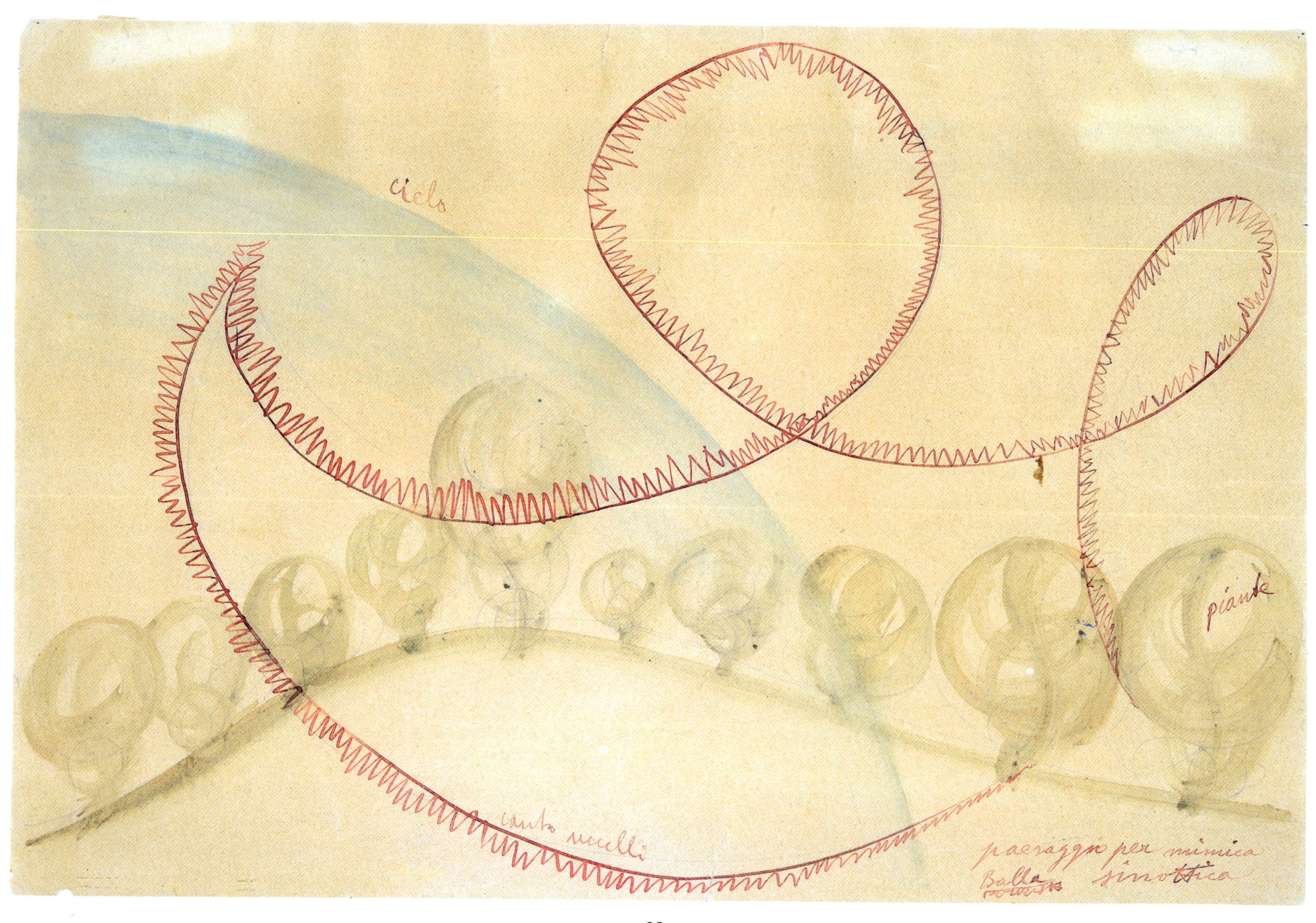

98

Mimica sinottica o Primavera – Paesaggio
(Synoptic Mimicry or Spring – Landscape), 1915
watercolour on paper, 22 x 32.5 cm

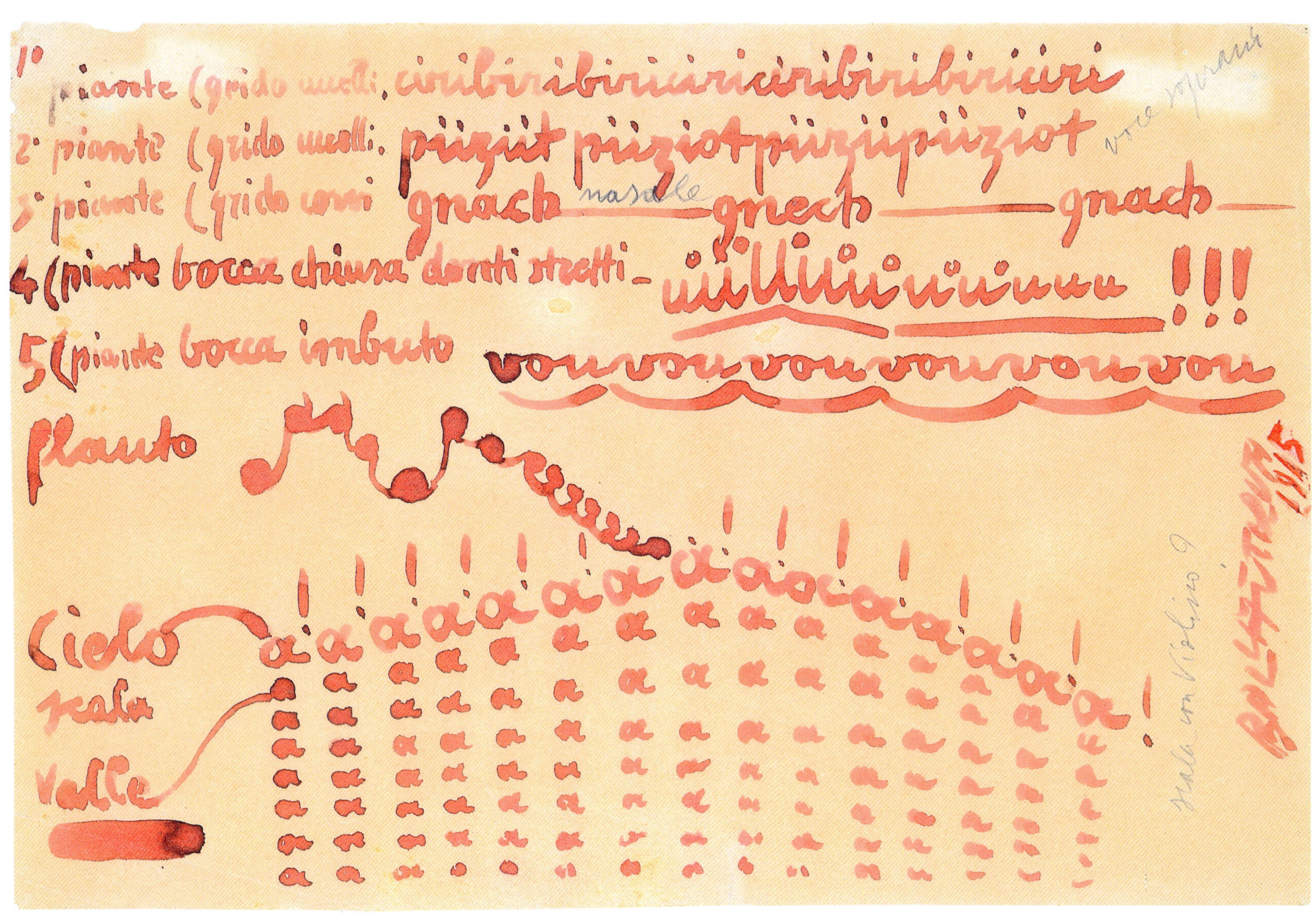

99

Mimica sinottica o Primavera – Testo rumorista
(Mimicry Synoptic or Spring – Noisist text), 1915
watercolour on paper, 22 x 32 cm

artist returned to nature, represented as an absolute in formal schemata of pure colour and geometry capable of expressing the cosmic energy of the natural cycles in association with sensations of sight, small and touch.

Some of these new works were exhibited in Balla's solo show at the Casa d'Arte Bragaglia, Rome, in 1918, on the occasion of which he also published his *Manifesto del colore*, stressing the abstract use of colour as an element amplifying cosmic energy.

In 1919 he took part in the national Futurist exhibition at Palazzo Cova in Milan, where he showed the plastic complex *Ritratto della Marchesa Casati* (*Portrait of the Marchesa Casati*).

The early 1920s saw a greater focus on decorative art. His home in the Parioli district was opened to the public and became a temple of creations inspired by the Futurist lifestyle. He had joined the editorial board of *Roma Futurista* in 1920 and the event was publicized in its pages. In 1921 Balla designed and produced the interior decoration of the nightclub Bal Tik Tak in Via Milano and the new premises of the Casa d'Arte Bragaglia in Via degli Avignonesi, only some evidence of which has survived.

Balla exhibited a series of Futurist tapestries in Paris at the Exposition Internationale des Arts Décoratifs in 1925.

He was forced to leave his beloved home in the Parioli district in 1926 but was able to stay nearby with friends. He developed still closer relations with his hosts, artists in their own right and the focal point of a group of intellectuals who habitually gathered at their home at Cotorniano, in the countryside outside Siena.

The same year saw participation together with Depero and Prampolini in the Exhibition of Modern Italian Art, which opened in New York at the Grand Central Galleries and then went on to Boston, Washington D.C. and Chicago.

Meanwhile, Fascism continued its advance with the support of Futurism, which saw it as a subversive movement capable of realizing its own revolutionary aspirations to modernize the country's culture and usher in a future era of progress. Balla produced works on the regime's key themes and presented Mussolini with a sculptural portrait in bronze in 1926.

The same year saw participation in the Venice Biennial with *S'è rotto l'incanto* (*The Spell is Broken*) and *Numeri innamorati* (*Numbers in Love*), both painted in the period 1922–23. The use of letters and numbers as elements of artistic construction recalls the Futurist Words-in-Freedom works but also the artist's interest in the aesthetic machine then taking shape on the international art scene and driven by the post-war spirit of reconstruction.

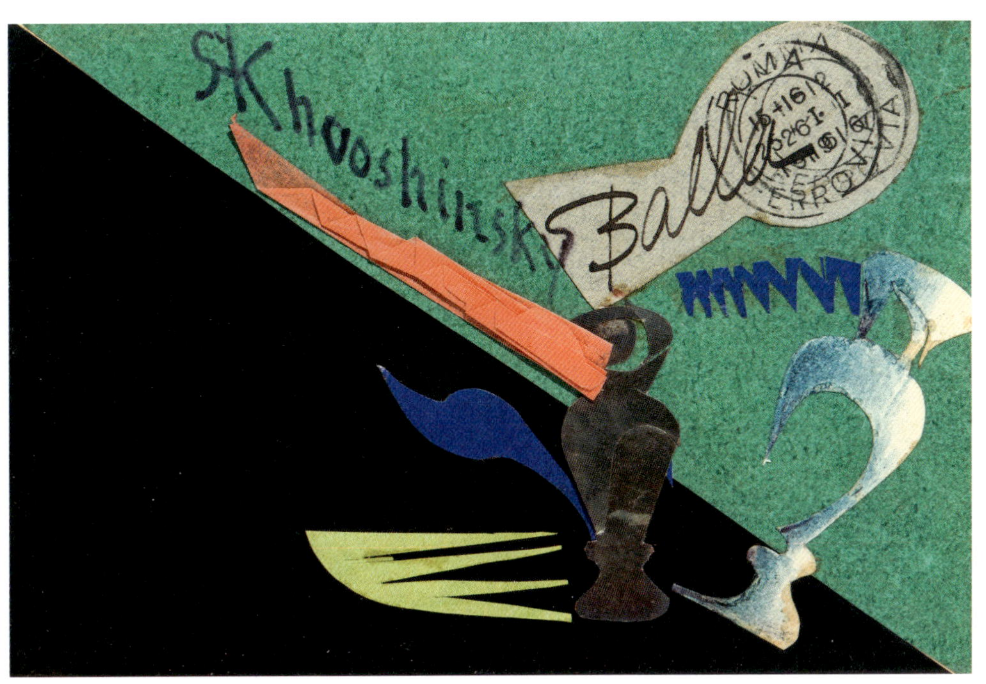

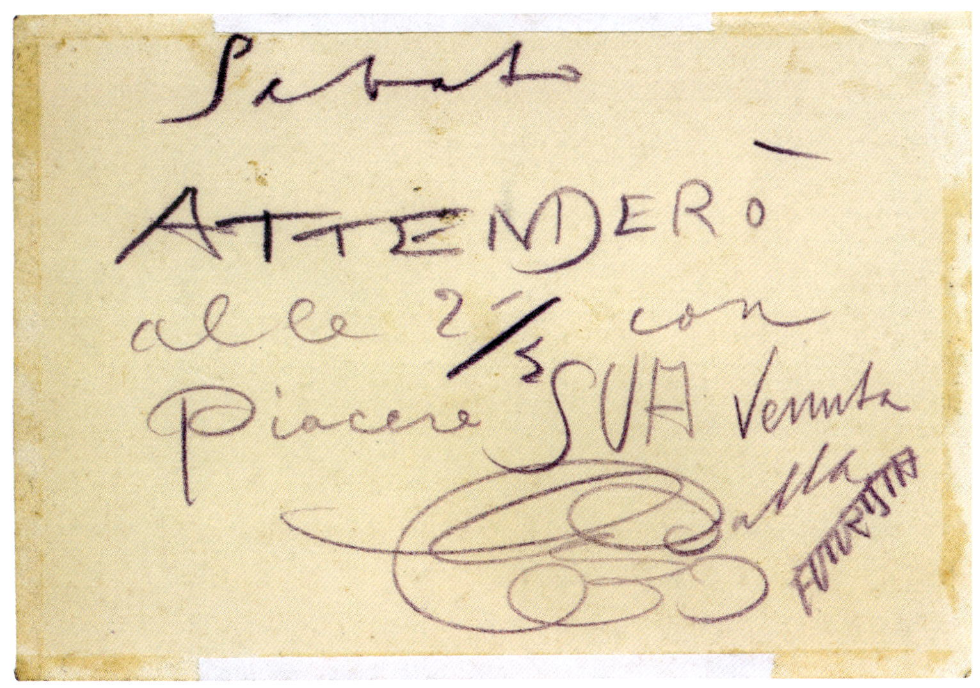

100a-b

Composizione astratta (Abstract Composition), 1916
(postcard to Rougena Khwoshinsky Zatkova,
26 January 1916)
mixed media on paper, 9.5 x 13 cm

Balla moved to Via Oslavia in 1929 and made his first journey in an aeroplane the same year. He also signed the *Manifesto dell'Aeropittura* together with the Neo-Futurists.

The artist rethought his position radically during the 1930s, feeling that Futurist had now run out of steam and returning to figuration "in the conviction that *pure* art lies in absolute realism". *Autocaffè* (*Self-Portrait with a Cup of Coffee*, 1928) already looked forward to a new phase of realism. Steering an independent course with respect to those of the national art scene, Balla returned to realism of a photographic character, which he had in fact never entirely abandoned, foreshadowing in some cases an aesthetic investigation whose vocabulary extended to images of current events and fashion.

Balla's definitive abandonment of the avant-garde experience coincided with recognition of his Futurist works at the international level.

Through the efforts of Margaret Scolari Barr, who visited Balla's home in 1934, and her husband Alfred Barr, director of the New York Museum of Modern Art, *Dinamismo di un cane al guinzaglio* was shown in the exhibition "Cubism and Abstract Art" in 1936.

Barr emphasized the painting's importance as a pioneering work in the letter of request, stating that its historic and almost revolutionary character made it indispensable in an exhibition featuring the various artistic movements of the 20th century. It was then bought by the collector Anson Conger Goodyear and subsequently entered the collection of the Albright-Knox Art Gallery in Buffalo. *Volo di rondini (Linee andamentali + successioni dinamiche)*, *Automobile in corsa* (*Racing Automobile*) and *Lampada ad Arco* were bought by the MoMA at different times.

A selection of Balla's most representative works were then shown at the MoMA in "Twentieth Century Italian Art" in 1949.

Balla's institutional and art-historical consecration began slightly later In Europe and Italy. In the 1950s, after a long silence, his work was "rediscovered" and major purchases were made for public and private collections.

While Balla went on producing figurative paintings mostly characterized by an intimate, family atmosphere, some members of the nascent Italian school of Abstract Art saw his Futurist period as a sort of revelation for their own work.

He met Ettore Colla and Piero Dorazio in that period and some of his historic works were shown in 1951 in an exhibition of the Gruppo Origine, to which the young artists belonged. In 1954 the Rose Fried Gallery in New York organized an exhibition on the Futurist group curated by Dorazio. His wife Virginia Dortch Dorazio, a photographer and writer, published *Giacomo Balla: An Album of His Life and Work* (1969), a precious contribution to our knowledge of the artist that takes us inside his home and studio on Via Oslavia. The period 1948–55 also saw participation in various editions of the Rome Quadrennial with Divisionist, Futurist and post-war works. On 1 March 1958, after a long illness, Balla died at the age of 87 surrounded by the love of his daughters.

In the years after the artist's death, the interest of American critics' in his work bore further witness to the recognition of his fundamental contribution to the art of the 20th century. In 1961 the MoMA in New York held the first exhibition on the Italian Futurist avant-garde, curated by Joshua Taylor, to mark the movement's fiftieth anniversary.

In Italy, it was Turin, the city of his birth, that celebrated Balla with an exhibition at the Galleria Civica d'Arte Moderna in 1963, just a few years after his death. Curated by Enrico Crispolti and Maria Drudi Gambillo, it was the first major Italian retrospective on the work of Giacomo Balla.

The quotations are taken from the following works:
Elica Balla, *Con Balla*, Multhipla Edizioni, 3 vols., Milan, 1984–86
Giacomo Balla, *Giacomo Balla. Scritti futuristi*, ed. Giovanni Lista, Abscondita, Milan, 2010
Gino Severini, *La vita di un pittore*, Edizioni di Comunità, Rome, 1965 (first edition: Garzanti, Milan, 1946)

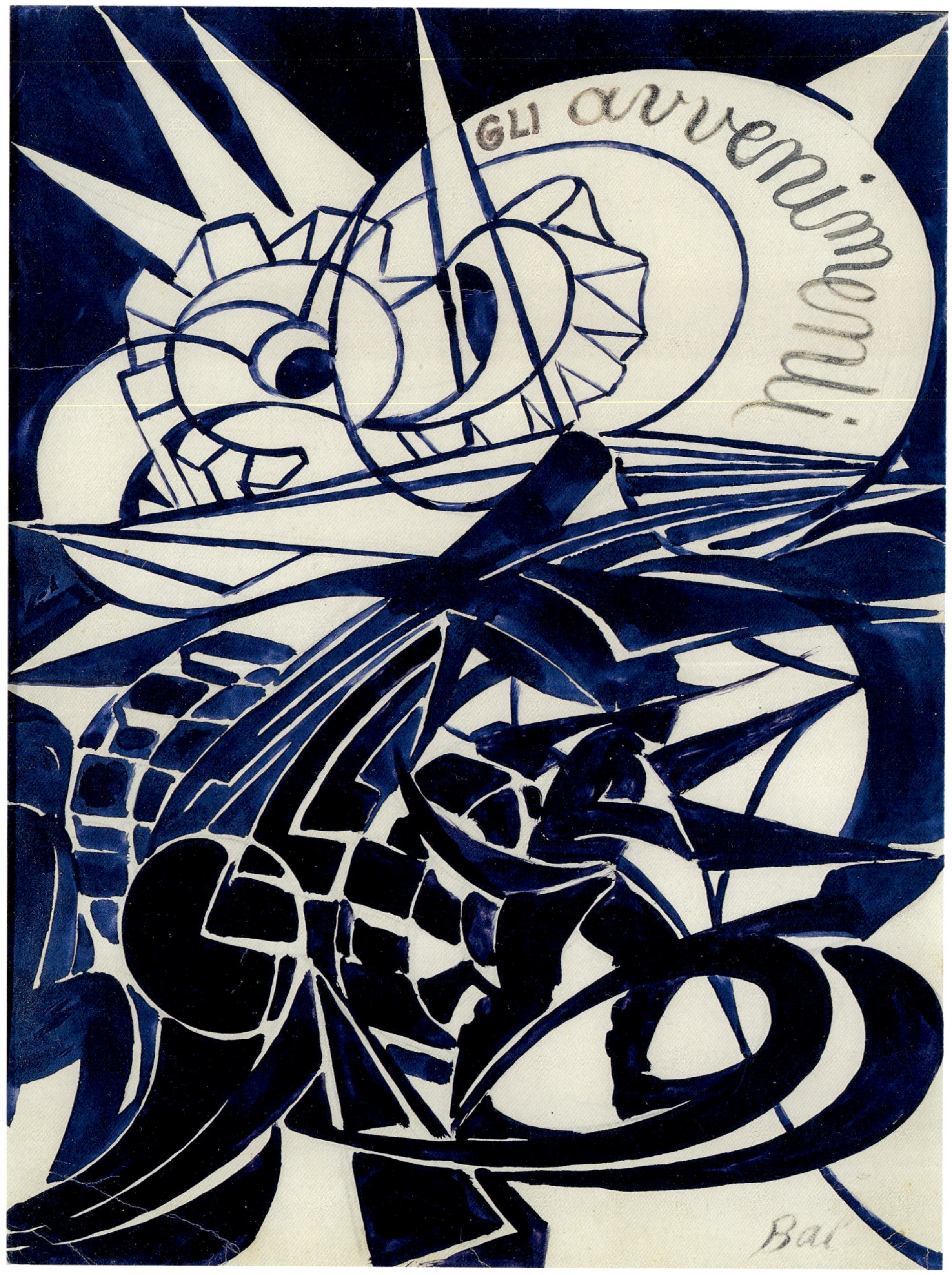

101

Gli Avvenimenti (Events), 1916
India ink on paper, 34 x 25 cm

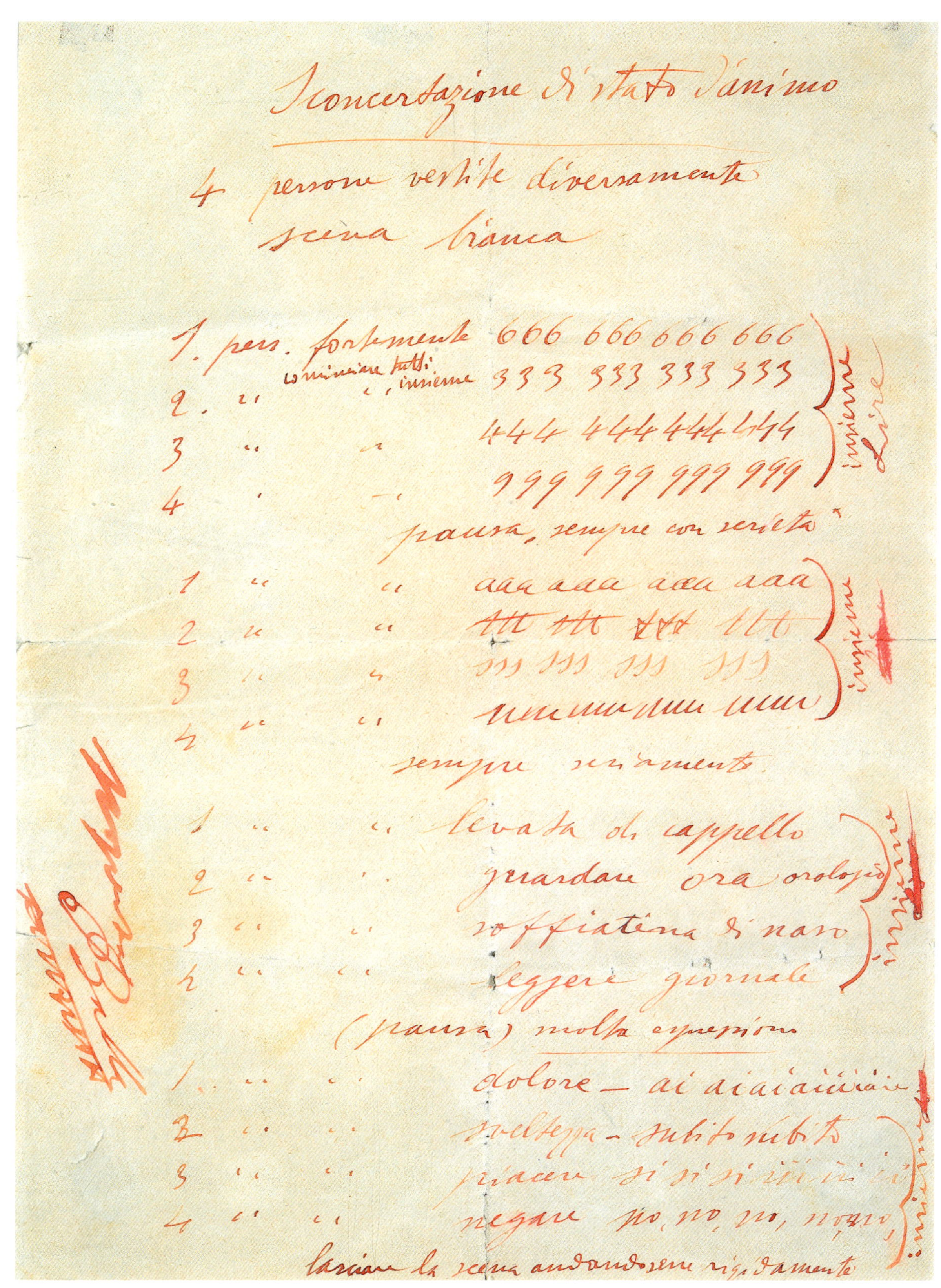

Sconcertazione di stato d'animo

4 persone vestite diversamente
scena bianca

1. pers. fortemente 666 666 666 666
2. " cominciare tutti insieme 333 333 333 333
3 " " 444 444 444 444
4 " " 999 999 999 999
pausa, sempre con serietà
1 " " aaa aaa aaa aaa
2 " " ttt ttt ttt ttt
3 " " sss sss sss sss
4 " " uuu uuu uuu uuu
sempre seriamente
1 " " levata di cappello
2 " " guardare ora orologio
3 " " soffiatina di naso
4 " " leggere giornale
(pausa) molta espressione
1 " " dolore – ai aiaiaiaiai
2 " " sveltezza – subito subito
3 " " piacere – si si si si si
4 " " negare no, no, no, no
lasciare la scena andandosene rigidamente

102

Sconcertazione di stati d'animo
(Disconcerted States of Mind), 1916
ink on paper, 30.5 x 22 cm

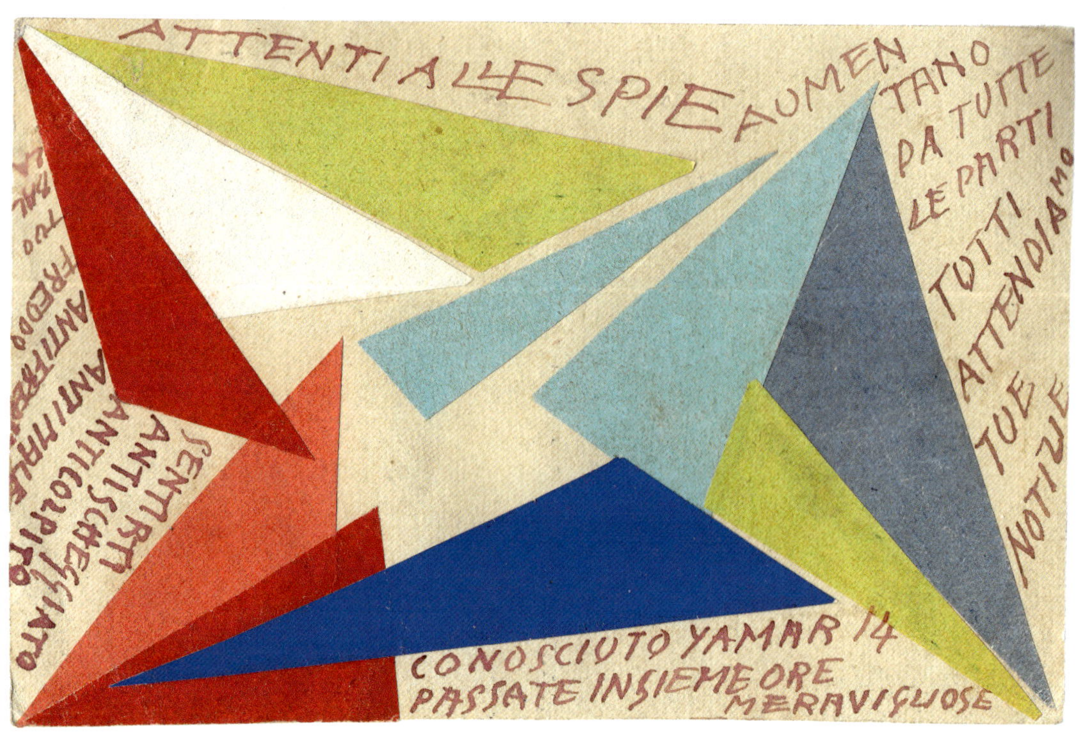

103

Attenti alle spie… (Watch out for spies …), 1917
(postcard to Filippo Tommaso Marinetti, 1917, the war zone)
tempera and collage on paper, 9.2 x 13.7 cm

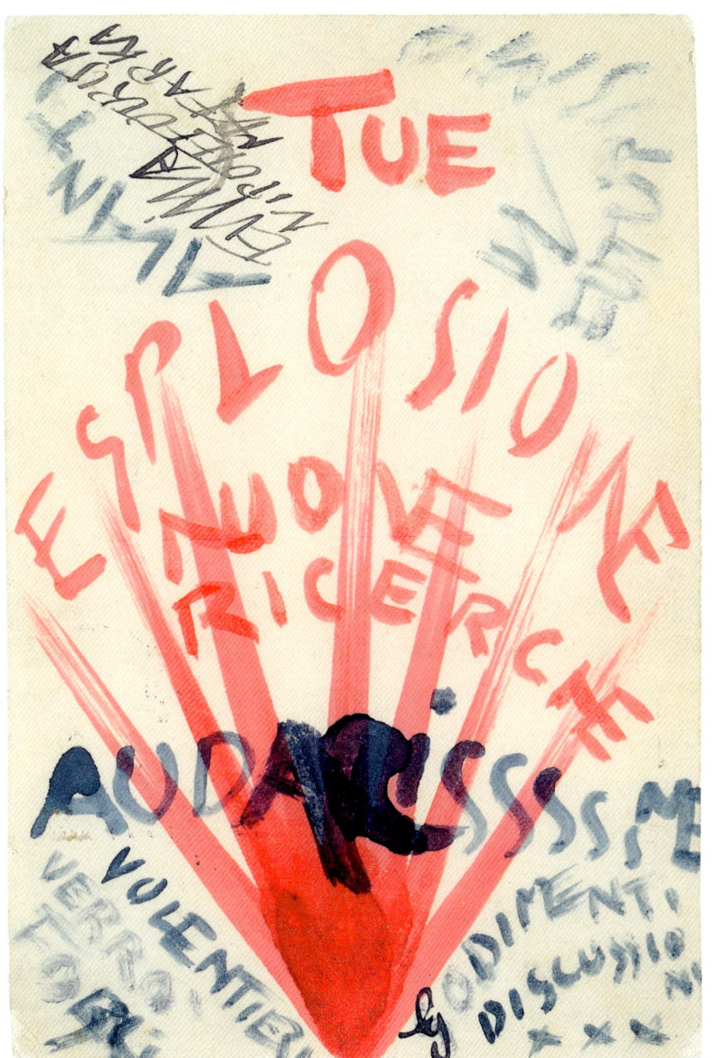

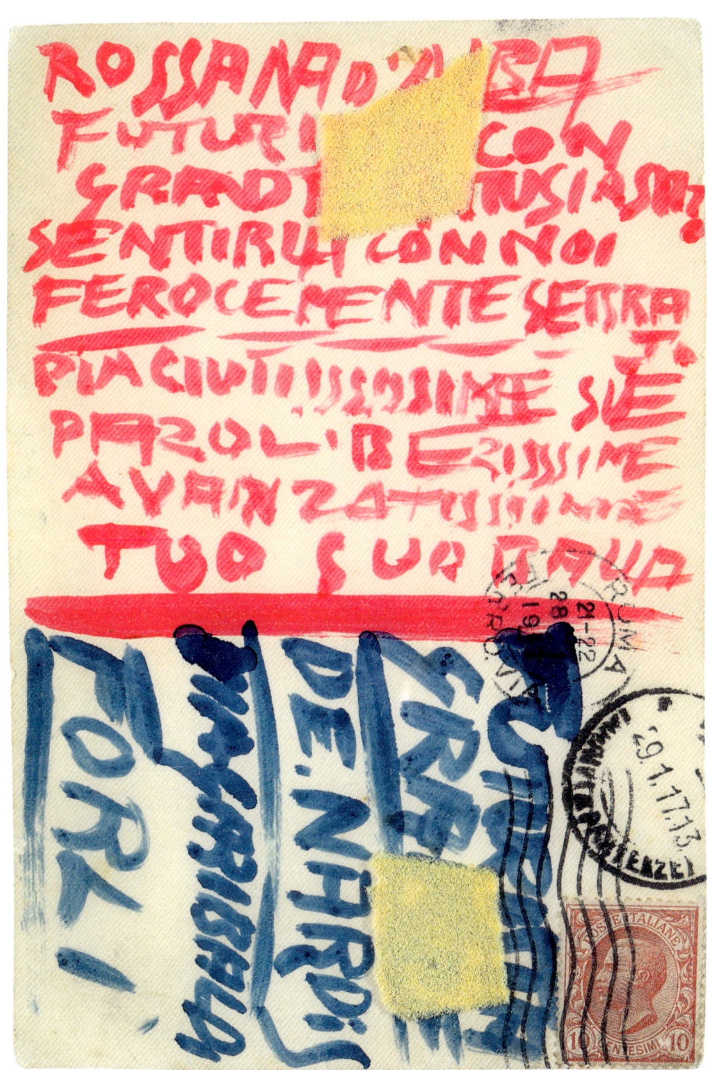

104a-b

Esplosione (Explosion), 1917
(postcard to Luciano De Nardis, 29 January 1917)
watercolour on pasteboard, 9 x 14 cm

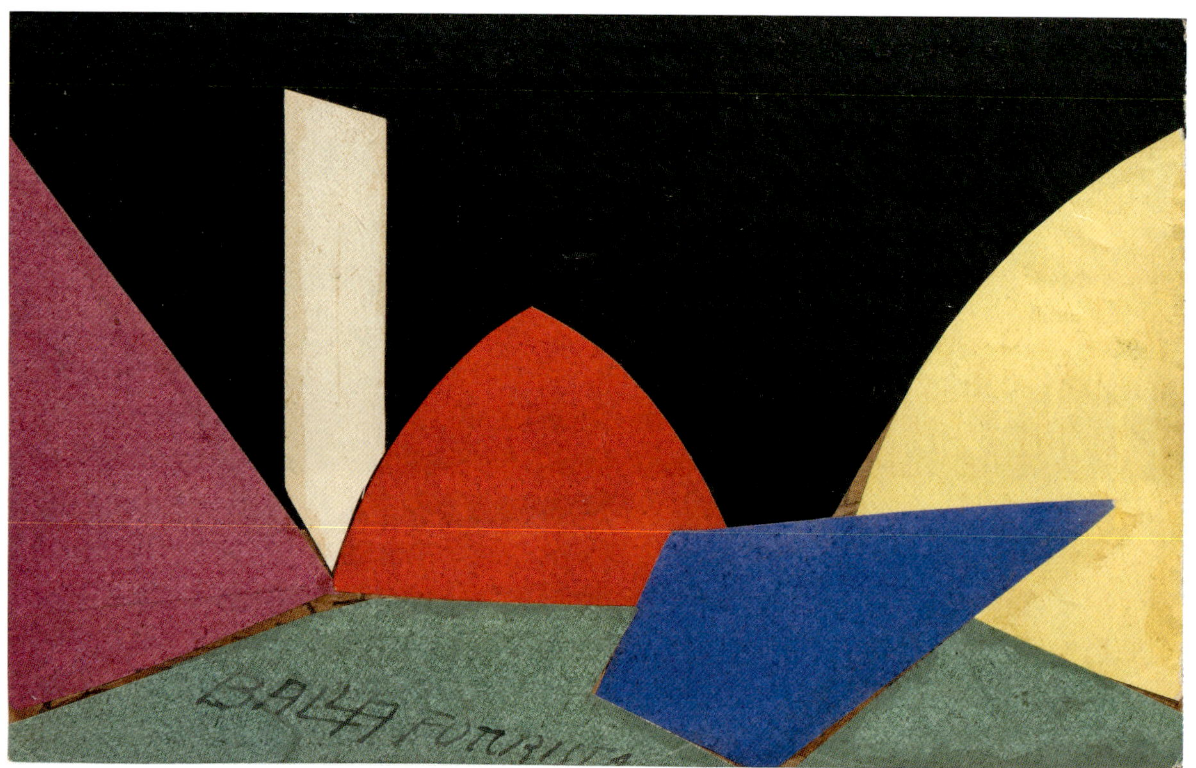

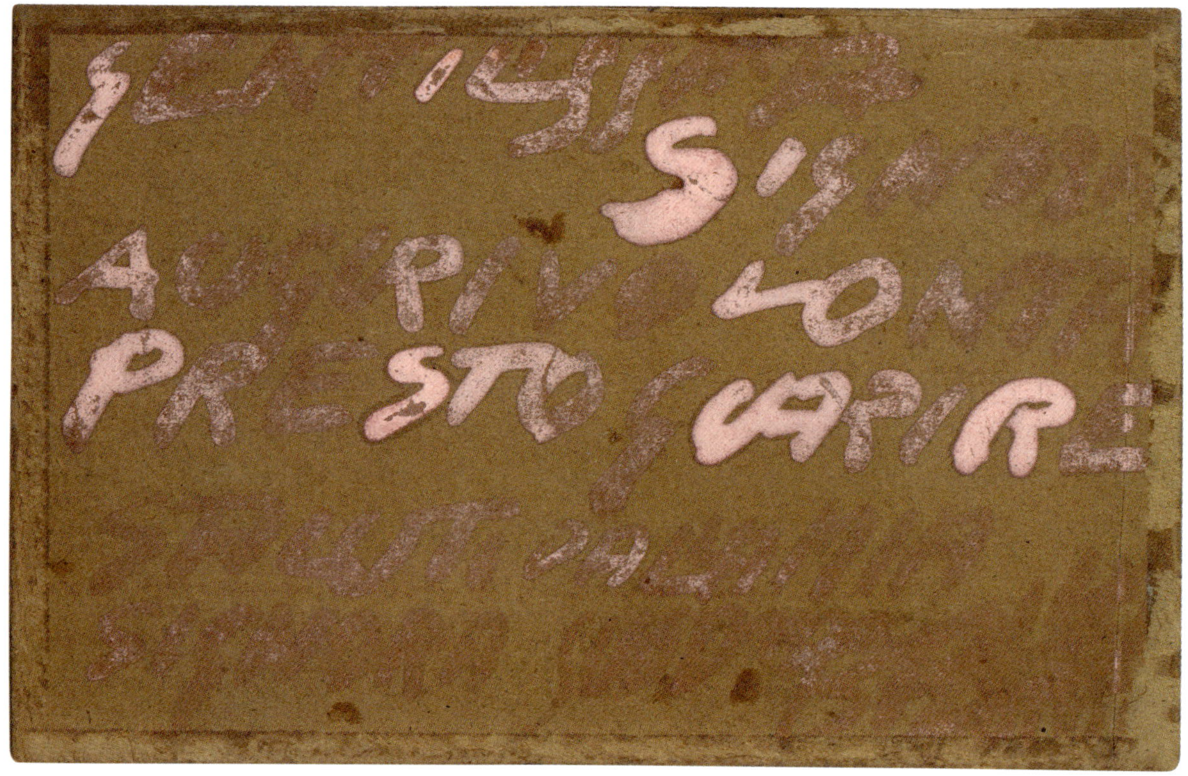

105a-b

Composizione astratta (Abstract Composition), c. 1917
(postcard to Rougena Khwoshinsky Zatkova, c. 1917)
collage on paper, 10 x 15.5 cm

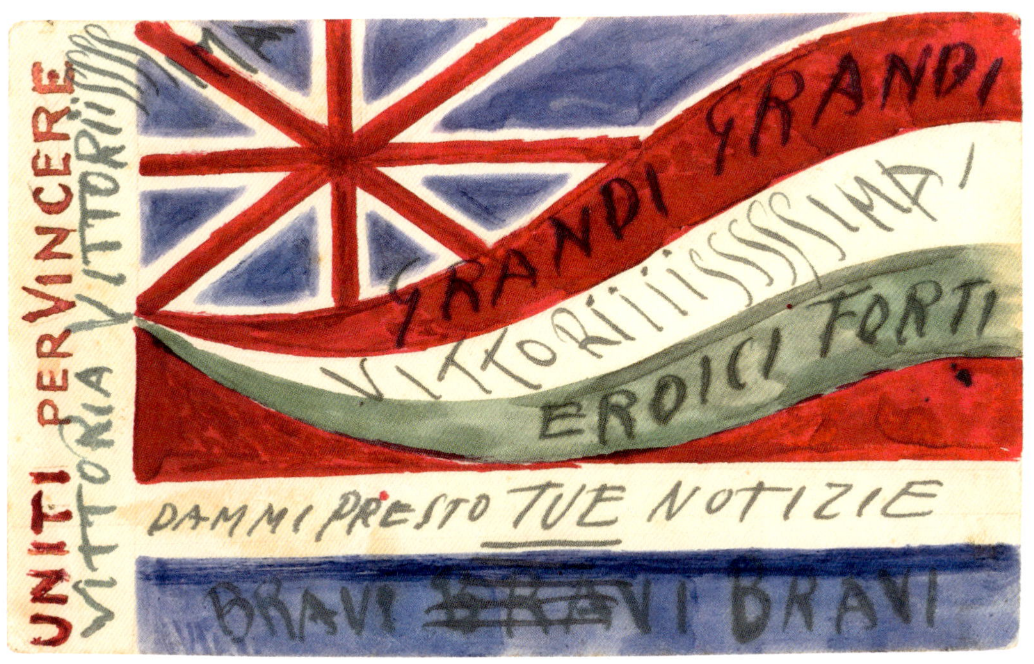

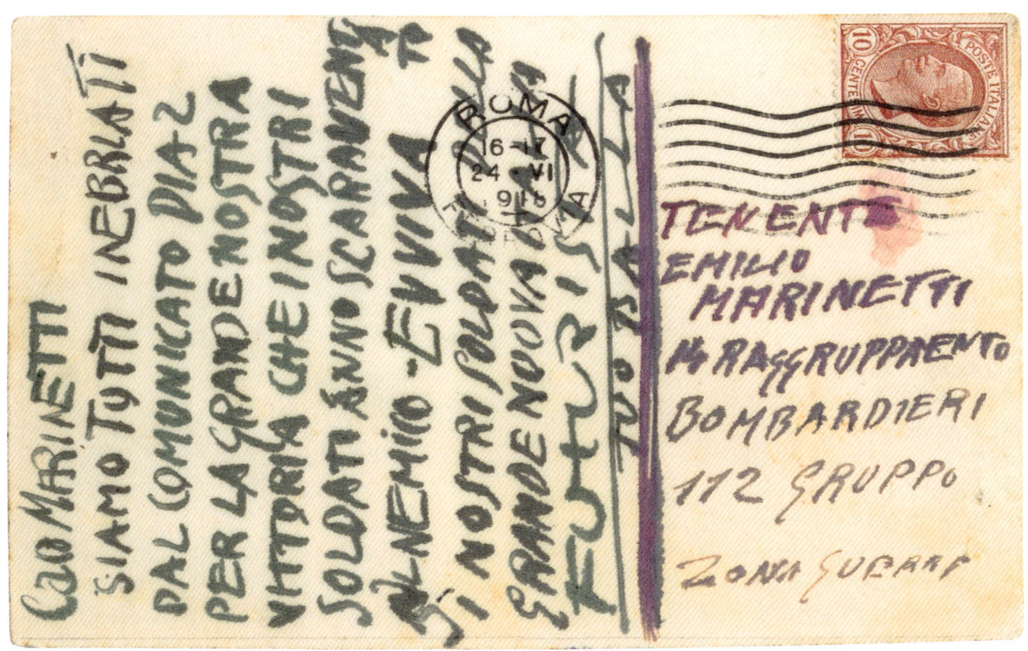

106a-b

Uniti per vincere Vittoria Vittorissima
(United to Win – Victory Victorissima), 1918
(postcard to Filippo Tommaso Marinetti, 24 June 1918)
watercolour on paper, 8.5 x 13.5 cm

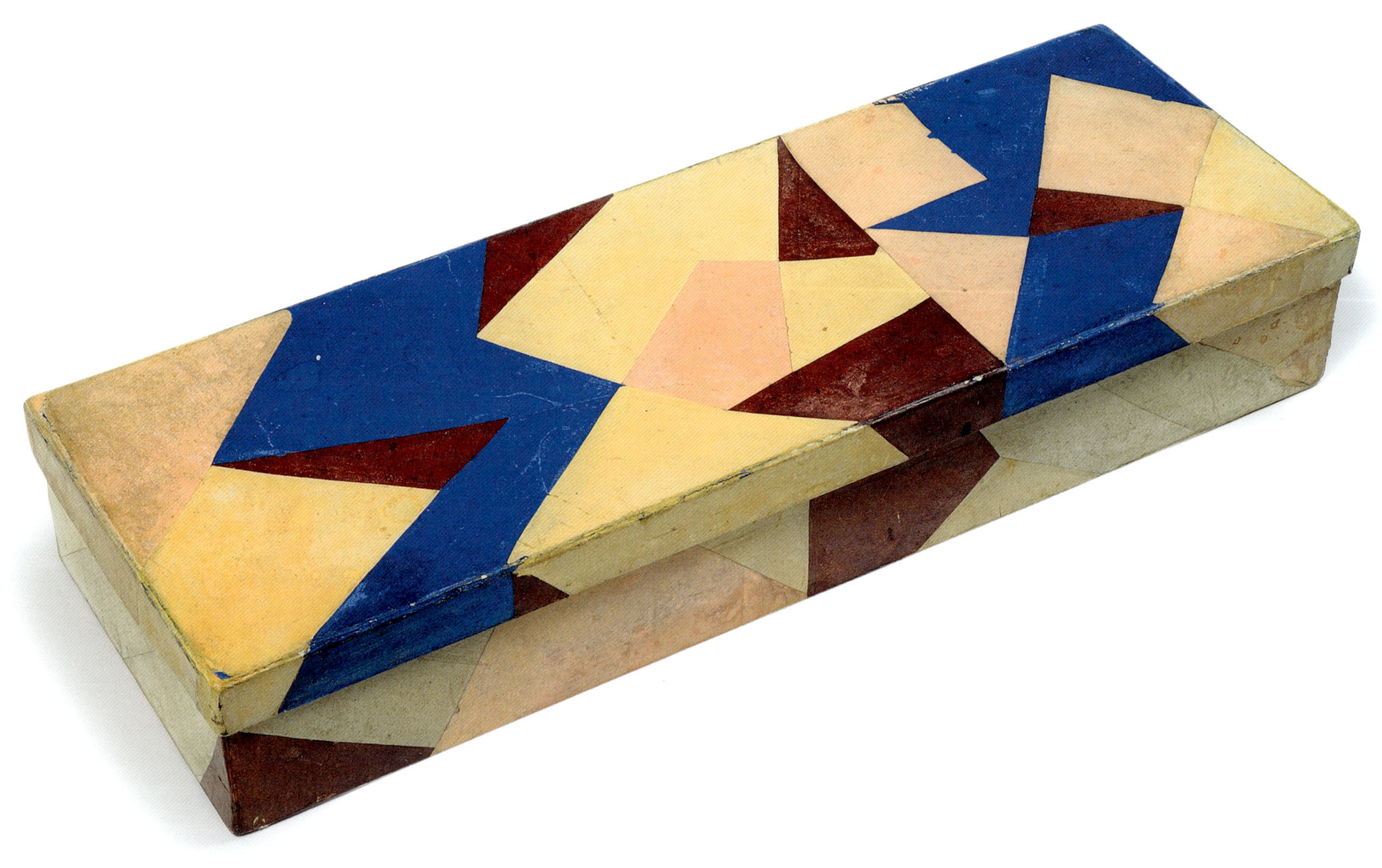

107

Box, 1919
collage, 10 x 60 x 20.5 cm

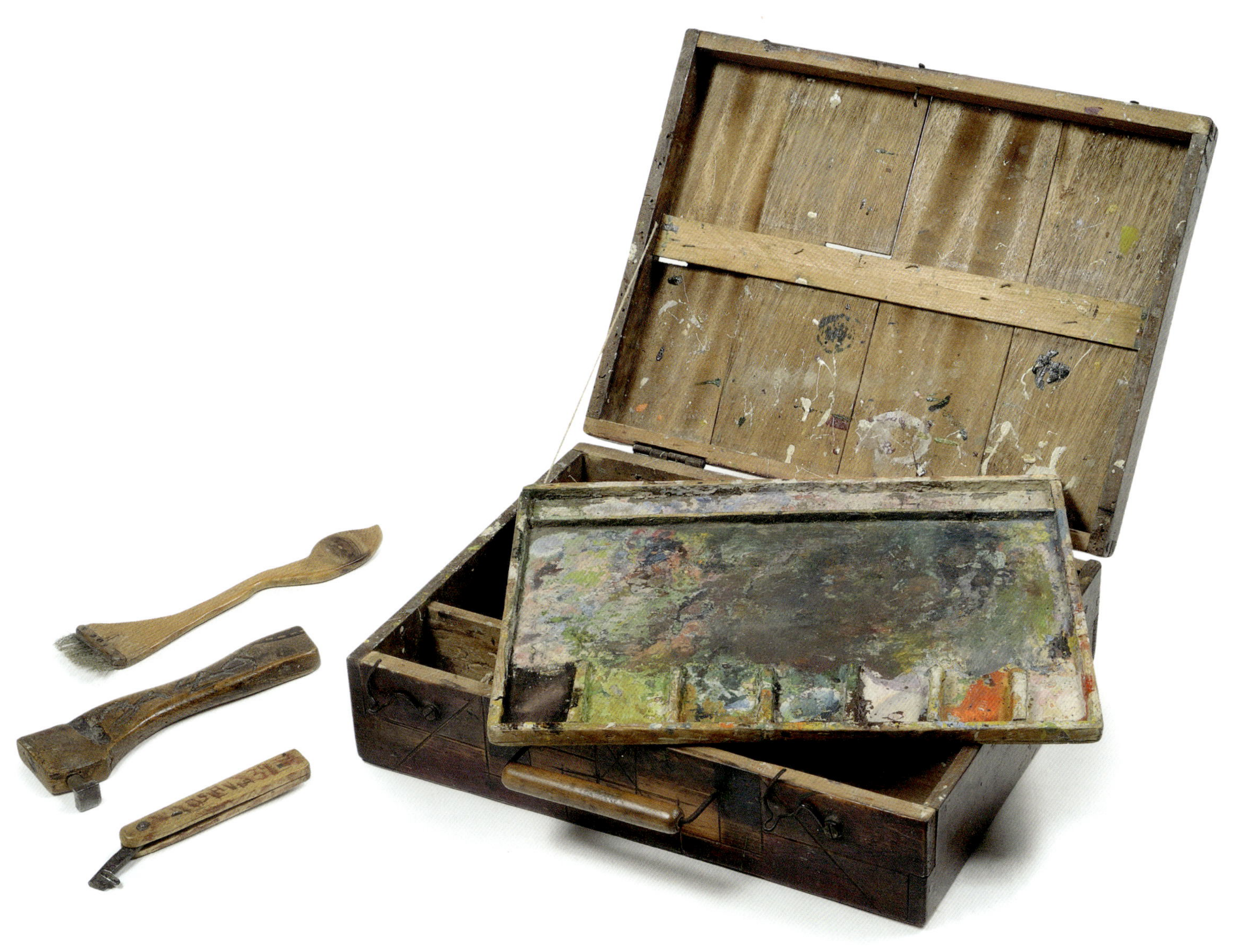

108

Box of tools for palette painting, undated
mixed media, 12 x 41 x 37 cm (open 41 x 41 x 42 cm)

109

Rack Object, c. 1925
oil and tempera on wood, 41 x 129 x 32.5 cm

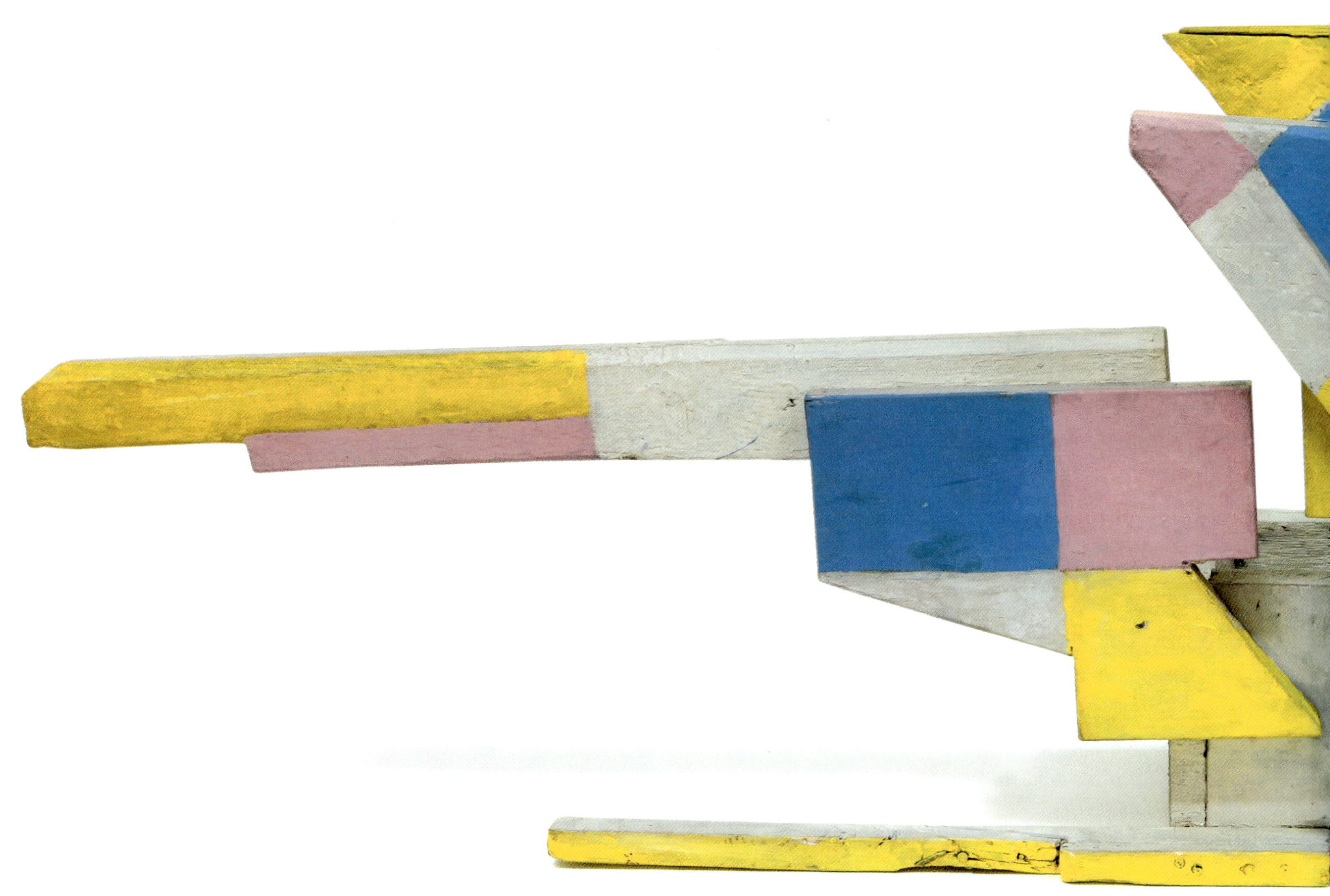

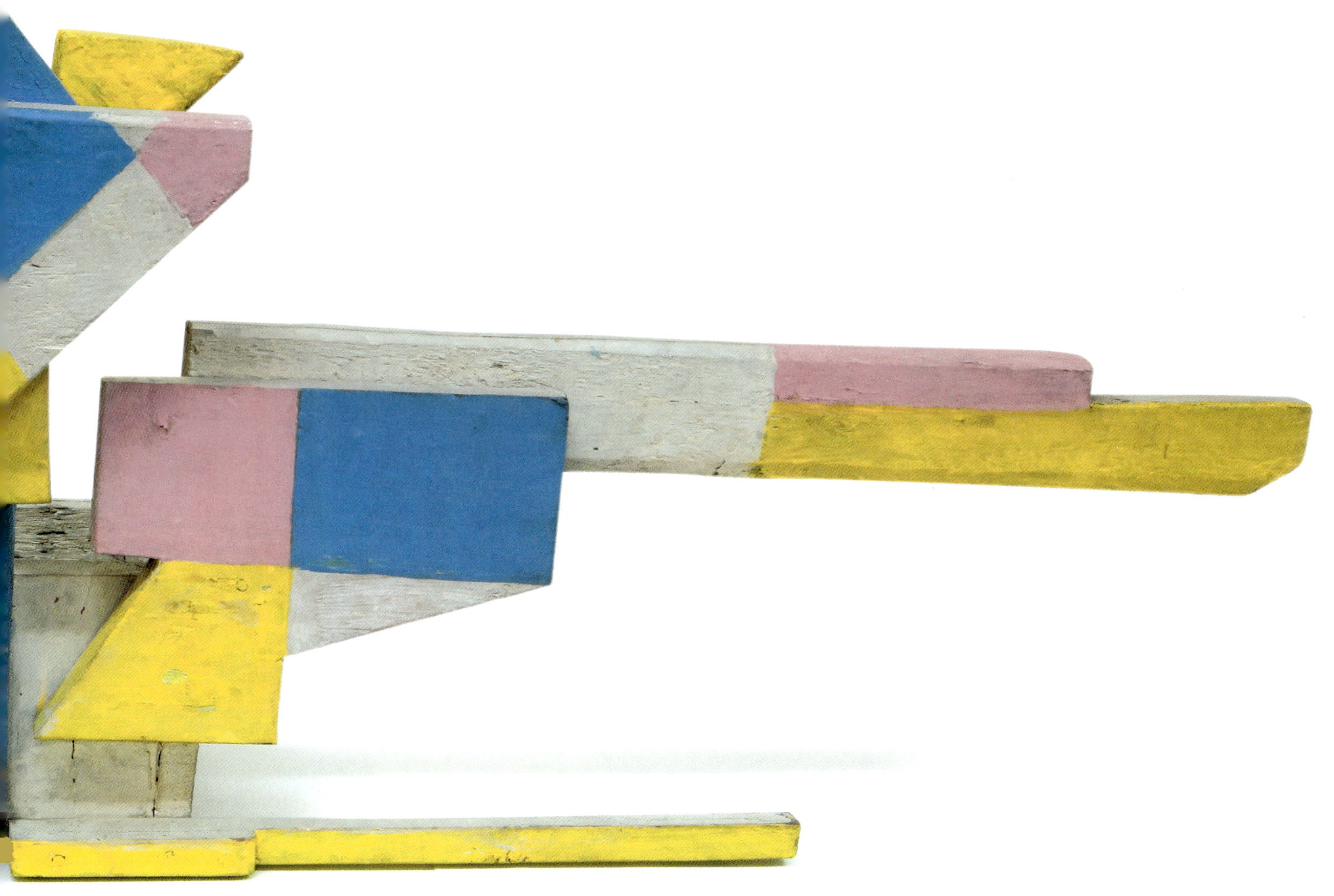

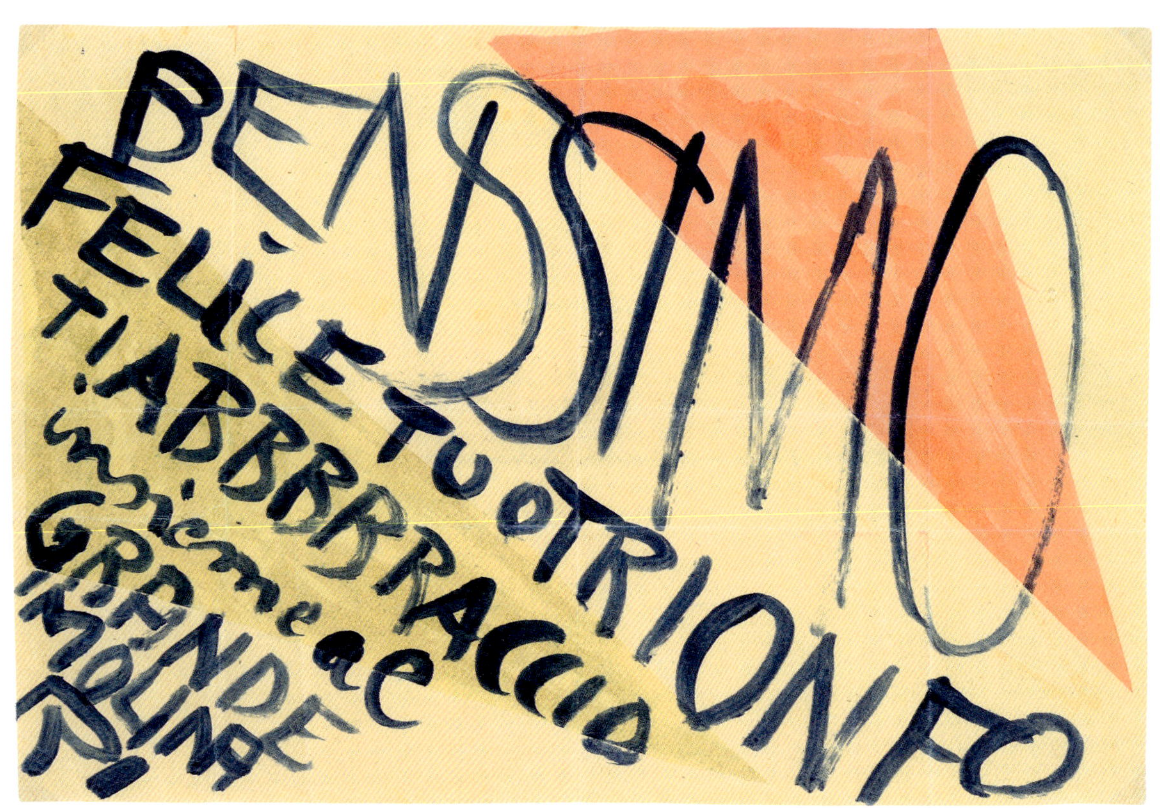
BENISSIMO
FELICE TUO TRIONFO
TI ABBRRACCIO
GRANDE

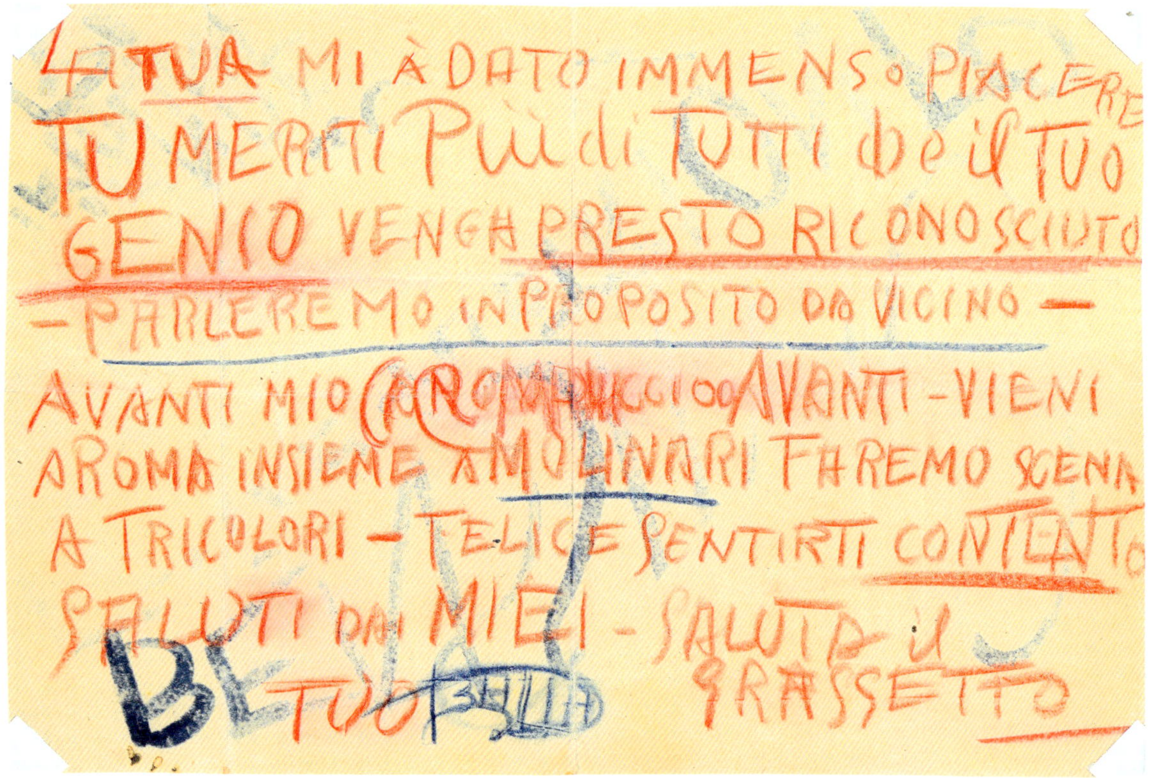
LA TUA MI À DATO IMMENSO PIACERE
TU MERITI PIÙ DI TUTTI CHE IL TUO
GENIO VENGA PRESTO RICONOSCIUTO
– PARLEREMO IN PROPOSITO DA VICINO –
AVANTI MIO CARO [illegible] AVANTI – VIENI
A ROMA INSIEME A MOLINARI FAREMO SCENA
A TRICOLORI – FELICE SENTIRTI CONTENTO
SALUTI DAI MIEI – SALUTA IL GRASSETTO
TUO BALLA

110a-b

Letter to Virgilio Marchi, 18 April 1920
India ink on paper, 18 x 22 cm

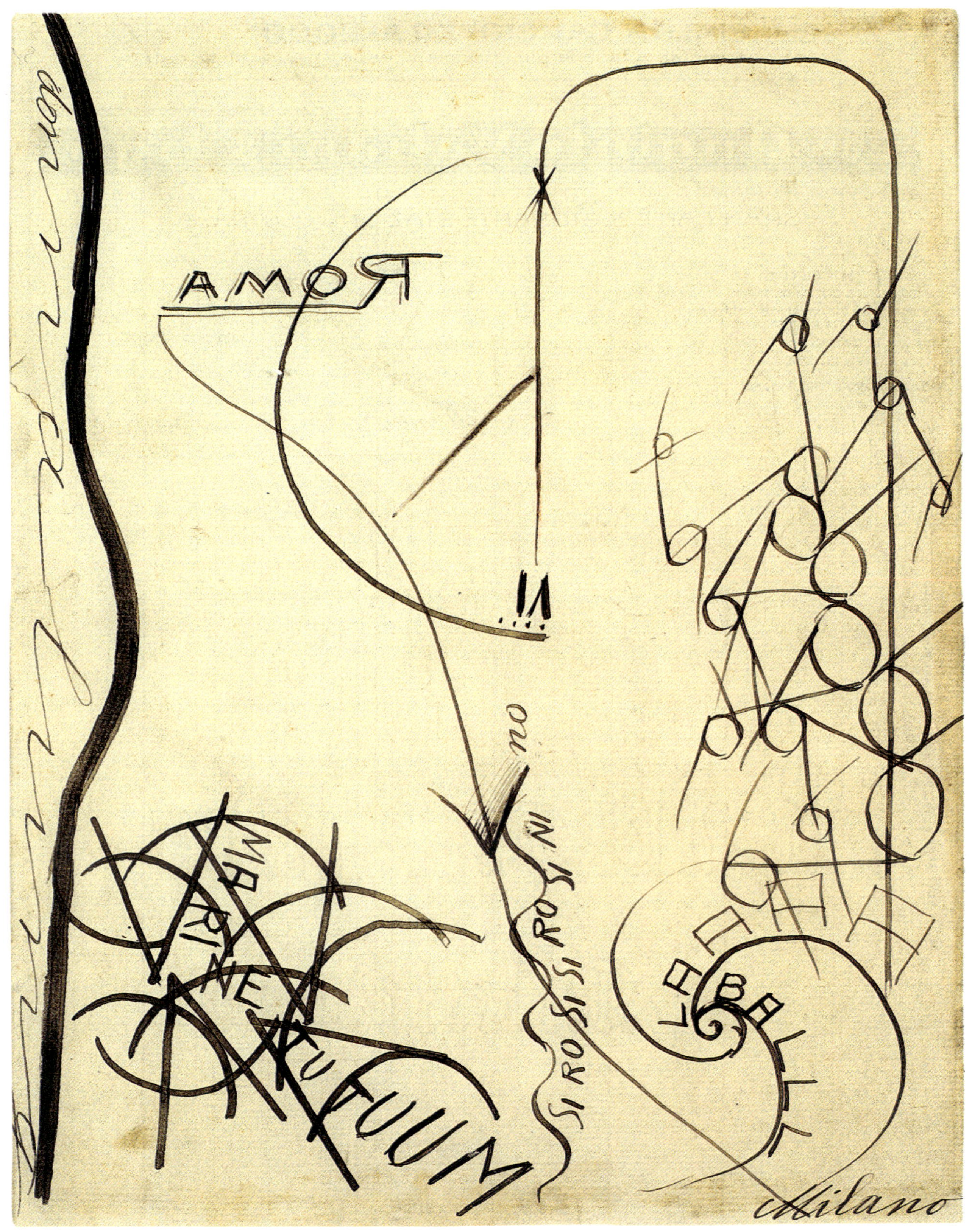

111

Partenza di Sironi per Milano
(Sironi's Departure for Milan), 1914
ink on paper, 28 x 22 cm

Opposite
113

Rumoristica plastica BALTRR (BALTRR Plastic Noisistics),
1914
ink, collage and mixed media on paper laid down on linen,
116 x 98 cm

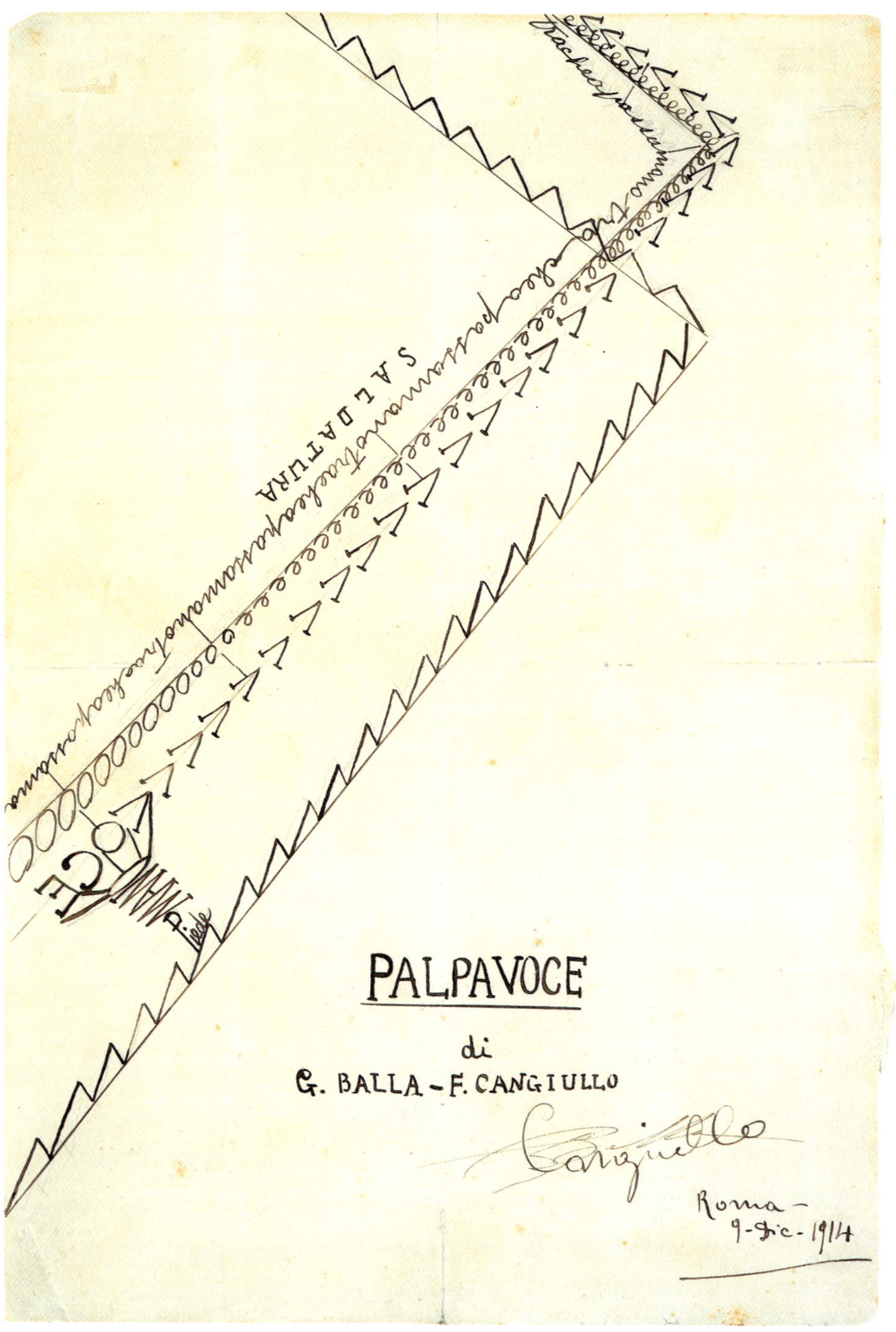

112

Giacomo Balla / Francesco Cangiullo
Palpavoce (Tactile Word), 1914
ink on paper, 37 x 24.5 cm

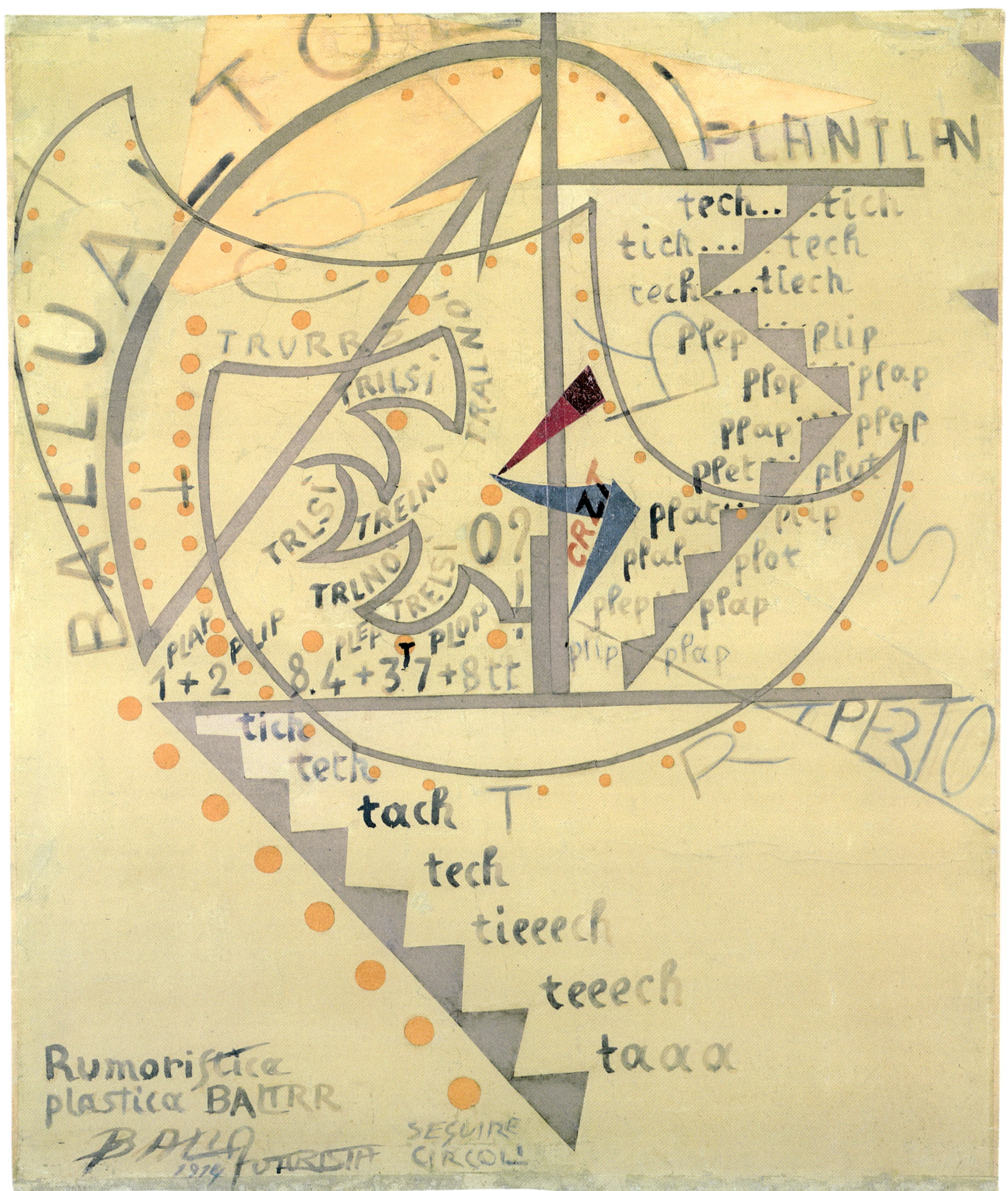
PLANTLAN
tech... tich
tich... tech
tech... tlech
plep... plip
plop... plap
plap... plep
plet... plut
plat... plap
plap plot
plep plap
plip plap
TRURR
TRILSI
TRALNO
TRLSI
TRELNO
TRLNO
TRELSI
0?
plap plip plep plop
1+2 8.4+37+8tt
tich
tech
tach
tech
tieeech
teeech
taaa
Rumoristica
plastica BALTRR
BALLA
1914 FUTURISTA
SEGUIRE
CIRCOLI

Autoritratto (Self-Portrait), c. 1894
oil on photographic paper, 33.9 x 29.8 cm
Rome, private collection
(cat. n. 1)

Fiera parigina (Parisian Fair), 1900
oil on canvas, 65 x 81 cm
Milan, Museo del Novecento
(cat. n. 2)

La fidanzata al Pincio (The Girlfriend at the Pincio), 1902
oil on canvas, 60.5 x 90 cm
Milan, Galleria d'Arte Moderna, Grassi Collection
(cat. n. 3)

Il contadino (The Peasant), 1902
oil and tempera on canvas, 175 x 115 cm
Rome, Accademia Nazionale di San Luca
(cat. n. 7)

Il mendicante (The Beggar), 1902
oil on canvas, 175.5 x 115 cm
Rome, La Galleria Nazionale
(cat. n. 9)

La seducente – Enrichetta (The Charmer – Enrichetta), c. 1902
crayon on paper, 45 x 36 cm
Rivoli, Fondazione Federico Cerruti per l'Arte
(cat. n. 4)

Il falegname Mariano (Mariano the Carpenter), 1903
graphite, charcoal and white lead on paper, 32.5 x 23 cm
Private collection
(cat. n. 12)

I malati (The Sick), 1903
oil on canvas, 175 x 115 cm
Rome, La Galleria Nazionale
(cat. n. 10)

La pialla nuova (The New Plane), 1903
crayon and charcoal on paper, 172 x 112 cm
Private collection
(cat. n. 11)

La giornata dell'operaio (The Worker's Day), 1904
pencil on paper, 8.8 x 10.8 cm
Private collection
(cat. n. 14)

La giornata dell'operaio (The Worker's Day), 1904
pencil on paper, 9 x 10.8 cm
Private collection
(cat. n. 15)

La giornata dell'operaio (The Worker's Day), 1904
pencil on paper, 12.6 x 10.3 cm
Private collection
(cat. n. 16)

La giornata dell'operaio (The Worker's Day), 1904
pencil on paper, 11.2 x 12.7 cm
Private collection
(cat. n. 17)

La pazza (The Madwoman), 1905
oil on canvas, 175 x 115 cm
Rome, La Galleria Nazionale
(cat. n. 8)

Ritratto di donna e due paesaggi (Portrait of a Woman and Two Landscapes), c. 1905
oil on panel, 40 x 97 cm
Private collection
(cat. n. 18)

Villa Borghese – Le torri del museo (Villa Borghese – The Towers of the Museum), c. 1905
crayon on paper, 38 x 52 cm
Rome, Gigli Collection
(cat. n. 19)

Villa Borghese – Tronchi (Villa Borghese – Tree Trunks), c. 1905
crayon on paper, 38.5 x 52 cm
Rome, Gigli Collection
(cat. n. 20)

Germogli primaverili – Paesaggio di Villa Borghese (Springtime Buds – Landscape of Villa Borghese), 1906
oil on canvas mounted on panel, 51 x 76.3 cm
Private collection
Courtesy Farsettiarte Prato
(cat. n. 21)

Il cesellatore – Ritratto di Duilio Cambellotti (The Painstaking Artist – Portrait of Duilio Cambellotti), 1906
charcoal and white lead on paper, 44.5 x 63 cm
Rome, Archivio dell'Opera di Duilio Cambellotti
(cat. n. 13)

Il dubbio (Doubt), 1907–08
oil on paper, 67 x 50 cm
Rome, Galleria d'Arte Moderna
(cat. n. 5)

Agave sul mare – Il mare di Anzio (Agave by the Sea – The Sea at Anzio), 1908
oil on canvas, 90 x 143 cm
Private collection
(cat. n. 22)

Affetti (Attachment), 1910
oil on canvas, 115.5 x 130 cm
Rome, Palazzo del Quirinale, Presidential Collection
(cat. n. 6)

Bambina che corre sul balcone (Girl Running on a Balcony), 1912
oil on canvas, 130 x 130 cm
Milan, Galleria d'Arte Moderna, Grassi Collection
(cat. n. 23)

Compenetrazione iridescente n. 1 (Iridescent Interpenetration no. 1), 1912
(postcard to Gino Galli, 11 December 1912)
watercolour on pasteboard, 14 x 9.5 cm
Private collection
(cat. n. 28 a-b)

Dinamismo di un cane al guinzaglio (Dynamism of a Dog on a Leash), 1912
oil on canvas, 89.85 x 109.85 cm
Buffalo, Albright-Knox Art Gallery, Bequest of A. Conger Goodyear and gift of George F. Goodyear, 1964
(cat. n. 54)

Finestra su Düsseldorf (Window in Düsseldorf), 1912
oil on panel, 28.5 x 35 cm
Private collection
(cat. n. 24)

La mano del violinista – Ritmi d'archetto (The Hand of the Violinist – The Rhythms of the Bow), 1912
oil on canvas, 52 x 75.2 cm
London, Estorick Collection of Modern Italian Art
(cat. n. 52)

Studio di volumi (Study of Volumes), 1912
pencil on pasteboard, 8.5 x 14 cm
Rome – Istanbul, Galleria Russo
(cat. n. 55)

Studio di volumi (Study of Volumes), 1912
pencil on pasteboard, 14 x 9 cm
Rome – Istanbul, Galleria Russo
(cat. n. 56)

Studio per compenetrazione iridescente n. 9 (Study for Iridescent Interpenetration no. 9), 1912
pencil and watercolour on paper, 20.5 x 12.5 cm
Turin, GAM – Galleria Civica d'Arte Moderna e Contemporanea
(inv. P/1825 verso)
(cat. n. 25)

Compenetrazione iridescente – studio (Iridescent Interpenetration – Study), c. 1912
watercolour and pencil on paper, 24 x 18.5
Turin, GAM – Galleria Civica d'Arte Moderna e Contemporanea (inv. P/2079)
(cat. n. 47)

Compenetrazione iridescente n. 11 (Iridescent Interpenetration no. 11), c. 1912
pencil and watercolour on paper, 57.5 x 38 cm
Turin, GAM – Galleria Civica d'Arte Moderna e Contemporanea (inv. P/1790)
(cat. n. 27)

Studi per compenetrazioni iridescenti (Studies for Iridescent Interpenetrations), c. 1912
pencil and watercolour on paper, 9 x 14 cm
Turin, GAM – Galleria Civica d'Arte Moderna e Contemporanea (inv. P/1822 verso)
(cat. n. 36)

Studio per compenetrazione iridescente (Study for Iridescent Interpenetration), c. 1912
pencil and watercolour on paper, 22 x 17.7 cm
Turin, GAM – Galleria Civica d'Arte Moderna e Contemporanea (inv. P/1792)
(cat. n. 30)

Studio per compenetrazione iridescente (Studio per manifesto Secessione) (Study for Iridescent Interpenetration – Study for Secession Poster), c. 1912
pencil and watercolour on paper, 22 x 17.7 cm
Turin, GAM – Galleria Civica d'Arte Moderna e Contemporanea (inv. P/1794)
(cat. n. 31)

Studio per compenetrazione iridescente (Studio per manifesto Secessione) (Study for Iridescent Interpenetration – Study for Secession Poster), c. 1912
pencil and watercolour on paper, 11 x 9.5 cm
Turin, GAM – Galleria Civica d'Arte Moderna e Contemporanea (inv. P/1799)
(cat. n. 32)

Studio per compenetrazione iridescente (Studio per manifesto Secessione) (Study for Iridescent Interpenetration – Study for Secession Poster), c. 1912
pencil and watercolour on paper, 22 x 17.7 cm
Turin, GAM – Galleria Civica d'Arte Moderna e Contemporanea (inv. P/1793)
(cat. n. 33)

Studio per compenetrazione iridescente (Study for Iridescent Interpenetration), from the Düsseldorf notebooks, c. 1912
pencil and watercolour on paper, 22 x 17.7 cm
Turin, GAM – Galleria Civica d'Arte Moderna e Contemporanea (inv. P/1800)
(cat. n. 34)

Studio per compenetrazione iridescente (Study for Iridescent Interpenetration), from the Düsseldorf notebooks, c. 1912
pencil and watercolour on paper, 21.9 x 17.7 cm
Turin, GAM – Galleria Civica d'Arte Moderna e Contemporanea (inv. P/1801)
(cat. n. 35)

Studio per compenetrazione iridescente (Study for Iridescent Interpenetration), from the Düsseldorf notebooks, c. 1912
pencil and watercolour on paper, 20.2 x 20.1 cm
Turin, GAM – Galleria Civica d'Arte Moderna e Contemporanea (inv. P/1803)
(cat. n. 26)

Studio per compenetrazione iridescente (per soffitto tondo) (Study for Iridescent Interpenetration – for round ceiling), c. 1912
pencil and watercolour on paper, 22 x 17.7 cm
Turin, GAM – Galleria Civica d'Arte Moderna e Contemporanea (inv. P/1813 verso)
(cat. n. 42)

Studio per compenetrazione iridescente radiale nel tondo (Study for radial Iridescent Interpenetration in tondo), c. 1912
pencil and watercolour on paper, 22 x 17.7 cm
Turin, GAM – Galleria Civica d'Arte Moderna e Contemporanea (inv. P/1815)
(cat. n. 43)

Studio per compenetrazione iridescente nel tondo (Study for Iridescent Interpenetration in tondo), c. 1912
pencil and watercolour on paper, 22 x 17.7 cm
Turin, GAM – Galleria Civica d'Arte Moderna e Contemporanea (inv. P/1816 verso)
(cat. n. 41)

a) Studio per compenetrazione iridescente b) Studio per Bambina che corre sul balcone (a. Study for Iridescent Interpenetration b. Study for Girl Running on a Balcony), c. 1912
pencil, pen and watercolour on paper, 22 x 17.7 cm
Turin, GAM – Galleria Civica d'Arte Moderna e Contemporanea (inv. P/1817)
(cat. n. 38)

Studio per compenetrazione iridescente (Study for Iridescent Interpenetration), c. 1912
pencil and watercolour on paper, 22 x 17.7 cm
Turin, GAM – Galleria Civica d'Arte Moderna e Contemporanea (inv. P/1821 verso)
(cat. n. 39)

Studio per compenetrazione iridescente a cerchi (Study for Iridescent Interpenetration with circles), c. 1912
pencil and watercolour on paper, 22 x 18 cm
Turin, GAM – Galleria Civica d'Arte Moderna e Contemporanea (inv. P/1823)
(cat. n. 40)

Studio per compenetrazione iridescente (Study for Iridescent Interpenetration), c. 1912
pencil and watercolour on paper, 18 x 13.3 cm
Turin, GAM – Galleria Civica d'Arte Moderna e Contemporanea (inv. P/1824)
(cat. n. 37)

Studio per Volo di rondini (Study for Flight of Swallows), c. 1912
pencil on paper, 22.4 x 24.3 cm
Rome, La Galleria Nazionale (inv. 9371)
(cat. n. 78)

Studio per Volo di rondini (Study for Flight of Swallows), c. 1912
pencil on paper, 30.8 x 31 cm
Rome, La Galleria Nazionale (inv. 9372)
(cat. n. 79)

Studio per Volo di rondini (Study for Flight of Swallows), c. 1912
pencil on ivory paper, 28.4 x 20.1 cm
Rome, La Galleria Nazionale (inv. 9373)
(cat. n. 80)

Studio per Volo di rondini (Study for Flight of Swallows), c. 1912
pencil on ivory paper, 16.3 x 21.5 cm
Rome, La Galleria Nazionale (inv. 9374)
(cat. n. 81)

Studio per Volo di rondini (Study for Flight of Swallows), c. 1912
pencil on paper, 11.4 x 17.1 cm
Rome, La Galleria Nazionale (inv. 9375)
(cat. n. 82)

Studio per Volo di rondini (Study for Flight of Swallows), c. 1912
pencil on paper, 15.4 x 21.6 cm
Rome, La Galleria Nazionale (inv. 9376)
(cat. n. 83)

Anton Giulio Bragaglia
Giacomo Balla davanti a Dinamismo di un cane al guinzaglio (Giacomo Balla in front of Dynamism of a Dog on a Leash), c. 1912–13
postcard, 9 x 13.5 cm
Private collection
(cat. n. 53)

Compenetrazione iridescente n. 4 (Studio della luce) (Iridescent Interpenetration no. 4 – Study of Light), 1912–13
oil and pencil on paper mounted on canvas, 55 x 76 cm
Rovereto, MART – Museo di Arte Moderna e Contemporanea di Trento e Rovereto
(cat. n. 49)

Studio di volumi (Study of Volumes), 1912–13
pencil on paper, 30.2 x 37 cm
Private collection
(cat. n. 57)

Studio per compenetrazione iridescente (Study for Iridescent Interpenetration), from the Düsseldorf notebooks, 1912–13
pencil and watercolour on paper, 17.7 x 21.9 cm
Private collection, Gian Enzo Sperone, New York (inv. GES00640)
(cat. n. 44)

Studio per compenetrazione iridescente (Study for Iridescent Interpenetration), from the Düsseldorf notebooks, 1912–13
pencil and watercolour on paper, 12.5 x 17.7 cm
Private collection, Gian Enzo Sperone, New York (inv. GES00641)
(cat. n. 45)

Studio per compenetrazione iridescente (Study for Iridescent Interpenetration), from the Düsseldorf notebooks, 1912–13
pencil and watercolour on paper, 20 x 17 cm
Gian Enzo Sperone, New York (inv. GES02497)
(cat. n. 46)

Compenetrazione iridescente n. 10 (Iridescent Interpenetration no. 10), c. 1912–13
pencil and watercolour on paper, 50 x 32 cm
Turin, GAM – Galleria Civica d'Arte Moderna e Contemporanea (inv. P/1791)
(cat. n. 48)

Compenetrazione iridescente n. 1 (Iridescent Interpenetration no. 1), 1912–14
oil and wax crayon on canvas, 99 x 59 cm
Private collection
(cat. n. 50)

Compenetrazioni iridescenti (Iridescent Interpenetrations), c. 1912–14
tempera on pasteboard, 20 x 13 cm
Private collection
(cat. n. 29a-b)

Auto in corsa (studio). Velocità astratta (Speeding Car – Study. Abstract Speed), 1913
gouache and watercolour on paper mounted on canvas, 67.5 x 99.6 cm
Amsterdam, Stedelijk Museum
(cat. n. 59)

Automobile + velocità + luce (Car + Speed + Light), 1913
watercolour and sepia on paper, 67 x 88.5 cm
Milan, Museo del Novecento
(cat. n. 60)

Compenetrazione – spazio (Interpenetration – Space), 1913
pencil on paper, 15 x 20.5 cm
Private collection
(cat. n. 58)

Alessandro Dell'Otti
Spessori d'atmosfera (Atmospheric Thicknesses), 1913
original photographic print with autograph signature, 12 x 14.5
Private collection
(cat. n. 77)

Espansione dinamica + velocità (Dynamic Expansion + Speed), 1913
paint on paper mounted on canvas, 65.6 x 108.5 cm
Rome, La Galleria Nazionale, gift of Luce and Elica Balla
(cat. n. 61)

Orbite celesti (Celestial Orbits), 1913
oil on canvas, 60 x 80
Rivoli, Fondazione Federico Cerruti per l'Arte
(cat. n. 76)

Studi per Dinamo – Dinamica (Studies for Dynamo – Dynamics), 1913
India ink on paper, 12.5 x 30; 12 x 30; 12.5 x 30 cm
Private collection
(cat. n. 62)

Velocità astratta (Abstract Speed), 1913
oil on canvas, 78 x 108 cm
Rivoli, Fondazione Federico Cerruti per l'Arte
(cat. n. 63)

Velocità astratta – L'auto è passata (Abstract Speed – The Car Has Passed), 1913
oil on canvas, 50.2 x 65.4 cm
London, Tate Modern, gift of the Friends of the Tate Gallery, 1970
(cat. n. 68)

Velocità di automobile (Automobile Speed), 1913
oil on paper mounted on cardboard, 64.7 x 93.8 cm
Milan, Galleria d'Arte Moderna, Grassi Collection
(cat. n. 66)

Velocità d'automobile (velocità n. 1) (Automobile Speed – Speed no. 1), 1913
ink wash on mounted paper, 46.5 x 60 cm
Rovereto, MART – Museo di Arte Moderna e Contemporanea di Trento e Rovereto
(cat. n. 65)

Volo di rondini (Flight of Swallows – Paths of Movement + Dynamic Sequences), 1913
oil on canvas, 96.8 x 120 cm
New York, Museum of Modern Art
(cat. n. 84)

Vortice (Vortex), c. 1913
pencil on paper, 13 x 17.7 cm
New York, Gian Enzo Sperone (inv. GES08280)
(cat. n. 70)

Velocità astratta + rumore (Abstract Speed + Sound), 1913–14
oil on board, 54.5 x 76.5 cm
Venice, Peggy Guggenheim Collection (Solomon R. Guggenheim Foundation, New York)
(cat. n. 67)

Compenetrazione iridescente n. 13 (Iridescent Interpenetration no. 13), c. 1913–14
tempera on paper mounted on canvas, 94 x 72 cm Turin, GAM – Galleria Civica d'Arte Moderna e Contemporanea, (inv. P/1789)
(cat. n. 51)

Autobiografia (Autobiography), 1914
ink on paper, 18 x 14 cm
Private collection
(cat. n. 88)

Automobile in corsa (Speeding Automobile), 1914
tempera and India ink on paper mounted on canvas, 53.8 x 73.3 cm
Jerusalem, The Israel Museum, Sam and Ayala Zacks Collection, Art Gallery of Ontario, permanent loan
(cat. n. 64)

Giacomo Balla / Francesco Cangiullo
Palpavoce (Tactile Word), 1914
ink on paper, 37 x 24.5 cm
Private collection
(cat. n. 112)

Composizione astratta – Linee di velocità (Abstract Composition – Lines of Speed), 1914
(letter to Filippo Tommaso Marinetti, 16 August 1914)
mixed media on paper, 11 x 13.5 cm
New York, Gian Enzo Sperone (inv. GES08177)
(cat. n. 89a-b)

Desideriamo tue notizie (We hope to hear from you), 1914
(postcard to Filippo Tommaso Marinetti, 1914)
watercolour on pasteboard, 9 x 14 cm
Private collection
(cat. n. 90a-b)

Futurismo Futurismo (Futurism Futurism), 1914
(postcard to Filippo Tommaso Marinetti, 11 November 1914)
watercolour on paper, 9 x 14 cm
New York, Gian Enzo Sperone (inv. GES08180)
(cat. n. 91a-b)

Letter to Umberto Boccioni, 1914
watercolour and India ink on paper, 18 x 22 cm
Private collection
(cat. n. 92a-b)

Linee di velocità astratta (Lines of Abstract Speed), 1914
tempera and watercolour on paper, 43 x 55.5 cm
New York, Gian Enzo Sperone (inv. GES00639)
(cat. n. 71)

Mercurio passa davanti al sole (Mercury Passing in Front of the Sun), 1914
tempera on paper mounted on canvas, 45 x 35.7 cm
Private collection, courtesy of Farsettiarte Prato
(cat. n. 74)

Partenza di Sironi per Milano (Sironi's Departure for Milan), 1914
ink on paper, 28 x 22 cm
Private collection
(cat. n. 111)

Mercurio passa davanti al sole (Mercury Passing in Front of the Sun), c. 1914
ink on paper, 27 x 19.4 cm
New York, Gian Enzo Sperone
(inv. GES08281)
(cat. n. 75)

Rumoristica plastica BALTRR (BALTRR Plastic Noisistics), 1914
ink, collage and mixed media on paper laid down on linen, 116 x 98 cm
Private collection, Property Care of Sotheby's Inc.
(cat. n. 113)

Vortice (Vortex), 1914
oil on paper, 65 x 83 cm
Rovereto, MART – Museo di Arte Moderna e Contemporanea di Trento e Rovereto, VAF – Stiftung
(inv. VAF 1141)
(cat. n. 72)

Folla + Paesaggio (Crowd + Landscape), 1915
collage of painted paper and tissue paper laid down on canvas, mounted on masonite, 152.5 x 66.7 cm
Private collection, Property Care of Sotheby's Inc.
(cat. n. 93)

Futuastrattismo Futudinamismo (Futuabstractism Futudynamism), 1915
(postcard to Filippo Tomaso Marinetti, 12 June 1915)
tempera and collage on pasteboard, 8 x 14.2 cm
New York, Gian Enzo Sperone
(inv. GES08178)
(cat. n. 94a-b)

Lettera metallica (Metallic Letter), 1915
(letter to Mario Broglio and Aldo Molinari, 1915)
tempera and pencil on paper, 20 x 28.5 cm
Private collection
(cat. n. 95a-b)

Linee di velocità (Lines of Speed) , 1915
(postcard to Carlo Carrà, 18 April 1915)
watercolour on pasteboard, 9 x 14 cm
Private collection
(cat. n. 96a-b)

Linea di velocità dell'aereo Caproni (Speed Line of the Caproni Aircraft), 1915
crayon on paper, 40 x 57.5 cm
New York, Gian Enzo Sperone
(inv. GES00988 – SW 93224)
(cat. n. 73)

Poster for the show at the Galleria Angelelli, Rome, 1915
tempera and watercolour on paper, 94 x 65 cm
Private collection
(cat. n. 97)

Mimica sinottica o Primavera – Paesaggio (Synoptic Mimicry or Spring – Landscape), 1915
watercolour on paper, 22 x 32.5 cm
Private collection
(cat. n. 98)

Mimica sinottica o Primavera – Testo rumorista (Mimicry Synoptic or Spring – Noisist text), 1915
watercolour on paper, 22 x 32 cm
Private collection
(cat. n. 99)

Gli Avvenimenti (Events), 1916
India ink on paper, 34 x 25 cm
Private collection
(cat. n. 101)

Composizione astratta (Abstract Composition), 1916
(postcard to Rougena Khwoshinsky Zatkova, 26 January 1916)
mixed media on paper, 9.5 x 13 cm
New York, Gian Enzo Sperone
(inv. GES08176)
(cat. n. 100a-b)

Sconcertazione di stati d'animo (Disconcerted States of Mind), 1916
ink on paper, 30.5 x 22 cm
Private collection
(cat. n. 102)

Attenti alle spie... (Watch out for spies ...), 1917
(postcard to Filippo Tommaso Marinetti, 1917, the war zone)
tempera and collage on paper, 9.2 x 13.7 cm
New York, Gian Enzo Sperone
(inv. GES07467)
(cat. n. 103)

Esplosione (Explosion), 1917
(postcard to Luciano De Nardis, 29 January 1917)
watercolour on pasteboard, 9 x 14 cm
Private collection
(cat. n. 104a-b)

Composizione astratta (Abstract Composition), c. 1917
(postcard to Rougena Khwoshinsky Zatkova, c. 1917)
collage on paper, 10 x 15.5 cm
New York, Gian Enzo Sperone
(inv. GES08179)
(cat. n. 105a-b)

Spazzolridente (The Laughing Sweeper), 1918
oil on canvas, 70 x 100 cm
Milano, Museo del Novecento, Riccardo e Magda Jucker Collection
(cat. n. 85)

Uniti per vincere Vittoria Vittorissima (United to Win – Victory Victorissima), 1918
(postcard to Filippo Tommaso Marinetti, 24 June 1918)
watercolour on paper, 8.5 x 13.5 cm
New York, Gian Enzo Sperone
(inv. GES08175)
(cat. n. 106a-b)

Box, 1919
collage, 10 x 60 x 20.5 cm
Private collection
(cat. n. 107)

Antonio Fornari
Giacomo Balla davanti a Fallimento *(Giacomo Balla in front of* Bankruptcy*)*, c. 1919
photographic print, 13 x 20 cm
Private collection
(cat. n. 69)

Letter to Virgilio Marchi, 18 April 1920
India ink on paper, 18 x 22 cm
Private collection
(cat. n. 110a-b)

Numeri innamorati (Numbers in Love), 1923
oil on canvas, 77 x 55 cm
Rovereto, MART – Museo di Arte Moderna e Contemporanea di Trento e Rovereto, VAF – Stiftung
(cat. n. 86)

Bozzetto per "LTI" detto Il grande T (Sketch for LTI or The Big T), 1923–24
enamel on hardboard, 29.5 x 44 cm
Verona, Galleria dello Scudo
(cat. n. 87)

Rack Object, c. 1925
oil and tempera on wood, 41 x 129 x 32.5 cm
Private collection
(cat. n. 109)

Box of tools for palette painting, undated
mixed media, 12 x 41 x 37 cm
(open 41 x 41 x 42 cm)
Private collection
(cat. n. 108)

SELECTED EXHIBITIONS

edited by Zelda De Lillo

• Turin 1891
L Esposizione della Società Promotrice delle Belle Arti, Room I, Palazzo delle Belle Arti, Parco del Valentino, Turin.

• Turin 1897
LVI Esposizione della Società Promotrice delle Belle Arti, Room VII, Palazzo delle Belle Arti, Parco del Valentino, Turin.

• Rome 1899
LXIX Esposizione Internazionale di Belle Arti, Società Amatori e Cultori di Belle Arti, Room C, Palazzo delle Esposizioni, Rome, February–June.

• Rome 1900
LXX Esposizione Internazionale di Belle Arti, Società Amatori e Cultori di Belle Arti, Room D, Palazzo delle Esposizioni, Rome, February–June.

• Rome 1901
LXXI Esposizione Internazionale di Belle Arti, Società Amatori e Cultori di Belle Arti, Room C, Palazzo delle Esposizioni, Rome, February–June.

• Rome 1902
LXXII Esposizione di Belle Arti, Società Amatori e Cultori di Belle Arti, In arte libertas, Room C, Palazzo delle Esposizioni, Rome, February–June.

• Turin 1902
I Esposizione Quadriennale della Società Promotrice delle Belle Arti, Room XIX, Palazzo delle Belle Arti, Parco del Valentino, Turin, April–November.

• Rome 1903
LXXIII Esposizione Internazionale di Belle Arti, Società Amatori e Cultori di Belle Arti, Room Q, Palazzo delle Esposizioni, Rome, February–June.

• Venice 1903
V Esposizione Internazionale d'Arte, La Biennale di Venezia, Piemontese Room O, Venice, 22 April – 31 October.

• Munich 1903
Münchener Jahresausstellung, Room 47, "Gruppo italiano e Associazione degli Acquarellisti in Rome", Glaspalast, Munich, from 25 June.

• Rome 1904
LXXIV Esposizione Internazionale di Belle Arti, Società Amatori e Cultori di Belle Arti, Palazzo delle Esposizioni, Rome, February–June.

• Düsseldorf 1904
Internationale Kunstausstellung, Room 25 A, Kunstpalast, Düsseldorf, 1 May – 23 October.

• Munich 1904
Münchener Jahres – Ausstellung, Room I, Temperagemälde, Glaspalast, Munich, from 25 June.

• Rome 1905
LXXV Esposizione Internazionale di Belle Arti, Società Amatori e Cultori di Belle Arti, Room B, Palazzo delle Esposizioni, Rome, February–June.

• Rome 1906
LXXVI Esposizione Internazionale di Belle Arti, Società Amatori e Cultori di Belle Arti, Room A, Palazzo delle Esposizioni, Rome, February–June.

• Milan 1906
Mostra Nazionale di Belle Arti. Esposizione di Milano. Inaugurazione del nuovo valico del Sempione, Room XLV, "Gruppo della Giovine Roma", Milan, March.

• Rome 1907
LXXVII Esposizione Internazionale di Belle Arti, Società Amatori e Cultori di Belle Arti, Rooms D – E; Rooms N – O – P, *Esposizione di Bianco e Nero*, Palazzo delle Esposizioni, Rome, February–June.

• Barcelona 1907
V Exposición Internacional de Bellas Artes e Industrias Artísticas, Room XXXII, *Italia*, Palau de Belles Arts, Barcelona.

• Rome 1908
LXXVIII Esposizione Internazionale di Belle Arti, Società Amatori e Cultori di Belle Arti, Rooms N – O, *Esposizione di Bianco e Nero*, Palazzo delle Esposizioni, Rome, February–June.

• Rome 1909
LXXIX Esposizione Internazionale di Belle Arti, Società Amatori e Cultori di Belle Arti, Rooms B, P, Palazzo delle Esposizioni, Rome, February–June.

• Paris 1909
Salon d'Automne, "Section d'Art Italien", Paris, October.

• Odessa 1909
Le Salon, Odessa, from 20 October.

• Rome 1910
LXXX Esposizione Internazionale di Belle Arti, Società Amatori e Cultori di Belle Arti, Room H, Palazzo delle Esposizioni, Rome, February–June.

• Buenos Aires 1910
Esposizione Internazionale di Belle Arti, Room VI, Museo de Bellas Artes, Buenos Aires, 12 July – 13 November.

• Milan 1910
Esposizione Nazionale di Belle Arti, Room VI, R. Accademia di Belle Arti in Milano, Palazzo della Permanente, Milan, 18 September – 6 November.

• Rome 1911
Esposizione Internazionale di Roma. Mostra di Belle Arti, Stand 74, Room XI, Palazzo delle Belle Arti, Valle Giulia, Rome; Capanna dell'Agro Pontino.

• Paris 1912
Les peintres futuristes italiens, Galerie Bernheim-Jeune, Paris, 5–24 February (*Lumière électrique* in the Catalogo but not in the Exhibition).

• Montecatini 1912
IV Mostra d'arte, Terme Tamerici, Montecatini, June–October.

• Rome 1913
Prima Esposizione Pittura Futurista, texts by Boccioni, Carrà, Russolo, Balla, Severini, Ridotto del Teatro Costanzi, Galleria G. Giosi, Rome, 21 February – 21 March.

• Rome 1913a
Fu Balla, Negozi d'Arte Giosi, Rome, 14–16 April.

• Rotterdam 1913
Les peintres et les sculpteurs futuristes italiens, Rotterdamsche Kunstkring, Rotterdam, 18 May – 15 June.

• Berlin 1913
Erster Deutscher Herbstsalon, Preface by H. Walden, Der Sturm, Berlin, from 20 September.

• Florence 1913–1914
Esposizione di Pittura Futurista di "Lacerba", texts by Boccioni, Carrà, Russolo, Balla, Severini, Soffici, Galleria Gonnelli, Florence, November 1913 – January 1914.

• Rome 1914
LXXXIII Esposizione Internazionale di Belle Arti, Società Amatori e Cultori di Belle Arti, Room N, Palazzo delle Esposizioni, Rome, February–June.

• Rome 1914a
Prima Esposizione della Probitas, Preface by M. Beduschi, Rooms T, Z, Palazzo delle Belle Arti, Rome, from 21 February.

• Rome 1914b
Esposizione di pittura futurista. Boccioni, Carrà, Russolo, Balla, Severini, Soffici, Preface by Boccioni, Carrà, Russolo, Balla, Severini, Soffici, Galleria Futurista Sprovieri, Rome, February–March.

• London 1914
Exhibition of the works of the Italian Futurist painters and sculptors. Boccioni, Carrà, Russolo, Balla, Severini, Soffici, Preface by Boccioni, The Doré Gallery, London, 28 – 30 April.

• Naples 1914
Prima esposizione di pittura futurista. Boccioni, Carrà, Russolo, Balla, Severini, Soffici, Preface by Boccioni, Carrà, Russolo, Balla, Severini, Soffici, Galleria Futurista Sprovieri, Naples, May–June.

• San Francisco 1915
Panama Pacific International Exhibition, Italian Futurists, Gallery One Hundred Forty One, Palace of Fine Arts, San Francisco, February–December (the Futurist Exhibition opened at the end of July).

• Rome 1915
Esposizione Fu Balla e Futurista, depliant with autobiography, Sala d'Arte A. Angelelli, Rome, December.

• Rome 1917
Collection de tableaux de Léonide Massine, Teatro Costanzi, Rome, February.

• **Lugo 1917**
Esposizione avanguardista e futurista, Salone Comunale, Lugo di Romagna, from 15 September (after Forlì and Ravenna).
• **Rome 1917a**
Mostra di bianco e nero a beneficio della Croce Rossa, Palazzo delle Esposizioni, Rome, from December.
• **Rome 1918**
Mostra del pittore futurista Balla, in the catalog the *Manifesto del colore di G. Balla*, Casa d'Arte Bragaglia, Rome, 4–31 October.
• **Milan 1920**
Mostra di artisti varii: Glicenstein, Balla (passatista), Costetti, Galleria Moretti, Piazza della Scala, Milan, March.
• **Ginevra 1920–1921**
Exposition Internationale d'Art Moderne, Preface by E. Faure, Geneva, 26 December 1920 – 25 January 1921.
• **Paris 1921**
Exposition des Peintres Futuristes Italiens et Conférence de Marinetti, Preface by Dudreville, Funi, Russolo, Sironi, Galerie Reinhardt, Paris, March.
• **Bologna 1922**
Esposizione d'arte italiana futurista, Teatro Modernissimo, Bologna, from 21 January.
• **Rome 1922**
Esposizione della Section d'Or de Paris, Galleria dell'arte moderna italiana, Via Veneto 6, Rome, 17 April – 2 May.
• **Turin 1922**
Esposizione futurista internazionale, Winter Club, Turin, 27 March – 27 April.
• **Macerata 1922**
I Esposizione Futurista, Preface by I. Pannaggi, Palazzo Convitto Nazionale, Macerata, June–July.
• **Turin 1925**
Mostra Futurista. Esposizione degli "Amici dell'Arte", exhibition curated by F.T. Marinetti, Palazzo Madama, Turin, January.
• **Rome 1925**
III Biennale Romana, Room 6, *Mostra collettiva futurista*, Preface by F.T. Marinetti, Palazzo delle Esposizioni, Rome, 1 March – 30 June.
• **New York 1926**
Exhibition of Modern Italian Art, Preface by A. Colasanti and C. Brinton, New York, January 1926 (after: Washington, D.C., Cleveland, Chicago, Denver, San Francisco, Philadelphia).
• **Bologna 1927**
Grande Mostra di Pittura Futurista, Casa del Fascio, Bologna, from 24 January.
• **Turin 1927**
La Quadriennale. Esposizione Nazionale di Belle Arti, Palazzo del Valentino, Turin, May–July.
• **Palermo 1927**
Mostra d'Arte Futurista, "Il Convegno", Palazzo Supercinema, Palermo, June 1927.
• **Turin 1927a**
Esposizione collettiva futurista, Circolo Novatore, Turin, October.
• **Milan 1927**
Mostra di trentaquattro pittori futuristi, Galleria Pesaro, Milan, November–December.
• **Imola 1928**
Grande Mostra d'Arte Futurista, Ridotto del Teatro Comunale, Imola, 29 January – 10 February.
• **Rome 1928**
XCIV Esposizione Internazionale di Belle Arti, Società Amatori e Cultori di Belle Arti, Room VII, *Il pittore futurista Giacomo Balla*, Preface by F.T. Marinetti, Palazzo delle Esposizioni, Rome, February–June.
• **Turin 1928**
Esposizione Internazionale degli Amici dell'Arte, Società della Promotrice, Turin, May–November.
• **Paris 1929–1930**
Peintres Futuristes Italiens, Preface by G. Severini, Galerie 23 – Rue La Boëtie, Paris, 27 December 1929 – 9 January 1930.
• **Rome 1929–1930**
Mostra del Centenario degli "Amatori e Cultori di Belle Arti" – Seconda Mostra del Sindacato Laziale Fascista di Belle Arti, Room G, *Mostra personale di Giacomo Balla*, Palazzo delle Esposizioni, Rome, December 1929 – January 1930.
• **Rome 1930**
Prima Mostra Nazionale dell'Animale nell'Arte, Preface by F.T. Marinetti, Palazzo delle Esposizioni e Giardino Zoologico, Rome, March–April
• **Rome 1930a**
Mostra del pittore Balla, Preface by G. Guida, F.T. Marinetti, Galleria del Dipinto, Rome, 22 June – 2 July.
• **Venice 1930**
XVII Esposizione Internazionale d'Arte, La Biennale di Venezia, Room 39, *Futuristi Italiani*, Preface by F.T. Marinetti, Venice, May–September.
• **Rome 1931**
I Quadriennale dell'Arte Nazionale, Rooms XII – XIII, Palazzo delle Esposizioni, Rome, January–June.
• **Rome 1931a**
I Mostra di aeropittura dei Futuristi Balla, Ballelica, Benedetta, Diulgherof, Dottori, Fillia, Oriani, Prampolini, Bruno Somenzi, Tato, Thayaht, Galleria La Camerata degli Artisti, Rome, 1–10 February.
• **Rome 1931b**
I Mostra Internazionale d'Arte Coloniale, Room XXVII, *Futuristi italiani*, Preface by F.T. Marinetti, curated by Ente Autonomo della Fiera di Tripoli, Rome, October–December.
• **New York 1934–1935**
Modern Works of Art: 5th Anniversary Exhibition, The Museum of Modern Art, New York, 19 November 1934 – 20 January 1935.
• **Naples 1934–1935**
II Mostra Internazionale d'Arte Coloniale, Room I, curated by Ente Autonomo Fiera di Tripoli, Naples, 1 October 1934 – 31 January 1935.
• **Rome 1935**
II Quadriennale d'Arte Nazionale, Room X, Palazzo delle Esposizioni, Rome, February–July.
• **Rome 1935a**
Mostra di disegni del Sindacato Interprovinciale Fascista Belle Arti di Rome, Room B, Circolo delle Arti e delle Lettere, Via Margutta 54, Rome, 11 April – 11 May.
• **Rome 1935b**
Mostra delle opere di pittura di Giacomo Balla di Luce e di Elica Balla, Preface by A. Silvestri, Galleria d'Arte Antonina, Rome, 9–14 November.
• **Hartford 1935**
Léonide Massine Collection, Wadsworth Atheneum, Hartford, Connecticut.
• **Rome 1936**
VI Mostra del Sindacato Fascista Belle Arti del Lazio, Room VII, Palazzo delle Esposizioni, Rome, February–March.
• **New York 1936**
Cubism and Abstract Art, ed. by A.H. Barr Jr., The Museum of Modern Art, New York, 2 March – 19 April.
• **Rome 1937**
VII Mostra del Sindacato Fascista Belle Arti del Lazio, Room XI, Mercati Traianei, Rome, April–June.
• **Rome 1938**
VIII Mostra del Sindacato Fascista Belle Arti del Lazio, Room XV, Mercati Traianei, Rome, 15 April – 30 June.
• **Rome 1939**
III Quadriennale d'Arte Nazionale, Room L, Palazzo delle Esposizioni, Rome, February–July.
• **New York 1939**
Art in Our Time: 10th Anniversary Exhibition, Preface by A.H. Barr Jr., The Museum of Modern Art, New York, 10 May – 30 September.
• **San Francisco 1939–1940**
Seven Centuries of Painting, California Palace of the Legion of Honour, San Francisco, 29 December 1939 – 28 January 1940.
• **Rome 1942**
Mostra personale di Giacomo Balla, Preface by G. Guida, Galleria d'Arte San Marco, Rome, 1–15 February.
• **Rome 1945**
Mostra della Campagna Romana a beneficio delle Scuole per i contadini dell'Agro Romano, Associazione Artistica Internazionale, Via Margutta 54, Rome, October–November.
• **Rome 1948**
Rassegna Nazionale di Arti Figurative, curated by Ente Autonomo Esposizione Nazionale Quadriennale d'Arte di Rome, Room X, Preface by B. Marinetti, Room XXIII, Galleria d'Arte Moderna, Valle Giulia, Rome, March–May.
• **Rome 1948a**
Prima mostra dei Sindacati Romani Pittori e Scultori, Confederazione Nazionale Artisti e Professionisti, Galleria di Roma, Rome, 2–15 April.
• **Baltimora 1948**
Themes and Variations in Painting and Sculpture, Museum of Modern Art, Baltimora, 15 April – 23 May.
• **New York 1949**
Twentieth-century Italian Art, ed. by J. Thrall Soby and A.H. Barr Jr., The Museum of Modern Art, New York, 28 June – 18 September.
• **Venice 1948**
La collezione Peggy Guggenheim, Preface by P. Guggenheim, catalog published for *XXIV Esposizione Internazionale d'Arte*, Venice, May–September.
• **Francavilla a Mare 1949**
III Premio Nazionale di Pittura "F.P. Michetti", Francavilla a Mare, August–September.
• **Paris 1950**
Exposition d'Art Moderne Italien, Preface by J. Cassou, Musée National d'Art Moderne, Paris, May–June.
• **Venice 1950**
XXV Esposizione Internazionale d'Arte, La Biennale di Venezia, Room VI, *I firmatari del primo manifesto futurista*, Preface by U. Apollonio, Venice, June–October.
• **Zurigo 1950**
Futurismo & Pittura Metafisica, ed. by R. Wehrli and

M. Bill, Kunsthaus, Zurigo, November–December.
• London 1950
Modern Italian Art (under the Auspices of the Amici di Brera and the Italian Institute), The Arts Council of Great Britain, Tate Gallery, London, 28 June – 30 July.
• Milan 1951
Arte astratta italiana. I primi astrattisti italiani, Preface by G. Le Noci, Galleria Bompiani, Milan, 20 March – 4 April.
• Milan 1951a
Giacomo Balla, ed. by G. Le Noci, Galleria Borromini, Milan, 10 November – 2 December.
• Rome 1951
Omaggio a G. Balla futurista, Galleria Origine, Rome, from 14 April.
• Bologna 1951
Mostra Nazionale della Pittura e della Scultura Futuriste, Palazzo del Podestà, Bologna, 11–25 November.
Rome 1951–1952
VI Quadriennale Nazionale d'Arte di Rome, Room 18, with a text by F.T. Marinetti, Palazzo delle Esposizioni, Rome, December 1951 – April 1952.
• Florence 1952
Futur Balla 1912–20, Preface by E. Prampolini, Galleria d'Arte Contemporanea Lungarno delle Grazie, Florence, from 8 November.
• Stockholm 1953
Nutida Italiensk Konst, Liljevalchs Konsthall, Stockholm, 6 March – 12 April.
• São Paulo 1953–1954
Futuristas e Artistas Italianos de Hoie: na segunda Bienal de São Paulo – Brasil, Special Room, *Il Futurismo*, São Paulo, 8 December 1953 – 8 February 1954.
• New York 1954
The Futurists. Balla Severini 1912–1918, Preface by J. Maritain and L. Venturi, Rose Fried Gallery, New York, 25 January – 26 February.
• New York 1954a
Futurism: Balla, Boccioni, Carrà, Russolo, Severini, Sidney Janis Gallery, New York, 22 March – 1 May.
• Milan 1954
X Triennale di Milano, Salone d'Onore, *I trent'anni della Triennale*, Palazzo dell'Arte, Milan, 28 August – 15 November.
• Madrid – San Sebastian – Toulon 1955
Bienal Hispanoamericana de Arte, Exposicion de Arte Italiano Contemporaneo, Preface by P. Bucarelli, Palacio del Retiro, Madrid, May–June (San Sebastian, July; Toulon, September).
• Buffalo 1955
Fifty Paintings from the Buffalo Fine Arts Academy, Albright-Knox Art Gallery, Buffalo, 14 May – 12 June.
• Lausanne 1955
Le mouvement dans l'art contemporain. Du Futurisme à l'art abstrait, Musée Cantonal des Beaux-Arts, Lausanne, 24 June – 26 September.
• Kassel 1955
Kunst des XX. Jahrhunderts Internationale Ausstellung im Museum Fridericianum, Preface by W. Haftmann, Documenta, Kassel, 15 June – 18 September.
• Ann Arbor 1955
20th Century Painting and Sculpture from the Collection of Mr. and Mrs. Harry L. Winston, curated by J. Paul Slusser, University of Michigan Museum of Art, Alumni Memorial Hall, Ann Arbor, Michigan, 30 October – 27 November.
• Rome 1955
Omaggio ai Maestri della Pittura Italiana Contemporanea, Preface by G. Marussi, Galleria d'Arte Selecta, Rome, 17 November – 2 December.
• Rome 1955–1956
VII Quadriennale Nazionale d'Arte di Roma, Antologia della pittura e scultura italiana dal 1910 al 1930, Preface by G. Castelfranco, Room A, Rome, November 1955 – April 1956.
• Houston 1956
Shadow and Substance. The Shadow Theatre of Montmartre and Modern Art, Contemporary Art Museum, Houston, March–April.
• Rome 1956
Balla, opere scelte del periodo futurista, Galleria d'Arte Selecta, Rome, 27 April – 11 May.
• Australia 1956
Italian Art of the 20th Century, exhibition curated by Art Club, Perth, Art Gallery of Western Australia, March–April (Adelaide, Melbourne, Hobart, Sydney, Brisbane, May–December).
• London – Plymouth – Birmingham 1956–1957
Modern Italian Art from the Estorick Collection, Preface by G.C. Argan, Tate Gallery, London, 21 November – 19 December 1956 (City Museum and Art Gallery, Birmingham, 23 February – 16 March 1957).
• Madison 1957
Sixteen works of Giacomo Balla, Mead Hall – Drew University, Madison, New Jersey, Spring.
• Milan 1957
Opere futuriste di Giacomo Balla, Galleria del Naviglio, Milan, 1–15 April.
• Paris 1957
Exposition de peintures, de gouaches et de dessins de Giacomo Balla, curated by C. Zervos, Galerie Cahiers d'Art, Paris, 12 April – 11 May.
• Munich 1957
Ausstellung Italienischer Kunst von 1910 bis zur Gegenwart, Munich, Haus der Kunst, 7 June – 15 September.
• Berlin 1957
Italienische Kunst im XX Jahrhundert. Sammlung Estorick London, Galerie Il Milione Mailand und Bronzen von Marcello Mascherini Triest, Akademie der Künste, Hochschule für Bildende Künste, Berlin, 21 September – 27 October.
• Cedar Rapids 1957
Italian Art of the 20th Century (opere della Collezione Slifka), Cedar Rapids Museum of Art, Cedar Rapids, Iowa, 1–22 October (after: in many American towns till October 1958).
• Turin 1957
Peintres d'aujourd'hui France – Italie / Pittori d'oggi Francia – Italia, V Mostra, Palazzo delle Arti, Parco del Valentino, Turin, October–November.
• Detroit – Richmond – San Francisco 1957–1958
Collecting Modern Art, Painting, Sculpture and Drawing from the Collection of Mr. and Mrs. Harry L. Winston, The Detroit Institute of Arts, Detroit, 27 September – 3 November 1957 (The Virginia Museum of Arts, Richmond, 13 December 1957 – 15 January 1958; San Francisco).
• Amsterdam 1958
Le renaissance du XXe siècle, Stedelijk Museum, Amsterdam, 4 July – 29 September.
• Milan 1959
Cinquant'anni d'arte a Milano dal Divisionismo ad oggi, curated by R. Taccani, A. Vallardi, Palazzo della Permanente, Milan, 31 January – 15 March.
• Rome 1959
Il Futurismo, Preface by A. Palazzeschi, catalog ed. by L. Drudi Gambillo, Palazzo Barberini, Rome, Spring–Summer.
• Saint-Étienne 1959
Peintres et sculpteurs italiens. Du Futurisme à nos jours, Musée d'Art et d'Industrie, Saint-Étienne, 27 May–December (Palais des Beaux Arts, Charleroi, from January 1960).
• Winterthur – Munich 1959–1960
Il Futurismo, Kunstmuseum Winterthur, Winterthur, 4 October – 15 November 1959 (Städtische Galerie und Lenbachgalerie, Munich, December 1959 – February 1960).
• Rome 1959–1960
VIII Quadriennale Nazionale d'Arte di Rome, Room 41, *Giacomo Balla*, Preface by E. Francia, Palazzo delle Esposizioni, Rome, December 1959 – April 1960.
• Milan 1959–1960
Futur Balla, curated by M. L. Drudi Gambillo, Galleria Blu, Milan, December 1959 – January 1960.
• Milan – Rome 1960
Arte italiana del XX secolo da collezioni americane, Preface by J. Thrall Soby, curated by P. Bucarelli, M. Calvesi, Palazzo Reale, Milan, 30 April – 26 June; Galleria Nazionale d'Arte Moderna, Rome, 16 July – 18 September (exhibition curated by The International Council at The Museum of Modern Art, New York).
• Milan 1960
Balla. Pittore futurista, Galleria Minima, Milan, 14–25 May.
• Venice 1960
XXX Esposizione Internazionale d'Arte, La Biennale di Venezia, Mostra Storica del Futurismo, Preface by G. Ballo, Venice, June–October.
• Paris 1960–1961
Les sources du XXe siècle. Les Arts en Europe de 1884 à 1914, Preface by J. Cassou, Musée National d'Art Moderne, Paris, 4 November 1960 – 23 January 1961.
• Hartford 1961
Salute to Italy: 100 Years of Italian Art 1861–1961, Wadsworth Atheneum, Hartford, Connecticut, 21 April – 28 May.
• New York – Detroit – Los Angeles 1961–1962
Futurism, curated by J.C. Taylor, The Museum of Modern Art, New York, 31 May – 5 September 1961 (The Detroit Institute of Arts, Detroit, 18 October – 19 December 1961; County Museum, Los Angeles, 14 January – 19 February 1962).
• London – Rome 1961
Some Aspects of Twentieth Century, Marlborough Fine Arts Ltd., London – Rome, Summer.
• Turin 1961
Da Boldini a Pollock. Pittura e scultura del XX secolo, curated

by F. Russoli, L. Carluccio, *Italia 61*, Turin.

• **Colonia 1962**
Europäische Kunst 1912 – Zum 50. Jahrestag der Ausstellung des "Sonderbundes westdeutscher Kunstfreunde und Künstler" in Köln, curated by H.R. Leppien, Wallraf-Richartz Museum, Cologne, 12 September – 9 December.

• **Turin 1963**
Giacomo Balla, curated by E. Crispolti and M. Drudi Gambillo, Galleria Civica d'Arte Moderna, Turin, from 4 April.

• **Strasbourg 1963**
La grande aventure de l'art du XXe siècle, curated by H. Haug, Château des Rohan, Strasbourg, 8 June – 15 September.

• **Rome 1963**
Giacomo Balla. Luce Balla, Galleria Il Bilico, Rome, 3–17 December.

• **Hamburg – Frankfurt 1963–1964**
Italien 1905–1925. Futurismus und Pittura Metafisica, curated by E. Rathke, Kunstverein, Hamburg, 28 September – 3 November 1963 (Frankfurter Kunstverein, Frankfurt, 16 November 1963 – 5 January 1964).

• **Baltimora 1964**
1914: An Exhibition of Paintings, Drawings and Sculptures, The Baltimore Museum of Art, Baltimora, 6 October – 15 November.

• **London 1964–1965**
The Peggy Guggenheim Collection, Preface by P. Guggenheim, Tate Gallery, London, 31 December 1964 – 7 March 1965.

• **Houston 1965**
The Heroic Years. Paris 1908–1914, The Museum of Fine Arts, Houston, 20 October–December.

• **Rome 1965**
Balla. I fiori 1916–1952, SM 13 – Studio d'Arte Moderna, Rome, from 6 November.

• **Mexico City1966**
Arte italiano Contemporaneo desde 1910, exhibition curated by Quadriennale di Roma, Museo de Arte Moderno, Mexico City.

• **Stockholm 1966–1967**
Peggy Guggenheims samling fran Venedig, Preface by P. Guggenheim, Moderna Museet, Stockholm, 26 October 1966 – 8 January 1967.

• **Florence 1967**
Arte moderna in Italia 1915–1935, curated by C.L. Ragghianti, Palazzo Strozzi, Florence, 26 February – 28 May.

• **Rome 1967**
Balla nel tondo, exh. curated by V. Orsini, text by M. Fagiolo dell'Arco, SM 13 – Studio d'Arte Moderna, Rome, April.

• **Spoleto 1967**
Tre secoli di disegni teatrali, IX Festival dei due Mondi, Palazzo Collicola, Spoleto, 25 June – 17 July.

• **Turin 1967**
Opere di Giacomo Balla, Galleria Notizie, Turin, March.

• **Washington 1967–1968**
Masters of Modern Italian Art from the Collection Gianni Mattioli, curated by F. Russoli, The Phillips Collection, Washington D.C., 2 December 1967 – 14 January 1968 (after: Dallas, San Francisco, Detroit, Kansas City, Boston, New York).

• **Rome 1968**
Balla pre-futurista, curated by M. Fagiolo dell'Arco, Galleria L'Obelisco, Rome, from 19 January.

• **Rome 1968a**
Balla: luce e movimento, curated by M. Fagiolo dell'Arco, Galleria L'Obelisco, Rome, from 23 February.

• **Rome 1968b**
Balla: stati d'animo, curated by M. Fagiolo dell'Arco, Galleria L'Obelisco, Rome, from 20 April.

• **Rome 1968c**
Balla. Ricostruzione futurista dell'Universo. Sculture 1913–1915, curated by M. Fagiolo dell'Arco, Galleria L'Obelisco, Rome May–June.

• **Strasbourg 1968**
L'art en Europe autour de 1918, Ancienne Douane, Strasbourg, 8 May – 15 September.

• **Venice 1968**
XXXIV Esposizione Internazionale d'Arte, La Biennale di Venezia, Quattro maestri del primo futurismo italiano, curated by M. Calvesi, Venice, July–September.

• **Turin 1968**
Giacomo Balla, sculture e fiori futuristi, Preface by R. Guasco, Galleria La Bussola, Turin, from 5 November.

• **New York – Geneva 1968**
Futurism, Preface by G. Ballo, Albert Loeb and Krugier Gallery Inc., New York, November–December (after: Galerie Krugier, Geneva).

• **New York 1968–1969**
The Machine, as Seen at the End of the Mechanical Age, curated by K.G. Pontus Hulten, The Museum of Modern Art, New York (after: Houston, San Francisco).

• **Rome 1968–1969**
Cento opere d'arte italiana dal Futurismo ad oggi, curated by G. De Marchis, Galleria Nazionale d'Arte Moderna, Rome, 20 December 1968 – 20 January 1969.

• **Strasbourg 1969**
Les ballets russes de Serge de Diaghilev 1909-1929, Ancienne Douane, Strasbourg, 15 May – 15 September.

• **Milan 1970**
Mostra del Divisionismo italiano, Palazzo della Permanente, Milan, 17 March – April.

• **Rome 1971**
Balla: disegni, studi, bozzetti dal 1897 al 1958, SM 13 – Studio d'Arte Moderna, Rome, 22 March – 14 April.

• **Rome 1971a**
Maestri europei, Galleria d'Arte Contemporanea La Medusa, Rome, Spring–Summer.

• **Rome 1971b**
Prima Mostra Nazionale Aeronautica di Pittura e Scultura, Preface by M. Venturoli, Ente Premi Rome, Rome, 8–25 October.

• **Rome 1971c**
Rassegna di Pitture e Documenti del Futurismo, curated by P. Perrone, Pinacoteca Galleria d'Arte, Rome, 21 October – 10 November.

• **Rome 1971d**
Balla 1871-1958. Tutte le sculture, Galleria dell'Obelisco, Rome, from 20 December.

• **Rotterdam 1971**
De metamorfose van het object, Kunst en anti-kunst 1910-1970, Museum Boymans-van Beuningen, Rotterdam, 25 June – 7 November.

• **Toronto 1971**
A Tribute to Samuel J. Zacks, Art Gallery of Ontario, Toronto, 21 May – 27 June.

• **San Diego 1971–1972**
Color and Form 1909–1914, Fine Arts Gallery, San Diego, 19 November 1971 – 2 January 1972.

• **Rome 1971–1972**
Giacomo Balla (1871-1958), curated by G. De Marchis, Galleria Nazionale d'Arte Moderna, Rome, 23 December 1971 – 27 February 1972.

• **Strasbourg 1972**
Occident – Orient. L'art moderne et L'art islamique, Ancienne Douane, Strasbourg, 15 May – 15 September.

• **Paris 1972**
Balla, curated by G. De Marchis, Musée d'Art Moderne de la Ville de Paris, Paris, 24 May – 2 July.

• **Rome 1972**
G. Balla – Arte applicata, SM 13 – Studio d'Arte Moderna, Rome, November–December.

• **Rome 1972a**
1870-1914 Aspetti dell'arte a Roma, curated by D. Durbé, Galleria Nazionale d'Arte Moderna, Rome.

• **Newcastle – Edinburgh – London 1972–1973**
Futurismo 1909–1919, Exhibition of Italian Futurism, Hatton Gallery, University of Newcastle, Newcastle, 4 November – 8 December 1972 (Royal Scottish Academy, Edinburgh, 16 December 1972 – 14 January 1973; London, Royal Academy of Arts).

• **Paris 1973**
Le Futurisme 1909-1916, Musée National d'Art Moderne, Paris, 19 September – 19 November.

• **New York 1973–1974**
Futurism – A Modern Focus. The Winston – Malbin Collection, The Solomon R. Guggenheim Museum, New York, 16 November 1973 – 3 February 1974.

• **Milan 1973–1974**
Boccioni e il suo tempo, curated by G. Ballo, Palazzo Reale, Milan, December 1973 – February 1974.

• **Düsseldorf 1974**
Futurismus 1909-1917, curated by J. Harten, Städtische Kunsthalle, Düsseldorf, 15 March – 28 April.

• **Turin 1974**
Giacomo Balla: trenta esempi, curated by M. Fagiolo dell'Arco, Galleria Martano, Turin, 8–31 May.

• **Verona 1976**
Giacomo Balla. Studi ricerche oggetti, Preface by L. Magagnato, exh. curated by L. Marcucci, Museo di Castelvecchio, Verona, February–March (Bolzano, March; Pescara, 14 August–September).

• **Rome 1976**
Balla 1871-1958. Tutte le sculture, Galleria dell'Obelisco, Rome.

• **Venice 1978**
XXXVIII Esposizione Internazionale d'Arte, La Biennale di Venezia, Sei stazioni per Artenatura. La natura dell'arte, curated by A. Bonito Oliva, J.-C. Amman, A. Del Guercio, F. Menna, Venice, 2 July – 15 October.

• **Milan 1979–1980**
Origini dell'Astrattismo. Verso altri orizzonti del reale, texts by G. Ballo, G.A. Dell'Acqua, P. Restany et al., Palazzo Reale, Milan, 18 October 1979 – 18 January 1980.

• **London 1980**
Abstraction: Towards a New Art. Painting 1910–1920,

texts by A. Bowness, P. Vergo, C. Green, J. Beckett, D. Ades, S. Compton, D. Brown, G. Levin, Tate Gallery, London, 6 February – 13 April.

• **Rome 1980**
Arte astratta italiana 1909-1959, catalog ed. by G. De Feo, I. Panicelli, L. Velani, P. Vivarelli, Galleria Nazionale d'Arte Moderna, Rome, 2 April – 11 May.

• **Paris 1980**
Œuvres Futuristes du Museum of Modern Art New York, curated by K.G. Pontus Hulten, Musée National d'Art Moderne, Centre Georges Pompidou, Paris, 16 April – 15 September.

• **Bologna 1980**
La Metafisica. Gli anni Venti, curated by R. Barilli and F. Solmi, Galleria d'Arte Moderna, Bologna, May–August.

• **Rome 1980a**
Roma 1911, catalog ed. by G. Piantoni, Galleria Nazionale d'Arte Moderna, Rome, 4 June – 15 July.

• **Turin 1980**
Ricostruzione futurista dell'Universo, curated by E. Crispolti, Mole Antonelliana, Turin, June–October.

• **Washington 1980–1981**
The Morton G. Neumann Family Collection, curated by E.A. Carmean Jr., National Gallery of Art, Washington, 31 August 1980 – 11 January 1981.

• **Rome 1980–1981**
Apollinaire e l'avanguardia, curated by B. Mantura, Galleria Nazionale d'Arte Moderna, Rome, 30 November 1980 – 4 January 1981.

• **Philadelphia 1980–1981**
Futurism and the International Avantgarde, curated by A. d'Harnoncourt, Philadelphia Museum of Art, Philadelphia, 26 October 1980 – 4 January 1981.

• **New York 1981**
Futurists: Italian and Russian 1912–1916, Carus Gallery, New York, October–December.

• **Modena 1982**
Giacomo Balla, Galleria Fonte d'Abisso, Modena, 13 February – 10 April.

• **Basel 1982**
Futur-Balla: un profeta dell'avanguardia, curated by P. Sprovieri, catalog by M. Fagiolo dell'Arco, Art 82, Basel, June.

• **Milan 1982–1983**
Boccioni a Milano, curated by G. Ballo, Palazzo Reale, Milan, December 1982 – March 1983.

• **Padua 1983**
Omaggio a Giacomo Balla, Galleria Civica, Padua, January–February.

• **Basel 1984**
Skulptur im 20 Jahrhundert, curated by E. Beyeler, R. Hohl, M. Schwander, Merian Park, Basel, 3 June – 30 September.

• **Frankfurt 1985**
Italienische Kunst 1900–1980, curated by P. Weiermair and M. Garberi, Frankfurter Kunstverein, Franckfurt, 22 February – 8 April.

• **Rome 1985**
Il Futurismo a Rome. Anni dieci-quaranta, curated by E. Crispolti, Galleria Editalia Qui arte contemporanea, Rome, 23 October – 30 November.

• **New York 1986**
Works by Giacomo Balla from 1905 to 1928, curated by M. Fagiolo dell'Arco, Kouros Gallery, New York, 15 March – 24 April.

• **Venice 1986**
Futurismo & Futurismi, curated by K.G. Pontus Hulten, Palazzo Grassi, Venice, May–September.

• **Venice 1986a**
XLII Esposizione Internazionale d'Arte, La Biennale di Venezia. Arte e Scienza, Venice, 29 June – 28 September.

• **Edinburgh – London – Oxford 1987**
Balla The Futurist, curated by M. Fagiolo dell'Arco, Scottish National Gallery of Modern Art, Edinburgh, 6 June – 19 July 1987 (Riverside Studios, London, 26 August – 27 September 1987; Museum of Modern Art, Oxford, 25 October – 6 December 1987).

• **Turin 1987**
1945-1965: arte italiana e straniera. Le collezioni della Galleria civica d'arte moderna di Turin, curated by P. Fossati, R. Maggio Serra, M. Rosci, Parco del Valentino, Turin, July–October.

• **Milan 1988**
Il Futurismo e la moda, curated by E. Crispolti, PAC, Milan, 25 February – 9 May.

• **New York 1988**
Aspects of Collage. Assemblage and Found Objects in Twentieth Century Art, The Solomon R. Guggenheim Museum, New York, March–May.

• **Naples 1988**
Balla a Capodimonte. La donazione Carelli, curated by M. Mormone, Museo di Capodimonte, Naples, 30 March – 30 May.

• **Amsterdam 1988**
Arte Italiana 1870-1910. Ottocento/Novecento, curated by G. Piantoni, Rijksmuseum Vincent Van Gogh, Amsterdam, 17 September – 27 November.

• **New York 1988a**
Futurism 1911–1918, curated by P. Baldacci, Philippe Daverio Gallery, New York, 10 November – 17 December.

• **Rome 1988–1989**
La donazione Balla e le altre opere dell'artista nelle collezioni della Galleria Nazionale d'Arte Moderna, curated by G. De Feo, P. Rosazza Ferraris, L. Velani, Galleria Nazionale d'Arte Moderna, Rome, 14 December 1988 – 19 February 1989.

• **London 1989**
Italian Art in the 20th Century. Painting and Sculpture, curated by N. Rosenthal, Royal Academy of Arts, London, 14 January – 9 April.

• **Milan 1989**
Arte Contemporanea per un Museo, 10 anni di acquisizioni delle Raccolte d'Arte di Milano, curated by M. Garberi, PAC, Milan, 23 June – 4 September.

• **Venice 1989**
Arte Italiana. Presenze 1909-1945, curated by K.G. Pontus Hulten and G. Celant, Palazzo Grassi, Venice, from April.

• **Rome 1989**
Casa Balla e il Futurismo a Roma, curated by E. Crispolti, Accademia di Francia, Villa Medici, Rome, 28 September – 3 December.

• **Kassel 1990**
Italiens Moderne, curated by L. Caramel, E. Crispolti, V. Loers, Museum Fridericianum, Kassel, 28 January – 25 March.

• **Trent 1990**
Divisionismo italiano, curated by G. Belli, Palazzo delle Albere, Trent, April–July.

• **Milan 1990**
Archivi Futuristi, curated by M. Verdone, Fonte d'Abisso, Milan, 7 April – 14 July.

• **Valencia 1990**
Avanguardia Italiana de entreguerras, curated by L. Caramel, E. Crispolti, V. Loers, IVAM Centre Julio González, Valencia, 9 April – 5 June.

• **Vienna 1991**
15 Masterpieces from the Vienna Museum of Modern Art Ludwig Foundation, curated by E. Badura-Triska, Thun-Hohenstein, Museum of Modern Art, Ludwig Foundation, Vienna.

• **Florence 1992**
Gli Uffizi. La donazione Balla, curated by A. Natali, Florence.

• **Japan 1992**
Futurism 1909–1944, traveling exhibit: Sezon Museum of Art, Tokyo; Hokkaido Museum of Art, Sapporo; Miyagi Museum of Art, Sendai; Museum of Modern Art, Otsu.

• **Milan 1992–1993**
La collezione Jucker, Preface by M.T. Fiorio, Palazzo Reale, Milan, 11 December 1992 – 17 January 1993.

• **Rome 1993**
Tutte le strade portano a Roma, curated by A. Bonito Oliva, Palazzo delle Esposizioni, Rome, 11 March – 26 April.

• **London 1994**
Italian 20th Century Masters from The Eric and Salomon Estorick Foundation, Grosvenor Gallery, London, 12–28 October.

• **Rome 1994–1995**
Roma. Sotto le stelle del '44. Storia arte e cultura dalla Guerra alla Liberazione, curated by C. Terenzi, Palazzo delle Esposizioni, Rome, 16 December 1994 – 28 February 1995.

• **Ferrara 1995**
Il pittore allo specchio – Autoritratti italiani del Novecento, curated by M. Fagiolo dell'Arco, Palazzo dei Diamanti, Ferrara, 21 July – October.

• **Catania 1996**
Futuristi e Aeropittori a Catania, Galleria d'Arte Moderna, Catania, March–May.

• **Barcelona 1996**
Futurismo 1909–1916, curated by E. Coen, Museo Picasso, Barcelona, 8 May – 21 June.

• **Naples 1996**
Futurismo e meridione, curated by E. Crispolti, Palazzo Reale, Naples, 18 July – 31 October.

• **Stuttgart 1997**
Magie der Zahl in der Kunst des 20. Jahrhunderts, Staatsgalerie Stuttgart, Stuttgart, 1 February – 19 May.

• **Comacchio 1997**
Casa Balla. Un pittore e le sue figlie tra futurismo e natura, curated by M. Fagiolo dell'Arco, Palazzo Bellini, Comacchio, 14 June – 12 October.

• **Genoa – Milan 1997–1998**
Futurismo. I grandi temi 1909-1944, curated by E. Crispolti, F. Sborgi, Palazzo Ducale, Genoa, 17 December 1997 – 8 March 1998 (Fondazione Mazzotta, Milan, 29 March – 28 June 1998).

• **Padua 1998**
Giacomo Balla 1895-1911. Verso il Futurismo, curated by M. Fagiolo dell'Arco, Palazzo

Zabarella, Padua, 15 March – 28 June.

• **Lausanne 1998**
Futurisme. L'Italie face à la modernité 1909–1944, curated by E. Crispolti, Fondation de l'Hermitage, Lausanne, 10 July – 11 October.

• **Rome 1998**
Minimalia. Da Giacomo Balla a…, curated by A. Bonito Oliva, Palazzo delle Esposizioni, Rome, 28 January – 6 April.

• **Milan 1998–1999**
Futur natura. La svolta di Balla 1916-1920, curated by M. Fagiolo dell'Arco, with E. Gigli, Galleria Fonte d'Abisso, Milan, 19 November 1998 – 20 February 1999.

• **Lisbon 1999**
Futurismo e Aeropittura, Palácio das Galveias, Lisbon, May–September.

• **Montreal 1999**
Cosmos. Du Romentisme à l'Avant-garde, curated by J. Clair, Musée des Beaux Arts, Montreal, 17 June – 17 October.

• **New York 1999–2000**
Minimalia: An Italian Vision in 20th Century Art, curated by A. Bonito Oliva, P.S.1, New York, 10 October 1999 – 9 January 2000.

• **Lucca 1999–2000**
Tempo sul Tempo. Carlo L. Ragghianti e il carattere cinematografico della visione, curated by M. Scotini, Fondazione Ragghianti, Lucca, 28 November 1999 – 30 January 2000.

• **Zurich 2000**
Balla – Boccioni – Severini, curated by M. Fagiolo dell'Arco, Thomas Ammann Fine Art, Zurich, 15 June – 30 September.

• **Rome 2000–2001**
Novecento. Arte e Storia, curated by M. Calvesi, P. Ginsborg, Scuderie del Quirinale e Mercati Traianei, Rome, 3 December 2000 – 1 April 2001.

• **Hannover 2001**
Italienischer Futurismus 1909–1918, curated by N. Nobis, Sprengel Museum, Hannover, 11 March – 24 June.

• **Brussels 2003–2004**
Futurismo 1909–1926. La bellezza della velocità, curated by A. Masoero and R. Miracco, Brussels, Musée d'Ixelles, 16 October 2003 – 11 January 2004.

• **Turin 2003–2004**
L'Officina del mago: l'artista nel suo atelier 1900-1950, curated by A. Masoero, B. Marconi, F. Matitti, Palazzo Cavour, Turin, 31 October 2003 – 8 February 2004.

• **Paris 2006**
Italia Nova. Une aventure de l'art italien 1900–1950, curated by G. Belli, Grand Palais, Paris, 5 April – 3 July.

• **Paris – Rome – London 2008–2009**
Le Futurisme à Paris. Une avant-garde explosive, curated by D. Ottinger, Musée National d'Art Moderne, Centre Georges Pompidou, Paris, 15 October 2008 – 26 January 2009 (*Futurismo Avanguardiavanguardie*, Scuderie del Quirinale, Rome 20 February – 24 May 2009, E. Coen, commissioner; *Futurism*, Tate Modern, London, 12 June – 20 September 2009, M. Gale, commissioner).

• **Milan 2008**
Balla. La modernità futurista, curated by G. Lista, P. Baldacci, L. Velani, Palazzo Reale, Milan, 15 February – 2 June.

• **Milan 2009**
Futurismo 1909-2009. Velocità+Arte+Azione, curated by G. Lista, A. Masoero, Palazzo Reale, Milan, 6 February – 7 June.

• **Helsinki 2012**
Uusi taide: Nopeus Vaara Uhma. Italian futurismi 1909–1944. A New Art: Speed Danger Defiance. Italian Futurism 1909–1944, curated by M. Ancora, G. Carpi, M. Valkonen, Espoo, EMMA Espoo Museum of Modern Art, Helsinki, 2 March – 10 June.

• **Barcelona 2013–2014**
Depero y la reconstrucción futurista del universo, texts by N. Boschiero, G. Lista, A. Pizza, La Pedrera, Barcelona, 17 September 2013 – 12 January 2104.

• **New York 2014**
Italian Futurism, 1909–1944: Reconstructing the Universe, curated by V. Green, The Solomon R. Guggenheim Museum, New York, 21 February – 31 August.

• **Mamiano di Traversetolo 2015**
Giacomo Balla Astrattista Futurista, curated by E. Gigli and S. Roffi, Fondazione Magnani Rocca, Mamiano di Traversetolo – Parma, 12 September – 8 December.

• **Madrid – Rovereto 2016**
Del Divisionismo al Futurismo, curated by B. Avanzi, D. Ferrari and F. Mazzocca, Fundación MAPFRE, Madrid, 12 February – 5 June (*I pittori della luce. Dal Divisionismo al Futurismo*, MART, Rovereto, 25 June – 9 October).

edited by Zelda De Lillo

Texts and manifestoes

• *Manifesto dei pittori futuristi*, Milan, 11 February 1910.
• *La pittura futurista. Manifesto tecnico*, Milan, 11 April 1910.
• *Gli Espositori al pubblico*, Paris–Florence, 1912–1913.
• *Il vestito antineutrale. Manifesto futurista*, Milan, 11 September 1914.
• *Ricostruzione futurista dell'universo*, Milan, 11 March 1915.
• *Fu balla – Balla futurista*, Rome, 15 December 1915.
• *La cinematografia futurista*, Milan, 11 September 1916.
• *Manifesto del colore*, Rome, 4 October 1918.
• *L'aeropittura. Manifesto futurista*, Turin, 22 September 1929.

• G. Balla, "Futurismo e futuristi", in *Perseo*, Milan, 1 February 1937.
• G. Balla, *Giacomo Balla. Scritti futuristi*, ed. by G. Lista, Abscondita, Milan 2010.

General texts

• "Esposizione di Belle Arti della Società degli Amatori e Cultori", in *Vita Nova*, Rome, III, April–June 1901.
• L'Italico, "Il ritorno dell'arte", in *La Tribuna*, Rome, 23 March 1902.
• Grita, "L'Esposizione a Roma", in *Fantasio*, Rome, 2, 29 March, pp. 12–13.
• Volframo, "Teatro e Arti", in *Nuova antologia di lettere, scienze ed arti*, Florence, 98, March–April 1902, pp. 730–731.
• E. Aitelli, "Esposizione Quadriennale di Belle Arti in Torino", in *Emporium*, Bergamo, XVI, 94, October 1902, p. 268.
• S.A. Nappi, "Visitando l'Esposizione di Belle Arti. Giacomo il notturno", in *L'Italia Moderna*, Rome, II–III, 13, issue I, July 1904, pp. 74–77.
• *Avanti della Domenica*, Rome, 1 May 1905, p. 7 (ill. by Giacomo Balla).
• O. Roux, "Esposizione di Belle Arti in Rome", in *Natura ed Arte*, Milan, XXVII, 1904–1905, pp. 771–772.
• V. Pica, "Arte Contemporanea: L'Esposizione degli Amatori e Cultori d'Arte a Roma", in *Emporium*, Bergamo, XXVII, June 1908, pp. 405–426.
• U. Antonelli, "Lottando. Una visita allo studio di Giacomo Balla", in *La Tribuna*, Rome, August 1908.
• G. Stiavelli, "LXXVIII Esposizione Internazionale di Belle Arti in Rome", in *Ars et Labor*, Milan, 63, I, 15 June 1908, pp. 438–445.
• L. Serra, "La mostra di Belle Arti a Roma", in *Natura ed Arte*, XXXV, Milan, 1908–1909, pp. 264–265.
• M. De Fiori, "Balla", in *Caffaro*, Genoa, 19 May 1909.
• V. Pica, "L'Esposizione degli Amatori e Cultori di Belle Arti in Roma", in *Emporium*, Bergamo, XXIX, April 1909, pp. 243–257.
• A. Colasanti, "L'Esposizione Internazionale d'arte in Roma", in *Emporium*, Bergamo, XXXI, May 1910, pp. 375–393.
• *Novissima*, X, Milan, 1910, tav. VIII.
• Aymerillot, "Il 1911 degli artisti Romani: Giacomo Balla", in *L'Alfiere*, Rome, II, 25, 24 January 1911.
• S. Brinton, "The International Art Exhibition at Rome: The Italian Section", in *The Studio*, London, 53, 220, July 1911, pp. 127–135.
• G. Apollinaire, "Les futuristes", in *Le Petit Bleu*, Paris, 9 February 1912.
• A.G. Bragaglia, "Fotodinamismo Futurista", Edizioni Nalato, Rome 1913.
• F. Mastrigli, "La mostra futurista al Costanzi", in *La Vita*, Rome, 23 February 1913.
• E. Cecchi, "Esposizioni Romane. La mostra futurista", in *Il Marzocco*, Florence, 23 March 1913.
• N. Pascazio, "La pittura futurista", in *Humanitas*, Bari, III, 16, 20 April 1913, pp. 95–97.
• U. Tommei, "Esposizione di pittura futurista a Firenze", in *Quartiere latino*, Florence, 24 December 1913.
• U. Nebbia, "Sul movimento pittorico contemporaneo", in *Emporium*, Bergamo, XXXVIII, December 1913, pp. 421–438.
• E. Prampolini, "Pittori futuristi. Prima esposizione italiana in Roma", in *L'Artista Moderno*, Turin, XII, XII, 1913, pp. 104–105.
• E. Prampolini, "Secessione. Prima esposizione d'arte Roma 1913", in *L'Artista Moderno*, Turin, XII, XII, 1913, pp. 149–155.
• D. Angeli, "Note d'arte. Il caso Balla", in *Il Giornale d'Italia*, Rome, 14 April 1913.
• U. Boccioni, *Pittura Scultura Futuriste*, Edizioni di Poesia, Milan 1914.
• A. Soffici, *Cubismo e Futurismo*, Edizioni La Voce, Florence 1914.
• G. Apollinaire, "Futurisme", in *Les Arts*, Paris, 31 May 1914.
• U. Boccioni, "Giacomo Balla", in *Gli Avvenimenti*, Milan, 6, 30 January 1916.
• *L'Italia Futurista*, Florence, I, 6, 26 August 1916 (cover illustration: *Pugno italiano di Boccioni* by Giacomo Balla).
• U. Boccioni, "L'arte di Carlo Fornara", in *Gli Avvenimenti*, Milan, 15, 2 April 1916.
• E. Settimelli, "La prima nel mondo della cinematografia futurista", in *L'Italia Futurista*, Florence, II, 1, 10 February 1917.
• "L'ultimo ballo russo al Costanzi", in *Il Piccolo Giornale d'Italia*, Rome, 27 April 1917.
• "I Balli russi al Costanzi", in *Il Giornale d'Italia*, Rome, 29 April 1917.
• *L'Idea Nazionale*, 30 April 1917.
• A. Gasco, "L'addio dei Balli russi", in *La Tribuna*, Rome, 29 April 1917.
• L. Venna, "Una visita a Giacomo Balla", in *L'Italia Futurista*, Florence, II, 37, 15 January 1918.
• G. Calderini, "Giacomo Balla", in *Il Fronte Interno*, IV, 302, Milan, 2 November 1918, p. 3.
• "La mostra di Giacomo Balla", in *Il Messaggero della Domenica*, Rome, 18 October 1918.
• A.G. Bragaglia, "Cronache d'Arte. Le Esposizioni della Casa d'Arte Bragaglia", in *Cronache d'Attualità*, Rome, II, II, 1, 5 February 1919.
• F.T. Marinetti, "Esposizione Nazionale Futurista che si apre oggi al Cova. Pittori futuristi combattenti e teatro plastico", in *Il Popolo d'Italia*, Milan, 21 March 1919, p. 111.
• G. Galli, "I nostri artisti: Giacomo Balla", in *Roma Futurista*, Rome, II, 51, 14 December 1919.
• "L'evoluzione futurista del vestiario", in *La Moda Maschile*, Rome, XIII, 5 May 1919.
• L. Corpechot, *Lettres sur la Jeune Italie*, Berger Levrault, Nancy–Paris–Strasbourg, 1919, pp.42–47.
• E. Santamaria, "Conversando con Giacomo Balla", in *Griffa*, Perugia, I, 10, 15 August 1920.
• Volt, "Giacomo Balla e la sua grande arte", in *La Testa di Ferro*, Milan, 11 November 1920.
• C. Caillot, "Une inauguration futuriste", in *Les Tablettes*, Genève, 1921, pp. 270–271.
• A. Cappa, "Giacomo Balla", in *La Rassegna dell'Arte e del Lavoro*, Bologna, 25 March 1922.
• S. Maurano, "Giacomo Balla. Il Futurista tipico", in *L'Impero*, Rome, 20 March 1925.
• G. Jannelli, "Giacomo Balla", in *Italia Nuova*, Venice, 1925.
• El Lissitzky, H. Arp, *Die Kunstismen: Les ismes de l'Art. The isms of Art*, Eugen Rentsch Verlag, Zurich–Munich–Leipzig, 1925.
• M. Sarfatti, *Le Arti Decorative Italiane a Parigi*, in *L'Italia alle Esposizioni Internazionali Arti Decorative e Industriali Moderne*, Paris, 1925, pp. 55–60.
• R. Papini, "Vecchio e nuovo nella Terza Biennale Romana", in *Emporium*, Bergamo, 365, LXI, May 1925, pp. 275–296.
• E. Prampolini, "I Futuristi Italiani alla XV Biennale Veneziana", in *Le Tre Venezie*, Venice, II, 5, suppl. May 1926, pp. 2–3.
• Fillia, "La pittura futurista alla Quadriennale di Torino", in *L'Impero*, Rome, 20 May 1927.
• F. Sapori, "L'Arte del

maestro Giacomo Balla", in *La Gazzetta del Popolo*, Turin, 3 February 1928.
• V. Marchi, "Giacomo Balla", in *La Stirpe*, Rome, March 1928, pp. 159–163.
• B. Randone, "Difendo Giacomo Balla", in *Cronache d'Arte Educatrice*, Rome, 6, VI, June 1928.
• M. Biancale, "I quadretti Romani di Giacomo Balla", in *Il Popolo di Roma*, Rome, 10 October 1929.
• F.T. Marinetti, "Giacomo Balla, artista torinese", in *L'Impero*, Rome, 22 November 1929.
• E. Prampolini, "I futuristi alla XVII Biennale", in *L'Impero d'Italia*, Rome, 18 May 1930.
• F.T. Marinetti, "Giacomo Balla e la pittura futurista", in *Oggi e Domani*, Rome, 16 June 1930.
• G. Dottori, "Una visita alla mostra", in *Oggi e Domani*, Rome, 30 June 1930.
• M. Sarfatti, *Storia della pittura moderna*, Cremonese, Rome 1930.
• N. Tarchiani, "Balla Giacomo", in *Enciclopedia Italiana di scienze, lettere ed arti*, Rome, V, 1930, p. 981, *ad vocem*.
• F. Sapori, "Balla il futurista", in *L'Amico degli Artisti*, Sapientia, Rome 1931, pp. 211–221.
• F.T. Marinetti, "Due pittori futuristi. Balla e Prampolini", in *Oggi e Domani*, Rome, 5 January 1931.
• V. Orazi, "I futuristi alla Prima Quadriennale", in *L'Impero d'Italia*, Rome, 6 January 1931.
• G. Jannelli, "Giacomo Balla", in *Oggi e Domani*, Rome, 6 April 1931.
• R. Papini, "Prima Quadriennale. Arte Nazionale esposta a Roma", in *Emporium*, Bergamo, LXXIII, June 1931, pp. 325–347.
• V. Marchi, "Il genio futurista di Giacomo Balla strapittore del Fascismo", in *Futurismo*, Rome, I, nn. 11–12–13, 20 November, p. 1; 25 November, p. 2; 4 December 1932, p. 4.
• V. Orazi, "Il pittore Giacomo Balla e primo realizzatore con Umberto Boccioni della pittura futurista", in *Futurismo*, Rome, I, 2, 30 June 1932.
• P. Cottini Agostinelli, "Un idolatra della realtà: il pittore Giacomo Balla", in *Corriere Diplomatico Consolare*, Rome, 20 February 1934.
• A. Costantini, *Pittura Italiana Contemporanea dalla fine dell'800 ad oggi*, Hoepli, Milan 1934, pp. 200–203.
• G. Dottori, "Un quarto di secolo d'arte futurista", in *La Città Nuova*, Turin, 20 February 1934.
• A.M. Comanducci, *I pittori italiani dell'Ottocento, Artisti d'Italia*, Milan 1934, p. 32, *ad vocem*.
• R. Huyghe, *Histoire de l'art contemporain: la peinture*, F. Alcan, Paris, 1935.
• A.H. Barr Jr., "Futurist painting", in *Cubism and Abstract Art*, The Museum of Modern Art, New York 1936, pp. 56–58.
• C.J. Bulliet, *The Significant Moderns and their Pictures*, Covici, Friede Publishers, New York 1936.
• F. Sapori, "Un grande pittore, Giacomo Balla ritrattista", in *Il Resto del Carlino*, Bologna, 1 March 1938.
• A.M. Brizio, *Ottocento Novecento*, II, Unione tipografico-editrice torinese, Turin 1939.
• U. Nebbia, *La Pittura del Novecento*, Soc. ed. libraria, Milan 1941.
• S. Cheney, *The Story of Modern Art*, The Viking Press, New York 1941, p. 468.
• R. Fanti, "Incontro con Giacomo Balla", in *La Gazzetta delle Arti*, Rome, 15–21 April 1946, p. 122.
• G. Severini, *Tutta la vita di un pittore*, Garzanti, Milan 1946 (II ed., Edizioni di Comunità, Milan 1965).
• A. Marcucci, "La Mostra del 1911", in *La scuola di Giovanni Cena*, Paravia, Rome 1948, pp. 57–6l.
• A. Podestà, "L'Arte Italiana in una mostra a New York", in *Emporium*, Bergamo, CX, June 1949, pp. 164–173.
• U. Apollonio, *Pittura italiana moderna: idea per una storia*, Neri Pozza, Venice 1950.
• C. Zervos, "Un demi-siècle d'art italien", in *Cahiers d'Art*, 25, 1, Paris, 1950, pp. 3–8.
• Benedetta, "Le Futurisme", in *Cahiers d'Art*, 25, 1, Paris, 1950, pp. 9–16.
• P. Buzzi, "Souvenirs sur le Futurisme", in *Cahiers d'Art*, 25, I, Paris, 1950, pp. 17–32.
• R. Carrieri, *Pittura e scultura d'avanguardia in Italia*, La Conchiglia, Milan 1950.
• G. Giani, *Il Futurismo*, Ed. del Cavallino, Venice 1950.
• E. Prampolini, *Lineamenti di scenografia italiana: dal Rinascimento ad oggi*, Bestetti, Rome 1950.
• E. Colla, "Segnalazione di opere di Giacomo Balla alla Galleria Origine", in *Spazio*, II, n. 5, 1951, p. 89.
• V. Costantini, "Perpetua giovinezza di Giacomo Balla", in *Corriere Lombardo*, Milan, 29 November 1951.
• E. Colla, "Pittura e scultura astratta di Giacomo Balla", in *Arti Visive*, I, 2, September 1952.
• A.H. Barr Jr., *Masters of Modern Art*, The Museum of Modern Art, Simon and Schuster, New York 1954.
• G. Ballo, *Pittori Italiani dal Futurismo a oggi*, Edizioni Mediterranee, Rome 1956.
• G. Castelfranco, M. Valsecchi, *Pittura e Scultura Italiane dal 1910 al 1930*, Quaderni della Quadriennale Nazionale d'Arte di Roma, De Luca Editore, Rome 1956.
• M. Seuphor, *Dictionnaire de la peinture abstraite: précédé d'une histoire de la peinture abstraite*, F. Hazan, Paris 1957.
• M. Drudi Gambillo, T. Fiori, *Archivi del Futurismo*, 2 vols., De Luca Editore, Rome 1958–1962.
• M. Valsecchi, *Profilo della pittura moderna*, Garzanti, Milan 1959.
• C. Maltese, *Storia dell'Arte in Italia 1785-1943*, Einaudi, Turin 1960, pp. 294–296.
• G. Marchiori, *Arte e artisti d'avanguardia in Italia (1910-1950)*, Edizioni di Comunità, Milan 1960.
• R. Modesti, *Il Futurismo*, Vister, Casatenovo Brianza 1960.
• R. Carrieri, *Il Futurismo*, Edizioni del Milione, Milan 1961.
• J.C. Taylor, *Futurism*, The Museum of Modern Art, New York 1961.
• E. Crispolti, "Il Bal Tic Tac di Balla, a via Milano", in *Palatino*, VI, nn. 9–12, Rome, September–December 1962, poi Edizioni Palatino, Rome 1962.
• G. Nicodemi, *Il dono di Carlo Grassi al Comune di Milano in memoria del figlio Gino*, Stab. Tip. R. Scotti, Milan 1962.
• G. Ballo, *La linea dell'arte italiana: dal simbolismo alle opere moltiplicate*, Edizioni Mediterranee, Rome 1964.
• G. De Marchis, "Acquisti della Galleria Nazionale d'Arte Moderna", in *Bollettino d'Arte*, V, L, I–II, 1965, p. 242.
• A. Barricelli, *Balla*, De Luca Editore, Rome 1966.
• F. Bellonzi, *Il Divisionismo nella pittura italiana*, Fabbri Editori, Milan 1967.
• M. Calvesi, *Il Futurismo*, 3 vols., Fabbri Editori, Milan 1967.
• M. Fagiolo dell'Arco, *Omaggio a Balla*, Bulzoni, Rome 1967.
• G. De Marchis, "Acquisti dei Musei e Gallerie dello Stato, Arte Moderna e Contemporanea", in *Bollettino d'Arte*, V, LII, IV, October–December 1967, p. 260.
• E. Crispolti, "Balla scultore", in *Arte Illustrata*, Milan, 2, February 1968, pp. 14–23.
• M. Fagiolo dell'Arco, *Balla pre-futurista*, Bulzoni, Rome 1968.
• M. Fagiolo dell'Arco, *Compenetrazioni iridescenti*, Bulzoni, Rome 1968.
• M. Fagiolo dell'Arco, "Futur-BALLA", in *Metro*, 13, Alfieri, Venice, 1968, pp. 54–77.
• M. Fagiolo dell'Arco, *Ricostruzione futurista dell'universo*, Bulzoni, Rome 1968.
• M.W. Martin, *Futurist Art and Theory 1909–1915*, Clarendon Press, Oxford 1968.
• L. Scrivo, *Sintesi del Futurismo: storia e documenti*, Bulzoni, Rome 1968.
• T. Fiori, *Archivi del Divisionismo*, 2 vols., De Luca Editore, Rome 1968–1969.
• V. Dortch Dorazio, *Giacomo Balla. An album of his Life and Work*, Wittenborn, New York 1969.
• G. De Marchis, *Pittura e scultura del XX secolo nelle collezioni della Galleria Nazionale d'Arte Moderna di Rome*, CNR, Rome 1969.
• E. Crispolti, *Il mito della macchina e altri temi del Futurismo*, Celebes, Trapani 1969.
• U. Apollonio, *Futurismo*, Mazzotta, Milan 1970.
• M. Valsecchi, *Futurismo italiano*, L'Italica, Venice 1970.
• M. Verdone, *Teatro italiano d'Avanguardia*, Officina, Rome 1970.
• A.M. Damigella, *Il Futurismo*, ITES, Catania 1971.
• A.M. Damigella, *Modernismo, simbolismo, divisionismo, arte sociale a Rome dal 1900 al 1911*, in *Aspetti dell'arte a Rome dal 1879 al 1914*, De Luca Editore, Rome 1972, pp. XLIII–LXIII.
• J.M. Nash, *Cubism, Futurism and Constructivism*, Thames and Hudson, London 1974.
• E. Crispolti, *Balla*, Editalia, Rome 1975.
• P. Fossati, "Balla pre-futurista", in *Prospettiva*, Florence, 3, October 1975, pp. 35–44.
• M. Verdone, *Poemi e scenari cinematografici d'avanguardia*, Officina, Rome 1975.
• G. Lista, *Théâtre futuriste italien: Anthologie critique*, 2 vols., L'Age d'Homme, Lausanne 1976.
• U. Piscopo, *Questioni e aspetti del futurismo: con una appendice di testi del futurismo a Napoli*, Ferraro, Naples 1976.

• G. De Marchis, *Giacomo Balla. L'aura futurista*, Einaudi, Turin 1977.
• G. Lista, *Marinetti e le Futurisme*, L'Age d'Homme, Lausanne 1977.
• G. Lista, *Futurismo e fotografia*, Multhipla Edizioni, Milan 1979.
• G. Ballo, *Origini dell'astrattismo 1885-1919*, Electa, Milan 1980.
• S. Barnes Robinson, *Giacomo Balla – Divisionism and Futurism 1871–1912*, UMI Research Press, Ann Arbor, Michigan 1981.
• G. Lista, *Balla*, Edizioni Galleria Fonte d'Abisso, Modena 1982.
• M. Fagiolo dell'Arco, *Balla: i taccuini*, 3-4-5, Martano, Turin 1982–1984–1985.
• G. Lista, *Giacomo Balla futuriste*, L'Age d'Homme, Lausanne 1984.
• E. Balla, *Con Balla*, 3 vols. (I: 1984; II–III: 1986), Multhipla Edizioni, Milan 1984–1986.
• A. Zander Rudenstine, *Peggy Guggenheim Collection Venice*, The Solomon R. Guggenheim Foundation, Harry N. Abrams, New York 1985.
• P. Baldacci, *Ricostruzione di casa Balla*, Mondadori, Milan 1986.
• E. Coen, *Futurismo*, Giunti, Florence 1986.
• E. Crispolti, *Il Futurismo e la moda. Balla e gli altri*, Marsilio Editori, Venice 1986.
• E. Crispolti, *Storia e critica del Futurismo*, Editori Laterza, Rome 1986.
• G. Lista, *Il Futurismo*, Jaca Book, Milan 1986.
• K.G. Pontus Hulten, *Futurismo & Futurismi*, Bompiani, Venice 1986.
• M. Fagiolo dell'Arco, *Balla The Futurist*, Mazzotta, Milan 1987.
• AA.VV., *Arte Italiana. Presenze 1909-1945*, Bompiani, Milan 1989.
• AA.VV., *Italian Art in the 20th Century. Painting and Sculpture*, Prestel–Verlag, Munich 1989.
• G. Lista, *La scène futuriste*, Éditions du CNRS, Paris 1989.
• G. Belli (ed. by), *Divisionismo italiano*, Electa, Milan 1990.
• M. Fagiolo dell'Arco, *Futur-Balla. La vita e le opere*, Electa, Milan 1990.
• M. Verdone, F. Pagnotta, M. Bidetti, *La Casa d'Arte Bragaglia 1918-1930*, Bulzoni, Rome 1992.
• F. Benzi, *Balla*, Giunti, Florence 2001.
• E. Gigli, *Giochi di luce e forme strane di Giacomo Balla: Feu d'artifice al teatro Costanzi, Roma 1917*, De Luca Editore, Rome 2005.
• AA.VV., *Italia Nova. Une aventure de l'art italien 1900–1950*, Skira, Milan 2006.
• P. Baldacci, "A propos du pavillon Futuriste Italien à la Panama Pacific International Exposition de San Francisco (février–décembre 1915)", in *Ligeia dossiers sur l'Art*, a. XX, 77–80, Paris, June–December 2007.
• F. Benzi, *Giacomo Balla. Genio futurista*, Electa, Milan 2007.
• G. De Marchis, *Futurismo da ripensare*, Electa, Milan 2007.
• *Balla. La modernità futurista*, exh. cat. (Milan, Palazzo Reale, 15 February – 2 June 2008), ed. by G. Lista, P. Baldacci, L. Velani, Skira, Milan 2008.
• E. Coen, *Illuminazioni: avanguardie a confronto: Italia, Germania, Russia*, exh. cat. (Rovereto, MART, 17 January – 7 June 2009) Electa, Milan 2009.
• E. Coen, M. Gale, G. Lista, J.-C. Marcadé, D. Ottinger, *Futurismo Avanguardiavanguardie*, 5 Continents, Milan 2009.
• G. Lista, E. Gigli, *Giacomo Balla: Futurismo e neofuturismo*, Mudima, Milan 2009.
• E. Gigli, *Giacomo Balla pittura dinamica = simultaneità delle forze*, De Luca Editore, Rome 2010.
• A. Nigro, "Roma, aprile 1917: le due serate di Giacomo Balla al Costanzi. Qualche precisazione sulla scenografia plastica per 'Feu d'artifice'", in *Contemporanea. Scritti di storia dell'arte per Jolanda Nigro Covre*, Campisano, Rome 2013, pp. 167–173.
• E. Gigli, *Balla Inventore Mago Profeta*, De Luca Editore, Rome 2013.
• E. Gigli, *Giacomo Balla. Coloratissimo e luminosissimo*, Edizioni Cinquantasei, Bologna 2013.
• AA.VV., *Italian Futurism, 1909–1944: Reconstructing the Universe*, exh. cat. (New York, Solomon R. Guggenheim Museum, 21 February – 31 August 2014), ed. by V. Greene, Guggenheim, New York 2014.
• E. Gigli, S. Roffi, *Giacomo Balla Astrattista Futurista*, Silvana Editoriale, Milan 2015.

UP 0182840559
FUTURBALLA LI
FE LIGHT SPEE
INGLESE
COEN ESTER
SKIRA